A.J. AYER

A.J. AYER

A Life

Ben Rogers

GROVE PRESS
New York

Originally published in Great Britain in 1999 by Chatto & Windus, Random
House, London, England

Printed in the United States of America

FIRST AMERICAN EDITION

Library of Congress Cataloging-in-Publication Data

Rogers, Ben.
    A.J. Ayer : a life / Ben Rogers.
      p.   cm.
    "Principal publications of A.J. Ayer": p.
    Includes bibliographical references (p.) and index.
    ISBN 0-8021-1673-6
    1. Ayer, A. J. (Alfred Jules), 1910– 2. Philosophers—England—
Biography. I. Title.

B1618.A94 R64 2000
192—dc21
[B]

                               00-030876

Grove Press
841 Broadway
New York, NY 10003

00 01 02 03   10 9 8 7 6 5 4 3 2 1

Contents

Illustrations

Section 1

1 Ayer's parents on their wedding day, London, 1909.
2 Freddie on his great-grandmother's knee, with his mother and his grandfather Dorus Citroën, 1912.
3 At Ascham, 1918, Freddie is eighth from right, front row, the smallest boy, with a fringe.
4 Freddie (at top of slope) with his cousins, Jack and Doris Holloway, Donald and Madge Kingsford, around 1918.
5 The College Wall XI, Eton, St Andrew's Day, 1928, Freddie fourth from right.
6 Part of the team, Freddie on left, second row.
7 Renée, Freddie and two friends in Paris, 1928.
8 With Martin Cooper in Vienna, 1933.
9 Freddie and Renée on their wedding day, 1932.
10 The Welsh Guards, May 1940. Guardsman Ayer second from right in front row.
11 Sheilah Graham with Wendy, Christmas 1942.
12 Freddie with Valerie and Julian in New York, 1943.
13 A.J. Ayer by Lee Miller, late 1940s.

Section 2

Acknowledgements

I would like to thank Su Rogers and John Miller, my mother and stepfather, for their great generosity and patience in lending me a room in which to write and a kitchen in which to lunch and for many other things beside. I owe a special debt to my friend Alison MacKeen who twice read through the manuscript offering suggestions and advice, and to Emma Kay. I am also extremely grateful to Richard and Ruthie Rogers.

There are many others whom I am keen to acknowledge for their time and kindness, not all of whom are, alas, still alive. They include: Rosie Alison, Brenda Almond, Shirley Anglesey (the Marchioness of Anglesey), Lord Annan, Robert Ashby, Mrs Doris Bamford, Priscilla and Martyn Beckett, Nicole Bedford (The Duchess of Bedford), William Bell, Anthony Benn, Daniele Besomi, Sir Isaiah and Lady Berlin, Mark Bonham-Carter, Sue Boothby, Sir Robin Brook, Philip Brownrigg, Jerome Bruner, Jemima Burrill, Sir Bernard Burrows, Nicholas Bunnin, David Butler, Sir Andrew Carnwath, Francis Carnwath, Miranda Carter, Mrs Madge Cave, Sir Nicholas Cheetham, Elisabeth Chilver, Karel Citroën, Nigel Clive, Chris Coope, Ian Crombie, Sir William and Lady Deakin, The Duke of Devonshire, Mathew Dickson, Colonel Sir Douglas Dodds–Parker, Francette Drin, Polly Drysdale, Michael Dummett, Anthony Dworkin, Hugh Euston (The Duke of Grafton), Peter Foges, M.R.D. Foot, Alistair Forbes, Sir Edward Ford, John Foster, Catherine Freeman, Princess Galitzine, Sylvia Guirey, Lord Glendevon, Celia

Goodman, Stephanie Goss, Anthony Grayling, Anthony Grey, Lord Hailsham, John Halpern, Pippa Hamilton, Stuart Hampshire, Francis Graham-Harrison, Jennifer Hart, Brian Hayden, Dennis Healey, Carl Hempel, Christopher Hitchens, Octavian von Hofmannsthal, Fred Holman, Veronica Hull, Mary James, Michael Judd, Cynthia Kee, Robert Kee, the Reverend Paul Kelly, Richard S. Kennedy, Heather Kiernan, Mimi Kilgore, Daniel Lang, Michael Law, Nigella Lawson, Dominic Lawson, Alice Lazerowitz, Patrick and Joan Leigh-Fermor, Jeremy Lewis, Peter Lipton, The Earl of Listowel, Marguerite Littman, Michael Lockwood, Peter Long, Lord and Lady Longford, Michael Luke, Adrian Maben, Graham MacDonald, Derwent May, Priscilla McBride, David McKenna, Karl Miller, Jonathan Miller, Nicholas Mosely, Nigel Nicolson, Vanessa Nicolson, Humphrey Ocean, Kathleen and Daniel O'Connor, Jane O'Grady, Hilda Oppenheimer, Vivien Oppenheimer, William Outram, Peter Parker, Jannetta Parladé, John Parry, David Pears, Tony Penrose, George Pitcher, Edo Pivcevi'c, Sir Edward Playfair, Giles Playfair, Patricia Plowright, Dorothy Pritchett, Richard Pring, Stuart Proffitt, V.W.O. Quine, Lord and Lady Quinton, Verity Ravensdale, Emily Read, Jenny Rees, Brooks Richards, Rosanne Richardson, Nina Rose, Alan Ross, Guy de Rothschild, Pauline Rumbold, Alan Ryan, A.G. Samuel, Arthur Schlesinger Jr., David Scrase, Lilian and Meyer Shapiro, Richard Sheahan, Martin Shearn, Peter Skiff, Natasha Spender, Timothy Sprigge, Edward St. Aubyn, Galen Strawson, Sir Peter Strawson, Olivier Todd, Jennifer Trusted, Peter Unger, J.O. Urmson, Peter Vansittart, Edward Vernon-Jones, Sir Geoffrey Warnock, John Watling, George Weidenfeld, Leon Wieseltier, David Wiggins, Reverend R.D.F. Wild, Paul Willert, Bernard Williams, Gaspard Willis, Robert and Elizabeth Willis, Raymond Winch, A.D. Woozley, Anne Wollheim, Jonathan Wordsworth, Mrs Marjorie Wyllie, J.Z. and Ray Young.

Many librarians, archivists and institutions have been of assistance to me. They include Cambridge University Library; Mrs Curthoys and Christ Church College Library, Oxford; Andrea Wathern and the English Speaking Union, London; Paul Quarrie, Michael Meredith and the Eton archives; Jane Blackstock and the Gollancz archives, London; The Houghton Library, Harvard; Rudolph Haller and the Institute of the Vienna Circle, Vienna; Sally Collins and Linacre College Library, Oxford; T.M. Farmiloe and John Handford and the Macmillan archives,

Basingstoke; The National Sound Archive, London; The Rights Department at the Open University, Milton Keynes; The Philosophy Library, Oxford; the archives of N.M. Rothschild and Sons, London; Kenneth Blackwell and the Russell Archives, McMaster University; Duncan Stuart, CMG, SOE Adviser to the Foreign and Commonwealth Office and the SOE archives, London; The Popper Collection, the Hoover Institution, Stanford; University College Library, London; Clifford Davis and Wadham Library, Oxford; Lieutenant Colonel C.F.B. Stephens, Regimental Adjutant, Welsh Guards and the archives of the Welsh Guards, London.

My apologies to anyone who has fallen off the list.

I am particularly grateful to a large group who have read through the manuscript or in other ways excelled themselves. They included Dee Ayer, Ted Honderich, Julian Ayer and Susan Butler, Nick Ayer, Wendy Fairey, Henry Hardy, Michael Ignatieff, Horatia Lawson, Jocelyn Rickards and Clive Donner, Scott Shapiro, Sally Toynbee, Beatrice Tourot, Gully Wells, Richard Wollheim, my agents Deborah Rogers and David Miller, and at Chatto, Jonathan Burnham, Alison Samuel, Beth Humphries, and in particular, Jenny Uglow, my incomparable editor.

Lastly I want to thank Harriet Gugenheim for her laughter and forbearance – for everything.

'So long as the bounds of logical possibility are respected, it is not for the philosopher to set any limit to the marvels of nature'.

A.J. Ayer, 'The Identity of Indiscernibles', 1953

'No more than the scientist is the philosopher specially privileged to lay down rules of conduct, or to prescribe an ideal form of life. . . . The question how men ought to live is one to which there is no authoritative answer. It has to be decided each man for himself'.

'The Claims of Philosophy', 1947

Preface

The complaint against twentieth-century analytic philosophy is familiar: it is shallow, arid, trivial and obscurantist; it completely fails in the task of philosophy, which is to tell us how to live. The great majority of educated people would be hard pressed to name one contemporary analytic philosopher and this itself indicates, the complaint continues, how obscure the subject has become.

Of course many people do know the name A.J. Ayer. When he died in 1989, the event made the front pages. His memorial meeting was attended not just by philosophers but by actors, politicians, writers, scientists and aristocratic socialites. Ayer was remembered for his girlfriends, dancing, and love of football, but chiefly as the voice of logical positivism, of atheism, of reason. His speed and clarity of thought, his rapid-fire delivery, his charm and left-wing views, made him a familiar face on Britain's televisions. He appeared thinly disguised in novels, was satirised on the stage, and denounced in newspapers and books. In America he was invited to lecture to the Kennedys and in the last years of his life stories about him appeared in the *New Yorker* and, more curiously, the *National Inquirer*. At one time, almost every undergraduate philosopher, on both sides of the Atlantic, had to read *Language, Truth and Logic*; most still do.

Yet there was an irony in Ayer's fame. For he did as much as anyone to professionalise philosophy, to divorce it from our everyday concerns. He set out quite deliberately to diminish its pretensions, to contain it, to tame it. No philosopher, or at least no English-language philosopher, did more to insist that philosophy had little to do with life. Isaiah Berlin recalled walking with Ayer around Christ Church Meadows in Oxford, early in the 1930s, when the two young men, both in their twenties, began to talk about the nature of philosophy. This, strangely, is a subject which has always worried philosophers, but Ayer was sure of his ground: 'There is philosophy, which is about conceptual analysis – about the meaning of what we say – and there is all of *this*' – an excited sweep of the hands – 'all of life.'[1] At the time this struck Berlin as strange, as it will strike most non-philosophers now. Ayer, however, never fundamentally departed from this view: 'I see philosophy as a fairly abstract activity, as concerned mainly with the analysis and criticism of concepts, and of course most usefully of scientific concepts', he was still saying in 1971.[2]

As Ayer conceived it, philosophy is essentially a second-order discipline. It cannot discover anything about the world; only empirical science can do that. Nor can it tell us how to live – at most, it can only remind us, as Ayer did again and again, that there is no truth in morals or art, no right answer to the fundamental questions of life. Instead, philosophy is the inquiry into what we mean when we refer to causation, the mind, infinity; into what we are asserting when we assert that a table is made up of indiscernible particles, that pain is caused by certain processes in the brain, that a nation is something above and beyond its members, that a murderer acted 'freely'. Philosophy is concerned with the analysis, paraphrase, translation or reduction of these and other perplexing statements, so that we can see precisely what sorts of claim are being made – in exactly what circumstances they are true. Moreover, philosophy is not merely a second-order subject – one that works at one remove from reality – it is necessarily also a very difficult one. Ayer thought it should be made as accessible as possible, and wrote some of the clearest, most elegant prose of the century. But the problems with which it deals are very abstract; their solutions, often deeply counter-intuitive, require a great deal of hard thought and technical ingenuity.

At first this way of thinking seemed to me, as Ayer's biographer, to pose an obvious problem. I worried that I might confront the difficulty faced by biographers of great mathematicians or scientists, where the connections between life and work must of necessity be fairly tenuous.

Who would want to read about a philosopher who believed that philosophy had nothing much to do with life? With time, however, I came to see that my problem contained its own solution. In seeking to refound philosophy as an analytic discipline, Ayer was not just trying to separate philosophy from life but to liberate life from philosophy.

As he saw it, philosophers had traditionally set out to establish themselves as authorities on the fundamental nature of the universe and of the character of right and wrong. They posited immutable laws of nature, claimed to show that the world was one, or pretended to demonstrate the existence of supersensible realms of being; they invented gods, divine commands and human ends, and sought in that way to tell people how to live.

To Ayer all this was not only unjustified – talk of supernatural reality, of beings existing outside space and time, or the fundamental unity of things was literally senseless – but also reactionary. In narrowing the possibilities of experience, in placing limits on the findings of science and in dictating what was right or wrong, philosophy had become a cramping, distorting discipline. The promise of life after death, the conception of earthly life as representing a punishment for inherited sin, the belief that pleasure was an evil, had terribly oppressive effects. With metaphysics banished, science could develop unfettered, and people would become more experimental, more open to other points of view, more tolerant in thought and practice. They would, in particular, become less likely to engage in religious and ideological wars. Above all else, Ayer hoped, men and women would realise that this life was the only life they have, and would thus become more appreciative of what it had to offer. Which is where the football, the dancing and the love affairs come in.

Here then was a very clear sense in which Ayer did live a philosophy – or at least in which philosophy informed the way he lived. He believed there was a richness to life, a wealth of things to be experienced and discovered, that metaphysics and its allies, religion, tradition, and unthinking conformity, worked to hide. The point of hiving off philosophy from life was not, or not only, to claim it as a specialism, but to free us to experience 'all of *this*'. Although, as Ayer often noted, most people are far too poor, ill-educated and oppressed to get any sustained enjoyment from life at all.

*

In writing Ayer's life, I had relatively few records to draw on. He was not much of a letter writer; one friend parodied his style: 'Dear X, I arrived according to plan yesterday. The journey was without incident. My bed is hard although not uncomfortable. The weather is cool but not unpleasant.'[3] Nor did he keep many letters, or other documents, at least until his last years.* The result is that one often has to turn to his two volumes of autobiography, *Part of My Life* and *More of My Life*, which while generally factually accurate, do not always convey the feelings with which he experienced the facts. I have, however, spoken to or corresponded with relatives, friends and colleagues, and made use of a wide range of broadcasts and interviews, as well as of any letters that I could find. I discovered that these sources showed him to be a stranger, more troubled but also a more human person than his remote and rather decorous autobiographical writings might suggest.

I met Alfred Jules Ayer only once. I was at school with his son Nick, who lived near our house in Camden Town, North London. One day in the mid-1970s, I dropped by. An old man with a kind delicate face, a well-tailored three-piece suit and, I think, a watch chain, answered the door. I recognised him as the famous philosopher. He said with a welcoming smile that Nick was out but would be back soon – would I like to come in? I said I might come back later. That was that.

Six or seven years later I studied PPE at Oxford, where not only *Language, Truth and Logic* but *The Problem of Knowledge* and *The Central Questions of Philosophy* appeared on our reading lists. These books attracted and disturbed me: I liked their simplicity, daring and cleverness, but reassured myself that the world could not possibly be the reduced and alien place they seemed to describe. When I had finished a doctorate, had become more tolerant of the idea that the world was, perhaps, a stranger place than naïvely I had imagined, and wanted to write about philosophy in a less academic way, biography seemed an obvious option. My first choice of subject was A.J. Ayer.

Early in 1994, I approached Dee Wells, Lady Ayer, Ayer's widow. She suggested I contact Ted Honderich, her co-literary executor and Grote

---

* Any records that Ayer's mother might have left him were destroyed during the war, when the warehouse in which she had stored her property was bombed. He kept virtually no lecture notes, and made no drafts of his books or essays, writing one copy by hand on double-lined foolscap, using every other line, to leave room for corrections. There were very few.

Professor of Mind and Logic at University College London – a position Ayer once held with great distinction. I did so, posting him a letter on a Friday evening, enclosing some examples of my writing. On Sunday morning, I woke to find a note dropped through my letterbox – Honderich had been cycling past – suggesting that we meet for lunch at UCL on Tuesday: 'You can see Freddie's old stomping ground.' Honderich warned me that writing Ayer's life would be a difficult and in some ways ungratifying task – 'Freddie had this capacity to evoke very strong feelings in people, often of a negative kind' – but if I still wanted to do it, he seemed inclined to let me. Honderich's kindness and promptness in those early days set the pattern. He has been unfailingly helpful and while remaining loyal to 'Freddie' (as I eventually learned to call him), has left me free to say whatever I thought needed saying.

A few days after my lunch with Ted, Dee invited me to the house in York Street. I looked at the portraits and photos of Ayer that covered the walls, along with a framed entry to a *Times* crossword competition. One snap captured him late in life, standing on a podium, in full academic regalia, receiving an honorary doctorate or some other prize. Another, evidently taken in the late 1960s or 1970s, showed him sitting on a stone bench in a leafy park, surrounded by a group of young boys: his face had a curious vulnerability so that he looked less like a teacher than the leader of a child sect. I browsed through his library, admiring a shelf, at least six feet long, entirely devoted to his own books in over a dozen languages. Then Dee found Freddie's address book, and we began to compile a list of the friends and colleagues whom I might want to contact.

Over the next four years, I spent many weeks in the house, exploring Ayer's files or just reading his books, and Dee and I often had lunch or dinner together. She was an encouraging and patient companion – and as deadlines receded into the future, I and my book became a very real test of patience. Throughout, Dee spoke about Freddie honestly but always with love and admiration.

To say that Dee loved Freddie is not to say that she altogether understood him – any more than I have succeeded in altogether understanding him. At one point, having both read Oliver Sacks's *Anthropologist from Mars*, we discussed whether Freddie might, like some of the individuals Sacks described, have been (mildly) autistic. It was an attractive idea that would have explained not only a number of physical characteristics – the constant fiddling and tendency to gabble – but also deeper psychological traits, like his devotion to games, love of facts and figures, and remarkable memory. Most obviously, it might have accounted for the remoteness that he sometimes displayed. Exploring the possibility further, I was excited to read that 'high functioning' autistic individuals or those with milder cases of 'Asperger's Syndrome' often speak with unusual precision in fully formed sentences, love routine and order, are capable of remarkable feats of concentration, and can display excellent abilities of logical abstract thinking; that they learn to ape many feelings without really experiencing them, and develop such social skills as they possess relatively late in life. These were all characteristics that seemed to find an echo in Ayer.

When I read further about the world inhabited by autistic children, I was struck by how closely it resembled the world as described by Ayer: a place of discrete sense-impressions, of patterned surfaces and disembodied stimuli.[4] In the end, however, I decided that this approach was unfruitful. Alongside traits that seemed to speak of a philosopher from Mars, Ayer displayed emphatically humanoid features: he formed some deep emotional bonds, was generally an astute judge of people, loved literature, and possessed a strong moral sense. If as a philosopher he had great powers of abstraction, he was not short of imagination and even wisdom: he never dreamed that morality might be reduced to a system or social conflict eradicated. Just before she died, Vanessa Lawson, Ayer's third wife, said, by way of making a larger point, 'Freddie's face looks fat, but really it's thin'. I think I understand what she meant: sometimes he seemed one thing, sometimes another.[5]

The ups and downs of Ayer's life led to many tensions among family, friends and lovers, some of whom, when I approached them, were understandably wary. In the end, however, almost every one agreed to be interviewed. (One exception, regrettably, was Guida Crowley, Ayer's secretary and friend, although she did agree to read and comment on a draft.) I can only say that while I have tried not to hurt anybody's feelings, I have done my best to do justice to all sides of the story.

Altogether I have corresponded with or interviewed over 150 people who knew Ayer, and have been struck by the variations in their impressions: Stuart Hampshire thought that no one had ever changed as much in the course of a life; Isaiah Berlin thought that no one had ever changed less. As Ted Honderich had predicted, while some remembered him fondly, others, especially perhaps philosophers, were more critical, if not positively catty. Once again I have tried to represent these various points of view fairly, and I hope that Ayer, who believed passionately in the truth and hated authorised versions in religion, philosophy and biography, would have approved.

I myself ended up liking and respecting him, and have often identified with a line from Philip Toynbee's diary of April 1947: 'Great affection for Freddie, his vanities, his nervous, lively warm face, his sharp, sham-destroying mind.'[6] He was serious, principled and courageous – the ardour with which, in his twenties, he set out to reform philosophy was stunning. But he combined these qualities, in an almost eighteenth-century fashion, with a guiltless appetite for life's pleasures and ironies. He possessed a quite childlike egotism, but he was without guile, malice or conceit. He had firm views on all the central questions of philosophy, but he welcomed disagreement. Tolerant, demanding, encouraging, he was a teacher of the highest rank.

My admiration for Ayer as a philosopher also increased the more I read his work, although his achievement is hard to place. He was not strikingly original, yet the position he defended was entirely his own, and he elaborated it with an unsurpassed elegance, imagination, verve and rigour. The empiricism, the philosophy of sensation, the rejection of authority in morals and science, all fitted him like one of his Savile Row suits. The result was something canonical – although Ayer, of course, did not really believe in canons.

I have throughout this biography treated Ayer's philosophy, public life and private life together. Given the distinction he drew between philosophy and life, I cannot of course claim that the two were, for him, entirely inseparable. He was not one of those philosophers – if there are any – whose ideas were dramatically changed by developments and encounters beyond the study. Nevertheless his thinking changed in important ways over the years, and it seemed right to mark these changes. For all his strictures about separating life from philosophy, Ayer also led a very full existence, in which abstract thought, friendship, politics and play were crammed together. 'There is philosophy and there is life', but in Ayer's case the two competed for space. I wanted to capture something of that.

1

Teachers, Bankers, Merchants, Wives

On the Abbey Road, in St John's Wood, right opposite the famous recording studio, there stands a pleasant six-storey block of red-brick mansion flats: Neville Court. St John's Wood first became popular in the early part of the nineteenth century with the erection of Lord's cricket ground and street upon street of elegant late Georgian-style villas. The area's tone was lowered somewhat in the 1880s and 1890s by the construction of a couple of railway lines, but at the turn of the century it still retained its reputation as one of London's most desirable suburbs. Throughout the Victorian and Edwardian eras the variety of its houses, the width of its tree-lined avenues and its proximity to the centre of the city attracted writers and artists from George Eliot to Edwin Landseer, as well as less notable representatives of the upper middle class. All that St John's Wood had against it, some said, was that it was terribly popular with wealthy Jews.

Number 8 Neville Court is an airy three-bedroom, first-floor flat, with high ceilings and large french windows in the main rooms, leading out to little balconies. It was in this flat that Alfred Jules Ayer was born on 29 October 1910, and here he was subject to the first of those formless, depthless sense-impressions that played such an important role in his later philosophy. An adult, he would say, is just a child who has learned to give order to the chair scrapings, breast patterns, hunger pangs, and milky flavours of the crib. Ayer's birth was difficult: it seems that his mother, Reine Ayer, was unable to have any more children, so he remained an only child. Reine was around twenty-three at the time, her husband, Jules Louis Cyprien Ayer, twenty years older. They had been married for just over a year.

Ayer could remember very little of his early childhood – he could recall almost nothing, for instance, of the schools he attended before he was seven. Nor did he preserve much in the way of contacts or possessions to remind him of his youth. In his sixties he did, however, write an autobiography, *Part of My Life*, in which, recalling what he could of his early years, he described a cosmopolitan, but otherwise conventional, affluent and relatively undramatic childhood – one that was not, apparently, unhappy. Ayer offered the picture of a remarkably precocious boy, a little 'highly-strung' perhaps, and 'unusually susceptible to childish terrors', but with a great zest for life, devoted to musical comedies, books and games.[1]

Against this account, however, many friends and family close to Ayer in later life came to feel that he had a bleak and difficult upbringing – one that hurt and in some ways limited him. Richard Wollheim, a friend from the 1950s, detected a sadness in Ayer which he associated with his being an only child. Wollheim was reminded of an autobiographical story by the late nineteenth-century Oxford aesthete, Walter Pater – 'The Child in the House' – in which Pater describes the development, in a book-loving, cosseted, philosophically minded little boy, of an enchanting awareness of the beauty of the world along with an aching recognition of the sorrow and suffering it contains.[2] There is much in Pater's creation, Florian Deleal, that has no counterpart in Ayer (Florian has a deep feeling for nature and religion, Ayer had almost none) but it is not hard to see why Wollheim made the connection. The boy in Pater's story combined a rare intensity of feeling and observation with a detachment from ordinary family relations in a way that is reminiscent of Ayer.

Yet although, as a young man, Ayer identified with Pater, there is no evidence that he read this particular story, or, if he did, that he made anything of it. Perhaps, then, Dickens offers firmer ground. Ayer never wrote about Dickens in any detail, but he returned to him again and again, and the novels are often a source of incidental reference in his philosophical writings. Dickens's stories abound with vulnerable, receptive and enterprising orphans – children 'of excellent abilities with strong powers of observation, quick, eager, delicate, and soon hurt bodily or mentally', more or less obliged to make their own way in an unfeeling world.[3] There was certainly much to which Ayer might have related in these creations. He was physically small, perceptive and determined; at once bookish and resourceful, sad and enthusiastic, gifted but emotionally perhaps a bit neglected.

Among the few photographs that he inherited from his childhood, there is one of his parents on their wedding day. It clearly shows the difference in age between them. Jules appears as a conventional, middle-aged man, short, dark, a little chubby, but moderately handsome; his narrow eyes, high cheekbones, and well tailored moustache all contribute to an air of neatness. Reine, by contrast, looks young, alert and vulnerable. She has a long neck, delicate features, and large sad eyes which stare out from under a crown of thick dark hair. Ayer never recorded how his parents met, but one cousin thought that they introduced themselves to each other on a boat – a cruise liner or a ferry.[4] They were both, in a sense, foreigners, and although their families came from different parts of Europe and rarely socialised together, each was cosmopolitan and business-minded. Perhaps they thought that, despite the age difference, they understood one another.

Freddie's birth certificate describes Jules's occupation as 'bank secretary'. He was in fact a secretary to Alfred Rothschild, one of three enormously rich brothers who requested the fourth generation of the Rothschild dynasty. As the first Jewish director of the Bank of England, a trustee of the National Gallery and an intimate of the Prince of Wales, Alfred Rothschild was at the nub of Britain's financial and political life. But he also had a reputation as a fast-living, showy dilettante, 'England's most eligible bachelor', who shared the Prince of Wales's taste for horses, actresses and night-life. It is not known exactly what Jules's duties as secretary entailed, but it appears, according to Ayer, that his connection with Rothschild gave him 'an entry into Edwardian Society'.[5] Although it is not easy to imagine a resident of Neville Court gallivanting with the Prince of Wales, Rothschild and Jules were certainly on good enough terms for Rothschild to agree to become young Alfred's godfather. Ayer never appreciated the honour – 'he gave me a silver christening mug which I have lost and a name which I do not like'. Nevertheless, Jules appeared to be prospering.[6]

When he met Reine, Jules was living near his French Swiss mother, Sophie, in the genteel south London suburb of Norwood. Little is known about Sophie, whom Ayer called *Bonne Maman*, although she was said to be clever. She had been born Sophie Henriette Raetz in the Canton of Berne around 1844, and was married at an early age to Jules's father, Nicolas Louis Cyprien Ayer, who merited an entry in the *Swiss Dictionary of Biography and History* as an important educationalist, geographer and linguist. Ayer never knew this grandfather, who died a quarter of a century before Ayer's birth, but he seems to have inherited certain character traits from him.

Nicolas Ayer, like his grandson, was an anti-clerical, Enlightenment thinker, a federalist and democrat. *Un radical fervent et militant*, he edited two prominent left-liberal papers in the late 1840s and was close to many of the leaders of the Radical party, including Numa Droz, twice president of the Swiss Confederation; his interests in education, in the vernacular languages of Europe and in the Continent's political geography were typical of the liberal nationalists of his age. Yet for all of his strongly held and controversial views, his textbooks, primers and statistical surveys, *Grammaire comparée de la langue française, Manuel de géographie statistique,* or *Introduction à l'étude des dialectes du pays romand,* make for very dry reading. A professor, simultaneously, of geography, French and political economy, eventually principal of Neuchâtel Academy, he preferred verifiable facts and figures to untestable speculation and excelled at sorting the rules of grammar, the constitutions of Europe and the peoples of the world into clear and simple classes. Not only the political radicalism and the anti-clericalism, but something of this devotion to hard fact would be passed down from grandfather to grandson.

Sophie and Nicolas had four children, of whom Jules, born in Neuchâtel in 1867, was the oldest. Their marriage, however, was not happy. Grandfather Ayer was said to be a brilliant but very difficult man – *un homme terrible*, in the words of a long-dead cousin – and at some point in the 1870s Sophie took the dramatic step of leaving him and moving to London. The children joined her only after their father's death in 1884, when Jules would have been around seventeen. Ayer wrote in *Part of My Life* that his grandmother worked as a governess in London and that 'she had had some Rothschild children among her pupils'.[7] The story sounds plausible – the Swiss had a reputation as teachers and often found work abroad as tutors and governesses – although one of Ayer's cousins believes that she lived not as a governess but as a companion with a branch of the family after befriending a Rothschild in Switzerland.[8] Whatever her relation to the Rothschilds, she was able to get both Jules and his brother employment in the family bank. Banking was, like teaching, a Swiss tradition, and both young men prospered. Their two sisters, Ayer's Tante Berthe and Tante Marie, married Swiss men. The first entered the Belgian diplomatic service and became Governor of the Belgian Congo. The second, Philippe Suchard, was a grandson of the confectioner and lived comfortably off the family firm in Switzerland. Freddie and his parents sometimes visited the Suchards in their house in Vevey on Lake Geneva. Again there is a suggestion that Freddie tended in his memoirs to downgrade the Ayers; but if they all ended living very comfortably, it was largely with the aid not of inherited wealth but of money they had either earned or married.[9]

Where the Ayers were descended from Swiss Calvinists, Reine Citroën, Ayer's mother, came from a family of Dutch Jews. Ayer had assumed that the Citroëns were descended from Sephardic Jews who fled from Spain in the sixteenth and seventeenth centuries, and it is indicative of his and his family's lack of interest in their own history that it was not until Ayer met a cousin in the 1970s that he learned that they were in fact Ashkenazim who came from Eastern Europe early in the eighteenth century. Over the next hundred years the family rose from its humble beginnings; Jacob Moses Limoenman, the earliest recorded ancestor, was an itinerant fruit seller; his son, Barend Roelof began as a working goldsmith, but became a retail jeweller, changing his name from Limoenman to the more genteel Citroën. The eldest of his fourteen children followed him into the wholesale jewellery business and a shop in Amsterdam still bears his name; another became a jeweller and it was his son, André Citroën, who started up the great car company. The photographer, Erwin Blumfeld, the artist, Paul Citroën, a friend of Kandinsky and a member of the Bauhaus staff, and Hanan Cidor, a post-war Israeli ambassador to the Netherlands were all descended from the same stock. A third son also became a wealthy wholesale jeweller, and his eldest son Dorus, born in Amsterdam in 1860, was Ayer's grandfather. A stern but loving patriarch, he lived until 1935 and was in many respects the most important figure in Ayer's life.

Although Dorus's father was rich, Dorus was required to make his own way in the world. He became a fruit trader in Antwerp and then prospected for diamonds in South Africa, in the 1880s, at the time of the great South African diamond boom; he seems to have prospered and was rich enough on his return to Antwerp to become a founder-partner in an engineering firm, Minerva, set up to produce the newly invented motorbike. He married Sarah Rozelaar, the daughter of a Dutch-Jewish diamond dealer who had settled in London; Reine, born in 1887, was the eldest of their three daughters. At some point in the 1890s the family moved to London, where Dorus, an Anglophile, deeply admiring of British tolerance and commercial spirit, set up a new branch of the Minerva company. At first he continued with the manufacture of motorbikes, but then, like his cousin, André Citroën, he turned to motor cars. During the First World War Minerva converted to the production of shells and fuses under the direction of Winston Churchill's Ministry of Munitions. According to Ayer, this experience left his grandfather with 'an abiding contempt for Civil Servants'. Dorus's role in the Ministry, however, must have been significant because at the end of the war he was offered a knighthood: his wife persuaded him to refuse it on the grounds that as foreigners 'it would make them look ridiculous'.[10]

Dorus, a stout, well turned-out man with a neat pear-shaped face, was a pioneer driver. Yet unlike André Citroën, he does not seem to have been technically minded; on official forms he described his profession as 'merchant', and the cars were, according to one of his granddaughters, 'just a business'.[11] They were, however, a very successful one: Minerva motor cars were well made and prestigious, 'the Rolls-Royces of Belgium', and they made the English Citroëns rich.

For most of Freddie's childhood his grandparents lived in a handsome red-brick villa in Hamilton Terrace, St John's Wood, moving for the duration of the war to a country estate in Essendon, Hertfordshire. Hamilton Terrace is an elegant tree-lined avenue and Dorus's double-fronted 1850 house (number 44) is still one of the finest on it. Like the Ayers, the Citroëns had family scattered over Europe. Dorus was well educated and multilingual (Dutch and French as well as English were often spoken in the house) and built up impressive collections of books, rugs, Chinese porcelain, clocks and other antiques. (When, however, he sold his Essendon house at the end of the war and moved back to London, he also sold his whole collection along with it, and started another, suggesting he was as much a collector as a connoisseur.) He had remarkable powers of mental arithmetic. 'He could run his eyes down a long page of figures and in seconds tell you their sum'.[12] There is evidence that Kenneth Ayer, a cousin from the other side of the family, had the same skill. If so then Freddie's own quickness of thought was a double inheritance.[13]

Dorus Citroën, astute, upright and practically minded, was a free-market liberal, with a strong sense of fair dealing. As Ayer recorded, however, he turned to the Conservatives when he became convinced that the country could no longer afford Free Trade.[14] He was atheistic and vehemently assimilationist, with an open hostility to Zionism – a much-debated subject in the drawing-rooms of St John's Wood and Bayswater when Ayer was growing up – and he more or less forbade his three daughters to marry Jews. This was in part because he believed in the genetic advantages of 'intermarriage', but also because he wanted to see his family integrated and disliked what he saw as the Jews' 'clannishness and religious obduracy'.[15] Dorus never converted and did not keep his Jewishness a secret; he merely considered it irrelevant to the modern age. Ayer never saw any reason to quarrel with this position.

This then was Ayer's ancestry: Swiss-Calvinist bankers and professors on one side, Dutch-Jewish merchants on the other.

When Freddie's father, Jules, met Reine Citroën, he had been working for the Rothschilds for about twenty years. Like his employer, Alfred Rothschild, he was a ladies' man, a gambler, and, with his tidy moustache and monocle, something of an Edwardian dandy. He spoke English fluently, although with a slight French accent, and pronounced his surname in the French way; it was Ayer and his cousins who Anglicised it. Isaiah Berlin never met Ayer's father, but his own father, also in the timber trade, did and described a frivolous character, 'the sort of man who would be drunk after two glasses of beer'.[16]

If the picture of a dandyish sociable man suggests someone rather dashing, Jules's two publications cast light on another aspect of his character. The first appeared in 1899. In his memoirs Ayer described it as 'a set of General and Comparative Tables of the World's Statistics' in two parts.[17] In fact it is simply a large and enormously detailed wall chart of global statistics, which sold for two shillings and which in spirit, if not in detail, owes a great deal to his father's figure-laden textbooks, most notably his *Tableaux de statistique générale et comparée* (1871). The second work, apparently unknown to, or forgotten by Freddie, was *A Century of Finance, 1804 to 1904: The London House of Rothschild*. This is also less than it sounds. Dedicated to 'the present Members of the great House' by 'their obliged and obedient Servant', it is not a full history of the bank but a summary, in table form, of its loan operations since its foundation. Like his wall chart, *A Century of Finance* is little more than a long and meticulous compilation of statistics. A related feature of Jules's character, and one inherited by his son, was what one cousin described as an 'obsession' with all sorts of games and puzzles.[18] He played bridge and other card games avidly, and loved not only solving, but also designing crosswords; at least one of his puzzles was published in the *Daily Telegraph*. In later life he took up bowls and golf. Freddie described his father as 'a very clever man', but his was a particular sort of intelligence – narrow, rule bound, pedantic.[19] He read very little and neither Freddie nor his cousins say anything to suggest that he held interesting views on politics, art or religion.

Reine read more than Jules, although she preferred historical romances to anything more highbrow. Born in Antwerp, she was educated in London, and spoke English as a first language. She was by all accounts a bright student who matriculated from school, which was more than many women of her background achieved. Ayer recalled that she 'would have liked to go to university, but my grandfather considered this a waste of time and money for girls and sent her instead to an art school for which she had no aptitude'.[20] As a result she seems to have lost any ambition she may once have had. Relatives mainly agreed in remembering her as 'fey',[21] 'an uncertain sort of woman, not very reliable and rather unpredictable, in fact a worry to her sisters'[22] or even 'highly strung, twitchy, neurotic': 'her father', one cousin suggested, 'had knocked it out of her'.[23] She was to tell Freddie's first wife that when she married at the age of twenty-two she had been ignorant of the facts of life – a startling admission, even by the standards of the day. In many ways Reine and Freddie were unusually close. They shopped, read and played together, and generally kept each other company – perhaps the amount of time they spent together explains Ayer's later ease with women. Yet their relationship was fraught and they often fought. She was proud of his precocity, but irritated by his show of it: 'She would have liked me to be more of what she regarded as a normal boy'. Freddie, in turn, resented her passivity, unworldliness and lack of imagination. 'She needed more affection than she received from me, or indeed, from my father.'[24] But perhaps she lacked the confidence, or was perhaps simply too selfish, to give him all the love and guidance a child wants.

Whatever Dorus's attitude to Jules and Reine's marriage (and for all of his beliefs about assimilation, he must have savoured the prospect of Jules's connection to the Rothschilds, the acknowledged head of Britain's 70,000-strong Jewish community), he quickly came to regret it. In 1912, when Freddie was about eighteen months old, Jules went bankrupt, the bailiffs were called in, and he was forced to leave Rothschild's. Freddie put his father's dramatic fall from grace down to his speculations on the foreign exchanges – 'He borrowed from moneylenders to make good his losses, speculated more heavily as his debts increased, and then had to borrow again'[25] – but one cousin suggests it was gambling of a more conventional kind; if so, it offers further evidence of his devotion to games.[26] The collapse in the Ayers' fortunes caused a crisis from which, one senses, neither Jules nor Reine, nor their relationship, ever quite recovered. Dorus, who came to suspect that Jules might have married his daughter as a means to pay off his debts, and who anyway considered bankruptcy a form of theft, was disapproving enough to offer to support Reine and Freddie, if she wished to leave her husband. Forced to choose between a domineering father and a bankrupt husband, Reine chose the latter, and Dorus helped Jules secure some sort of a job in Belgium. Here the Ayers lived for two years, until the outbreak of the First World War brought them back to a small house in Kilburn, St John's Wood's poorer neighbour. Once again Dorus stepped in, this time to help Jules purchase a partnership in a timber firm in the north London suburb of Finchley.

Jules was not a natural businessman – 'his adventurousness,' Ayer suspected, 'alarmed his partner'[27] – but a wood business could hardly fail in time of war, and by 1918 the Ayers had moved to 41 St John's Wood Park, a four-storey house not far from Hamilton Terrace. They were not rich, but, with a cook and a housemaid, they were independent and secure. Ayer was much too young to remember the bankruptcy or the bailiffs, and must have pieced together the story later. He seems, nevertheless, to have felt the humiliation of the situation. Later in life he tended to dwell on, even exaggerate, his family's poverty and always worried about money. The whole experience, Dee Ayer suggests, contributed to his sense of being an outsider – to his looking at the world with 'big desiring eyes'. Dorus worried that Ayer might inherit some of his father's 'weakness', but if anything Jules's failure seems to have worked in an opposite direction: Ayer became especially determined to get on in life. It spurred his ambition and fostered a desire to be someone else, someone stronger and more successful. Alongside his sense of being an outsider, Ayer tended to think of himself as self-made.

The Ayers' marriage was far from happy. Freddie's father had lost his social standing and 'hated' his new employment.[28] He had been used to the company of Alfred Rothschild, friend of the Prince of Wales. Now he had to make do with that of his partner, Mr Bick, a Russian Jew who lived with his large family in a house in suburban Finchley. The Ayers sometimes visited the Bicks at the weekend and Freddie enjoyed 'the hot-house domestic Jewish atmosphere' that he found there, so different from the hush of home. His father, however, did not. He drank heavily and in later years spent ever more time on crossword puzzles. 'I did not,' Ayer wrote in his memoirs, 'see him as an unhappy man, but he must have been more unhappy than I realised.'[29]

If Jules was disappointed, so was Reine. She had enjoyed working as a VAD nurse during the war, but otherwise lacked a focus for her talents and 'suffered', Ayer thought, 'from too little to do'.[30] Perhaps it is revealing that one of the few memories Ayer had of his early life was of a dreary domestic routine: his mother's weekly account-settling tour of the local shops. Speaking many years later to a journalist, he described Reine's position as typical of women of her period who were denied education and opportunity:

My mother, although she was an intelligent woman, led a vapid existence. We were not particularly rich and only had a small house, but servants' wages were minimal, so we had a cook and a housemaid. Therefore she had very little to do. In the morning she might shop; in the afternoon she sometimes had tea parties or saw friends; in the evening she would have dinner with my father – mostly in silence because after twenty years of marriage they had very little to say to each other. It was a great waste of a fine intellect.[31]

Ayer had many happy family memories: of his mother playing Coleridge Taylor's *Petite Suite de Concert* on the piano, of holidays spent in France, of shopping expeditions to the West End on open double-decker buses, and of visits to Christmas pantomimes and musical comedies, his favourite treat. Ayer loved the theatre – it appealed to the performer in him – and learned the words to many of the musicals' songs, taught himself to tap-dance and dreamed of going on stage. Yet people who knew him in later life tend to agree that his home must have been a rather joyless and unstimulating place to grow up.

Jules's friends dropped him after his bankruptcy and Reine had only a few friends of her own. In the absence of a social life to bring them together or much attachment between them, their families helped to fill the vacuum. Jules's French-speaking mother, Sophie, was alive until Freddie was about thirteen. Freddie visited her Norwood home, where she lived with her widowed daughter, Tante Berthe and Berthe's much adored pet monkey. Tante Berthe was an intelligent woman, warm and attractively eccentric (on her death she left money to London Zoo so that the monkeys could have bananas on bank holidays) and Freddie felt close to her. 'She disapproved of the way in which my parents were bringing me up, though she did not feel entitled to interfere. She thought that I was nagged too much and also too much cosseted.'[32]

It was the other family, however, that exerted the stronger force; Dorus in particular. Not everyone Ayer writes about in his memoirs comes alive, and it is significant that Dorus does. The picture is somewhat ambivalent, but judging by the accounts of his remaining relatives, it is true to life. The Dutch merchant was a strict and intimidating patriarch. 'He had,' in the words of one granddaughter, 'a terrible temper and what he said went.'[33] He was ambitious for his grandsons, probably excessively so, and urged Freddie to take Disraeli as his model. Years later, after the Second World War, at a time when his job prospects looked bleak, one of Dorus's grandsons killed himself. Freddie was to write: 'To the extent that this was due to his seeing himself as a failure, he may well have been a victim of the pressure to which we were subjected in our boyhood by my grandfather's desire for our success.'[34] Dorus, though, was also devoted and kind, with a strong sense of family. He kept a close eye on Ayer's education, paying for the greater part of it, and in other ways fed the tendrils of his talent, introducing him to Shakespeare, Pepys, Rousseau, and Disraeli's novels.

The family in which Freddie grew up thus formed a close and doubtless rather claustrophobic unit. The two Citroën grandparents, the three daughters and their five children lived close together in north London and saw each other on a daily basis until, early in the 1920s, at around the time Freddie left his prep school, Dorus and his wife Sarah (later only remembered as 'a kind old woman') moved to Trellick Towers near Eastbourne on the south coast.[35] Dorus's new address was a large late nineteenth-century estate (now a college) with a team of gardeners, an orchid house, grape house, rose garden, and tennis court. A man came in from the town twice a week solely to wind up Dorus's collection of clocks. The rest of the family visited often, and in the holidays Freddie would sometimes be chauffeured from London to stay with his grandparents alone, practising cricket on the lawn, climbing trees in the orchard, or poring over Dorus's map collection. One of his cousins' birthdays was on Christmas Eve and, as the eldest grandson, it fell on Freddie, much to his delight, to make a little speech wishing her happy returns. With Grandpapa Citroën in the background and a mother, two aunts and a grandmother to fuss over him, Freddie had a pampered upbringing, even by Edwardian standards. As his wives would later complain, he never had to learn to do anything for himself.

A small, nervous and precocious boy, Freddie was, by his own admission, 'unadventurous except in thought'.[36] He had his younger cousins to play with but few friends, and, in the way that only children do, he seems early on to have developed a rich, consoling and rather narcissistic fantasy life. One gets the sense, in fact, that the five- or six-year-old Freddie – the neat little dark-haired boy with big eyes and a quizzical smile, dressed in a sailor suit, gliding down Baker Street on the back of a gleaming Minerva – already possessed the qualities he displayed as an adult: an acute intelligence, a capacity to lose himself in the flow of life and a love of praise and admiration. Together they helped ward off an inner sadness.

Freddie was unusually clumsy, so that the models and Meccano sets that other boys built were beyond him, but, like David Copperfield, he read early, read everything, and found it easy to identify with whatever he read. The first books he could remember included the Brer Rabbit stories and *Robinson Crusoe*, but he also read comics like the *Boy's Own Paper*, poems and rhymes, adventure stories, and school life novels whose upright young protagonists could be relied on to vanquish playground bullies and sports-field cheats. At eight he discovered Kipling, winning *The Jungle Book* as his first school prize, and quickly moved on to Dumas's *Three Musketeers*. At around the same time Dorus gave him fondly inscribed copies of two jingoistic histories: *Deeds that Won the Empire* and *Fights for the Flag*. 'There was always a bit of *Deeds that Won the Empire* in Freddie,' Dee Ayer suggests.[37] It is true: the values of the schoolboy hero – courage and emotional resilience married to a steadfast conviction of what was right and wrong – remained with Ayer for the rest of his life.

At the age of about five Freddie became, like his grandfather, a collector, not of clocks and paintings, but of books, stamps and cigarette cards. He also quickly developed a lifelong devotion to games. He remembered that he and his mother were happiest when playing together – tennis and ping-pong, board, card and spelling games: anything at all. Above all he displayed an extraordinary memory, although less for events or people than for verse and facts. At an early age he could recite from memory the list of all the English league football teams in the order in which they stood, what he took to be the strongest eleven for every one of the sixteen first-class county cricket teams (a mental list, excluding dozens of rejected players, 174 items long), or the whole of the 500-line poem about Horatius from Macaulay's *Lays of Ancient Rome*. His adoring family encouraged their little prodigy in his dazzling mental feats and he delighted in their applause. A star was born.

Yet although Freddie was precociously clever, he was also cocky, quarrelsome and hard to control. One cousin recalls an early but inevitably formal birthday party at which he jumped on the table, ran down it, picked up a piece of cake and ran back: it was apparently characteristic.[38] In *Part of My Life* Ayer himself recalled how when André Citroën came to visit Dorus in London, Ayer pulled away the chair on which Citroën was about to sit. Perhaps these can be discounted as everyday examples of boyish high-spiritedness, but his cousin Doris

Bamford confirms what Freddie himself described: he and his mother fought together, he would talk down to her, and there would be embarrassing scenes in public.[39] Jules deliberately distanced himself from their quarrels, and Freddie repaid his remoteness in kind. Although father and son both loved games, they hardly ever played together.

Ayer himself had little to say about these tensions, and it is not easy to make sense of this aspect of his life. Yet there seems to have been something in his upbringing which combined with his father's bankruptcy and his foreignness to make him feel small and angry. Perhaps he understood as much as Jules and Reine did about the evasions and compromises on which their lives were founded.

2

School-days

Towards the end of the First World War, as his parents were moving from Kilburn back to their new larger home in St John's Wood, Freddie was sent to a preparatory school outside Eastbourne. He was only seven, young even by the standards of the day – so young in fact that at first he slept in the same room as the headmaster's wife, a maternal woman popular with the boys. Later he attributed his being sent off at such an early age to two causes: 'My mother was highly strung and could not control me, and in addition it was the end of the war and there were air raids.'[1] Freddie was a timid boy and must have been alarmed at the thought of leaving home. He would have been a good deal more so if he had known what the next ten years had in store for him. It was the beginning of a very English, which is to say a very unhappy, education.

Resorts on the south-eastern coast were popular venues for a growing number of private schools and by 1914, at the outbreak of war, there were about fifty boys' prep schools in and around Eastbourne devoted to the intensive farming of young Englishmen. Ascham St Vincent's, the school that had been selected for Ayer, was a large late-Victorian red-brick building close to the sea and the Downs, housing around seventy boys aged from seven to thirteen. It was average in size, as it was in everything else. Ascham had been founded by Reverend William Newcombe Willis in 1889 and he was still headmaster when Freddie arrived three decades later. Willis 'was not', in the faintly praising words of his son, 'a great scholar, but he had his Cambridge degree and he was also a keen sportsman and an outstanding soccer player'.[2]

The routine was that of prep schools everywhere. For six days of the week the boys got up at 7.25, 'drill' was at 7.50, breakfast at 8.00, chapel at 8.40, and then lessons went on, with a short break, until noon. Classes continued after lunch, although two afternoons a week were given over to sport. On Sundays the boys swapped their blazers and grey flannels for Eton suits and a stiff collar. There were two services and a scripture class but the rest of the day was free: usually the headmaster took his charges for a walk, crocodile fashion, along the cliffs.

Latin was taught from the beginning, as were maths and history, some French, English, music and drawing, but scarcely any science. A few of the brighter boys took up Greek at ten or eleven. 'Gawgy', the carpentry teacher, tried unsuccessfully to initiate Freddie into the mysteries of dowelling, dovetailing and mortise and tenon, and two or three times a term the boys could look forward to special evening lectures: Mr Perl would make explosions and talk on the discoveries of modern science; Miss Baker, the headmaster's sister-in-law, might give a travel lecture illustrated with lantern slides; if the boys were lucky a magician or a comedian would be brought in to perform. Unfortunately for Freddie, his grand-parents Dorus and Sarah did not move to the area until around the time he left the school, but his parents sometimes visited on Sundays, taking him out to tea at Eastbourne's Grand Hotel. With no half-terms, the twelve-week terms seemed to go on for ever.

Ascham's was not an academic school. In fact according to (Sir) Robin Brook, a pupil slightly senior to Freddie, later a power in the City, it was 'academically pretty dud'; he once had to take over a maths class, the master not being up to it.[3] Yet the cleverer boys, including Freddie, received extra outside tuition, and after the war, as the school's standing improved, a decent number managed to get scholarships to public schools, the touchstone of prep school success.[*] Like other schools of its kind, Ascham took sport at least as seriously as it did learning and a great deal of endeavour went into what the prospectus of 1889 described as

---

[*] The school seems to have been particularly good at getting its students into Eton and eight pupils gained scholarships there between 1918 and 1928.

'cricket, football, gymnastics and other manly exercises'. There was also a shooting range, which although not compulsory, was especially popular during the war. Ascham could boast fifty old boys who had died in that conflict, each one honoured with an obituary in the school chronicle. Here was a vindication of what Cyril Connolly, who attended the nearby St Cyprian's, described as the prep school creed: 'Not once or twice in our rough island's story/ The path of duty was the way to glory'.[4] The school's rules were strictly enforced: the only thing that made it excusable to leave one's desk during class and rush madly to the window was the still rare sight of an aeroplane or zeppelin. The headmaster in particular was 'a good disciplinarian' – so good that he once whipped his own son just to verify that his new cane worked.[5]

Freddie was caned only once, towards the end of his prep school career, but it is clear that his first years at Ascham's were traumatic and most of his time there fairly miserable. A school photograph taken soon after his arrival shows a vulnerable, feminine boy, notably smaller than his peers, with a childish fringe, large hamster cheeks and big dark eyes. He remembered the buildings as 'ugly', the food as 'atrocious' and in conversation described the place as 'a little Belsen'.[6] As if in protest, he came down early on with what was vaguely described as 'brain-fever' – Ayer suggested it might have been caused by overwork – walked in his sleep and experienced a series of fantastic although not unpleasant dreams in which he starred as a pirate.[7] Worst of all, he was bullied and he recalled hiding in the lavatories during break to escape his persecutors. His size cannot have helped – 'a handkerchief sucking little thing' was how one boy described him – nor his cockiness. But the main problem seems to have been that he was foreign, although not, apparently, that he was Jewish: an American and French boy were victimised in much the same way.

Very often Ayer's autobiographical interviews and broadcasts cast his life in a very different light from that of his two volumes of memoirs, and so it was with Ascham. In *Part of My Life*, he makes light of his years there, claiming, incredibly, that he did not suffer from homesickness.[8] But when asked on *Desert Island Discs* whether he looked back on his childhood as a happy time he replied, 'Not really; I was sent away to boarding-school at the age of seven and at that time those places were fairly barbarous'.[9] In another interview of the same year he was even more forthcoming: 'I was sent away to school at seven and I was dreadfully unhappy. It never occurred to me to tell my parents what went on there. There was a sense of shame, and I think I had the feeling that it was none of their business.'[10]

As unhappy as he was, Freddie could always look forward to holidays. Christmas and Easter and most of the summer were spent in London, but every August the Ayers went abroad. In the early years they stayed in Normandy's less fashionable seaside resorts, Berneval, Paramé and Etretat, where playing with children in the hotel and on the beach helped improve his French. Ayer enjoyed these breaks, in which he spent most of his time reading or playing tennis in local tournaments.

Ayer was around seven when his liking for games turned into a lifelong passion for sport. Cricket and football would occupy a very large place in his life. Cricket came first, and here Ayer naturally enough followed Middlesex, whose ground, Lord's, was only a short walk or a penny bus ride from home. Although his school term and August holidays meant that he missed many of Middlesex's most important games, he was happy to watch whatever was on. By the time he was ten or eleven, on nearly every fine day in the early part of the summer, Freddie went to Lord's, with a lunch-box under his arm, not only to watch Eton versus Harrow (in those days an occasion which required top hat and tails) but other public school matches, a series which culminated in Lord's School against the Rest and the Public Schools against the Army. In each case he plumped arbitrarily for a team, and then found that he had the capacity to identify himself entirely with its fate. Ayer fantasised about playing for England and Dorus duly paid for him to have private coaching at Lord's. 'He once came to watch me and characteristically took the professional aside to ask him if I was ever likely to be any good at the game. The professional frankly told him that I had no chance at all, but my grandfather was kind enough not to report this to me until I had realised it for myself.'[11]

It was a year or two more before Freddie became interested in football. There was no reason why he should support one London team rather than another, but he chose Tottenham Hotspur partly because he liked the bravado of their name, partly because they were doing unusually well, winning promotion to the First Division in the 1919–20 season, and the FA Cup a year later. Spurs' White Hart Lane ground was some distance from St John's Wood, and as neither Dorus nor Jules would have enjoyed the plebeian spectacle of a football match, Ayer did not get to see his team play very often. But on the few occasions when his cousin Kenneth Ayer took him, the cheering crowds and the speed of the game made an overwhelming impression. The company of his handsome worldly cousin, seven years his senior, added to the excitement: it was on one of these trips that Kenneth told Freddie the facts of life.

Whenever Ayer looked back on his career as a sports fan, he always stressed the arbitrariness of the process by which he chose the teams he supported: it was as if he felt some connection here with his larger sense of the contingency of all our moral commitments – their ultimate groundlessness. Ayer, of course, liked the way these sports kept his extraordinarily receptive mind busy. He collected almanacs, annuals and football cards and read the sports pages in his father's *Times*. He had to fill up those memory banks with something. But part of the appeal for him, as for most boys, was the outlet that sport provided for his fantasies. It was a short step from the hope that one day Freddie Ayer might play for the Ascham cricket first eleven to the hope that one day he might score a winning run for England. It was the stuff this foreign boy's dreams were made of.

Although he claims not to have been especially hard-working, Ayer did consistently well at Ascham in all subjects except maths. Despite being more than a year younger than most of the boys in his class, he often came top of his year. Both his teachers and his parents were naturally looking for a scholarship place at one of the better public schools, and at some point his name was put down for Charterhouse. In the summer of 1923, however, an Ascham boy a year older than Freddie was entered for a scholarship at Eton, and Freddie was sent to take the exams with him, on the reasoning that the exam practice would be good for him. In the event, the older boy came thirteenth out of forty-six; a good performance but not quite good enough to secure a scholarship. Ayer came third.

Freddie himself was afraid of Eton – he imagined the famous school as a snobbish place – but his parents, encouraged by Dorus, accepted the scholarship. This meant he could have gone free, although in the end Dorus, fearing this might be held against Freddie, paid the fees. The fact that he had won a scholarship to Eton would always be important to

Freddie. He was proud of having 'made my own way from the age of twelve'.[12]

Cyril Connolly once compared Eton's system of government to the division of power in medieval Europe. He could have added that it was just as old-fashioned in its ethos and methods of education. As Connolly's analogy implies, the boys were subject to bewilderingly complex hierarchies of status and power. The adult order began with the Provost, M.R. James (better remembered for his ghost stories) and just below him the headmaster, an Anglican clergyman called Cyril Alington, an open-minded classicist alive to the needs and interests of the boys in his charge. The Provost's post, however, was largely honorific, and the headmaster had little direct authority, so that in day to day matters, power rested with the housemasters, or in Ayer's case the Master in College, who housed the boys, dined with them and kept them in order.

This adult hierarchy reached down to but also overlapped with the hierarchy of boys. At the apex was the Eton Society, or Pop, a self-selecting oligarchy of around thirty boys, made up largely of the school's leading athletes. These were allowed to wear coloured waistcoats and other distinctive clothing, and to carry tightly rolled umbrellas – and also to punish younger boys with a knotted cane. Pop connected with and competed against Sixth Form, the top twenty boys in the school's academic order, who in theory ruled the school, and were entitled to employ fags, cane junior boys and wear stiff collars on their shirts. Below them, in an intermediate position between lord and serf, came a small group of boys known as 'Liberty', and finally, at the bottom of the pyramid, the great mass of junior boys. All these hierarchies were reflected in the sports field where dress code and other privileges varied depending on a boy's skill and accomplishments. Ayer started off on the football pitch in knickerbockers before moving into shorts.

With over a thousand pupils, and extensive grounds and buildings, dotted on either side of the High Street, Eton was not so much school as a small town. To its pupils, it was a world in itself. If it could terrify, it also offered rare privileges and intimacies. The boys could be caned for breaking some trifling law or convention – on one occasion Ayer was caned for running along a passage through which junior boys were supposed to walk, on another for reading in bed after lights out – but unusually for a public school, they had their own rooms and ate most of their meals at the same table as their housemaster and his assistants. The education was narrow, but a great deal of it took the form of cosy tutorials with able, often distinguished, scholars. If sporting achievement was valued above almost everything, the school also had a proud academic tradition: the boys were encouraged to make use of the library's priceless collection and to join literary and artistic societies. Thus Ayer read Shakespeare with the Provost, who ran the Shakespeare Society, and, in his last years at the school tried his hand at witty essays modelled on Shaw and Strachey, in the Essay Society.

Indeed, despite the ever-present threat of punishment, the boys were treated for the most part like the important gentlemen they were destined to become. Their uniforms were taken away by prior arrangement to be cleaned by 'people' in the town. If a boy damaged his top hat, or simply wanted a new ribbon, he took it to a man in New and Lingwood's outfitters on the High Street. The food served by the housemasters was generally adequate, but if it wasn't the boys could supplement it with teas ordered in from the town. Senior pupils were invited to dine in the headmaster's or Provost's lodgings where they discussed the issues of the day with Oxbridge dons and London politicians. Royal visits were still a regular occurrence, and the Fourth of June, Eton's anniversary celebrations, remained one of the highlights of the Season. After the speeches and the games, the day ended with a candlelit boat procession and a spectacular firework display. It is little wonder, as Ayer would say later, that 'among Etonians, you find a kind of natural assumption of superiority'.[13]

As a King's Scholar, Ayer joined College, a group of seventy pupils who occupied a special place in this special world. Scholars or Collegers, as they were also known, came together with the other boys – Oppidans – in the Corps, on the sports field, and in chapel. Nevertheless, College was an institution peculiar to itself, 'an intellectual elite thrust in the heart of a social elite', in Bernard Crick's nice phrase.[14] Whereas the Oppidans were distributed in 'houses' outside the school, Collegers lived at its very centre, on one side of the graceful cobbled front quadrangle, School Yard. They had their own terminology and dress code and a game in which they specialised, the Wall Game, a muddy joyous battle, spent in an almost constant scrum over a ball. Among the well-born and wealthy boys in College, Freddie's year contained the son of Reginald McKenna, a liberal Chancellor of the Exchequer and Neil Hogg, brother of Quintin Hogg, later Lord Hailsham. But Scholars, or 'Tugs', were generally less aristocratic and more academic than the rest of the school. Where the Collegers cast the Oppidans as hearty toffs, they in turn were cast as swots.

Ayer went to Eton in September 1923, a month before his thirteenth birthday; he was certainly the youngest scholar and probably the youngest boy in the school. His year or 'election' was exceptionally small, settling down to only eight boys in all, and in later years Freddie was to judge them rather 'a dim lot', not to be ranked, for instance, with the vintage of 1916 and 1917, which included George Orwell and Cyril Connolly, and which for a while had virtually abolished caning.[15] The new arrivals lived in 'Chamber' for their first couple of years, small and basic semi-public stalls in a larger hall, before moving into their own private rooms. There were some initiation rites to endure, but they were not severe: Freddie stood on a table and gave a high-pitched rendition of 'My Darling Clementine'. School photos show that once again he was the smallest of the new intake, still dressed in Eton jacket and large stiff collar after the others had reached the required five feet four inches and moved into black suits with morning tails. One boy, a year younger (Edward Ford, later to become equerry to the Queen), recalls his first impression of Freddie: 'a bright, bumptious little boy, trying rather self-consciously to be clever and looking round for approval after one of his quips'.[16]

For the first three years the boys studied for the school certificate. This involved some maths, English, history and foreign languages, but the emphasis was on classics. As at Ascham, there was hardly any science. Teaching methods were old-fashioned and the boys had to learn great swaths of classical and modern verse by heart; a good student, like Freddie for instance, seems to have been expected to recite a great part of the *Odyssey* from memory. Freddie found much of this narrow and boring, but he later insisted on the benefits of a formal education: it taught discipline, rigour and the value of accuracy. And anyway, Eton did have one great advantage: the boys were expected to do an unusual amount of work on their own, which gave those, like Ayer, who worked quickly a great deal of free time; 'this was what I most prized at Eton, the amount of leisure you had to do your own reading'.[17]

Much of Ayer's school life comes across only very dimly from his autobiographical writings, but he vividly remembered his sporting career at Eton, down even to the detail of individual matches. He was in many respects an unpractical and badly co-ordinated boy. He could barely swim or climb a rope and even as an adult he never learned to drive a car or change a plug. But, oddly, Ayer had some facility for field sports, where his cunning and intense competitiveness seem to have given him an edge, and he played the Field and Wall Game for College and rugby and football for the school. One of his contemporaries remembered that 'He was quite a good player of the Field game (a variation on soccer), in which dribbling (keeping the ball close) was important, and contrived his own way of doing this, keeping his elbows stuck well out . . . I think this was considered contrary to the spirit of the game, but there was no rule against it.'[18] Another describes him as 'a very good Wall player. He was a small chap and could crawl about the mud beneath the larger players'.[19]

As with Ascham, so with Eton: Ayer's writings tend to make light of his time at the school, but later in life he often spoke to friends and lovers about his unhappiness there. Going back to the place with Dee Ayer, he stumbled as he took her up some stairs to his old room; later he confessed to an attack of nerves.[20] Returning to the school in 1980 to contribute to an Open University programme, he admitted, 'It was pretty brutal in my time, a lot of beating of boys by other boys.' At first, it seems, Ayer's size and youth ensured him some indulgence and his fag master was a kind boy, the son of his Ascham headmaster. Robin Brook, however, who had preceded Ayer from Ascham to Eton, recalls that in time Ayer became the victim of bullying: 'I was able to act as a buffer to some extent and protect him, but I remember clearly him being singled out for rough treatment'.[21] This 'rough treatment' was, of course, unofficial, but Ayer was beaten formally five times (he remembered the number), always for minor misdemeanours, most characteristically being 'noisy and obstreperous' – 'a charge against which', as he said, 'it was difficult to make any defence'. Quintin Hogg, a highly strung Colleger who was later to rise to near the top of the Conservative party, particularly enjoyed wielding the cane and although Freddie claimed in public not to bear any grudge, he spoke about him in different terms in private. He was not, however, beyond administering minor punishments himself: one boy only a year younger remembered being placed on the 'perch', a ledge about eight feet high and a foot square, on one side of the fire in Chamber. 'Freddie would watch one's unease and probably relent after about seven minutes'.[22]

To the extent that Freddie did suffer at Eton, a great part of the blame can be laid on the Master in College, H.K. Marsden, a sadist and, Ayer later surmised, a repressed homosexual. Marsden, a tall lanky man in his thirties with a drooping moustache, had himself been educated at Eton, and was fanatically devoted to the place in a petty, bigoted way. He had a passion for rules and penalties: the only time he worked outside Eton, during the Second World War, he found a job regulating railway timetables. Many of Freddie's contemporaries remembered Marsden with affection: he was devoted to 'his boys', escorted some to France every summer, and took great pride in their achievements. Nevertheless, one boy admitted that he was a bit of 'a rough diamond' who 'had his favourites',[23] and Wilfred Blunt, a master at Eton in the 1930s, went much further, condemning him as 'the most unattractive species of the genus *schoolmaster* that I encountered in the course of thirty-six years of teaching'.[24]

'Bloody Bill', as Marsden was known, took over College about the time that Ayer arrived and set about eradicating the tolerant, mildly homo-erotic climate that had developed under his predecessor, encouraging the boys to spy on one another and spying himself. Freddie's friend and contemporary, Andrew Carnwath, recalled how Marsden would 'turn up to chat just as you were getting into the little tin baths we had in our rooms' and according to Freddie himself, 'I could not go to the lavatory after lights out without his coming in to my room and asking me where I had been'.[25] While he was not allowed to beat the boys himself, he contrived to have them beaten, and indeed later on, according to Ayer, broke the rules at least once by beating a boy. As an adult, Ayer campaigned against corporal punishment, often pointing out the licence it gave to sexual sadists: he must have had Marsden in the back of his mind. Freddie, it is clear, was not one of Marsden's favourites – he distrusted foreigners, and did not approve of Freddie's ability to think for himself or his tendency to answer back. Ayer's memoirs give only one example of Marsden's picking on him: prowling about the corridors one night, he persuaded Ayer to admit to what he cryptically describes as 'sado-masochistic fantasies', and then later betrayed him to Dorus. But it seems likely that Marsden victimised him in other ways. Ayer certainly came to despise him and would sometimes admit that Marsden was the only person he had ever really hated.*

Ayer's progress continued much as it had at Ascham, which is to say that he did well and retained his competitiveness, without working unusually hard. In the summer of 1916 he took his school certificate and got a distinction in everything except higher maths, which he failed. He was now expected to specialise in a single subject and would have liked to concentrate on history, but was persuaded to do classics – the best policy for anyone judged Oxbridge material. The emphasis was still very much on the translation and memorisation of the major classical authors, and Ayer was taught very little about ancient history and almost nothing about classical society, art or philosophy. Given the fact that the first twelve years of his formal education were devoted almost entirely to classics, it left remarkably little imprint on him. Throughout the enormous range of his publications, there is nothing, not even a book review, about ancient philosophy or an ancient philosopher.

Most of Ayer's contemporaries were extremely impressed by his ability, and not just in classics. Philip Brownrigg, in the year below, reckoned Freddie 'the most intelligent boy I ever knew'; Freddie's classmate, Bernard Burrows, remembered that 'he was much more sophisticated than the rest of us. He had a grounding in Continental literature and history that set him apart'; and A.G. Ogstan agreed: 'I always had for him a feeling of respect, not only for his cleverness but also for his apparently greater experience of the great world'.[26] The puzzle, indeed, is not that Freddie did well at school, but that he did not do better. He retained but did not improve on the position at which he had entered his election, above five of the boys but below Burrows and McKenna, and he 'never came at all close' to winning the main classical prize, the Newcastle Scholarship.[27] Burrows came to feel that Freddie had been holding

* The hostility in what Freddie had to say about him in Part of My Life is striking, especially so as in every other respect the book is a model of self-restraint. Nor was this the only time his feelings against the man got the better of him; Sir Edward Ford remembered that Ayer caused much resentment many years later, by repeating his denunciation at an Old Collegers' dinner (Sir Edward Ford, LTA, 22 December 1994).

himself back – he was turned off by what Burrows described as the 'mechanical literary exercises' to which they devoted their time.[28] Another contemporary agreed: 'My feeling is that at Eton he was more or less consciously biding his time and giving very little away'.[29]

It is clear from both the evidence of his contemporaries and from what Ayer himself recalled about the authors he liked, that, intellectually at least, he was advanced for his age. He had read most of Shakespeare's plays before he saw his first performance, albeit often in the company of the Shakespeare Society, and by sixteen had developed an early taste for the nineteenth-century poets – Shelley, Keats and Swinburne especially. At around the same time, he began to take an interest in contemporary literature, politics and ideas, including the most advanced: he read H.G. Wells, Bernard Shaw, Lytton Strachey, Clive Bell and Bertrand Russell. He even got leave from Eton in the summer of 1925 to go to see the first public London performance of Pirandello's famously avant-garde *Six Characters in Search of an Author* at the New Oxford Theatre.

Yet until Ayer discovered Russell and Clive Bell in his last year, he does not seem to have read any philosophy, and one gets little idea of whether he thought about questions that he would learn to call philosophical. Did he, for instance, look up into the sky and wonder whether the universe was infinite? Or did he ever close his eyes and then consider whether perhaps he was destined to close them? Did these thoughts give rise to others about the mechanism that connected his will to his body? Why was it that no matter how hard he concentrated, he could not experience anything between his decision to close his eyes and their closing? And what happened to the world once they closed? Common sense said that it continued to exist, but how could one know for certain? Ayer's silence is itself revealing: even if philosophical problems interested him, they never really troubled him, as they troubled many other young philosophers, including his two great heroes, Hume and Russell. Philosophy became a vocation for Ayer – a supremely important and serious subject. But it was not one for which he *suffered* as a boy, or later on.

The one subject of obvious philosophical significance that does seem to have interested him, almost in fact obsessed him, was religion. As Ayer told it, he first began to have doubts about Christianity not on philosophical but on pragmatic grounds, when his prayers failed to get him into Ascham's first eleven. Ayer had been baptised as a baby, and the hated Marsden enlisted Reine and Jules in pressuring him into confirmation, with the very unphilosophical argument, 'Now, you're already an oddity. You don't want to be even more different from the other boys than you are.' Ayer later came to regret having given in to this pressure, for by the time he was confirmed his prep school doubts about the efficacy of prayer had begun to harden into something deeper. One day, 'I suddenly asked myself, "Do you believe this?" and I answered "No!" And I thought about it quite a lot and it seemed to me the Christian religion was not intellectually tenable ... I came to the conclusion that if one did believe the world had been created, it was much more plausible that it had been created by the devil than by God. And rather than believe in a malevolent deity, I chose to believe it came about by chance'.[30]

In another school, Ayer's hostility to religion might not have been tolerated, but he was lucky in being taken up by the Reverend Cyril Alington, Eton's headmaster, who, despite being a traditionally minded Christian himself, seems to have liked Freddie and recognised his talents, inviting him into his house for special Greek tuition. Ayer in turn thought him 'marvellous' and 'revered him'.[31]

Alington insisted that he attend chapel, but, as his divinity teacher, allowed him free rein. Ayer quickly mastered the conventional arguments for the existence of God – the argument from design, the ontological argument and the rest – and their standard refutations, but like Russell he also prided himself on knowing more about Church history and doctrine than many clergymen and made special studies of the Gospels and their inconsistencies. It was Alington who pointed him towards W.E.H. Lecky's *History of Morals*, a sceptical history of Christianity, which made a great impression on him, as it did on Russell at a similar age. Lecky's volumes offered a veritable mine of information on the self-denial and suffering religious fanaticism had caused. Freddie could read about the unhealthy habits of such early Christians as Silvia, a famous virgin who 'though she was sixty years old, and though bodily sickness was a consequence of her habits, resolutely refused, on religious principles, to wash any part of her body except her fingers'. Or about the horror in which sex was held by some primitive Christian ascetics like St Ammon who, 'on the night of his marriage, proceeded to greet his bride with a harangue upon the evils of the married state'.[32] Later chapters charted the abominable cruelties inspired and carried out by the medieval Church.

Freddie's peers recognised his intelligence, but although he was not entirely without friends, he was not much liked. He was rarely invited to 'mess' or eat with the other boys in their rooms, and he was passed over again and again by the College Debating Society, although in normal circumstances election was more or less automatic for anyone of a certain age:

> The club met in the evening two or three times a half, and when elections had been held, the successful candidates, who had already gone to bed, were usually told of the fact by someone's coming to their rooms. I used to lie awake on those nights, hoping for a knock on my door and suffering when I heard the footsteps pass and the hand knock on another door instead. I had to wait until all the members of my own election and almost all of my junior election had been chosen, before I was allowed to join.[33]

When finally invited to join, early in 1928, he wrote that he cried – from joy but also from humiliation.

Ayer's loneliness was due in part to factors outside his control. There was, all seem to agree, very little conscious anti-Semitism in College. Ayer mentions only one incident when a 'loutish' boy in his election passed him a note about his tabernacle being in St John's Wood. Yet there does seem to have been a sense that he was 'different'. One contemporary remembered him as 'a one off', whose 'family was always shrouded in mystery'.[34] Another agreed: 'One knew extraordinarily little about Freddie Ayer's parents'.[35] Andrew Carnwath, in the same year as Freddie, detected an 'inferiority complex' – 'I always felt that he was uncomfortable about his social position'.[36] Ayer himself put his problems down to his never learning 'how to get on with boys from a different social class to my own'.[37]

Yet whatever the role played by religious or social background, some of the responsibility for his difficulties lay with Ayer himself. His schoolfellows remember what one describes as 'rather a cocky manner'[38] –

a fast, sharp tongue which could get him into trouble, as when he offended Miss Oughterson, the matron in College:

> She used to entertain a group of the younger boys in her room when they returned from the holidays and on one such occasion was telling us how an anonymous telephone-caller had repeatedly disturbed her sleep. 'I can't think why anyone would want to do that,' she said. 'Can you?' Even though I could see the question was rhetorical, I heard my voice saying, 'It depends how much they disliked you, Miss Oughterson', causing an intake of breath throughout the room.[39]

But beyond what he insisted was just a display of cheekiness, not malice, Freddie could be assertive, indignant and hectoring – 'a bumptious, aggressive, difficult boy', too pleased with his own cleverness.[40] A fellow pupil, writing about a football match in which Freddie played, described him as 'continually up in arms over somebody or something' and Ayer himself recognised the justice of Marsden's comments, in one of his reports, that Ayer's problem was that he never knew when he was not wanted.[41]

Ayer's religious views, in particular, became a source of aggravation. With distance, his atheism looks admirably precocious, clear-sighted and brave. He was repelled by what he saw as an irrational creed of guilt, damnation and blood sacrifice and did his best to convince his peers of his point of view. It is not surprising though, that they found his harangues 'a colossal bore'. 'That is one reason I think [why] I was not particularly liked by my companions. I went about trying to make converts, saying, surely you see this passage in Mark conflicts with that one in Matthew.'[42]

3

Apprentice

Some adults look back on childhood as the best period of their lives, but not Freddie Ayer. He was naturally resilient, and always had the capacity to enjoy himself – to lose himself in cricket, books or the theatre. But there is a hint of repression in his failure to remember anything about his early years and he did not contemplate the later ones with much nostalgia. His childhood, one senses, was associated in his mind with the longer history of irrationality and superstition that he denigrated as a philosopher: it was something to be escaped rather than cherished. Ayer's life, however, began to change in his last years at Eton, years in which, among other things, he discovered philosophy and romance. The young man who went up to Oxford in 1929 was a good deal happier and more confident than the boy who took the school certificate in 1926. And that was so, despite the death of his father.

Early in the 1920s, the Ayers began to forsake the beaches of Brittany and Normandy for Thun or other picturesque lakeside resorts in the area of Interlaken in Switzerland. These summer breaks were less than exciting. Freddie spent his days reading and playing tennis, the only game he ever played well; after supper in the hotel, he and his mother played cards or occasionally went to hear a concert or lecture. He nevertheless enjoyed himself, all the more so when one year his older cousin, Kenneth, kept him company.

In the summer of 1927, in between Freddie's fourth and penultimate year at Eton, the Ayers took what would prove to be the last of these holidays, staying with Marie and Philippe Suchard at their house in the rich, chocolate-producing town of Vevey on Lake Geneva. Freddie found his father in particularly high spirits: 'I felt closer to him than I had at any time since my early childhood.' There was a Walter Mitty side to Jules that had always exasperated Ayer; he had not made a success of his career, and for all his devotion to facts and figures, did not have the sharp, knowing grasp on reality that, in different ways, both Freddie and Dorus possessed. But he was a clever man, proud and ambitious for his son – 'he used to encourage me and comfort himself by repeating, not quite accurately, that the younger Pitt had become Prime Minister at the age of twenty two' – and with time Ayer might have learned to forgive him his shortcomings.[1]

As it turned out, however, the relation between Jules and Freddie had little further time to develop. Nine months later, Freddie was at home in St John's Wood for the Easter holidays. Father and son were together in the bathroom when Jules, aged just over sixty, suddenly collapsed with meningitis. On the principle that it is best to shield children from what really matters to them, Freddie was sent away to his grandparents in Eastbourne and was recalled to London too late to see Jules alive. He was there, though, to attend a dismal service at Golders Green Crematorium and was disturbed to see the coffin disappear towards the flames. 'Except at that moment,' Ayer wrote, 'I do not think that I felt the loss of my father very keenly, though later on, when I had come to learn more about his life, I regretted that I had not known him better and that I had not been more of a companion to him.'[2]

Perhaps if Freddie had appeared more upset, his Easter plans would have been altered. But it had been arranged that he should spend part of the holidays with a French family in Auteuil, in the suburbs of Paris, and he went. The family ran a finishing school for girls, but they accepted boys in the holidays, when most of their female pupils were away. Freddie quickly fell in with a group of students of both sexes, and particularly with one small dark, very attractive girl, Renée Lees, a year and a half his senior. Ayer admitted forty years later that 'due to the dreadful English boarding-school system, I hardly spoke to a girl until I was seventeen; I was shy and romantic in a Shelleyesque way and surrounded the girls I met with a mystical aura'.[3] That he was soon exchanging confidences with Renée must, then, have been important to him.

Renée Lees, born in 1909, was the victim of a miserable childhood. Her father, Thomas Hans Orde-Lees came from distinguished Protestant Anglo-Irish stock, the Lees of Blackrock, County Dublin. His father was Chief Constable of the Isle of Wight, a responsible position when Queen Victoria was at Osborne. Having passed through public school and Sandhurst, Orde-Lees became a captain and later colonel in the Royal Marine Light Infantry, serving in China during the Boxer Rebellion, before becoming superintendent of physical training at the naval college in Portsmouth. An attractive, athletic man, 'very susceptible to women', Orde-Lees was always on the lookout for a new adventure. An accomplished acrobat, trick-cyclist and mountaineer, he was also, like Dorus, a pioneer driver, although his preference was for motorbikes and, in the snow, motor-sledges.

Renée's mother, from a middle-class family, was seven years older than Orde-Lees, and, when she met him, already a widow with two almost grown-up children. Unhappy at home, she had run away, marrying her first husband at sixteen: he had died of delirium tremens when dispatched by his family to South Africa. She was also an alcoholic.

Both families were opposed to her marriage to Orde-Lees in 1902, and Renée left behind the beginning of an autobiography – written with Freddie's co-operation when they were both in their twenties – from which it is clear that her parents' life together was very unhappy. Orde-Lees hated his wife's drinking and jealousy, which drove her to further extremes of jealousy and drunkenness.

One of my earliest recollections is of seeing her collapse in her drunkenness against some railings, so that one of the spikes pierced her arm, making a wound of which she bore the scar all her life. I remember watching the blood saturate her dark-blue cotton dress and being surprised that it appeared black instead of red. A still more vivid memory is that of myself as a child of four standing at the head of a flight of stairs and watching my mother walk drunkenly across the hall below. I saw my father go angrily towards her and was suddenly terrified that he was going to hurt her. Then, half deliberately, in order to divert him, half overcome by my horror and fear, I threw myself head first downstairs. When my father picked me up I was unconscious.[4]

Renée was, by her own account, an exceptionally ungovernable child, who early on acquired her father's taste for physical adventure. Almost before she could walk, her father (who had wanted a boy) built her a tiny cycle: it marked the beginning of a lifelong love affair with bicycles and motorbikes. Left to her own devices, she roamed around the streets of Portsmouth, stealing and fighting, and making friends with the local working-class boys. 'Once I scratched a child's face so badly that we narrowly escaped being taken to law'.[5]

Orde-Lees had always wanted to 'go polar exploring one day' and had tried unsuccessfully to join Scott's last expedition to the Antarctic in 1910. When Renée was five he managed to attach himself to Shackleton's ill-fated trans-Antarctic expedition of 1914–16. Cantankerous and pessimistic, he was unpopular with the other men in Shackleton's team; it was said that when it appeared that the group might have to resort to cannibalism, he was chosen as the first to be eaten.

With Orde-Lees off in the Antarctic, there was no point in staying on the south coast, and, when the First World War broke out, Renée's mother moved with her to London, where, according to Renée, she spent most of her days in the pub, leaving her daughter to play on the pavement outside. Renée had, at least once, to accompany her mother to the police station after she had been arrested for drunkenness. Soon after this incident, the Orde-Lees family intervened and Renée was taken away, first to stay with her paternal grandparents and then with a guardian in Petersfield.

I was well cared for at Petersfield, but I felt the loss of the freedom that I had enjoyed when I lived with my mother. . . The children with whom I now played and went to school were so very insipid in comparison with my playmates of the streets. I could not deny myself the pleasure of shocking them. This eventually caused my expulsion from the local school, the occasion being my use of the word 'bloody' in class.[6]

Although Orde-Lees's family, the Lees of Blackrock, County Dublin,

40

were Protestants, he converted to Catholicism at the end of his Antarctic adventure and on his return in 1916 he sent Renée to a gloomy convent school on the outskirts of London. The experiment was inevitably unsuccessful. From the beginning Renée and the nuns were at loggerheads; at ten, she was suspended for removing her knickers and standing on her hands; at twelve, her parents were told to take her away for good.

> If the nuns did not achieve their aim of breaking my spirit, they did at any rate succeed in destroying my self-confidence. They told me so often that I was a moral outcast, destined to come to grief at the first opportunity, that I came not only to accept this view myself but also to believe that it was shared by everyone who met me. As a result, I grew to regard every stranger as a potential enemy and acquired a shyness and self-consciousness which increased as I grew older and made every new social contact an ordeal.[7]

Renée's autobiography runs out at this stage, but there is much in the twelve-year-old child – the physical vitality, the love of boyish pursuits, the identification with the oppressed, the bravado, insecurity and mischievousness – that remained with her for the rest of her life.

After returning from the Antarctic, Orde-Lees had joined the Royal Flying Corps, where he quickly alienated his superiors by starting a campaign to have the newly invented parachute installed in the Air Force's planes. To publicise his ideas, he and a lady companion travelled round the country giving demonstration jumps: in one stunt he jumped from Tower Bridge into the Thames. Sent on a military mission to Japan, he resigned his commission, found employment teaching English and settled down.

After her expulsion from the convent, Renée left her mother and joined her father in Tokyo, where she lived for the next five years. This was a formative period. She went to school in the city, learned Japanese, and developed a taste for the simple elegance of Japanese arts and design. More than that, she came to identify with the subservience expected of Japanese women. 'She had a way of formalising human relationships, and introducing regularity and ritual into them,' her son Julian recalled. 'She was more Japanese than English.'[8]

When Freddie met her in Paris, where she had been sent to round off her education, Renée had already failed to reconcile herself to several finishing schools, before alighting on Auteuil. Patricia Watkins (later Patricia Johnson, then Patricia Plowright), who was to become her closest friend, first met her in Paris at this time and remembered Renée's 'enormous sense of fun'. 'No sooner had we met than she tried to convert me to Catholicism. It was a game, really. She was a tomboy, and had been thrown out of a number of schools for climbing trees, showing her knickers and that sort of thing.'[9] Freddie recalled her as 'a remarkably pretty girl, small and vital, with brown hair, bobbed in the current fashion, a generous mouth and mischievous blue eyes'.[10] They liked each other immediately, although at this stage there was no question of a love affair. Here was someone utterly different from Freddie, yet also very much an outsider: a strong, unconventional young woman, who shared his instinctive radicalism.

Freddie had a wonderful time in Paris, where he found he could afford to be himself for the first time: enthusiastic, boisterous and clever. Here at last he knew easy friendship and perhaps also began to discover his effect on women: they were more impressed than men by his intelligence and more willing to be an audience. 'We went about Paris,' he wrote later, 'in a group with [another] English boy and one or two of the girls from the finishing-school, travelling in buses and on the Métro, talking incessantly, noisy young tourists, indifferent to the impression that we made. We went to the races at Auteuil and Longchamp, dallied in the Tuileries and explored the Bois de Boulogne. It was the first of many visits to Paris and the most idyllic.'[11] It is easy to forget, as he describes this happy episode in his memoirs, that his father had died only weeks before.

Ayer returned to Eton in April, for what was to be his last summer term and the beginning of his last full year. The records of the Eton College Debating Society for this time furnish the first contemporaneous record of his thinking. He had finally been elected the term before. In *Part of My Life* he wrote that he at once made the electors regret their decision by taking the debates much too seriously and the Debating Society's journal, in which each participant recorded his own contribution, seems to bear this out.[12] By the following spring feelings were running high, with criticism centred upon the 'three Ciceros, or at least Ciceros in their estimation' who, it was complained, dominated the debates. Judging by the way Ayer's regular but minuscule script covers the journal's pages, it seems likely he was one of the trio.

Although Ayer's arguments tend to be tight and lucid, it is not easy to recognise him in these pages. This is, in part, because the conventions of the forum, modelled on the debates of the Oxford Union and ultimately the Houses of Parliament, were constrainingly adult – so unlike the atmosphere in Paris. But the views he defended when he was seventeen were also very different from those for which he became famous.

True, in the first debate he spoke out against corporal punishment, and commended (in homage perhaps to his new friend Renée) 'Japanese methods of education in which the cane is anathema'.[13] But for the most part his values are those of a priggish adolescent. A debate on religion shows his atheism to have been of a very high-minded kind: he argued that it might 'have been necessary to create this fantastic, ludicrous, pathetic, monstrous picture of a personal God in order to frighten fools into being good', but hoped and believed that there would come a time when the need to believe in such a deity was outgrown, and men would learn to be good without the threat of divine sanction.[14] In a debate on medicine he talked disparagingly about 'the demon God of the progress of science' and in another he argued, along with most of his fellows, against the vote for women.[15] (This was ten years after its introduction, although just before the qualifying age for the female franchise was reduced from thirty to twenty-one in July 1928.) At points Ayer's argument descends into parody – 'often when meditating upon the designs of the creator we may have been tempted to speculate why women were created in this masculine world' – but the proposition that women were not fit to vote seems to have been urged seriously enough.

The pose struck most often, though, is not that of the misogynist, but the cultural pessimist. In one debate, on the culture of the United States, Ayer painted a hostile picture of America as a place where 'personal aggrandisement' is 'combined with a complete intolerance of spiritual non-conformity'. In another, on the motion that 'Practical science is detrimental to the culture of a nation', he attacked 'the counterfeit culture' of the industrial age:

I offer you four pictures taken from the pages of a daily newspaper on the morning after a bank holiday. The first, a jam of immobile cars. The second a huge crowd waiting on the elephants at the zoo. The third a seething mob at Brighton endeavouring to capture Lobby Lud. The fourth, an all night queue for a musical comedy. In every case a crowd of persons herding uncomfortably together in pursuit of some unattractive and uncomfortable goal ... Culture requires industry, discrimination, perhaps genius in its devotees. And genius ... can not be bought but it can be stifled, and the wireless and the civilisation that they represent are utterly repugnant to the free sphere of individualism in which culture must be sought ... You do not become cultured by being led in a crowd round an art gallery; you recede in fact from culture because your own perceptions are atrophied by the standards imposed upon them.[16]

Ayer may have alienated some of the other boys in the debating society, but in other respects this summer 'half' of 1928 was a good one for him. For the Fourth of June celebrations, there was a tradition that older pupils recited speeches or put on performances, always in their original language. In June 1928 Ayer did both, reciting Lord Randolph Churchill's famous 1884 speech attacking the profligacy of Gladstone's government and, with a group of other boys, staging a few scenes from a nineteenth-century comedy, La Farce de l'Avocat Pathelin. Ayer played the cloth merchant. Of the performances that day, the Eton Chronicle recorded, 'The French play received the greatest applause of all. This was largely due to the acting of Ayer, K.S. [King's Scholar], who is very much to be congratulated on the pace at which he spoke, while remaining perfectly audible'. In the same month, Ayer came second in the Examination of the First Hundred, an annual exam sat by all the senior boys, and first in its classics section. He was beaten only by Fitzroy Maclean, a brilliant linguist.

Freddie and his family must have taken pride in his successes, but he also had other things on his mind. His intellectual horizons were expanding, and for this Eton can take some of the credit. As he moved up the school, he came into more frequent contact with a number of unusually good teachers, including Alington, who had indulged Ayer's precocious atheism, and two younger men, Jack McDougal and Richard Martineau, both gifted classicists. One of them organised some classes on the pre-Socratic philosophers, offering Ayer an early taste of philosophy. Later in life Ayer would argue that if philosophy was to be taught in school, it should be done in this way, by an enthusiastic amateur.

Yet it was not Eton that introduced Ayer to modern philosophy. He seems to have initiated himself. One way into the subject was provided by Russell's *Sceptical Essays*, which Ayer seems to have read when it first came out in the middle of 1928, the beginning of his last year at Eton. Russell was fifty-six when these essays appeared, and his best philosophical work was behind him, but the collection displays all his usual verve and style. The essays cover a wide range of topics – machines and emotions, Eastern ideals of happiness, and puritanism – and Ayer would have found something to interest him in all of them.

He seems to have identified in particular with the opening essay, 'On the Value of Scepticism', in which Russell defends the 'wildly paradoxical and subversive' doctrine that 'it is undesirable to believe a proposition when there is no ground whatever for supposing it true'.[17] (Quoting this himself, Ayer once described it as having served 'as a motto throughout my philosophical career.')[18] As Russell argued, the widespread adoption of this doctrine would bring immense benefits, diminishing 'the incomes of clairvoyants, bookmakers, bishops and others who live on ... irrational hopes' and more generally undermining nationalist, political and religious prejudice:

In the modern world, those whom we effectively hate are distant groups, especially foreign nations. We conceive them abstractly, and deceive ourselves into the belief that acts which are really embodiments of hatred are done from love of justice or some such lofty motive. Only a large measure of scepticism can tear away the veils which hide this truth from us. Having achieved that, we could begin to build a new morality, not based on envy and restriction, but on the wish for a full life and the realisation that other human beings are a help and not a hindrance when once the madness of envy has been cured. . . This is no impossibly austere morality, yet its adoption would turn our earth into a paradise.[19]

Here, then, Ayer found a bold defence of the old empiricist belief in the value and importance of testing a proposition before believing it true.

Sceptical Essays, however, also contains articles devoted to specifically philosophical topics. It is here that Ayer would have first read about F.H. Bradley, William James, Bergson and the great German logician Gottlob Frege; it is here too, that he would first have learned about the challenge to traditional notions of time and space posed by Einstein's theories. In one essay in particular, 'Philosophy in the Twentieth Century', Russell offered a brief sketch of the development of philosophy over the previous forty years, which must have served Ayer as a guide in his subsequent reading. Russell described the process by which the Hegelian or Absolute Idealism of the 1890s, with its religious doctrine that neither time nor space is real, and that the universe consists of a single thinking, spiritual whole, had gradually been undermined by a new, more scientific philosophy – one that he himself had helped to develop:

> The first characteristic of the new philosophy is that it abandons the claim to be a special philosophic method or a peculiar brand of knowledge to be obtained by its means. It regards philosophy as essentially one with science, differing from the special sciences merely by the generality of its problems and by the fact that it is concerned with the formation of hypotheses where empirical evidence is still lacking. It conceives that all knowledge is scientific knowledge, to be ascertained and proved by the methods of science. It does not aim, as previous philosophy has usually done, at statements about the universe as a whole, nor at the construction of a comprehensive system. It believes, on the basis of its logic, that there is no reason to deny the apparently piecemeal and higgledy-piggledy nature of the world. It does not regard the world as 'organic', in the sense that from any part, adequately understood, the whole could be inferred as the skeleton of an extinct monster can be inferred from a single bone. In particular, it does not attempt, as German idealism did, to deduce the nature of the world as a whole from the nature of knowledge. It regards knowledge as a natural fact like another, with no mystic significance and no cosmic importance.[20]

There was much in this passage with which Ayer came to disagree. Where Russell was inclined to run science and philosophy together, Ayer would insist – it became almost a hallmark of his thought – on the distance between them: one was concerned with the empirical world, the other with solving conceptual problems, in particular those thrown up by scientific advancement. Yet Ayer always shared the spirit, if not the detail, of Russell's outlook, and identified wholeheartedly with his rejection of mysticism and philosophical idealism, his commitment to a broadly scientific view of the world, and his belief in the importance of scepticism, rigour and clarity of thought. Philosophy was not science, but Ayer agreed with Russell that it needed to be put on a scientific footing.

A book of a rather different nature but equally important to Ayer at this time was G.E. Moore's *Principia Ethica*. If *Sceptical Essays* gave him an overview of modern analytic philosophy, Moore's intricate and difficult treatise gave him a taste of the thing itself. Ayer's route to the book began in Paris, where a trip to the Louvre stimulated him to buy Clive Bell's *Art* (1914). In defending its famous doctrine that the value of a work of visual art lies not in its representational qualities but in its possession of a mysterious 'significant form', Bell had appealed to the authority of *Principia Ethica* and Ayer promptly went out and bought it.

When it first appeared in 1903, *Principia Ethica* had made a great impression on Strachey, Keynes, Bell and other future members of the Bloomsbury group, and it had a similar impact on Ayer. Later he came to reject Moore's argument that 'good' was a simple and therefore indefinable quality and also a non-natural one – something apprehended directly as a property of states of affairs, like the property 'yellow' – and his principle that the rightness of an action depends entirely on the goodness of its consequences. He also came to reject Moore's narrow conception of the good life as nothing more than 'the pleasures of human intercourse, and the enjoyment of beautiful objects' (although it is easy to see how this Bloomsbury ideal could have chimed with the high-minded aestheticism evident in his contributions to the Debating Society). Nevertheless there was a central feature of Moore's views which spoke to Ayer as a young man, and which he never gave up. This was Moore's insistence on the logical fallacy ('the naturalistic fallacy') in supposing that normative statements might be derived from descriptive statements – or to put it another way, in supposing that questions of morality might

47

be reduced to questions of fact. There was no way of demonstrating, Moore argued, and Ayer agreed, that a certain course of action is right or a certain feeling good, in the same way that one can demonstrate, say, that blood circulates around the body: morality is not a branch of science.

As Moore developed this argument, it proved to have wide application; he used it to criticise those Utilitarians like Bentham, Mill and Sidgwick whom he took to have identified good with pleasure, and those Social Darwinians who had reduced it to the survival of the fittest. But Moore also argued against Christians, mystics and idealists who suggested that morality can be founded on God's commands or intentions. For Ayer the anti-metaphysical, anti-religious dimension of Moore's argument – his contention, essentially, that it is right and proper to ask whether God's commands are good – must have been especially appealing.

In the summer of 1928 Freddie went with his mother to stay with relations in Holland. It was the first time he had visited this side of his family, entering a large network of great uncles, aunts and cousins and, beyond them, a more Jewish world than any he had known before – a cultured, self-reliant, commercially minded world soon to be destroyed.

Looking back from a distance of fifty years, Freddie remembered little of this visit, except for the hospitality and the endless meals, but he dated his love of seventeenth-century Dutch art to the time he spent in the Rijksmuseum in Amsterdam and the Mauritshuis in The Hague. Vermeer, in particular, became one of Ayer's favourite painters, and it is not hard to see why. The world of nature, as Ayer was the first to admit, remained a completely closed book to him; it gave him none of the sense of belonging to a larger world; it could not make him feel happy, though one has a sense that it could make him feel lonely. Vermeer's interior world of neat and elegant sunlit rooms, however, was one that he would always try to create around him.

That autumn, Ayer was back at Eton in time for his eighteenth birthday. Having moved into the senior election, he further aggravated his old enemy Marsden by leading an unsuccessful campaign to end corporal punishment – an early glimpse of Ayer in his role as moral campaigner. The initiative failed, but Freddie was now beginning to make friends. Nicholas Cheetham, from the year below, has fond memories of him at this time and recalled that he was popular, too, with the other boys.[21] Ayer also developed what he described as 'a sentimental friendship' with David Headley, a homosexual boy a year below him.

Unlike many of his new friends, Freddie had no family ties to Oxford or Cambridge, but Eton had informal connections with Christ Church and Robert Willis, a boy in Ayer's senior election and another new friend, had got a scholarship to 'the House' (as Christ Church was known) the year before. Freddie had tried for a scholarship along with him, but if he hoped to repeat the coup that had got him into Eton, and come victorious out of what was meant to be 'a trial run', he was disappointed. He had better luck in the winter of 1928, when he obtained the first of three Christ Church scholarships in classics.

There was little point in staying on for the summer term – especially as by this time Marsden wanted rid of him, and even hinted to Reine that he might have him removed – so in March he left Eton for good.

Ayer now had six months free before going up to Oxford and his grandfather suggested that he should learn Spanish, on the grounds that it would prove a useful asset should he ever go into business. It was arranged for Freddie to stay with a local family in Santander, a busy port on the northern coast of Spain, where a professor from Liverpool ran a summer school. Before he left, Renée turned up in London, having travelled from Tokyo by train. When he died, Ayer possessed a copy of Bernard Shaw's *The Intelligent Woman's Guide to Socialism and Capitalism*, inscribed 'Renée Lees, Trans-Atlantic Railway, February, 1929'. It seems likely that he sent it to her, or at least urged her to buy it, for he had read the book a year before and had been greatly influenced by it. In the time that she had been away, Renée had entered into an informal engagement with a major, fifteen years older than her, but she did not take the commitment seriously. In Paris she and Freddie had been friends. 'There had been nothing in our letters, either, to foreshadow our behaving differently from the way we had in Paris, but almost as soon as the first moment of shyness had passed we fell into each other's arms'.[22]

Renée decided it would be more adventurous for Freddie to go to Spain by steamer, and rather against his inclination, he took a boat from Liverpool across the Bay of Biscay. In Santander he lodged with a local teacher, his large family and their cats. Ayer had no problem picking up the language and was able for the rest of his life to get by in Spanish.

Santander had a certain glamour: the Spanish court resided there during the summer, frequenting the tennis club where Freddie went to play so that later he was able to boast that he had competed against the King's younger son in what was grandly known as the Championship of Northern Spain. But the flea-infested beds of his temporary home, its daily diet of kidney beans, and the smelly streets around it, offered a version of continental life different from anything he had known before. To a pampered eighteen-year-old, it was an exhilarating although sometimes unnerving experience. He managed, with mixed feelings, to sit through a bullfight, but fled in horror from a brothel to which an older boy led him. The girls called after him, *'Que loco'* – 'What a madman!'

4

Student

Ayer went up to Oxford in the month of the Wall Street crash. The day on which it ended, 'Black Tuesday', 29 October 1929, was his nineteenth birthday. The crash, however, had very little immediate effect on university life. The brightest of the bright young things – Evelyn Waugh, Harold Acton, Cyril Connolly, Anthony Powell – were all long gone and a new generation, who were to become swept up in the battles of the 1930s, was taking its place. W.H. Auden, Cecil Day-Lewis, and Hugh Gaitskell had left in the summer of 1928; Richard Crossman was in his final year; Louis MacNeice and Stephen Spender had been there for two years. Michael Foot, Denis Healey and Edward Heath were still to come. Politics, though, had not yet come to overshadow the university as it would later in the decade, and Ayer and his contemporaries lived what in retrospect seemed a gilded life.

The Oxford of the 1930s was still dominated overwhelmingly by students from the public schools; women and grammar school boys, although growing in number, had had little impact on the place. Regulations were relatively lax, and the academic demands on the students easily met. Labour was cheap and the pedestrian had not yet been marginalised by the motor car. There was, one contemporary recalled, hedonism in the very architecture of the place 'with its bells and towers, meadows and rivers and crumbling sandstone'.[1] This was a unique moment. Ayer's generation lived by very different values from their

51

parents; they were worldly, fun-loving and experimental. Yet their privileges were still Victorian. It is not surprising that so many, including Ayer, looked back on this time with a sense of loss.

Christ Church was a large college, aristocratic, religious and snooty, although with a strong academic tradition. Ayer was given Auden's old rooms, an elegant oak-panelled set on the north-west corner of the eighteenth-century Peckwater Quad. He breakfasted and sometimes lunched here, the meals usually brought from the kitchen by his scout or scout's assistant. Dinner in the beautiful candlelit hall was compulsory four nights a week—as was chapel. The university set the courses and the exams, and provided optional lectures, but undergraduate education was centred on the college. Ayer was expected to turn up with an essay to one or two tutorials a week. The classics course normally took four years, with the first five terms being devoted to honour moderations – a continuation of the kind of close study of Latin and Greek texts with which Ayer had grown impatient at Eton. He was however permitted to skip a year and move at the beginning of his second term straight into Greats, essentially a combination of philosophy and ancient history. At Christ Church, ancient history was in the hands of a conservative bachelor-don, Robin Dundas, whom Ayer did not like and who in turn found Ayer 'frigid'; it was lucky, then, that he was farmed out to 'Tom Brown' Stevens, a young and inspiring Greek historian. In philosophy Ayer managed early on to alienate one of his tutors, Michael Foster – an old-fashioned philosopher and a strict Christian – but got on with the other, Gilbert Ryle.

Later in life, Ayer would always talk of Oxford as a liberation. He learned, at least to some extent, to control his pugnacity, and, with a larger pool from which to search out friends, his views were not experienced as a threat or a provocation, as they had been at Eton. In time he would discover that he liked big cities best, but Oxford gave him space in which to become himself.

This raises the question of who that self was. There was a tension in Ayer. He was both a Lothario and a crusader, an aesthete and political radical, a lounger and an iconoclast. These figures are not entirely dissimilar – they share a disdain for puritanism, for moral hypocrisy, for pomposity, for the morality of the establishment – but neither are they always reconcilable. Like the hands at either end of a two-man saw, they have a common project but that does not always stop them pulling in different directions. In Ayer's undergraduate years, though, it was the aesthete who had the stronger purchase, at least outside philosophy. The crusader gathered his strength as the decade went on.

Ayer was still attracted by the Bloomsbury aestheticism he found in Moore and Clive Bell. He subscribed, at least until he read Hume in his second year, to the view defended in *Principia Ethica* that good, and by implication beauty, inhered objectively, although not materially, in objects or conduct, that they were not reducible to anything 'practical' and could only therefore be appreciated by a refined and educated sensibility. He decorated his rooms with prints by Cézanne and Van Gogh, then still a radical gesture, although here perhaps he was encouraged by Renée, always the more visual and more modern in her tastes.

Literature would always be more important to him than art, or for that matter music, and during these years he discovered or was guided to an impressive range of authors: Thomas Love Peacock (a lifelong favourite), Walter Pater, George Moore, W.B. Yeats, James Joyce, William Empson, Siegfried Sassoon, T.S. Eliot, Robert Graves, J.B. Priestley, Compton Mackenzie and Cyril Connolly, among others. Robert Willis, his old friend from Eton who remained a close friend at Christ Church, remembers him urging the merits of Proust, and by this time Ayer was reading French authors almost as much as English, including Racine, Stendhal, Balzac, Verlaine (a favourite poet), Baudelaire, Mallarmé, Valéry, Malraux, Céline, and Jules Romains. According to a neighbour and friend, William Outram, 'He was always most courteous and polite in his rather high, clearly articulated voice; which often I heard around midnight reciting poets, etc. into the night – possibly through his window. He had a wide range of lit. interests, I think Keats, Shelley and W.S. [William Shakespeare] were three. Reading or quoting aloud he could sound distinctly melancholy in tone of voice'.[2]

Ayer's feeling for literature was deep and genuine. He was a confident, independently minded judge, who returned to his favourite authors again and again, and was always eager to recommend works that he thought unjustly neglected, like W.H. Mallock's *The New Republic* or R.L. Stevenson's and Lloyd Osbourne's *The Wrong Box*. He also, at the end of his life, described himself as 'addicted to literary criticism'.[3] Yet for all literature's importance to him, he wrote no more than a dozen paragraphs on the philosophy of art in the course of his life, and while he wrote a little more by way of literary appreciation, his efforts in this area tend to be disappointingly bland. The blandness in his writing was in part, admittedly, almost deliberate: as a subjectivist in aesthetics as well as morals, Ayer was wary of foisting his own tastes on others. But it was in part traceable to the fact that, as Ayer understood it, 'the purpose of aesthetic criticism is not so much to give knowledge as to communicate emotion', and emotion was something Ayer found it hard to communicate.[4] The result was that whatever feeling he got from literature tended to remain locked up inside him.[5]

Dorus Citroën supplemented Ayer's scholarship with a monthly allowance, so he could afford to live in style. He always cared about his appearance and, encouraged by Renée, dressed smartly. Outram remembered him as 'a rather neat and dapper young figure, often in darkish clothes' and Isaiah Berlin recalled that he carried a silver-topped cane. At about this time, Ayer, who now took up smoking, started atavistically collecting cigarette cards again, but otherwise his interest in sport seems to have fallen off. His model in all things was first provided by Noël Coward's *Private Lives* and then by Oscar Wilde's great hero, Walter Pater, whose 'precious aestheticism' Ayer claimed 'represented my attitude to life'.*[6] He identified in particular with the famous, obliquely erotic passage in the conclusion to *The Renaissance*:

The service of philosophy, of speculative culture, towards the human spirit is to rouse, to startle it into sharp and eager observation. Every moment some form grows perfect in hand or face: some tone on the hills or the sea is choicer than the rest; some mood of passion or insight or intellectual excitement is irresistibly

---

* Ayer saw Coward's play on its first run in 1929 and it had 'a very deep' impact on him. Ayer suggested that he had been most impressed by the sophistication of the male lead, played by Coward himself, yet the play centres on a couple of misfits who, much to the world's bemused disapproval, find a perverse, compulsive, raucous pleasure in quarrelling and, indeed, hitting each other. Their conduct is hardly 'sophisticated' in the normal sense of the word. Did Ayer perhaps recognise himself in the play? As time would show, he too was something of a sexual misfit with strange enjoyments, unable to remain faithful to one woman for long. Although steady, moderate and judicious in most areas of his life, his relations with women were always running out of control. Perhaps it was Coward's plea for tolerance, his sympathy for odd, unconventional private lives, as much as the charm and style of the play's characters, that spoke to him.

real and attractive for us – for that moment only. Not the fruit of experience, but experience itself is the end.

And although Ayer never came very close to attaining Pater's ideal of a life of fresh sensation, he was dandyish enough for rumours to go round that he was 'effeminate'. Like Noël Coward, Ayer would have been pleased by the comment of his philosophy tutor Michael Foster on an end of term 'Collections' report: 'Exceptionally able, and, I think, industrious, though he takes pains to conceal the fact that he has taken pains.' After being invited to dinner in Ayer's rooms for the first time, Giles Playfair, a contemporary at Merton who became a friend, wrote in his diary entry: 'I like him, although he is rather precious'.[7]

Others too found him mannered. In his first year, Ayer involved himself in the Oxford Union and contributed to a wide range of debates, speaking in favour, for instance, of vivisection and the League of Nations. But it was not until the very end of the year that he was given a leading part, when he supported the motion that 'The blame for whatever decadence exists today in the universities should be laid on the public schools'. The *Oxford Magazine* reported that 'Mr A.J. Ayer certainly has the makings of a debater but loses much in effect by a certain affectation both of manner and matter', while *Isis* judged that 'Mr A.J. Ayer made a good point when he said that the secondary schools were in some ways more public school than the public schools themselves . . . He did not improve his speech . . . by making a prolonged gurgling noise which he announced to be a foreign tongue into which he had inadvertently dropped. Mr Ayer is a good enough speaker not to need to indulge in such intellectual snobbery'.[8]

Ayer, short at five feet seven inches, with narrow shoulders, thick dark hair, and what he liked to describe as a 'Bourbon nose', struck most of his fellows, as he had struck his peers at Eton, as unusually worldly and mature. This is how Henry Harvey, a Christ Church contemporary, remembered him:

> I see him walking past to get to the open south side [of the Quad], in a manner and gait quite unlike other undergraduates. He was hardly older than I was if at all, but he was already very much grown up, purposeful, looking neither to right or to left . . . He'd be likely to have a woman friend with him, as unlike Oxford women as he

was unlike Oxford men. She looked worldly, perhaps Spanish, smart, house-boots probably.[9]

Ayer's seeming sophistication had much to do with his 'foreign' appearance, European background and his advanced tastes in literature and art, but as this recollection suggests, his having a girlfriend or a 'mistress' was also counted 'a terrific thing'.[10]

Freddie and Renée had picked up their love affair on his return from Spain, and it continued after his removal to college. She was often up in Oxford to see him, and occasionally he would visit her in London, getting the last train – 'the fornicator' – back, to arrive just before college shut after midnight. Edward Playfair, an ex-Etonian (and Giles's cousin), recalls an encounter with Renée and Freddie, at the end of Freddie's first year, while spending a weekend with his Oxford friend, Guy Chilver:

> It was a glorious Summer: Oxford was looking at its best . . . It was all thoroughly enjoyable and at the end Guy took me to a restaurant with an upstairs room for dinner before taking me to the station to catch the train home. As we were leaving, and had reached the landing on the stairs above the entrance, the swing doors opened, and in there bounded a very exotic cat, attached by a silken thread to a beautiful girl in a rich fur coat; after her came a man of exotic good looks, wearing that get-up which soon became fashionable among intellectuals but which was then new to me, green shirt, darker green tie, black slouch hat; the three came upstairs; Guy started to introduce me but in vain; they went past us upstairs. Just the same, I looked at the man; he looked at me; when he was several steps above me he shot a hand down and said, 'oh, yes, I do know you, don't I?' This was Freddie, whom I only remembered as a rather inky little fag.[11]

Old mores were breaking down and on one trip to London, Freddie and Renée spent a night together, in the Royal Hotel in Russell Square. 'Renée had not entirely thrown off her Catholic upbringing, and her conscience was a little troubled. Mine was not. I was just nineteen and very much in love'.[12]

At this stage, Renée was the more political of the two. Ayer seems to have thought of himself as a radical liberal, but he was not especially interested in politics, going so far as to join, on social grounds, Oxford's most fashionable Conservative club, the Canning, and even becoming its secretary. 'I read one or two papers to the club and remember not without shame that in one of them I expressed some sympathy for an authoritarian form of government. I suppose that I had been influenced by Plato's arguments against democracy.'[13] In a separate venture, he and Giles Playfair joined Derek Walker-Smith, later a Conservative minister, in forming a group in emulation of the nineteenth-century 'fourth party' which made the fortunes of Randolph Churchill and Arthur Balfour. The idea was to interrupt the Oxford Union's proceedings, liven up debates and draw attention to themselves, rather than advance any one political cause. 'We were all,' Playfair said, 'fairly middle of the road in those days.'[14] The group soon fizzled out, but having launched themselves in this way, Playfair and Walker-Smith moved to the centre of undergraduate public life; hardly an issue of the student magazine *Isis* or *Cherwell* goes by without mentioning their involvement in one student organisation or another. Ayer on the other hand, after his poor performances at the Union, devoted his energies mainly to philosophy, literature and friends, although he did become president of the undergraduate philosophy group, the Jowett Society.

Of the friends Ayer made in his first year, the one who made the greatest impression was Maurice Bowra, a gifted classicist and literary critic and the most famous Oxford figure of his day. Bowra, 'short and sturdy, with a massive head, small watchful eyes and a resonant voice, delivering words like rapid musketry', was a decade and a half older than Ayer and already Dean at Wadham.[15] Nevertheless, he had an eye for young men and liked to cultivate the smarter undergraduates, inviting them to dinner parties in his rooms. Ayer met him almost by accident, in the rooms of a common friend, and was invited to dinner by him in his first term; although rendered dumb by drink on that occasion, he redeemed himself on others.

Bowra had witnessed terrible things in the trenches in France but had put these behind him, to become one of the brightest of the 1920s bright young things: promiscuous, pleasure loving and irreverent, with a passion for all things Mediterranean. His pornographic verses and catty *bons mots* were the stuff of legend – he said of one ill colleague, 'While there is death there is hope' – but in addition he had the capacity of the most gifted conversationalists to bring out the best in friends and guests.

There was a dark side to Bowra: he was troubled by his homosexuality (he lived in constant fear of blackmail) and by his inability to write as well as he spoke. But to those undergraduates lucky enough to be taken into his circle – to be appointed to his 'immoral front' – he was a liberating force: a living alternative to the values of the pre-war era. The art historian Kenneth Clark recalled how 'his priggish fears and inhibitions were blown to smithereens' by Bowra: 'the chief quality of his wit was its audacity. He said all the dreadful things one longed to hear said, and said them as if they were obvious to any decent man'. For Anthony Powell, 'Here was a don – someone by his very calling (in those days) suspect as representative of authority and discipline, an official promoter of didacticism – who, so far from attempting to expound tedious moral values of an old-fashioned kind, openly practised the worship of Pleasure'.[16] Bowra's writing on poetry and Greek literature is strangely uninspired but he had strong feelings for all forms of literature and could talk brilliantly about Proust, Yeats, Eliot and other modernists; some of Ayer's interest in these must have been picked up from him.

When it came to the crunch – the General Strike or appeasement – Bowra's sympathies were left-liberal, but he was not much interested in politics, and had been put off philosophy by the experience of being taught it by H.W.B. Joseph, his tutor at New College. He seems, though, to have admired Ayer's intellectual fervour, describing him as 'a young genius' in his memoirs, and Ayer in turn identified with his combination of irreverence and academic brilliance.[17] The two never became intimate – Ayer recalled that 'when we were alone there was a feeling of unease' – but Ayer was nevertheless 'influenced by him to the point of copying some of his mannerisms of speech and modelling [my] wit upon his'.[18] Here was a better, more appropriate model than Pater or Coward.

Like Ayer, Isaiah Berlin was quickly swept up in Bowra's circle but as Berlin remembered it, he and Ayer met independently. Early in his first year (Berlin's second) Freddie and his close friend Andrew Wordsworth arrived in Berlin's rooms at Corpus Christi in search of a meeting of the Jowett Society. Berlin, who had read *War and Peace* at ten, was already what he was to remain: a brilliant talker ('always using two words, where one will not do'),[19] learned in European history and literature, with an almost clairvoyant ability to bring the past to life. Wordsworth and Ayer were immediately taken by this babbling prodigy and invited themselves to stay. 'They behaved very badly,' Berlin recalled: 'they treated me like a curiosity and I had to send them away'.[20]

At first glance Berlin and Ayer had everything in common. Berlin's Jewish parents had emigrated from Russia to London in 1921, and his and Freddie's fathers, both in the timber trade, had known each other. Both young men, cosseted and indulged as children, experienced Oxford as a liberation, and each was amused by the other's company. Broadly sympathetic to the new philosophy emanating from Cambridge, they spent a great deal of their twenties arguing about logic, epistemology, political philosophy and ethics.

Yet for all the affinities, it was never an easy friendship. Towards the end of his life, Ayer was to say to Berlin, 'we are familiar but not intimate', although 'familiar but wary' might have done just as well.[21] As a young man Ayer was the more confident philosophically, and initially this must have impressed Berlin, who spent a good deal of the 1930s unsure of exactly what he believed. But Berlin was a timid, prudish youth, who recoiled from the very thought of sex, and even in later life he never managed to reconcile himself to the way Ayer behaved towards women: 'He was like the Don Giovanni of the Champagne Aria – he was obsessed with women.' And with time Berlin became disillusioned with Ayer as a philosopher, coming to feel that his work relied on a small set of formulae: 'He was the best writer of philosophical prose since Hume, better even than Russell, but he never had an original idea in his life. He was like a mechanic, he fiddled with things and tried to fix them.'[22]

Ayer, on other hand, was exasperated by Berlin's political moderation and intellectual caution. Berlin remembered Ayer reproaching him at one point in the 1930s: 'You're not much of a crusader are you?'

In fact the differences between the two men went much deeper than either of them can at first have understood: both were passionately liberal in politics and, for rather different reasons, both men doubted the possibility of establishing a rigorous ethical system: morality was a matter of often conflicting intuitions and sentiments. But where Ayer thought the job of philosophy was to systematise and simplify, Berlin always insisted on the limits of systematic thought. Where Ayer wanted to see the development of an empirical social science, Berlin came to insist on the irreducible diversity of ways of life. Where Ayer criticised nationalism and religion, Berlin argued that we cannot live without group identities. It is typical that while Ayer, without in any way denying his Jewishness, wished to leave it behind – 'it simply was not important to him' – Berlin became a Zionist.[23]

Not all of Ayer's friends flew as high as Bowra and Berlin. His closest companion was Andrew Wordsworth, a good-looking student from Marlborough, who had come just below Ayer and John Cheetham in the competition for Christ Church's three classics scholarships. Wordsworth had little of Ayer's intellectual sharpness, but Ayer remembered him as 'more worldly than I was, and much better read, at least in modern literature. He had spent some time in Paris before coming up to Oxford and had discovered the Surrealists, of whom I had not previously heard. It was under his influence that I began to read Proust, and James Joyce's *Ulysses* and the works of D.H. Lawrence.'[24]

Wordsworth, a great-grandson of the poet, had been brought up a Christian, but he combined religious beliefs with an active sexual life and a good deal of drinking. Isaiah Berlin does not seem to have liked or approved of him, but Richard Wollheim, who was taught by him at Westminster later in the 1930s, describes a very engaging character – 'a friend of the [1930s] poets and a poet himself'.[25] He was 'totally unconventional in all ways: bohemian, unambitious, but also very serious and emotional'.[26] In *Part of My Life* Ayer recalled a dinner party he and Wordsworth gave together in their first year, to which they invited all the people they agreed were most brilliant in the university, including Berlin and Bowra. During the summer vacation of 1930, Ayer went to stay with Andrew and his mother in their house in Lulworth Cove.

At the end of Freddie's first year, he and Renée were as much a couple as ever and wrote to each other almost every day: 'If I had not heard from her in the morning,' he recalled, 'I used to wait anxiously for the evening post, going down repeatedly to the foot of the staircase to see if it had been delivered.'[27] Renée remained close to the friend she had made at Auteuil, Patricia Watkins, and often stayed at Patricia's parents' house in Hampstead. Freddie charmed her mother and was allowed to stay the night, although Mrs Plowright would have been less welcoming if she had known what he was doing upstairs. Sometimes the couple stayed in hotels together in London and elsewhere, always, of course, presenting themselves as a married couple and using false names. On one occasion in Paris, Freddie nearly got himself in trouble, insisting, when the proprietor recognised him from an earlier visit, that he was not himself but his cousin.

Renée was certainly a catch, and although one or two of Freddie's friends found her eccentricity affected, most of them remember her as gutsy and sexy – there was nothing of the bluestocking about her. On the contrary, she had acquired a way with machines from her father, and had become, like him, a motorbike fanatic. On the weekends she and Patricia would drive to country fairs together so she could ride her Harley-Davidson on 'the wall of death'.[28]

At the end of Ayer's first year, Renée returned to Tokyo to spend six months with her father, taking the Trans-Siberian railway to Vladivostok, stopping off in Moscow on the way. Freddie went with her as far as Berlin. In Germany he met up with his friend John Cheetham, and made a tour of Bavaria, travelling by train and bus and staying in comfortable, although not the best, hotels.

Amongst Oxford's undergraduates, the cult of Weimar – the land of sexual freedom, progressive politics and avant-garde culture – had just begun to establish itself, but if either Ayer or Cheetham encountered the sort of *demi-monde* that Christopher Isherwood wrote about, it went unrecorded. In his memoirs Ayer simply mentioned finding Bavaria's baroque architecture 'particularly attractive'. Cheetham, a tall handsome man who was later to become ambassador to Mexico, remembered Ayer well: 'The flow of his talk was fascinating; he never seemed to get bored ... Although he could appear scathing about stupid people, he was someone unusually kind and nice ... What did strike me, knowing him both at Eton and Oxford, was that his family seemed such humble people, not socially but in character – almost pathetically proud of having a successful son, from an intellectual and social point of view.'[29]

Ayer spent most of what was left of the summer with his mother in London. After Jules's death, she had moved with a maid into a flat in Eyre Court, a large and gloomy mansion block not far from their old home in Swiss Cottage, with a room for Ayer and another for a maid. Ayer had had a good year. He had found new friends and inspiring models and felt happier and more confident than ever before. Yet he still lost his patience with his mother and her fussing, unworldly ways, and they continued to quarrel.

5

Homecoming

Ayer returned to Oxford in October 1930 for the beginning of his second year. He kept his rooms and life went on much as it had before, although Renée was in Japan until after Christmas. He continued to enjoy himself, moving in ever smarter circles and making several friends, including Gilbert Highet, an older classicist who eventually became a professor at Columbia and Martin Cooper, a gifted pianist with whom Maurice Bowra had fallen in love. Cooper used to tell the story of how he asked Freddie what he had been doing and Freddie replied, 'dreaming and reading Racine'.[1]

The most important new friend was Goronwy Rees, another of Bowra's handsome young men. Rees, the only one of Freddie's companions from these years not to have been to public school, had been brought up on strictly Calvinist principles by his father, a preacher and theologian from Aberystwyth. From Cardiff High School he won a place at New College where his philosophy tutor, H.W.B. Joseph, attempted, as Rees put it, to 'wheedle, cajole, threaten and bully' him into the 'Platonism he thought appropriate to a scholar of the College'. When he met Ayer, however, Rees was in full revolt against religion, his father and Joseph.

A dazzling talker, he combined the looks of a film star with an extraordinarily receptive mind and an ability to live for the moment which none of his pleasure-loving peers could quite equal. Despite New College's chaplain's prediction that Rees was 'far too great a social success' ever to get a first, he not only secured one, but was subsequently elected to All Souls, where he published a well received novel, *The Summer Flood*. Later he moved to London, working first on the *Guardian* and then the *Spectator*, and published a second novel *A Bridge to Divide Them*. Yet in the end things did not go well for Rees, whose many careers – novelist, historian, journalist, businessman, educationalist, spy – were dogged by drink, depression and scandal. He was certainly extremely clever and extraordinarily charming, but as Stuart Hampshire observed, he 'could never be tedious enough for his own good' – his social gifts outweighed his emotional stability.[2]

Ayer, however, remained closer to Rees than he did to any other Oxford friend. It is not hard to see what drew them together. They were both outsiders who achieved whatever status they gained by virtue of their intelligence. Both were left wing, and both shared what Ayer described as 'a zest for experience'; Rees was a sexual adventurer from the beginning, seducing both Elizabeth Bowen and Rosamond Lehmann in his twenties, while Ayer became one.

Beyond these affinities, though, perhaps there was something deeper. Each man was aware of experiencing the world in an unusual way; neither had a strong sense of his life as a narrative or as part of a larger whole. Rees, in fact, used to say that Hume's description of the self as 'a collection of perceptions which succeed each other with inconceivable rapidity and are in perpetual flux and movement', described his experience of his own self exactly. Critics of Rees's 1960 memoir, *A Bundle of Sensations*, in which he elaborated this account of himself, have questioned his sincerity, arguing that like everyone else he had strong traits of character of which he must have in some sense been aware. Yet some people do experience life in a more episodic fashion than others and there is grounds for thinking that Ayer too fell into this class. Both men had what Ayer described as 'an unusually strong capacity to live intensely in the moment', but very little sense of the inner self as a thing worth exploring; neither had a strong feeling of connectedness to other people or to nature.[3] Isaiah Berlin remembered Ayer once saying, 'I don't think in the first person but the third person singular: I say not "I am going to do this or that" but "Freddie is going to do it"'.[4] Like Rees, he experienced the world in a way that was 'intense' but also 'thin'.

Ayer's remoteness from some of the more ordinary human emotions became especially evident when he was touched – or rather, untouched – by death. In November of his second year, his Citroën grandmother died. 'Her funeral, like my father's, was held at Golders Green Crematorium', Ayer impassively recorded. 'There was no service, but my grandfather, standing by the coffin, made an emotional speech in which he called upon his grandchildren to prove themselves worthy of her. I believe that we were all very fond of her, as she undoubtedly was of us, but the livelier image of my grandfather overshadows her in my memory'.[5]

That Christmas Freddie accompanied Dorus, and presumably Reine, on a Mediterranean cruise.

A month or two later Renée arrived back in London with some dramatic stories to tell. She had taken a boat from Japan to California and then bought a motorbike and driven across the country, via the Southern states, to New York. Apparently, she was the first woman to make the journey in this way, and her arrival in New York was greeted by a flurry of journalists and photographers. She made an odd figure, having cut off a bit of fur from her coat and strapped it across her nose in order to protect it from the sun. Freddie, always reluctant to commit himself too thoroughly, had written to her in Tokyo trying to end their relationship, but they quickly picked up where they left off. Renée now moved into a small flat in Limerston Street in Chelsea, where Freddie would visit her, and they began to take most of their holidays together, keeping their expeditions a secret from their parents.

Ayer certainly loved her, but their relationship was always stormy. She was exceptionally pretty, with many admirers, and he would often give way to jealousy. Ayer, for his part, claimed that at this stage he never had eyes for any other women. William Outram, though, remembers how, as a student, Ayer took a fancy to a good-looking American who was reading a 'haphazard' course in English literature. Ayer asked her to tea and Outram met her some days later: 'Billy, it was *awful* and I'll never go again; he diagnosed me, dissected me, metaphorically, analysed me, asked endless questions and, not content with *that* showed decidedly amorous inclinations'. Later Outram met Freddie in the quad: 'You know Willy, I shouldn't have thought she was any good to you. Intelligent and amusing, but *absurdly* chaste and ridiculously virginal'.[6]

Almost nothing that Ayer wrote as an undergraduate has survived. The exceptions are one or two unremarkable reviews (one of a

production of Flecker's *Hassan* in *Cherwell* and another of a book by
Ernest Dimnet on psychology in Isaiah Berlin's *Oxford Outlook*), and a
letter sent in his third year to the *New Statesman* defending Russell's *The
Scientific Outlook* from a hostile reviewer. We get glimpses of his interests
and ideas from other sources, however, and it is not hard to reconstruct
the outlines of his intellectual development.

At the end of his first term his tutors were already marking him out as
an 'extremely penetrating, and unsentimental thinker' (Gilbert Ryle)
with 'scant respect for' his superiors (Robert Longden, an ancient
historian) and, although a number of them complained about a certain
coldness in him ('Praise would benefit and might melt him': Longden),
they continued to commend his intellectual independence and preference for 'self-help'. By the middle of his second year, Stevens and the
other ancient historians recognised that although Ayer worked hard
enough for them, his real interest was in philosophy.

William Outram shows that Ayer's philosophical passions spilled from
his tutorials into his conversation:

> He was a ready talker and appeared to be fond of arguments,
> discussions, often drawn out into wordy locutions on almost any
> subject – such as some people might dispose of in a few phrases. He
> liked pros and cons, premises, 'fors and againsts', proofs and
> disproofs; and where none were available, possibly suspension of
> such conversations . . . 'I don't believe in a God, as I can't prove his
> existence, Willy' he said once. 'But you know, your conversation is
> good; you ought to make it work harder – on more important
> subjects . . .' 'Such as?', I asked. 'Oh, the meaning of Existence or
> Being – Is it or isn't it, etc. But everything needs its own proof'. He
> became quite worked up over what I considered everyday problems.[7]

As this suggests, atheism continued to be intensely important to him –
here was an issue where philosophy seemed of very real relevance, with
the power not only to expose the fallacies in the arguments for the
existence of God, but to break down the unthinking acceptance of moral
and political authority which belief in God tended to encourage.

Ayer often argued about atheism with his friend Andrew Wordsworth
or with anyone else he could find, but it was not until his second year

that he found an opponent really worthy of him. Martin d'Arcy, in his early forties with striking El Greco looks and a 'fine slippery mind', had studied philosophy at Campion Hall, a Jesuit college affiliated to the university, before the war. He returned to the Hall as lecturer and tutor a few years before Ayer's arrival.[8] A worldly conversationalist and a powerful preacher, he fast established himself as the country's most important Catholic apologist, winning over a series of high-profile converts including Waugh himself. Ayer, however (no doubt setting out with Hume's *Dialogues Concerning Natural Religion* under his arm), was unintimidated, and a seminar which D'Arcy ran once a year on Thomas Aquinas degenerated, under the impact of Ayer's objections, into a running argument on the existence of God. Father d'Arcy paid Freddie the compliment of describing him to Evelyn Waugh as 'the most dangerous man in Oxford' and Ayer in turn, while he can't have thought much of D'Arcy's florid prose or snobbish devotion to the Anglo-Catholic aristocracy, seems to have respected his teacherly patience.

Respect, however, did not enter into Ayer's feelings towards most of his philosophical superiors.

The Oxford sub-faculty of philosophy of the 1920s and 1930s was by far the largest in the country, but the philosophy it produced was uninspiring, and is now virtually never read. A variety of factors contributed to this sorry state of affairs, but perhaps the most important was the First World War, which effectively killed off the generation, including the philosophical generation, immediately before Ayer's own. The Kant scholar H.J. Paton and R.G. Collingwood, an idealist peculiar to himself, were among the few philosophers to return to Oxford from the war, and they both remained on the edge of things. The result was that when Ayer and his contemporaries took up philosophy they found the subject in Oxford still dominated by pre-war traditions. This seems to have exacerbated the usual inter-generational conflict. Students and teachers, Gilbert Ryle remembered, looked bitterly at each other over 'a boundless military cemetery'.[9]

The neo-Hegelianism of the 1890s was still represented in Harold Joachim, Professor of Logic. He had been an influential figure in his time but was in his sixties by the time Ayer took up philosophy and like most Oxford philosophers was chiefly interested in the history of the subject. The same was true of Michael Forster, the senior of Ayer's two tutors at

Christ Church, who schooled Ayer in the intricacies of Plato and Kant, but otherwise contributed nothing to his development.

With Hegelianism more or less an exhausted force, Oxford philosophy of the 1920s and early 1930s was dominated by the 'Oxford realists', H.A. Prichard, Professor of Moral Philosophy, and H.W.B. Joseph, a ferociously energetic college tutor. The main forum of philosophical discussion at the time – 'the philosophers' tea' – always resolved itself into an argumentative duel between them. Yet these too were men in their sixties, who had arrived at their ideas, such as they were, decades earlier. The only book Prichard published, *Kant's Theory of Knowledge*, had come out in 1909, while the first edition of Joseph's main work, *Introduction to Logic*, appeared as early as 1906.

Whereas the majority of the Cambridge philosophers were trained mathematicians or scientists, the Oxford realists had read classics, a training which, it seemed to Ayer, had given them a stubborn disapproval of new ideas. It is, in fact, much easier to say what they were against than what they were for. Both followed the earlier Oxford realist Cook Wilson in rejecting Bradley's Hegelianism and Sidgwick's Utilitarianism; both stood out against Einstein's relativity theory and Russell's logic. Joseph had written against Marx's labour theory of value and against the Darwinian 'cult of evolution'. Prichard in particular was suspicious of all philosophical systems and made a virtue of a cautious and *ad hoc* approach to philosophical problems; at the beginning of every year his name appeared on the lecture list: 'The Idea of Moral Obligation (continued)'. In ethics they were, like Moore, intuitionists, only a good deal sounder on morality and religion. Joseph was intensely religious: he liked to say that a favourite hymn, 'Immortal, Invisible, God Only Wise', expressed his sentiments exactly. Ayer does not seem to have had much contact with either philosopher as an undergraduate, but in so far as he did, he remembered them as 'two terrible old monsters', 'reactionary', and 'narrow and dogmatic'.[10]

It is not surprising, then, that the tradition inaugurated by Moore and Russell in Cambridge had made hardly any inroads in Oxford. Prichard had attacked Russell's theory of knowledge in an article in *Mind* in 1915 and Joseph quarrelled with Russell's follower, Susan Stebbing, in an exchange of articles in the same journal in the early 1930s. For the most part, however, Oxford philosophy simply ignored the ideas flowing from

Cambridge. Sturt's guide for Oxford undergraduates, *Philosophy in Lit. Hum. Practical Hints for Students of the School*, which came out two years before Freddie arrived, does not mention a single name associated with the new Cambridge school, except C.D. Broad, who is cited only in passing.

Yet there were one or two figures around who were beginning to take an interest in the new currents and whom Ayer found personally sympathetic. One was Henry Price, a tutor at Trinity until in 1935 he succeeded Joachim as professor of logic. Price, a shy, reclusive figure, belonged to no school or group, but had studied as an undergraduate at the Cambridge of Moore, Russell and Broad and was the first to launch the idea that young Oxford could learn from them. In his last year as an undergraduate Freddie went to Price's lectures on the role of sense-data in perception and found them 'wonderfully stimulating'.[11]

The more important figure, however, where Ayer's development was concerned, was his tutor, Gilbert Ryle. Ryle was ten years older than Ayer and had just missed fighting in the war. He had got a first in Greats and then another in PPE; the school of politics, philosophy and economics was new and Ryle had been invited to take finals in it in order to set the standard for a first-class degree. When Ayer first met him he was still writing about the German phenomenology of Brentano, Husserl and Heidegger, but he does not seem to have interested Ayer in that tradition. Anyway, his attention was turning towards the Cambridge school and in Ayer's last year he published his first major article, 'Systematically Misleading Expressions', in which he commended and developed what was most fundamental in their approach.

Ryle argued that the job of philosophy was to provide philosophical paraphrases of statements so as remove any weird ontological commitments which they might seem to contain – to reformulate, for instance, sentences like 'Unpunctuality is reprehensible', which might appear to be of the logical form 'The Parthenon is in Athens', and so give unpunctuality the same sort of reality as the Parthenon, into something like 'Whoever is unpunctual deserves that other people should reprove him for being unpunctual.' Anticipating Ayer's own arguments in *Language, Truth and Logic*, Ryle suggested that by disregarding the distinction between the grammatical appearance of statements and 'what the statements really record', metaphysicians are often led into talk which at best 'is systematically misleading ... and at worst ... meaningless'.[12]

Ryle, 'a confirmed bachelor' in the code of the day, was a complicated character. He was a very conscientious teacher and a writer of brilliance, with an informal playful style all his own. But he affected a bluff boat-club sensibility and his tastes in everything except literature were militantly middlebrow. When Isaiah Berlin, bumping into him in the street, told him that he had just heard a moving rendition of Bach's B-Minor Mass in the Sheldonian, Ryle responded, 'Oh been listening to tunes again have you?'[13] If Freddie was 'an aesthete', Ryle liked to present himself as a 'hearty', and so Ryle had mixed feelings about his dazzling student. He seems to have disapproved of his flamboyance and was wary of his zeal, but he recognised his intellectual qualities, describing Ayer in his last report (Easter 1932) as 'the best philosopher that I have yet been taught by, among my pupils'. Ayer, in turn, found that they did not have a great deal in common outside philosophy, but was immensely grateful for the inspiration and encouragement Ryle provided; he made philosophy at Christ Church seem important and exciting.

Early on in his time at Oxford, Ayer would have read the eighteenth-century Scottish philosopher David Hume and it is surprising that he left no record of what must have been a crucial moment in his intellectual development: Hume was to remain, with Russell, the philosopher he most admired.* Thus while Ayer agreed with the British empiricists in general that all knowledge has its source in experience, and is built out of sense-impressions, he followed Hume, rather than Locke or Berkeley, in his account of exactly what we can be said to know on the basis of these impressions. Hume's empiricism, as Ayer read it, offered him a criterion of significance against which to test the meaningfulness of a concept. With this in place Hume could demonstrate that many cherished metaphysical entities – God, absolute values, necessary causation, the self as a substance underlying our impressions and ideas – had no counterpart in our experience, and were, to that extent, illegitimate. For both men, the greatest challenge posed by philosophy was to escape the private

---

* Ayer does write, in *Part of My Life*, that on first reading Hume's *Treatise of Human Nature*, he scrawled on its flyleaf, 'In order to discover what he means, he studies the phenomena by which his proposition is verified' (*PML*, p. 116). This is, of course, an anticipation of the verification principle that he is later supposed to have borrowed from the Vienna Circle.

world in which their doctrines of sense-impressions threatened to imprison them, and to justify our beliefs in the external world, the past and other entities of common sense. Like Hume's, Ayer's philosophy represents a protracted attempt to navigate a course between the Scylla of metaphysics and Charybdis of extreme scepticism.

Ayer also deepened his knowledge of Russell, Hume's successor, working mainly by himself, but helped along by Price and Ryle. Although the more technical parts of Russell's formal logic did not interest him, and were to some degree beyond him, he mastered the basic ideas behind Russell's philosophy of mathematics and enjoyed the series of more general works that started with *The Problems of Philosophy* (1912), *Our Knowledge of the External World* (1914) and *The Analysis of Mind* (1921).

As a philosopher, Russell wanted to make the world fit for science; he wanted to place empirical knowledge on a firm foundation by trying to reconstruct it with as few assumptions as possible. He faced, however, the problem faced by any scientifically minded philosopher: that our language seems to commit us to entities hardly compatible with science, like classes, numbers, propositions, non-existent and imaginary characters, such collectives as the family or the state – objects which too easily took on a fantastic life of their own.

Part of Russell's achievement as a logician, as Ayer came to see it, was to show us ways of freeing ourselves from these commitments by developing techniques enabling the translation of philosophically perplexing propositions into less troubling forms. A famous example of this attempt to get beneath 'grammatical' to 'logical structure' was provided by Russell's 'Theory of Descriptions', which purported to show how statements that refer to things that do not exist – and which might thus suggest the existence of a shadowy realm of non-existents – can be translated into statements containing covert existence claims. We could never speak this logically pellucid language – it would be impossibly cumbersome. But its existence warrants the use of ordinary language: it enables us, or the philosophers among us, to understand just what is, and what is not, being said.

For Ayer, however, Russell's work in philosophical logic was only half his achievement. He also applied his new logical techniques to problems in the philosophy of mind and perception, thus giving fresh impetus to the old empiricist project. In accordance with the most fundamental principle of empiricism, Russell took it as axiomatic that 'every proposition which we can understand must be composed of constituents with which we are acquainted',[14] and he never veered from his belief that the only perceptual objects of which we are directly aware are our own private sense-impressions or sense-data. Starting from the truism that 'if several people are looking at a table at the same moment, no two of them will see exactly the same distribution of light', it seemed evident to Russell, as it did to Ayer, that 'the real table, if there is one, is not the same as what we immediately experience by sight'.[15]

Where Russell did change his views was on the relation between the sense-experiences on which our knowledge of the external world is founded, and the external world itself. Before the First World War and again from around 1927 he developed a causal theory, reminiscent of Locke's, and argued that one could assume the existence of the physical world as the best explanation for sensory experiences. In the intervening period, however, in line with the principle 'wherever possible substitute constructions out of known entities for inference to unknown entities', he adopted a phenomenalist position. According to this, every statement of common sense or science could be reduced to a statement about our actual and hypothetical sensory experiences. From what Ayer says in his autobiographical writings, he seems from the beginning to have found this phenomenalist approach the more promising. He seems, also, to have been convinced by *The Analysis of Mind* of 1921, in which Russell took his phenomenalism a stage further and, developing a theory akin to William James's 'neutral monism', argued that both mind and matter are logical constructions out of sense-data, which are themselves neither mental nor physical. This theory has more than a hint of mind–matter dualism about it, in that it admits the existence of states of consciousness which are not definable in physical terms. But then neither Russell nor Ayer was ever an out-and-out materialist.

In the summer holiday of his second year, Freddie went with some friends of Renée to St Raphael in the south of France. Ayer liked the town, 'but my relations with Renée became tense, as they usually did when we were in the company of others, especially if they were people that I did not know very well'.[16] From St Raphael they went on their own to visit Arles and Avignon.

They had been lovers for over two years and now began to talk about marriage, although both approached the possibility with conflicting emotions. Ayer wrote unrevealingly about his own feelings, admitting to 'a half conscious reluctance to assume the responsibilities of marriage' while feeling himself 'to be committed' and not wanting 'to separate from her'.[17] But one gets the sense of a couple deeply attached to each other, although not always for the best of reasons. They had both suffered humiliations and needed love and admiration; she looked after him and he seemed destined for success. They made each other feel secure.

The summer of 1931 was Ayer's last as a student. On the national stage as well, an old world was passing. While Freddie and Renée were in France, Britain plunged into financial crisis, and the Prime Minister, Ramsay MacDonald, without consulting his Labour cabinet, formed a national government with his Liberal and Conservative opponents. It quickly set about raising income tax while cutting wages and state benefits. The repercussions of MacDonald's 'great betrayal' and the worsening depression were enormous. To many Labour party members, and those like Ayer who sympathised with it, the events of that summer and autumn offered an early demonstration of the bankruptcy of the established order. There were many other demonstrations – Abyssinia, the Spanish Civil War, appeasement – to come. The sense of economic insecurity was obvious even in Oxford, where, as Isaiah Berlin remembered, 'The whole atmosphere changed' almost overnight. Students found their allowances cut; suits gave way to tweed jackets and trousers; the last traces of aestheticism evaporated like a splash of eau-de-Cologne.[18] The Wall Street crash had marked their overture, but with the events of that summer, the 1930s had really begun.

Back in Oxford early in the autumn, Ayer retained his rooms in Christ Church and continued his studies. October's general election fell two days before his twenty-first birthday, which debarred him from voting, but in principle (and much to Dorus's annoyance) he now supported Labour. Yet Ayer always remembered the autumn term of 1931 less for its devastating landslide, ushering a decade of complacent Conservative rule, than as the moment when he discovered Wittgenstein's *Tractatus Logico-Philosophicus*.

Once again he was fortunate to have Ryle as his tutor. Ryle had already made contact with Wittgenstein on the latter's return to

Cambridge in 1929 and now directed Ayer to his one published work, the *Tractatus*. 'Wittgenstein,' Ayer wrote, 'did not then figure in the Oxford curriculum, and I knew nothing about him at all until I started to read this book. Its effect on me was overwhelming . . . This was exactly what I wanted, the very conclusions I had been groping towards on my own. All the difficulties that had perplexed me were instantly removed.'[19]

The *Tractatus* is a very difficult book – at places almost incomprehensible; to have been converted by it at such a young age, and at a time when it was hardly known in Oxford, was stunning proof of Ayer's precocity. Yet, as his recollection makes clear, for all of the impact it had on him – and no book was ever to impress him in quite the same way – it did not so much change his views as help articulate and clarify them. Ayer's encounter with Wittgenstein recalls his quick and easy assimilation of Russell and Moore at Eton: it was not so much an intellectual conversion as a homecoming.

In his excitement, Ayer argued about the *Tractatus* at length with Ryle and Isaiah Berlin, and in his final term gave a paper on it at a meeting of the Jowett Society held at Christ Church. It was almost certainly the first occasion on which Oxford was treated to any public discussion of Wittgenstein's work. Berlin, who replied to the paper without himself having read the *Tractatus*, remembered Ayer that evening, resplendent in black tie and red carnation, and later described the occasion as 'the opening shot of the great positivist campaign' that he waged over the next ten years.[20] Quintin Hogg, Ayer's old enemy from Eton, now a fellow at All Souls, was there and, worried by the moral and religious implications of Wittgenstein's doctrines, kept asking questions. Berlin recalled him saying 'I am wondering . . .' and Freddie jumping in with 'Quintin, you always are.'[21]

Although Ayer's paper has not survived but it is not hard to see what so excited him about the *Tractatus*. He would have liked the ambition of the book, its authoritative tone and, above all, the way it claimed to have found 'the final solution of the problems' with which it dealt.[22]* More

---

* It must have helped Ayer's identification with the book that in 1932 Wittgenstein was a relatively young man, in his early forties, and that, after a decade spent in Austria, he had recently returned to nearby Cambridge. As is well known, Wittgenstein's ideas had changed in the period between the publication of *Tractatus* and Ayer's first encounter with it, but Ayer was not aware of this. To him, Wittgenstein was the *Tractatus*.

than anything, though, he liked the ideas it contained – or at least the ideas that he found in it, for he read it in a way that made it even simpler and bolder, though less original, than it was.

Like Russell, Wittgenstein saw that the major task of philosophy was to get below the surface of ordinary discourse in order to display the real logical form of a proposition. Wittgenstein, in fact, explicitly credited Russell with having been the first to enunciate and develop this understanding of philosophy: 'All philosophy is "critique of language" . . . It was Russell who performed the service of showing that the apparent logical form of a proposition need not be its real one'.[23] Wittgenstein, though, took Russell's ideas to their extreme, offering solutions to many problems that had afflicted Russell's work. As the *Tractatus* conceived it, the world is fundamentally made up of a set of atomic facts: all of reality, on Wittgenstein's account, is 'of a level'. There are no different kinds of being, superior or inferior facts. Language reflects the shape of the world, in that it is made up of elementary propositions that picture actual or possible atomic facts, and a small number of logical constants, like 'and' and 'not', used to link these elementary propositions. To have any literal significance, a sentence must express a true or false elementary proposition, or assign a certain distribution of truth or falsehood to elementary propositions. Despite appearances to the contrary, then, all language, in its buzzing, careering variety, and for all its nuances and ambiguities, possessed this simple structure.

Wittgenstein characteristically offered no examples of the atomic propositions which play such a key role in his scheme of things. Ayer, however, following Russell, simply took it for granted that they were descriptions of sense-experience, and took the *Tractatus* to be saying that all meaningful talk about the world amounted either to simple sense-data statements, 'There is a yellow patch now', or was translatable into such statements.

In addition to propositions that picture the world, the *Tractatus* allowed only one other class of propositions: tautologies and contradictions, which have nothing to say about the world but merely about the arbitrary meaning of words. Both maths and logic were held to fall into this class. In this way Wittgenstein avoided the conclusion that there were certain truths that were somehow written into the very structure of the universe, as Plato and Descartes had believed, or at the very least provide the conditions of our apprehension of it, as Kant had suggested. When language works, according to Wittgenstein (not an ideal language but language we all use) it either describes a world of contingent facts – 'the propositions of natural science' – or it draws out the implications of definitions.

Unhelpfully Wittgenstein suggested that the propositions of philosophy (including his own), not themselves falling into either category, were meaningless: 'My propositions serve as elucidation in the following way: anyone who understands me eventually recognises them as nonsensical'.[24] Ayer dismissed this as a frivolity, and preferred to say that philosophical propositions were themselves tautologies. Philosophy was about the translation or reduction of difficult statements into an equivalent but less perplexing language – it was, as Ryle liked to say, 'talk about talk'. Indeed, in so far as it was Wittgenstein who had convincingly shown that there were essentially only two types of proposition, statements of empirical fact and tautologies, it was Wittgenstein who, Ayer believed, had given him the authority for this view.[25]

Wittgenstein's radically simple view of the world and of language appealed to Ayer, but there was something else that he admired in the *Tractatus*, namely the use to which this doctrine was put. For Russell, philosophy was a search for certainty – for a sure foundation for knowledge. Wittgenstein never denied that certainty could be achieved. On the contrary, language, as he saw it, had the capacity to describe the world exactly as it was. But the motivation behind the *Tractatus* was less to give propositions of science and common sense a certain foundation, than to purify language. The *Tractatus*'s concern, as its preface made clear, was to show how language works but also to point to its limit – to gesture to what was unsayable by establishing what could be said. 'The whole sense of the book might be summed up in the following words,' Wittgenstein had written: 'what can be said at all can be said clearly, and what we cannot talk about we must pass over in silence.'[26] And Wittgenstein drew the cords of language very tight, contending that most of the concepts used by philosophers – and indeed all discourse about ethics, God and the meaning of life – violated the bounds of meaning. This was a message Ayer wanted to hear.

Admittedly the *Tractatus* itself seemed, at the end, to take a mystical turn. In the book's last few pages Wittgenstein gnomically suggested that even though nothing could meaningfully be said about God, beauty or good, values might nevertheless be apprehended, realised or lived in some non-linguistic way: Ayer simply dismissed this part of the *Tractatus* itself as so much nonsense.[27]

At about the time he first encountered the *Tractatus*, Ayer began to think seriously about his future. His grandfather wanted him to become a barrister and the idea had its appeal. Ayer would have enjoyed the combination of dramatic and intellectual skill that the Bar requires and liked to say that he would have excelled in the job. But the life of a philosopher, as Ayer conceived it, combined the same elements – performance and cleverness – and feeling that he had a talent for it, and wanting to stay on at Oxford at least a little longer, he decided to apply for a year-long research lectureship at Christ Church.

There was another motive too. Although Freddie and Renée had mentioned the possibility of marriage to their families, neither approved. The objections of Renée's guardians appear mainly to have been based on snobbery, although they also found Freddie cocky, while Dorus felt (rightly, as Ayer would later admit) that he was too young to marry. He also hoped that Ayer would later be able to make a more advantageous match. With the prospect of a family conflict looming, Ayer wanted the financial independence that a fellowship would bring.

In the event he was offered not the research position but something better: a lectureship in philosophy. This would normally have led to his being made an Official Student (as fellowships were called in Christ Church) a year or two later – quite a coup for a twenty-one-year-old. Things in fact turned out differently. Ayer had been offered the lectureship on the assumption that Michael Foster would get the professorship he was applying for elsewhere, but the position went to someone else. Nevertheless, Ayer was given a lectureship in philosophy and it was assumed that in time he would find a fellowship at Christ Church or somewhere else if that was what he still wanted.

He celebrated his success with a raucous party at the George and was summoned to be disciplined by a proctor the next morning. 'Being, I suppose, a little worse for drink, I took this as an affront to my dignity and went on so much about it that Robert Willis, who was one of the party, remarked very truly that there were lacunae in my character.'[28]

With Renée he went away at Christmas to Wiltshire, and that Easter they took a house in Cornwall. Back in Oxford he worked steadily for his final exams in June, winning the Slade exhibition, a college prize worth a helpful £60, during the Easter term.

Ayer sat six papers for his finals and there was at first some doubt about his degree. Initially his ancient history examiners, led by H.T. Wade-Gery, gave him beta alpha on all his papers. His philosophy tutors were divided; two old-fashioned figures, Murphy and Pickard-Cambridge, mainly gave him beta marks while J.D. Mabbot, complaining that Ayer had shown little evidence of having read any political theory or Aristotle's *Ethics*, wanted a viva. Wade-Gery, however, perhaps knowing something of Ayer's reputation, suspected that he was being marked down because of the nature of his views. On the morning of the viva he surprised the philosophy examiners by announcing that he had taken Ayer's papers home again and re-read them. Having become convinced that Ayer was first class, he had then taken them round to a second history examiner, who had agreed. This ensured an automatic first, although in ancient history not philosophy, and the viva became a formality.

The story has a characteristic end. Ayer had already alienated his philosophy examiners by what he had written. He now went on to answer the few questions that it fell on Wade-Gery to ask him, in 'a cheeky manner', so antagonising him.[29] David Stephens, a fellow undergraduate, reported to Isaiah Berlin in a letter at the end of June that Ayer was 'humiliated by Wade-Gery: you must have heard about it. We laughed a good deal.'[30]

6

Marriage among the Scientists

Freddie and Renée had spent much of his last year at Oxford together. They quarrelled but they also loved each other. She at least was eager to get married. Ayer was less sure, but by the time of his finals it was more or less understood that they would wed. Despite the initial opposition of both families, once Renée had been introduced to Reine and Dorus, they quickly came round to her and to the match. 'In the course of giving his consent,' Ayer wrote, 'my grandfather said "You've had other girls of course?" and seemed rather dismayed when I told him I had not.'[1]

The wedding was put off until autumn as Ayer wanted to try for a fellowship at All Souls and calculated that his chances would be better if he were single. That summer they went away on a tour of Spain; Freddie always believed in the conceivability of backward causation and this was a premature honeymoon of sorts. Renée wanted to go by motorcycle, which they did. She drove, with Freddie travelling in a sidecar, packed tight with luggage and camping equipment. In a diary that Renée kept of the holiday, since lost, she wrote about his ability to read and even write while in the sidecar: he could work in almost any circumstances. Doubtless, too, Freddie read or wrote while Renée put up the tents. 'At that time not many tourists went to Spain, fewer still rode motor-cycles, and only gypsies camped,' Ayer recalled in Part of My Life. 'Our reversal of the customary roles of driver and passenger also drew attention to us, but the interest which we aroused in the villages where we bought provisions was always friendly.'[2]

They drove through France to Burgos and on to Madrid, which they used as a base for excursions to Avila, Segovia and Toledo. The ragged poverty they saw shocked them. Later they rode to Seville, where they witnessed General José Sanjurjo's failed attempt at a coup against the newly formed Republican government, and on to Granada. Ayer was not especially impressed by the Alhambra but the evidence this part of Spain offers of the history of the expulsion of Moors must have been another reminder, if any were needed, of the crimes committed in the name of Christianity. All in all it was an especially happy trip which Renée later recalled with nostalgia. It gave them both an affection for the wild, romantic culture of Spain, which would make their opposition to Franco much more than a matter of principle.

By the time he finished his degree, Ayer was Oxford's most ardent Wittgensteinian. Ryle and Wittgenstein had met at a philosophical conference in 1929 and had since become friends – Ryle was one of the few people who both liked him and did not fear him. It was in June 1932, soon after Ayer's exams, that Ryle drove him to Cambridge to meet the great man.

Wittgenstein's rooms were situated at the very top of a high staircase in Whewell's Court, Trinity College. The sitting-room was like a monk's cell, with no ornament, paintings or photographs, and no armchairs or reading lamps. Ryle and Ayer were ushered in, and two deck chairs were produced. The meeting passed more or less without incident, although Wittgenstein, with no small talk, earnestly asked Ayer what he had been reading. He replied that it had been Calderón's play *La vida es sueño* and added frankly that he did not think he had understood it. He meant at least in part that he had found the Spanish difficult. Wittgenstein, however, was impressed by what he thought was an indication of Ayer's humility before the hidden depths of the play and henceforth treated him as a protégé. At a dinner party fifty years later, Ayer was to say to a neighbour, 'What, of course, I did not realise was that he had a crush on me.' Ayer, for his part, was awed by Wittgenstein's quiet intensity, so much of which emanated from his piercing blue eyes. Yet there was no question of Ayer becoming one of Wittgenstein's young disciples. Ayer disapproved of intellectual deference, whether it was paid to a religious or a mere philosophical seer. Anyway, philosophically, he was fast becoming his own man.

On the same visit Ayer was invited by Richard Braithwaite, to return to Cambridge that autumn and give a paper to the Moral Science Club, as Cambridge's principal philosophy seminar was called. Wittgenstein and Moore would be present. It says something for Ryle's confidence in Ayer that the invitation was issued, and for Ayer's confidence in himself that it was accepted. He was not yet twenty-two.

Christ Church had granted Ayer leave of absence from teaching until the summer term of 1933, so he now had time on his hands. His first thought had been to work under Wittgenstein at Cambridge. Ryle, however, argued that the veneration that Wittgenstein expected from his students was bad for both teacher and pupil. He must have realised that Ayer was particularly ill-suited to sit at anyone's feet. Instead he suggested that Ayer go to Austria to work under Moritz Schlick, one of the leaders of the Vienna Circle. News of the circle of radical philosopher-scientists was just beginning to trickle into the US and Britain, with, for instance, an article by A.E. Blumberg and H. Feigl, 'Logical Positivism, a New Movement in European Philosophy' appearing in the American *Journal of Philosophy* in 1931. Ryle had been impressed by Schlick when they met at a conference in Oxford in 1930.

In early November Ayer gave his paper to the Moral Sciences Club on 'General Propositions'. The issue that Ayer set out to address concerned the nature of propositions of the form 'All As are B'. These had long worried Russell and Wittgenstein and other logical atomists, because they posed a challenge to the principle that the only sort of facts were atomic facts. It was a basic tenet of logical atomism that all sentences can be reduced to elementary observations, joined by a few logical constants. It was hard, though, to see how general propositions could be translated in this way. It is tempting to suggest that the proposition 'All men are mortal' or 'All gases expand when heated' is just a summary statement of a number of atomic facts – 'this gas expands', 'that gas expands', and so on. But the general proposition claims more than this; it claims that if anything is a gas, it will expand: it tells us something about the class of gases.

The logical atomists developed different ways of dealing with general propositions; Wittgenstein simply denied that they posed a problem, while Russell felt obliged to admit their irreducibility. Frank Ramsey, a brilliant Cambridge logician and a close friend of Wittgenstein, who had died at a tragically young age in 1930, had sketched another position. With impressive tenacity, he had argued that if general propositions could not be translated into conjunctions of elementary ones, then they could not be propositions at all. Instead he suggested that they should be understood as rules for guiding our expectations – rules that we may adopt or reject, depending on their usefulness.

In his paper Ayer made it clear that he was persuaded by Ramsey's pragmatic solution. It was Ramsey, in fact, who first roused Ayer's interest in the American pragmatists. For the most part, however, he stuck to attacking what Richard Braithwaite, writing in the records of the Moral Science Club, described as 'the Oxford view' that they 'assert a necessary connection between universals'.[3] A slightly later draft of the paper has survived.[4] The most striking aspect of it is the extent to which Ayer was already stressing the distinction between meaningful and meaningless utterances, happily arguing that the claim that events are related to each other by a mysterious relation of necessity was not wrong but literally nonsensical. The paper was well received and, fortunately for Ayer, Wittgenstein took his part in the discussion that followed, defending and elaborating upon Ayer's position. For such a young student, 'General Propositions' is a remarkably deft and accomplished piece of writing, even if, as Ayer admitted, 'I have occupied myself almost entirely with criticism of other philosophers' views'.

If Ayer's performance at the Moral Science Club was a boost to his confidence, it was soon to take a knocking. In October he sat the exam for entry into All Souls, the most prestigious academic community in Britain. Goronwy Rees had won a fellowship the year before and Ayer would have set much store by doing the same. In the event, he did not even come close. The question that Ayer chose to answer on the philosophy paper – that metaphysics, though violating logic, is demanded by experience – could almost have been laid as a trap for him, and Ayer's dismissive response did not go down well with his examiners. His slightly cocky manner at the candidates' dinner, where he resuscitated his father's theory that the Ayers were counts of the Holy Roman Empire, also failed to please. It was Isaiah Berlin, sitting the exams alongside Freddie, who won the distinction of being the first Jew to be accepted into the college.

Renée was as happy as Freddie with the prospect of a honeymoon in Vienna, but they found it harder to agree on the venue for their wedding. Ayer wanted a civil marriage, but Renée held out for a Catholic ceremony and won: although no longer religious herself, she did not want to upset her father's family. They were married at the Brompton Oratory – about the grandest Catholic church in the country – on 25 November 1932 and held a reception at one of London's big hotels. Renée wore a pale grey dress with orange carnations, and photographs show Ayer looking dapper in top hat and tails. His old schoolfriend David Headley was best man, with Reine as the second witness. The wedding went off well enough but Ayer spoke about the ceremony with regret for the rest of his life. His objection to religion was not just a matter of philosophical principle. He was repelled by the sight of intelligent men and women indulging in the nonsense which he very literally believed religion to be. It was debasing, superstitious, stupid.

The Ayers left for Vienna the day after their wedding, catching the ferry to Ostend and the train through Germany. Freddie's Oxford friend, Martin Cooper, was in the Austrian capital studying music and found them lodgings with an expatriate American, Frau Jones, at 25 Schönberg-strasse, a large nineteenth-century building close to the Südbahnhof station. The Ayers were on a tight budget and the neighbourhood was poor and dreary, but they were only a short tram ride from the centre and it offered a good base from which to explore the city.

With a population of nearly two million, the Austrian capital was a busy, crowded city that retained much of the sparkle of its late nineteenth-century heyday, and Freddie and Renée found that they liked 'almost everything about it'.[5] It was a wonderful architectural showcase, from its medieval cathedral, through baroque imperial buildings to the Secession architecture of Otto Wagner and Josef Hoffman and the functionalism of Adolf Loos. Horse and cart still rivalled the car and the city's café culture continued to thrive: for the price of a cup of coffee one could spend a morning in an elegant salon reading newspapers in three or four languages.

Vienna, of course, was famous for its music and with Martin Cooper as their guide, the Ayers went to concerts and to the beautiful opera house where Freddie discovered the charms of light opera, of Mozart, Verdi and

Richard Strauss. He also liked the cheap dance halls, where you could drink beer, eat *Wurst* and waltz late into the night. The Kunsthistorisches Museum housed one of Europe's great art collections and he and Renée formed a special affection for Tintoretto's sexy *Susannah and the Elders*.

Vienna was a place, too, with a strong and markedly Jewish intellectual culture. Freud was still practising, as was Alfred Adler, who ran an influential educational institute, loosely associated with Vienna University, where the young Karl Popper had studied. According to the economist Friedrich von Hayek, who taught at the university in the early 1930s, it was a place of 'great intellectual excitement' – the result of an unusual degree of interaction between the various departments, and a remarkably open relationship between the university and the rest of the world.[6]

Yet if Viennese traditions lived on, the city had changed dramatically since the war. The elections of 1919 had given the Socialists absolute control of Vienna's powerful municipal government and they set out on a uniquely ambitious and radical project: the creation of a participatory proletarian society, intended, quite self-consciously, to serve as an alternative to both decadent bourgeois ways and the authoritarian Bolshevik model. For Freddie and Renée, the work of the new administration was most visible in the great modernist housing complexes, like the Karl Marx-Hof, completed in 1930. But this was only one aspect of 'Red Vienna' that was attracting the attention of progressively minded politicians and writers all over Europe. Other initiatives included the extension of public health and social welfare services and the promotion of worker libraries, study groups, theatres, sports grounds and festivals. The Ayers only just missed the International Workers' Olympics of 1931. Municipally funded lectures, pamphlets and films extolled the virtues of an orderly home, exercise and education; a great deal of effort, in particular, went into getting women into school and the workplace. Renée, with her taste for modern architecture and an interest in progressive education and family planning, was especially impressed by what she saw.

There was, however, a darker side to Austrian politics, one that cannot have escaped the Ayers' notice. With the collapse of the Austrian Empire and the abolition of its monarchy, Vienna had become the capital of a small and depressed clerical republic which experienced the same terrible levels of unemployment and poverty as its larger Weimar neighbour. Although the Socialists had control of Vienna, the National Government was in the hands of a right-wing alliance of reactionary Christian Socials and pan-Germans, the latter wanting to see the incorporation of Austria into a larger German ethnic state.

The two political camps quarrelled about everything, especially religion. In 1928 they had clashed over posters of a scantily clad Josephine Baker announcing a forthcoming tour; in another incident the Church threatened to excommunicate Catholics who took a hand in the construction of a municipal crematorium. Every attempt by the Socialists to introduce new laws or build new facilities was opposed by the Church, and as both left-wing and right-wing parties had paramilitary wings, violent confrontations were commonplace. Indeed, by the early 1930s, Austria seemed on the brink of civil war. As was inevitable in Central Europe, the conflict had an anti-Semitic dimension. While many leading Socialists were Jewish, the parties of the Right were anti-Semitic. The arrival in Vienna of thousands of poor Orthodox Jews, refugees from Poland, exacerbated the tensions.

All these movements and conflicts informed the arguments of the Vienna Circle. Some of the circle's members were socialists and worked closely with the city government in developing its educational and cultural programmes. Others tried to remain aloof from politics. But whatever their position, their philosophy placed them firmly among the enemies of the clerical party. As Ayer quickly discovered, in Vienna, unlike in Oxford or Cambridge, philosophy was inescapably political.[7]

In his memoirs Ayer recalls meeting Moritz Schlick, the circle's leader, soon after his arrival, but his letters from Austria – the first of Ayer's letters to have survived – reveal that he bided his time. Apart from exploring the city with Renée, he seems to have spent the first month trying to improve his very rudimentary German; he took lessons, read the newspapers and, in the university library, began to study German philosophy journals. He and Renée spent Christmas in the city, and then went to stay in a cottage belonging to a friend of Martin Cooper, high up in the Wienerwald, the snow-covered mountains to the south-west of Vienna. Writing to Isaiah Berlin towards the end of his stay, Ayer is evidently apprehensive about approaching the Viennese philosophers, but is otherwise enjoying himself:

It is very beautiful here . . . and we are learning to ski. I would much prefer to remain here but I really must take some steps about learning German and seeing Schlick. From next week, therefore we shall be in Vienna . . .

I have no gossip for you. We have been occasionally to the Opera here. I liked Verdi's *Don Carlos* very much and also *Don Giovanni*, though it ought to have been better staged. We go at least three times a week to the cinema and see practically no one except Martin. Next week perhaps I shall risk my life at the University: I shall anyhow obtain somewhere an interview with Schlick.

I have grown a beard. It is very black and said by Renée to be handsome. But Christ Church senior common room will certainly not tolerate it, so you may never see me with it: or at least not until my job there is secure.[8]

The same letter contains what Ayer described as 'a long hasty and confused rigmarole about the laws of nature'. After characterising philosophy as 'the attempt to give definitions of various sorts', he turns to the question ('the only important question in philosophy') of the nature of scientific theories and their relation to the commonsense world observable by 'the plain man'. Although the line of argument is far from clear, Ayer concludes with the suggestion that scientific theories represent 'fictional' constructions capable of accounting for the observable facts in the simplest possible way: 'In principle you can always translate [the language of science] back [into the language of observation], i.e. I maintain that nothing is said with electrons etc. that could not in principle be said without: but in practice the enumeration of all the facts the electrons explain is hardly possible'. Whatever the exact nature of his views at this time, it is clear that Ayer's enthusiasm for Frank Ramsey was greater than ever: 'such a great philosopher: really very great – goes for the important things more than Wittgenstein who suffers from not being really interested enough in the actual world'.

Ayer need not have worried about introducing himself to Schlick. A suave, silver-haired German, Schlick had married a wealthy American and spoke English fluently. After calling on him in his elegant apartment on Prinz Eugen Strasse, Ayer reported back to Gilbert Ryle that he had found him 'very cordial though really too busy to take much interest in

85

me'.[9] Yet after reading a testimonial Ryle had written and talking with Ayer for half an hour, Schlick was sufficiently impressed to invite him not only to attend his lectures and classes but also to join the meetings of the Vienna Circle. 'I was pleased and excited by this invitation,' Ayer later wrote, 'but not so surprised as I now think that I should have been.'[10] The circle only had about twenty regular members and they were nearly all established philosophers or scientists – at least seven held university chairs – so Ayer was right to be surprised. Indeed, Ayer was one of only two visitors ever to join the circle. The other was W.V.O. Quine, a brilliant American logician, only a year or two older than Ayer, who was in the city at the same time. Like Ayer, he was hugely influenced by what he discovered.

Schlick, born in 1882, trained as a physicist and in 1922 became Professor of the Philosophy of Science at Vienna University, a position which had already been held by two of Austria's most important philosopher-physicists, Ernst Mach and Ludwig Boltzmann. Soon after arriving in Vienna, he formed a discussion group, in association with the mathematician Hans Hahn, known simply as 'Schlick's Circle' before becoming the Vienna Circle. The circle met once every week or two in a university room. In addition to Schlick and his assistant Friedrich Waismann, its other leading participants were Rudolf Carnap and Otto Neurath. Wittgenstein, who was in Vienna from 1925 to 1929, was never a member but he often met with Schlick and Waismann (the latter becoming his amanuensis and lifelong disciple) and shaped the circle's development in important ways: twice in the mid-1920s the circle devoted a series of meetings to the *Tractatus*, discussing it proposition by proposition.[*]

The young American philosopher Sidney Hook, later to become a friend of Ayer, spent a year studying and travelling in Germany in 1929 and on his return published an account of his impressions in the *Journal*

---

[*] 'Neurath made frequent interjections, "metaphysics", during the Circle's reading and discussion of Wittgenstein's *Tractatus*, to the irritation of Moritz Schlick who finally told him he was interrupting the proceedings too much. Hans Hahn, as conciliator, suggested to Neurath just to say "M" instead. After much humming – so C. G. Hempel was later told – Neurath made another suggestion to Schlick. "I think it will save time and trouble if I say 'non-M' every time the group is not talking methaphysics"' (editors' note in M. Neurath and R.S. Cohen (eds), *Otto Neurath, Empiricism and Sociology*, Dordrecht, Holland, 1973, pp. 82–3).

of Philosophy which helps put the circle into context. Hook, it is true, shared the positivists' anti-metaphysical bias, but that in a sense is just the point: he saw German philosophical scene in the same light as the Vienna Circle or Ayer would have done.

Two aspects in particular struck Hook. In the first place he emphasised the extent to which the tradition of German metaphysical idealism – the tradition of Kant, Schelling, Fichte and Hegel – reigned supreme. There was a quite open hostility to science amongst most of the philosophers he encountered, and a widespread assumption that it was the duty of philosophy to advance the cause of religion, morality, freedom of the will, the *Volk* and the organic nation state. In fact Hook got the impression that the whole point of German philosophy was to vindicate, through the close study and reconstruction of the major idealistic texts, our a-priori, extra-empirical knowledge of time, space, God or the Absolute, the laws of morality and beauty. 'The typical German professor of philosophy', Hook wrote, is prepared to tell his students 'the eternal truths of any science irrespective of what its particular findings at any moment may be' and 'resents the suggestion that he must go to school to the physicist to unlearn what he knows about causality, space, time and the nature of system'.[11]

The second feature noted by Hook was 'the importance of philosophy in German life'. There were, Hook observed, 'more books published in philosophy in Germany than in the rest of Europe combined'. And, he continued, 'Few students of biology, engineering, history or law feel satisfied that they have mastered their subject matter unless they have heard some professor lecture' on its philosophy. '"This is what we are going to study", I heard a lecturer in human physiology say, pointing to an enlarged chart of the human body, "but if you want to know what man is you must ask our friends the philosophers".'[12] This then was the tradition, metaphysical, insular and anti-scientific, against which the Vienna Circle was reacting.

The members of the circle differed in their origins; at least three, Feigl, Neurath and Waismann, were Jewish; some, like Schlick and Carnap, came to Vienna from Germany, others were Austrian. It says a great deal about this group that all its members without exception had, like Mach and Holtzmann, Frege and Russell before them, a scientific or mathematical training – most had come to philosophy from theoretical physics. The circle were champions of what they called the 'Wissenschaftliche Weltauffassung' – the world scientifically conceived – and saw it as their mission to put philosophy on a scientific footing.

Philosophy, as the Vienna Circle conceived it, had a simple double task. Negatively, its purpose was to warn people off falling into metaphysics, and particularly to do battle with the Romantic and idealistic tradition of German philosophy. More positively, it saw philosophy's job as clarifying the logic of science and commonsense observation – what, back in Cambridge, was described as the 'analysis' of scientific concepts. The Viennese positivists revered Einstein, and Schlick was among the first to write about the philosophical implications of relativity theory. They delighted in the fact that Einstein had shown that the fundamental principles of Newtonian physics, the basic laws of time and space, which Kant had contended that we know a priori were not even truths, let alone a-priori ones. What could better illustrate the error of letting philosophy dictate to science?

Like positivists and empiricists everywhere, the Vienna Circle believed in progress, in fact and science. They argued, indeed, that science alone, stretched to encompass commonsense observation, is the only source of real knowledge. Since what we know – about the external material world, the laws of nature, other minds, or about the ultimate constitution of the universe – is built up from, and ultimately reducible to, sense-experience, any proposition which does not make reference to this experience cannot lay claim to the title of knowledge. The positivists were all, to a lesser or greater degree, united in rejecting the distinction, central to German idealism, between the empathetic methods of the social sciences and the inductive methods of the natural sciences. As Carnap put it, 'There is only one science (Unified Science), not separate subjects ... for all knowledge stems from one source of knowledge: experience – the unmediated content of experience such as red, hard, toothache and joy.'[13]

The Vienna Circle, however, elaborated on older empiricist and positivist traditions in bringing new developments in logic to their aid, and in advocating the verification theory of meaning.

The precise formulation of the principle which it was claimed could be found, at least implicitly, in Wittgenstein's *Tractatus*, proved famously elusive. However, it stated roughly that an utterance is meaningful if and only if it expresses a proposition the truth or falsehood of which can be determined by empirical observation or solely by reference to the meaning of the terms it contains. The idea here was ultimately very simple. We learn language, at least at the beginning, by learning what events, objects or experiences make statements – 'this is a chair', 'that is a dog' – true or false. At this very elementary level, what a proposition means can be described in terms of the simple empirical facts or experiences that verify it. According to the Viennese positivists, however, this is true all the way up: even the complex propositions of science are translatable into basic observation statements, the meaning of which is given by the experiences that render them true. It followed that if a descriptive statement could not in principle be verified – if its truth could not be tested empirically – then it was meaningless. At the time Ayer was in Vienna, Popper had not yet published his famous alternative to the principle, in which he substituted falsifiability for verifiability as a defining attribute of scientific propositions.

The verification principle radically transformed the nature of the positivists' argument, making the impossibility of metaphysics depend not upon the nature of what can be known, but on what can be said. The Vienna Circle no longer attacked propositions about the soul, God, the Absolute, the after-life, historical destiny, national spirit, or transcendent values, as being false or unduly speculative. Instead it maintained that in so far as they were unverifiable, they were literally meaningless. Nor did Schlick and his circle restrict their attack to metaphysics of a traditional kind; they argued that a great part of mainstream philosophy – the questions at issue, for instance between monists and pluralists or materialists and idealists – was spurious. For what empirical test could possibly count as deciding whether the world is one or many, or whether the things we perceive are or are not independent of anyone's mind?

Like all the best philosophies, the circle's 'logical positivism' gave expression to an exhilaratingly simple vision: the world as the scientists describe it is all there is; everything, even the great achievements of art and literature, are accountable in its terms. But also like the best philosophies, it was capable of advancing its vision in powerfully subtle ways, employing and feeding off the latest developments in maths and science.

When Ayer met him, Schlick was around fifty, tall, soft-spoken and aristocratic. Ayer likened him to a patrician American senator, although he was not especially impressed by him as a philosopher. In politics he was a liberal, rather than a socialist, and was on what was known as the 'right' of the circle, although this label referred to philosophical as much as political commitments. By contrast, the circle's two other leading figures, Rudolf Carnap and Otto Neurath, were firmly on the left.

Carnap, a decade younger than Schlick, was also a German and, by training, a theoretical physicist. A high-minded, rather earnest radical, with a devotion to Esperanto, he had studied with Frege and corresponded with Russell before, in the mid-1920s, taking up a teaching post in Vienna. Ayer was enormously impressed by his first major work, dating from this time, *The Logical Construction of the World* – an attempt to show how the major domains of empirical knowledge could be reconstructed in terms of the data of direct experience and the single relation of remembered similarity between them. Later Carnap changed tack, arguing that the basic propositions of science are physical not phenomenal, thus jumping from the pan of solipsism into the fire of behaviourism. He never, though, gave up his view that the task of philosophy was to analyse all meaningful language into elemental observation statements.

Where Carnap became known as a rigorous and thorough logician, Neurath was a generalist. A huge, fat, enormously energetic man, he struck Ayer as the strongest personality of the group. He had begun by studying maths in Vienna and then moved on through linguistics, ancient history, the philosophy of science, economics, sociology and statistics. He was an ardent socialist and acted as an economic adviser to the left-wing Spartacist government that took over Bavaria at the end of the war. After the defeat of the Spartacists, Neurath was imprisoned and then expelled from Germany.

Back in Vienna, he worked closely with the municipal government. Among other projects he founded a workers' museum devoted to the display and propagation of a system of pictorial statistics which he had developed, capable of illustrating facts about social conditions in a universal language of graphs and images. (Just as Neurath believed that all meaningful statements could be reduced to a simple language of observation, so he hoped to translate abstract statistics into a simple

visual form.) A description by a young student of his first encounter with
Neurath gives a flavour of the man:

> Neurath was asleep on a couch. As soon as his wife had roused him
> he was at once wide awake. Carnap introduced me. Neurath's first
> question was: 'What is your study?' I answered 'philosophy'. 'Do you
> read mathematics, physics?' 'No,' I said, 'pure philosophy.' 'Do you
> devote yourself to anything as dirty as that? Why not straight
> theology?' I was shocked but in less than an hour had already fallen
> under Neurath's spell.[14]

Neurath's interest in housing and his work on picture statistics naturally
brought him in contact with modern artistic movements in Austria and
Germany, and both he and Carnap had close relations with the Bauhaus,
Europe's leading school of avant-garde art and design. Neurath was at the
opening of the Dessau Bauhaus in December 1926 and both men lectured
there on a number of occasions over the next six years, as did several
others from the circle. There was much that bound the Bauhaus and the
Vienna Circle, or at least its left wing, together. Both worshipped science
and were correspondingly hostile to all religious and national traditions;
both identified with Red Vienna and its attempt to create a new classless
and cosmopolitan man. Both sought to refound and purify their
disciplines using a transparent, elemental and universal language – the
language of engineering and observation respectively. Carnap and
Neurath were quite explicit in endorsing the functionalism of the
Bauhaus as the architectural counterpart to their own empiricist views.[*]
    Carnap and Neurath were not only responsible for the Vienna Circle's

---

[*] It has sometimes been argued, by Anthony Quinton among others, that if artistic and literary
modernism had a philosophical counterpart, it was the existentialism of Heidegger and Sartre. As the
connections between the Vienna Circle and the Bauhaus suggest, however, logical positivism also
represented a species of modernism, albeit modernism in its most Enlightenment and optimistic
form. Neurath's preference for primitivism over 'sophisticated' European culture was, for instance,
very much in keeping with the broader tendencies of modernism: primitive cultures had magic, but
that was a crude form of science; they did not have metaphysics, the direct counterpart to empty
ornament in art and design. For Quinton's argument, see 'Which Philosophy Is Modernistic?', in
Thoughts and Thinkers, London, 1982. For the links between the Bauhaus and the Vienna Circle see
Peter Galison, 'Aufbau/Bauhaus: Logical Positivism and Architectural Modernism', *Critical Inquiry*,
xvi (Summer 1990).

ties to the Bauhaus, they were also behind the publication in 1929 of the short manifesto that launched the circle as a public entity: *Wissenschaftliche Weltauffassung: Der Wiener Kries* (The Scientific Conception of the World: The Vienna Circle). Schlick was abroad when the manifesto was written and might not have approved of some of its more political gestures, but Neurath and Carnap skilfully implicated him in its publication by dedicating it to him and emphasising his role in the formation of the circle.

Wissenschaftliche Weltauffassung was as clear a statement of the circle's beliefs as one could wish for, identifying as the two hallmarks of its approach, its empiricism and its commitment to logical analysis, and distinguishing both from the belief, common to rationalists, Kantians and Hegelians, that there were certain metaphysical facts about the world we know independently of experience:

> The scientific world-conception knows no unconditionally valid knowledge derived from pure reason, no 'synthetic a-priori' of the kind that lies at the basis of Kantian epistemology and even more of all pre- and post-Kantian ontology and metaphysics. . . It is precisely in the rejection of the possibility of synthetic knowledge a-priori that the basic thesis of modern empiricism lies.[15]

After listing the fourteen members of the circle, Neurath and Carnap ended their pamphlet by paying tribute to Einstein, Russell and Wittgenstein, the three 'leading representatives of the world scientifically conceived'.

With the manifesto of 1929, 'Schlick's Circle' moved from being just another of Vienna's many discussion groups to an organised intellectual movement – 'The Vienna Circle' – set on broadcasting its ideas and building bridges with other like-minded groups. Carnap took over the journal in which Wittgenstein's *Tractatus* had first been published and renamed it *Erkenntniss* (Knowledge). The circle also launched a series of pamphlets under the general title of 'Unified Science', a series of philosophical books, 'Writings on the World Scientifically Conceived', and finally a multi-volume *Encyclopaedia of Unified Science*, which quite self-consciously placed itself in the tradition of the Enlightenment *Encyclopédie*. The circle made formal contact with similar groups in

Berlin and Prague, as well as informal contact with sympathetic philosophers elsewhere, like Ryle and Ayer.

By the time the Ayers arrived in Vienna, the circle was past its prime, although this is more obvious with hindsight than it was at the time. Hitler was elected Chancellor of Germany in March 1933, the month the honeymooners returned to England; in the same month (a few days before they left the city), the Austrian Chancellor Engelbert Dollfuss dissolved parliament, threw his lot in with Mussolini and set about constructing a Catholic-Fascist state. Describing this time, Karl Menger, another member of the circle, remembered that working conditions were already nearly intolerable: 'Groups of young people, many wearing Swastikas, marched along the sidewalks singing Nazi songs. Now and then, members of one of the rival paramilitary groups paraded through the wider avenues'.[16] The university was inevitably a political hotbed and Ayer sometimes arrived to find it closed by disturbances.

For as long as the Ayers were in Vienna, however, the circle's twice-monthly meetings went on as before. Quine, who attended some of the meetings with Ayer, recalled them taking place in a great barn-like space,[17] but according to Ayer the group gathered around a table in a small room in an institute outside the university.[18] Carnap had already left for a professorship in Prague, so Ayer did not get to meet him until later, which left Schlick, Waismann, Neurath and Hahn as the main participants. The only woman present was Olga Hahn, Neurath's large, blind, cigar-smoking wife, a mathematician by training. The meetings Ayer attended were almost entirely taken up with a dispute about the nature of 'protocol statements' – the basic observation statements to which, the positivists claimed, all meaning had reference. Schlick contended that they were descriptive of sense-experiences – what Cambridge called sense-data – about which the subject could not be mistaken. Neurath on the other hand believed that one had to start at the level of physical objects and that no beliefs were sacrosanct. In other words, he had come to hold the sort of coherence theory of truth now associated with pragmatism and post-modernism, according to which the things we believe can only be checked against other beliefs.

Ayer, always a foundationalist, was later to side with Schlick in this debate. In Vienna, however, he found it hard enough to follow the circle's discussions, let alone contribute to them. As he admitted in his

A.J. Ayer

letters to Oxford, language was proving a real stumbling block, and he was getting 'very little' from either the circle's meetings, or Schlick's university lectures. Nevertheless, he did come away with at least some general impressions and wrote enthusiastically to both Berlin and Ryle about what he had found:

Dear Shaya [Isaiah]

When I last wrote to you ... I had not yet met Schlick and his colleagues. Now that I have attended some of Schlick's lectures on *Naturphilosophie*, and a series of their fortnightly club meetings, I can give you some information that might amuse you. I have myself got little more than amusement out of them. That is the fault of my German which does not yet enable me to understand them well enough to obtain the instruction they are certainly able to give me.

The best of them are Waismann, Hahn and Gödel. Schlick seems to be a man of about the same calibre as Broad, with this superiority that he has been content to follow Wittgenstein instead of going into jealous opposition. In his lectures he discusses the views of Eddington and Poincaré on the function of science and so forth. Wittgenstein is a deity to them all, not mainly on the strength of the *Tractatus* which they consider a slightly metaphysical work ('metaphysical' is the ultimate term of abuse) but on the ground of his later views which I myself (again the insufficiency of my German) have not been able to learn from them fully. Philosophy is grammar. Where you would talk about laws they talk about rules of grammar. All philosophical questions are purely linguistical. And all linguistical questions are resolved by considering how the symbol under consideration is in fact *used*. All contemporary philosophers in Germany are rogues or fools. Even to think of Heidegger makes them sick. No modern English philosophers have ever been heard of except Russell and Ramsey. Russell is thought of as in many respects an old fashioned metaphysician but definitely a forerunner of the Christ [Wittgenstein], Ramsey as an intelligent pupil of Wittgenstein. The history of philosophy is, I believe, taught but I have never heard the views of any philosopher older than Frege or Bolzano discussed and I am acquainted with only one philosopher here who thinks that ethics is a serious branch of philosophy and he

94

is a South American business man who only took up the subject at an advanced age three years ago.[19]

Writing to Ryle, Ayer again emphasised the circle's adulation of Wittgenstein, 'treated here as a second Pythagoras', but he also made clear his own attitude towards the master:

> With your help I have already got from Wittgenstein all that he has to offer, and that is the correct attitude towards philosophy, the appreciation of what is and what is not a genuine philosophical problem. His actual handling of these problems does not interest me so much. I am bold enough to want to attempt that on my own.[20]

There were, of course, other things to do in Vienna apart from attend philosophical seminars, and Renée and Freddie had a merry time. At one point, Freddie's old class-mate, Bernard Burrows passed through the city. Burrows, who was to have a successful career as a diplomat, had not been close to Ayer at Eton, but he and Renée took to each other immediately and he was pleased to find that she had 'humanised' Freddie – 'domesticated him'.[21] The trio went to Budapest for a long weekend together, where they saw a memorable performance of *Don Pasquale*, and the Ayers also went alone to Prague.

Back in Vienna they enjoyed the company of Quine and his wife during the short time that they were all in the city together. Ayer 'admired' Quine as a man, and immediately recognised his powers as a logician, even if, as he wrote to Ryle, 'the problems of pure logistic do not interest me very much'.[22] What seems chiefly to have stuck in Quine's mind was Renée's resourcefulness in the kitchen and her imaginative use of a tight budget. In addition they spent a great deal of time with Martin Cooper. A friend of Renée also turned up, 'an attractively feckless English girl', who helped add to what Ayer described as 'the atmosphere of *la vie de Bohème*'.[23] They drank in Vienna's great cafés and often went to the cinema, where they sat in cheap wooden seats, as well as the opera. They also visited working-class night clubs and dance halls where, convention had it, one could ask strangers for a dance. In his autobiography Ayer described how one evening he danced with a woman who made a pass at him. Before, he had been happy to make nervous advances towards women, but had never known the success of some of his handsomer and more confident friends. Now for the first time he realised with 'a thrill of excitement' that perhaps he could be attractive to other women.[24] It was an inauspicious end to a honeymoon.

7

Apostle

After almost four months in Vienna, the Ayers were back in Oxford by the beginning of April 1933. It would not be quite right to say that Freddie had been converted by the Vienna Circle. He was already more or less a logical positivist before he went out, having picked up much of the circle's empiricism from Hume and Russell. Then he had read the *Tractatus* almost as closely as anyone in the circle and he and they had taken from it many of the same views: that all meaningful propositions were either true or false; that necessity was analytic; that propositions of morality, religion and metaphysics have no truth value. Ayer's encounter with the Viennese positivists, however, gave him a mission. Here was an organised movement that thought like him, seemed to have the future on its side, and about which he knew more than anyone else in Britain. He would be its English-language apostle. That logical positivism was a foreign movement added to its allure. Ayer felt – had been made to feel – a foreigner. It was only fitting that he should spearhead the invasion of foreign ideas.

Almost the first thing Ayer seems to have done on his return was to write an article, 'Demonstration of the Impossibility of Metaphysics', in which he offered a highly condensed version of the positivist attack on religion and metaphysics. Ayer acknowledged at the outset that he had drawn heavily on articles in *Erkenntnis* by Schlick and Carnap, although, characteristically, his effort was a good deal more trenchant than theirs.

Ayer's central contention is simply put. He argues that 'It is not necessary to take a list of metaphysical terms such as the Absolute, the Unconditioned, the Ego and so forth, and prove each of them to be meaningless.'[1] For, given the task that metaphysics sets itself – to discover the nature of the reality underlying or transcending the phenomena which the empirical sciences study – it follows that all its assertions are of necessity nonsensical. How could you deliberate about a sphere with which human experience never comes in contact? 'Demonstration' was not published until a year after it had been written, but once it appeared in *Mind* it quickly provoked a flurry of objections and replies in the philosophical journals. It was a taste of the controversy to come.

In Oxford the Ayers took a small first-floor flat in the centre of the city (58 High Street) and acquired two Siamese cats. The menagerie was completed by a donkey which Renée had bought after discovering it being abused by its owner, and which they kept in a field on the edge of the city. Renée herself had rather Siamese features and bow legs, and further cultivated an oriental look by wearing her hair in a long pig-tail and walking round town with the donkey, laden with groceries, behind her. She and Freddie furnished their flat with second-hand Second Empire couches, and placed a large reproduction of Tintoretto's *Susannah and the Elders* over their bed. Isaiah Berlin found it all terribly gaudy: 'It was like Violetta's apartment in *La Traviata* – there wasn't a natural colour in it'.[2] But Freddie and Renée liked the effect.

Ayer was now a member of Christ Church Senior Common Room and was given a set of rooms in Killcanon Quad. Women, however, were not permitted even to dine in college, and Renée was largely excluded from his life there. Although Ayer was appointed to a research lectureship he was allowed to undertake a little teaching, taking Christ Church undergraduates for the philosophy components of both PPE and Greats. Many of his students were the same age or older than him; indeed his first, though unofficial, student was his old schoolfriend John Cheetham, who entered Christ Church the same time as Freddie, but had taken an extra year to complete his course. Cheetham remembered Ayer as a 'marvellous' teacher. 'He simplified the whole thing in the most extraordinarily clever way. He had written a vast number of essays on philosophy, many of them typed. I remember him saying, "Oh, I've written short papers on all these subjects, I will send them along, you will read them carefully and get a first." I did get a first and I put it down to him – I only got a second in my mods.'[3]

In addition to his teaching, in the autumn of 1933 Ayer also gave a series of Saturday morning lectures: 'The Philosophy of Analysis (Russell, Wittgenstein, Carnap)'. This was the first time any of these names had appeared on the lecture list; indeed it seems to have been the first time anyone in Oxford had ever given a lecture series on a living philosopher. The subject was recondite and Ayer found it hard not to gabble, but he retained a small and loyal audience.

No notes to these lectures have survived, but a series of articles he wrote around this time – most notably 'Atomic Propositions' and 'On Particulars and Universals' – gives us some idea of the direction of his thought. Apart from their sheer virtuosity, two other qualities stand out. The first is the boldness with which they dismiss a whole range of positions out of hand – not just those defended by Hegel and Heidegger but even those associated with Russell and Wittgenstein – as 'metaphysical' and therefore nonsensical. Ayer for instance rejected as 'senseless' the theory advanced by both Wittgenstein and Russell that the world is ultimately made up of elemental atomic facts. It was not for philosophers to affirm or deny anything about reality; their concern was not with the truth or falsehood of propositions but with their meaning.[4]

The second striking feature of these early papers is the extent to which they accept, entirely without argument, the fundamental tenets of logical positivism in its most extreme form. There is much to be said for the verification principle in one version or another: it seems right to say that in order for a statement to have meaning, one must be clear about how to confirm its truth. But the very extreme construal which Ayer put on this principle produced radically counter-intuitive implications. As Ayer understood it, at least at this time, it committed him to the doctrine that statements about the past, about other minds, about material objects, really 'tell you what you will experience in a given situation'.[5] My statement that Hume was born in 1711 is really a statement to the effect that if I check certain church records and other documents I will find that Hume's birth is identified as having taken place in '1711'. Church records, in turn, are themselves really logical constructions out of a set of sense-impressions, as indeed was Hume – both as others experienced him and as he experienced himself. Yet Ayer not only believed these strange doctrines; the degree of his conversion was such that they hardly seemed strange to him. It was only towards the end of the decade that he began to apply himself to defending his version of verificationism. And by that time he was already moving towards a weaker, less counter-intuitive position.

Ayer's colleagues at Christ Church appear to have recognised his qualities as a teacher, but relations between him and the Senior Common Room did not run smoothly. It is hard, in fact, to imagine a college to which he was less suited. Christ Church, an ecclesiastical chapter as well as a college, was the most religious of all Oxford colleges, and also among the most aristocratic. The Cathedral canons sat on the college's governing body, and there was a disproportionate number of theologians amongst its dons. The head of the college, Dean White, was a good old-fashioned snob whose voice, as one contemporary recalled, 'trembled with pleasure at the mention of a duke'.[6] The Dean admittedly concentrated mainly on ecclesiastical matters but the two senior figures in the college, Ayer's old Greek history tutor Robin Dundas and J.C. Masterman, a historian, were apparently cast from a similar mould. None of them looked kindly on Ayer's ideas: it was one thing, perhaps, to be a left-wing atheist and quite another to display, as he did, an open contempt for religion. Ayer himself only hints at the animosity he provoked, but Julian Ayer, his son, remembered Renée describing how she would beg Freddie to show a little more tact in the way he dealt with his superiors in the college. On the rare occasions when she herself met Dundas, she did her best to smooth the feathers Ayer had ruffled.[7]

Ayer, nevertheless, had his allies. There was a group of younger more liberal-minded dons who plotted and schemed together, including Patrick Gordon Walker, then a student in modern history, to whom Freddie and Renée both became close. This was the first of many friendships Freddie struck up with the generation of bright and generally middle-class Oxford graduates – Hugh Gaitskell, Douglas Jay, Tony Crosland, Roy Jenkins – who would rise to the top of the Labour party after the war.

There were other older men whom he also found sympathetic, including Roy Harrod and F.A. Lindemann, later Lord Cherwell, both, like so many Christ Church dons at this time, homosexual or at least bisexual. A well-connected left-wing Liberal and a friend of the

Bloomsbury Group, Harrod ranged widely and, like his mentor Keynes, wrote on probability and the philosophy of induction, as well as on economics. He and Ayer talked philosophy together and commented on one another's writings. Ayer admired his rationality and seems to have learned from his example: 'Unlike many professing utilitarians,' Ayer observed, 'he really did seem to judge actions by their probable consequences; and he always had the courage to act on his beliefs.'[8]

Lindemann, however, was the bigger figure. 'The Prof', as he was known to his friends, had trained as a physicist, and had undertaken some heroic airborne experiments during the war, before being appointed Professor of Physics in 1919. He was still in his early thirties. He was a rich man, who kept very aristocratic company, and, in addition to the college servants, retained a butler and a chauffeur for his Rolls-Royce. Politically he was well to the right, a close friend and adviser to Churchill, who would bring him into the government during the next war. He had no sympathy, however, for religion or metaphysics and at a time when most Oxford dons still held science in suspicion, made it his mission to bring physics up to Cambridge standards. In a biography that Harrod wrote of Lindemann, he describes a memorable debate in his rooms in Christ Church in the early 1920s, during which H.W.B. Joseph and Oxford's Professor of Metaphysics J.A. Smith tried to rebut Einstein's theories with their usual appeals to common sense. Lindemann was snobbish and reactionary, and given to anti-Semitic remarks – Isaiah Berlin found him 'one of the most disagreeable people I have ever known.'[9] But Ayer somehow forgave him his faults.[10]

In Harrod and Lindemann, Ayer found both allies and patrons – and in Lindemann he grew close to a philosophically minded physicist rather in the Viennese mould. Lindemann, in turn, was, as Harrod wrote, 'delighted' by this brilliant and attractive young man: 'He had a personal regard for him and ranked his abilities high; and of course he was immensely pleased by his onslaughts on the established school of Oxford philosophy'. 'In the talk of Ayer,' Harrod recalled, 'his absolute integrity shone out; it was plain that he was straining every nerve and using every muscle to make the point that he had in mind and convince his interlocutor.'[11]

Lindemann and Harrod led a campaign to get more scientific research fellows appointed to Christ Church, much to the chagrin of Masterman and others, who worried that they would upset common room life. It was Lindemann who managed in the early 1930s to secure a studentship for Einstein, leading one don to complain that the college's endowments had not been given to subsidise 'some German Jew'.[12]

Einstein paid his last visit in June 1933, at the end of Ayer's first term back from Vienna. He stayed for less than a month but Ayer sat next to him at high table on two or three occasions and they got on well together, continuing their conversations after dinner was over. Ayer spoke to him in his rather rudimentary German and Einstein enjoyed learning about the Vienna Circle. As Ayer would often recount, the great scientist described him as 'that clever young man' and Ayer, in turn, while finding Einstein's humour surprisingly unsophisticated, was impressed by the interest that he, like Moore and Russell, took in young people. 'One thing,' Ayer was to write just before he died, 'which contributes to my regarding [Einstein] as the greatest man whom I have ever met, . . . was his talking to me, a very young man of no importance, as though he could learn something from me.'[13]

A few days after Einstein's departure, it fell to Ayer, as junior lecturer, to give the 1933 Gaudy oration, a speech delivered at the beginning of Christ Church's annual old boys' banquet. The speaker was expected to offer an appreciation of one of the college's many illustrious members and Ayer chose Ruskin, who had been Slade Professor there in the 1870s. Ayer got off to a bad start by mislaying his one stiff shirt and keeping the guests waiting for a quarter of an hour while he borrowed another. 'The Dean felt he had been made to look a fool in front of his distinguished guests, and never altogether forgave me'.[14] The event is recorded, in the librarian's hand, on a copy of the oration in the college library – 'John Ruskin by A.J. Ayer, B.A. (who arrived 15 minutes late)'. Nor was the speech, which contains a barely hidden argument with Christian asceticism, designed to please.

While admiring Ruskin's sensitivity 'to beauty and the good things of life', Ayer objected to his puritan streak, which he traced back to Ruskin's mother, a rigid Christian:

In his own nature [Ruskin] was no enemy to pleasure. He had a passion for collecting pictures and manuscripts and geological specimens and precious stones, he was given to extravagance in dress and wore blue socks to match his eyes, he was critical and appreciative of good food and wine; . . . at all times he was naturally disposed to value travelling and drawing and writing for their own sake. Yet he could not allow himself, his mother would not allow him, to take pleasures as pleasures. He had to rationalise his enjoyment of them, to pretend in the case of some that they were not really pleasurable, in the case of others that though pleasurable they were undertaken solely in virtue of the good that they produced. These pieces of self-justification were seldom plausible. The important point is that he found it necessary to make them.

On Ayer's account, Ruskin's Christianity had not altogether killed his capacity for pleasure but it had distorted it, and forced him into something very like cant.

Under the guise of praising an 'old boy', Ayer was also able to make some telling political points, commending Ruskin's support of state education, wage agreements and the nationalisation of the means of transport. In particular, he endorsed Ruskin's analysis of the way unfettered capitalism fosters war – a good League of Nations sentiment, perhaps, but one for which there cannot have been as much approval amongst Ayer's audience as he pretends to assume. The final paragraphs, too, hit a radical note; Ayer asked the banqueters to remember Ruskin not as Slade Professor nor as a progenitor of neo-Gothic architecture but as the man after whom the left-wing workers' institute, Ruskin College, was named. It was a confident, generous and insightful paper, alive to the many tensions in Ruskin's life and character, and it showed none of the affectation that had got Ayer into trouble when he spoke as an undergraduate at the Union. Yet even had he arrived on time, it would have been a provocative performance.

Soon after the Gaudy, in early July, Ayer and Ryle went up to Birmingham to attend the Joint Session of Mind Association and the Aristotelian Society – British philosophy's annual get-together. The conference then, as now, changed location every year but was always held over a weekend and consisted of a presidential address and four symposia. This was Ayer's first taste of a philosophical conference, and he liked it.

Although he did not deliver a paper, he spoke passionately in support of the Vienna Circle whenever he got the chance. Everyone who knew Ayer at this time agreed that he was best in this sort of situation; he loved the cut and thrust of verbal argument and enjoyed the chance to perform before a crowd. As Isaiah Berlin remembered, 'he pirouetted'. Yet on this occasion Ayer's contribution was almost too vehement; as he later admitted, he 'startled the company' by the violence of his onslaught upon metaphysics. 'I did not mean to be offensive, but my delight in argument, my conviction of the truth of my opinions, my desire to convert others to them and my impatience with those who refused to see the light were so strong as to obliterate any tact or any respect for person that I might otherwise have mustered'.[15]

Perhaps it was at Birmingham, as part of this onslaught, that Ayer declared that the utterances of philosophers should have been published in the literary journal London Mercury rather than in Mind, meaning that most of them were 'emotive' or poetic rather than meaningful. They expressed a mood but said nothing verifiable about the world. Certainly by the next winter the philosopher C.A. Mace was citing this in Analysis as 'the deservedly-much-quoted epigram of Mr Ayer'.[16]

No one, alas, has left an eyewitness account of Ayer's performance but it says something for its force that it was being talked about by people who had not even attended the conference. In an article, 'Impressions and Appraisals of Analytic Philosophy in Europe', that appeared in the American Journal of Philosophy in 1936, the New York philosopher Ernest Nagel recorded that 'It was reported to me that in England some of the older men were dumbfounded and scandalised when, at a public meeting, a brilliant young adherent of the Wiener Kreis threatened them with early extinction since "the armies of Cambridge and Vienna were already upon them"'.[17] There can, surely, be no doubt about the identity of this young Turk. Nagel's source may well have been the philosopher Margaret MacDonald, who later told the American philosopher Alice Ambrose about Ayer's impact at 'a joint meeting of the Mind Association and Aristotelian Society', reporting his dramatic deliverance. '"You're lost, you're lost. The forces of Cambridge and Vienna are descending upon you!"'[18]

If, at Birmingham, Ayer was the most outspoken enemy of old-fashioned ways, he was not alone in the fight. He and a group of mainly young, like-minded philosophers including John Wisdom, Margaret

MacDonald and Austin Duncan-Jones, many of whom met at the Birmingham session, founded the journal *Analysis*. As the house journal of the new scientific philosophy, it encouraged short articles concerned with the close, quasi-technical analysis of facts, 'the general nature of which . . . is already known, rather than with attempts to establish new kinds of facts about the world, of very wide scope or on a very large scale'.[19]

The first issue came out four months later. It opened with an article by Ayer, 'Atomic Propositions', on the vexed question of the corrigibility of 'protocol statements' – statements describing our most basic observations. In three exhilaratingly bold paragraphs Ayer quickly reached the heart of the problem, arguing that one can make a mistake in even the most basic observations, like 'this is green' or 'I am in pain' on the grounds that one might misuse language (describing what is blue as green), deceive oneself, or simply mis-identify an object.

During the autumn term of 1933, Ayer worked hard on his Saturday morning lectures on 'the philosophy of analysis' but found time to sit the annual exam for the John Locke Prize in Philosophy, alongside another brilliant young philosopher, his future sparring partner, J.L. Austin. Isaiah Berlin had got the John Locke two years before but on this occasion the examining board, which included two of Oxford's grand old men, J.A. Smith and Prichard, declared that they could not see enough merit in any of the candidates to justify its award. By now Ayer had got what was in effect a second in his finals' philosophy papers, failed to get into All Souls, and failed the John Locke, each time running against the same problem: examiners unsympathetic to his views. Other setbacks were soon to follow.

It was also during this autumn term of 1933 or the Christmas vacation after it that *Language, Truth and Logic* was conceived. 'I had been expatiating to Isaiah on some aspect of the Positivistic system,' Ayer wrote, '[when] he suggested to me that I should get it all written down before my enthusiasm had been given time to stale.'[20] Ayer was immediately taken by the idea, but did not want to begin writing without securing the backing of a publisher. 'A girl' whom Ayer met at a dinner party given by Richard Crossman in New College – in fact Sheila Lynd, an attractive communist who worked for Victor Gollancz and with whom

Gollancz was in love – introduced Ayer to the publisher, who agreed to take the book.

The subject was not especially suited to Gollancz, who was much more interested in politics than philosophy – his Left Book Club would soon become one of the great publishing successes of the 1930s. Berlin, however, seems to have worked behind the scenes, visiting Lynd at Gollancz's offices. 'This afternoon Isaiah B. came in to talk to me about an admirable little "academic" book on Modern Logic . . .' Lynd wrote in a memo to Gollancz, 'which an extremely brilliant young man called Freddy Ayers [sic] is writing and would like us to publish'.[21] And Ayer himself also talked the book up, assuring Gollancz that it would be the most important philosophical work since the *Tractatus*, a definitive solution to all outstanding philosophical problems, and so forth. Perhaps as much to get him out of his office as anything else, Gollancz offered him a deal. The contract, drawn up on 26 January, shows the title simply as 'Logical Positivism', although Ayer from the beginning felt that this was not quite right: the book was meant to serve as an introduction to the doctrines of the Vienna Circle but also to be a reformulation and development of its ideas. It was going to be a combative, innovative work, not simply a survey. Ayer toyed with 'Logic and Experience' before finally arriving at *Language, Truth and Logic*, a somewhat uninspired title which draws heavily, as Ayer admitted, on Waismann's unpublished 'Logik, Sprache, Philosophie'.

Ayer started work on the book straight after Christmas. He told Gollancz it would only take him six to eight months, and was frustrated that in the end it took eighteen. Precocity was, in Freddie's eyes, a leading virtue. He had begun his Gaudy oration by pointing out that Ruskin was twenty-four when he published his first book, and he would have been well aware that Hume was only twenty-three when he began work on the *Treatise* and twenty-seven when it appeared in print. Ramsey, Isaiah Berlin suggested, was an even more important model: he had not had the chance to finish a book before he died at the age of twenty-six, but his review of Wittgenstein's *Tractatus* appeared when he was twenty and by the time he was Freddie's age, he had written a handful of dazzling logical papers. As Henry Price observed around this time, Ayer was 'a young man in a hurry'.[22]

8

Language, Truth and Logic
or, the Philosophy of Nonsense

Aged twenty-three, Ayer found himself in a very uncertain position. Many of his peers and elders already recognised him as a very remarkable young man. He had published two or three widely discussed articles, was working hard on a book, and had proved himself an inspired public performer. And yet he had made enemies at Christ Church and elsewhere. For all his promise, his future was worryingly insecure.

The lectureship Ayer had so precociously secured in 1932 had been intended to serve as a stepping-stone to a Christ Church studentship. With this lectureship due to expire in June, however, there was still no permanent position for him to move into. So it came as a blow when, after announcing the creation of a new studentship which paid £1,000 a year, triple Ayer's lectureship, and interviewing Ayer for the position, Christ Church appointed Frank Pakenham (later Lord Longford), a high-minded young Anglo-Irish aristocrat who had been lecturing in politics at Christ Church for just over a year. The college, it was true, needed a politics tutor, but the fact of Pakenham's birth and Freddie's values also seemed to have entered into the balance: there was snobbish talk in the Senior Common Room about 'the importance of bringing the upper classes on board'. Neither Ayer's chagrin, nor Pakenham's zealous Catholicism prevented Ayer becoming close to Pakenham and his wife Elizabeth, who were both in the process of switching their loyalties from the Conservatives to Labour. Nevertheless, while most of his Oxford friends and contemporaries were now settled, Ayer had to make do with a year's extension of his lowly lectureship. It was, as one friend remembered, 'humiliating'.[1]

Around this time, in the summer or autumn of 1934, the Ayers left Oxford for London. It was Renée who characteristically orchestrated the move. She had taken his failure at Christ Church 'very ill', believing that the decision had not been taken on purely academic grounds; and in any case disliked the clannishness of Oxford life. Ayer acquiesced. He had begun to think that he might have to take up law after all. He even went so far as to enrol again at the Bar.

It is important to an understanding of the character of Language, Truth and Logic that Ayer now had a little over a year of paid income in which to write the book, after which it seemed he might be forced to give up philosophy. He was, of course, enormously excited by the ideas he was writing about and this accounts for much of the work's flair and zeal. But it also looked as if Language, Truth and Logic might well be not only a first but a valedictory work. This, and his struggles in writing it to secure a position for himself, helped give it its urgency, iconoclasm, and its aspiration to definitiveness. Its author was writing from conviction but also from anger. As he put it in a letter to Neurath a few weeks before the book finally appeared: 'At Oxford, where I work, metaphysics still predominates. I feel very isolated here and have been made to suffer economically for my views'.[2]

Ayer worked hard on Language, Truth and Logic, and, as one might expect, compared to the rate he achieved after his return from Vienna – five periodical publications in nine months – his production of articles fell off. Renée found a quaint, crooked, two-floor red-brick maisonette above a tobacconist's in Foubert's Place, a narrow street in west Soho, just behind Liberty's and a minute's walk from Oxford Circus. Freddie had a small room on the top floor where he worked when he was not in Oxford. It was during this time that he developed his habit of setting himself a goal of a certain number of words – anything between 300 and 1,000 – every morning. Like Russell, he thought hard about what he was going to say before writing. He found it almost impossible to think without playing with something like a cigarette-holder, a set of keys or a chain, and paced up and down as he thought. Then he wrote (or in the case of this first book, typed) a fair copy straight on to the page. No drafts of *Language, Truth and Logic* survive, but drafts of other works show that he made virtually no corrections.

Renée, in the meantime, looked after him. Although a radical in politics, she played, almost overplayed, the role of subservient housewife. She liked to describe herself as 'a Japanese doormat' – it was something, she said, she'd been taught in the East. The Ayers were not rich; in fact they had less money than most of their friends. But with the Christ Church lectureship and an allowance from Dorus, they had enough money to live with a certain style, and Soho, with its French and Italian restaurants, theatres, night clubs, shops and markets, lent itself to the sort of bohemian life they enjoyed. They ate out alone or with friends, went to the cinema two or three times a week, often in the afternoon, and Renée bought clothes more or less whenever she wanted them. Looking back at the end of his life, Ayer judged this the greatest period for both French and American cinema, and he and Renée saw almost everything that came out.[3] Freddie indeed became a film enthusiast, learning the names and remembering the roles not just of the great stars, Jean Gabin and Louis Jouvet, Clark Gable, Gary Cooper, Mae West, Cary Grant, Humphrey Bogart, Marlene Dietrich and Fred Astaire (his favourite), but of minor character actors as well. Cinema, for a while, seems to have become more important than sport.

Ayer found he liked life in London, with its endless amusements and distractions, but his social life still centred on Oxford. It was around this time that he became close to a number of gifted young Oxford scientists, including J.Z. Young and Solly Zuckerman. They naturally approved of the intellectual campaign that Ayer was waging. Freddie and Zuckerman, who had just published his celebrated *Social Life of Monkeys and Apes*, became especially close. He recalled how, 'During the period in which he was writing his first book . . . [Freddie] was often in my flat in Museum Road, pacing up and down my sitting room, twirling a silver chain as he declaimed his views.'[4] Zuckerman was four or five years older than Ayer and Isaiah Berlin but the three were often seen as a group – 'Oxford's three brilliant Jews', as Stuart Hampshire described them.[5] '[Isaiah], Freddie and I were much in demand,' Zuckerman wrote in his autobiography, 'and on one occasion when Isaiah and I were walking home after a dinner party, he remarked "I can just hear them saying now, 'those two were very bright and amusing, but where did they come from?'"[6] No doubt they asked the same about Ayer.

Another, very brilliant, Jewish friend Freddie made in the winter of 1933–34 was the American jurist Felix Frankfurter, in Oxford as Eastman Visiting Professor, with his wife Marion, a gracious New Englander. Frankfurter, although a distinguished jurist then in his fifties, was quite unlike the conservative establishment figures that then very largely ruled Oxford. The son of a poor immigrant family, he had risen to become Professor of Law at Harvard. He had helped found the American Civil Liberties Union, and had fought a courageous although ultimately unsuccessful campaign to save the Boston anarchists Sacco and Vanzetti, who had been wrongfully convicted and executed for murder in the 1920s. As a personal friend of President Roosevelt and a close adviser on the New Deal, Frankfurter represented, to Ayer and his friends, a living, breathing alternative to the *laissez-faire* policies of the National Government. Yet it was not just his politics but his personal qualities, above all his invigorating disregard for the proprieties and hierarchies of Oxford life, that accounted for what Ayer described as Frankfurter's 'spectacular' social success.[7] Berlin recalled that he possessed an 'over-flowing gaiety and spontaneity . . . which contrasted almost too sharply with the reserve, solemnity and, in places, vanity and self-importance' of the Oxford establishment.[8] According to Bowra, 'Felix believed in the paramount importance of the law'. Yet he tempered 'this somewhat abstract loyalty by strong personal attachments . . . He had a boundless curiosity about human beings and liked almost anyone who had something to say for themselves and was not stuffy or cagey.'[9]

There was a memorably hilarious dinner party in the beginning of the summer term of 1934 at the Frankfurters' house in Oxford. Freddie and Renée, Goronwy Rees, Bowra, Guy Burgess and the lawyer and banker Sylvester Gates were there, and towards the end of the evening Gates and Freddie began arguing about whether Wittgenstein's sentence 'Whereof one may not speak, thereon one must preserve silence' occurs once or twice in the *Tractatus*. Freddie said it was once, Gates twice. Bets were taken. Freddie jumped in a taxi and fetched a copy of the book from his flat, to discover the sentence was to be found once in the main body of the book and once in the preface. The dispute was now about whether the preface counted as part of the book and Frankfurter agreed to sit as judge on the case. Freddie was in his element, defending his brief with the energy of 'an Arab steed', although in the end Frankfurter's ruling went against him. Talking twenty-five years later, Frankfurter remembered these Oxford friends as an 'extremely clever, almost excessively clever young crowd'.[10]

For the summer of 1934 the records almost run dry. In June Ayer lunged and parried at the Joint Session in Cardiff. Soon after, he and Renée visited his grandfather in Eastbourne and stayed with an elderly aunt and uncle of Renée at their country house in Kent. Here Freddie worked hard on his book, but still found time to begin his lifelong love affair with Dickens. He would read the novels over and over again for the rest of his life, as he did those of Jane Austen, Thomas Love Peacock and a few other favourites. By the end of the summer, when 'Logical Positivism' was meant to have been submitted to Gollancz, Ayer still barely had a draft. He promised to finish it by Christmas. As before, however, his teaching got in the way. Christmas, and then Easter, came and went. It was not until July 1934 that the manuscript was delivered, a full year late.

In the meantime, Freddie's family life was changing. His mother, Reine, was lonely by herself and in the autumn of 1934 she remarried. Ayer's new stepfather, Richard Vance, was an elderly Irish accountant whom Reine had met at a seaside hotel. After their marriage they lived together in her flat off the Finchley Road. Wedding pictures show a large moustached man with what Ayer describes 'as a rather ugly florid face but considerable charm of manner'.

> He treated her as the child that she had in many ways remained and
> I think that she was happier with him than she had been with my
> father, at any rate in their later years ... I liked him very much,
> admired the way in which he managed my mother, and enjoyed his
> company.[11]

Freddie and his new stepfather were both cricket enthusiasts and in the summer holidays often spent the afternoon together, walking the short distance from the Eyre Court flat to Lord's. Then, after Christmas, on 25 January 1935 (Ayer always remembered the date) Dorus Citroën died.

A year before Dorus, too, had remarried, to a South African, Dehra Hadfield, whom he had known for many years. She had originally been brought into the Citroën household as a companion to one of the daughters, and was then sent off when Freddie's grandmother began to suspect (or discovered) that she and Dorus were having an affair. Dorus was around seventy-four at the time of the marriage; Dehra must have been at least twenty years younger. In accordance with Dorus's instructions, his cremation was unreligious and informal. He divided most of his wealth between his five grandchildren, characteristically depositing the sum in a trust, which after several attempts over the years, has yet to be broken. In addition, each of the grandchildren was allowed to choose one item from the Eastbourne house. Freddie and Renée eschewed the antiques in favour of a new radio-gramophone. It was a modern-minded choice that went with a recently acquired glass dining table in the Bauhaus style, but it was, as Ayer acknowledged, 'lacking in sentiment', and became something of a Citroën family joke.

Ayer always looked back on his grandfather with something close to reverence. Dorus had offered him an education, a private income, a knowledge of how the world worked and a degree of social confidence, but perhaps something less tangible as well. Dorus came from generations of jewellers, and was himself a collector. 'He knew the value of things,' as a granddaughter put it,[12] and had an eye for what was bogus and what was genuine – like the painting that Freddie's father owned and claimed was by the Dutch painter Wouwermans, and which Citroën quietly knew was not. Perhaps he was overbearing and set too much store by worldly success, but he was clear-headed, unsentimental and unpretentious. These of course were Ayer's qualities, too, and to this extent his philosophy was cast from an old familial mould. It is surely revealing that in his article, 'Demonstration of the Impossibility of Metaphysics', and again in Language, Truth and Logic, he offered as an example of a meaningful non-metaphysical question the issue of whether picture X was painted by Goya. To the extent that this was the sort of question on which Dorus's mind centred and which he knew exactly how to go about answering, he represented a model empiricist.

Ayer had been working on Language, Truth and Logic for a year when his grandfather died; he had another six months left of his fellowship, which he calculated would just see him through. In addition to the legacy Dorus Citroën had left all the grandchildren, he had made a provision in his will releasing funds for any of his three grandsons who wanted to change professions – a provision evidently drawn up partly with Freddie in mind.

Ayer's future remained, indeed, as unsettled as ever. In a letter to Roy Harrod, now his principal champion at Christ Church, written early in the new year of 1935, he gave frank expression to his doubts and worries:

> . . . I know that you are right and Gilbert [Ryle] wrong with regard to the question of my views being obstacles in the way of my getting an Oxford job. I count more on the chance of a post falling vacant in Cambridge or London, in the course of the next few years.
>
> It was charming of you to say 'that I could always follow in the footsteps of Hume' [and earn a living as a man of letters] but I am not sure that this is true. I do not write with facility. Even when I have something definite to say, as is the case with my present book, it takes me a very long time to say it: I have periods, lasting weeks, even months, of great sterility, from one of which I am only just now emerging. And when I have no case to argue, or no important information to impart, I cannot write at all. In short I can only write about subjects in which I am more or less an expert, and at present philosophy is the only subject in which I can claim to be an expert. I mean to learn others, but I doubt if I could learn fast enough, or write quickly enough about them to enable me to embark on a profitable literary career.[13]

Nor was Ayer the only one worried about his future. Stuart Hampshire, a young philosopher at All Souls, first met the Ayers at around this time, and remembered that 'Renée was in a terrible state'. He also recalled that Freddie's supporters, led by Harrod, appealed to Isaiah Berlin to do whatever he could to drum up support, although to no effect. The affair required 'a partisanship that was not Isaiah's style'.[14]

Harrod, however, was not easily deterred. Having hit upon the plan of reviving the research studentship that had been created for Einstein and left empty by his move to Princeton, he succeeded in securing references from G.E. Moore at Cambridge, Henry Price at Oxford, and A. N.

Whitehead, Russell's old collaborator on *Principia Mathematica*, at Harvard. Whitehead's reference could not have been more enthusiastic, likening Ayer to 'J.M. Keynes, Bertrand Russell, and others of that type among my old pupils'. Those of Moore and Price, however, who knew Ayer personally, are more revealing.[15]

Moore wrote that he was 'one of the ablest philosophical disputants that I have ever met' although 'in his writings he does not seem to me as yet to have done full justice to the powers which he displays in oral discussion'.[16] Price agreed that Ayer was at his best in public discussion – 'he expounds and defends his views with enthusiasm, almost with passion, and his quickness and ingenuity have full scope' – and credited him with having almost single-handedly familiarised Oxford with 'the Russell–Wittgenstein school'. 'On the other hand', he went on,

> it must be admitted that he has certain compensatory weaknesses – a narrowness of interest and a certain indifference and contempt for some quite respectable but old fashioned ways of thinking. Perhaps we might say that Mr Ayer has at present both the defects and merits of the man with a system . . . It must be admitted too that his uncompromisingness in controversy has antagonised a certain number of people, including some of those who would admit on reflection that they have learned a good deal from him.[17]

Despite Price's reservations, all three references were, in the main, extremely enthusiastic, and on 8 May 1935 Ayer was finally elected to a five-year research studentship. It was Einstein's position captured by another Jew, although at least this time not a German. A few weeks later he tried for a permanent fellowship at Pembroke College, although once again to no avail. 'Oxford,' as Berlin said in a letter to Frankfurter, 'is afraid of him.'[18]

Ayer continued to apply for other fellowships, although without success. In 1938, a position became available at Trinity. Ayer was furious to discover that Michael Foster, his old philosophy tutor, had been consulted as to Ayer's qualities and had reported that he did not think him fit to teach the young. Ayer burst into his rooms 'and railed at him, saying that this was a monstrous way to treat a colleague and accusing him of being jealous'. Foster listened to this tirade in pained and embarrassed silence. Later Ayer would say that he felt 'ashamed' of his conduct: 'his opinion of me, whether or not it was justified, was undoubtedly honest, and having been asked for his advice, he had every right to give it'.[19] Yet his feelings against Foster were surely excusable.

With Dorus's legacy and a fellowship to support them, the Ayers seem to have decided they were rich enough to start a family, and early in the summer of 1935 Renée became pregnant. At around the same time, her father paid a rare visit to London. To Renée's disapproval, he had married his young Japanese housekeeper, Hisako, who accompanied him. 'The argument which he put to Renée to justify his choice,' Ayer wrote,

> was that what he was in search of was not an attractive younger woman who would expect him to lavish attention on her, but someone who would cause him no anxiety, make few demands on him, and care for all his wants; and these were conditions that he already knew that Hisako satisfied. Here he miscalculated. No sooner were they married than she developed arthritis . . . and he found himself waiting upon her. During the months that they spent with us, she sat like an idol, with her hands half-clenched in front of her, saying very little, but taking notice of everything that went on.[20]

This was the first time Freddie had met his father-in-law and although the Catholic officer and the radical positivist did not have much in common, Freddie seems to have found the situation funny rather than awkward. In June the two couples took a camping holiday in Switzerland, driving on to spend a few days in Venice. Renée's father, as befitted an explorer, took charge of the expedition and it also fell to him, despite his age, to do most of the heavy work. His wife was crippled, Renée was pregnant, Freddie was useless. Ayer had often been to Switzerland but this was his first time in Italy. 'No one,' he wrote to Isaiah Berlin from Como, 'appears to mind one being English, but I can not find much to like in the Italians. They have neither the good nature of the Spaniards nor the intelligence of the French'. Still, Venice itself 'in July is delightful.'[21]

In 1934 Ayer met Carnap for the first time, when he gave a series of lectures at London. Otherwise he had had little contact with the philosophers in the Vienna Circle in the two years since he had left Austria. In September 1935, however, Neurath helped organise the first and the largest of the International Congresses for the Unity of Science, a great gathering of over 150 philosopher-scientists at the Sorbonne. He invited Ayer to speak. Ayer offered papers on 'The criterion of Truth and Falsehood' (a contribution to the quarrel over the nature of basic statements of science and experience, later published in *Analysis*, in which he continued to deny that there were any empirical judgements that were incorrigible), and an outline of 'The Analytic Movement in Contemporary British Philosophy'. Neurath preferred the latter.[22]

The conference attracted philosophers from fifteen countries, and marked the high point of logical positivism as an organised international movement. Russell, the honorary president of the proceedings, gave an opening address and Neurath made an impassioned plea for international co-operation, ending his contribution with *Vivent les nouveaux encyclopédistes*.[23] But the highlight of the conference was Tarski's exposition and defence of the semantic theory of truth, which re-converted Carnap to correspondence theory. Carnap and Schlick were there from Vienna, as was Karl Popper whom Ayer met for the first time and befriended. Popper was not himself a member of the Vienna Circle and liked to stress his differences from it. His first and most famous book, however, *The Logic of Scientific Discovery*, had just been published in one of the circle's monograph series and Ayer always insisted, to Popper's annoyance, on viewing him as a fellow traveller.

Looking back after the war, Russell recalled that he had been most impressed by the international co-operation that the congress displayed: 'In their official sittings [the philosophers] discussed highly abstract matters, but in their spare time they would touch on all the most thorny questions of European politics. I observed, with astonished admiration, that national bias hardly ever showed itself in these discussions. The severe logical training to which these men submitted themselves had, it appeared, rendered them immune to the infection of passionate dogma . . .'[24]

Ayer no doubt enjoyed himself; he loved France and welcomed the chance to show off his French, but his paper was unexceptional. He acknowledged that the conception of philosophy as the analysis of common sense and scientific observation, far from being a novelty in

England, was implicit in the work of all the British empiricists from Locke to Mill. He credited Russell and Moore with the rehabilitation of this approach in the teeth of the British idealists of the late nineteenth century. He singled out Russell, above all, for having arrived by the end of the war at something very close to logical positivism, although he regretted his tendency to slip into metaphysical language by talking about ultimate constituents of the world, and somewhat misrepresenting the nature of philosophical analysis by suggesting that it is concerned not exclusively with the relationship of symbols, but with 'the resolution of complex objects into their ultimately simple constituents'. Once again, Ayer was stressing the importance of distinguishing conceptual analysis from science.[25]

What Ayer did not say in his paper was that he himself had just finished the first book-length treatment of logical positivism to be written in English. The preface to *Language, Truth and Logic* signs off '11 Foubert's Place, July 1935' and was written a few days before the Ayers and Orde-Leeses left for the Continent. In the end it had taken nineteen, not nine months to write, although Ayer could still claim to have completed it before his twenty-fifth birthday. The preface singled out Ryle and Berlin for thanks. Berlin, in particular, remembered discussing almost every paragraph in it.

A.J. AYER

Interlude: *Language, Truth and Logic*

It has often been said, not least of all by Ayer himself, that *Language, Truth and Logic* is not original, to which Ayer might have replied by quoting Pascal: 'Let no one say that I have said nothing new; the arrangement of the material is new.' Whether or not material newly arranged and elaborated entitles a work to be called original, it is here, in the tight, bold and lucid integration of Moorean analysis, Russellian logic and Viennese positivism, that the book's brilliance lies. The clear-headedness with which Ayer elaborated his key ideas – the conception of philosophy as offering 'definitions in use', the verification principle, the distinction between empirical and analytic propositions, the emotivist theory of morals – and then used them to cut a swathe through the traditional problems of philosophy, set a new standard for philosophical debate. Sixty years on, the book's vigour, elegance and ease is as remarkable as ever. Never has philosophy been so fast, so neat.

A great deal has been written about the irreverence and audacity of *Language, Truth and Logic*, from the bravado of its opening declaration, 'The traditional disputes of philosophers are, for the most part, as unwarranted as they are unfruitful', to the finality of its final chapter, 'Solutions of Outstanding Philosophical Disputes'.* And, of course, Ayer's arguments *are* wonderfully irreverent. Those who have written about the book, however, including Ayer himself, have generally made sense of its arguments by placing them in the long tradition of anti-metaphysical philosophy that flows from the Ancient sceptics and atomists, through Hume and Auguste Comte, to Ernst Mach and Russell. It is worth stepping back in a slightly different direction, and viewing it in the context of its times.

The 1930s, like the 1960s, was an age of youthful rebellion, a rebellion that had its roots in the depression and the rise of Fascism and, perhaps more deeply, in the rejection of the values associated with the First World War. The hard-headed, unsentimental, scientifically minded verse of the 1930s poets – Auden, Day Lewis, Spender, MacNeice – gave

---

* The model here, of course, is the *Tractatus*, where Wittgenstein says, 'I am, therefore, of the opinion that the problems have in essentials been finally solved'. However, Ayer's book lacks Wittgenstein's qualifier, 'And if I am not mistaken in this, then the value of this work secondly consists in the fact that it shows how little has been done when these problems have been solved'.

famous expression to this rebellion. Yet a similar disdain for comfortable bourgeois conventions found voice in Surrealism, Mass Observation, the cults of psychoanalysis and Marxism and a range of other movements. It is not, perhaps, too fanciful to see the interest in logical positivism in general, and *Language, Truth and Logic* in particular, as a part of this broad revolt.* Viewed from this perspective, the really defining feature of the book is not so much its attack on metaphysics as a more far-reaching rejection of philosophical authority in both knowledge and morals.

Much of this rejection is worked by Ayer's empiricism. The hallmark of rationalist and metaphysically minded philosophers, in Ayer's view (and he presented them with lofty disregard for history, as a single undifferentiated block), was their distrust of science and common sense. They saw it as the business of philosophy to 'furnish speculative truths, which would, as it were, compete with the hypotheses of science . . . [or] . . . to pass *a priori* judgements upon the validity of scientific theories'.[26] Thus they sought, like Descartes, to deduce the existence of God and other truths about the universe in an almost mathematical fashion. Or like Kant to establish, a priori, from the nature of experience itself, supposedly universal and necessary truths concerning the structure of space, of the causal order and the like. To Ayer, these attempts to go beyond or regulate experience represented an incoherent and obnoxious form of philosophical imperialism, and a great part of *Language, Truth and Logic* was devoted to their refutation.

As Ayer explained at the outset, his most essential contention was that 'all genuine propositions' fall into one of two classes: those which concern the a-priori propositions of logic and pure mathematics and those which concern matters of fact. All a-priori truths, he argued (following Wittgenstein) are analytic or tautologous in character: 'the reason why they can not be confuted in experience is that they do not

---

* Stuart Hampshire, a radical young philosopher and a friend of the poets, drew a parallel between 1930s poetry and philosophy in his essay 'W. H. Auden' (in *Modern Writers and Other Essays*, London, 1969). 'There was', he wrote, 'a respectful veiled hostility between the generations' that expressed itself in different approaches to poetry and philosophy. 'For a generation made literal-minded by the new political brutalities and by the probability of war, it was no longer possible to give licence to half-serious beliefs which seemed poetic playthings and which, taken by themselves, were just incredible'. He offers as examples 'Eliot's magnificent middle manner' and 'fine Bradleyian philosophy'.

make any assertion about the empirical world. 'They simply record our determination to use words in a certain fashion'.[27] There is a sense in which these propositions do give us new knowledge. 'They call attention to linguistic usages, of which we might otherwise not be conscious, and they reveal unsuspected implications in our assertions and beliefs'. But there is also a sense 'in which they may be said to add nothing to our knowledge. For they tell us only what we may be said to know already'.[28]

The synthetic propositions of empirical science, on the other hand, are, Ayer maintained, a genuine source of knowledge – the only source of knowledge of the world, rather than of language, that there is. Ayer famously argued that all these propositions were hypotheses analysable into the language of 'sense contents'. He contended in particular that statements about the past were really statements about the future (or at least 'rules for the prediction of those "historical" experiences which are commonly said to verify them'), and statements about other minds are really statements about bodily behaviour. What matters, in the present context, however, is not the details of his argument, but that in arguing this way, he sought to slay once and for all the idea that 'philosophy or some other discipline has the power to reveal to us authoritatively the nature of objects which we have never observed'.[29] The whole thrust of this part of his work was to liberate science and common sense from philosophy, to free it from 'the system builders'. There is no source of truth, Ayer argued, but experience. The desire to go beyond it, to supplement or rival the evidence of the senses, is utterly misconceived.

This was already an uncompromisingly anti-authoritarian position, but Ayer's empiricism in science was paralleled by his emotivism in morals.[*] As usual his position had a history traceable to Hume and beyond. More recently a number of philosophers, including Ogden and Richards, in *The Meaning of Meaning* (1923) and Carnap had at least gestured towards the sort of analysis Ayer defended. It seems fair to say, however, that Ayer's infamous sixth chapter, 'Critique of Ethics and Theology', offered a much tighter, more developed defence of the emotivist thesis than anything before it. It became, almost immediately, the defining statement of the

---

[*] Here, in fact, Ayer was parting from an important strand of the empiricist tradition. Utilitarians like Bentham and Mill were inclined to assimilate judgements of value to judgements of fact and contend that the claim that a certain course of action is right or just, is the claim that it will maximise happiness.

position – its *locus classicus*. In the process Ayer did much to kill off a number of rival theories; G.E. Moore's *Principia Ethica*, for instance, never recovered its prestige. This is one of those instances where *Language, Truth and Logic* clarified the debate and moved it on.

Ayer began in fact, by following lines already laid down by Moore, in arguing against the position, common to classical Utilitarianism and certain species of relativism, that the right or the good can ever be equated with an empirical state of affairs – the greatest happiness of the greatest number, say, or the customs of a given country. It always remains possible, Ayer argued, to ask about any state of affairs, 'Is it good? Is it right?' He also, however, rejected the view (common to Moore and Oxford intuitionists like Prichard) that good was an objective but non-empirical property detected by a faculty of moral intuition. Ayer's militant empiricism allowed no place for talk of such mysterious entities. Instead he advanced the 'radically subjectivist' argument that judgements of value (aesthetic as well as moral) do not say anything at all, but simply express the speaker's approval or disapproval:

> If ... I ... say, 'Stealing money is wrong' I produce a sentence which has no factual meaning – that is, expresses no proposition which can be either true or false. It is as if I had written 'Stealing money!!' – where the shape and thickness of the exclamation marks show, by a suitable convention, that a special sort of moral disapproval is the feeling which is being expressed.[30]

There is in our moral and political discourse, Ayer acknowledged, room for dispute, but only because moral judgements are generally made up of an assertion of an empirical fact, the truth of which one can legitimately contest, as well as an expression of feeling towards the fact. ('You acted wrongly in stealing that money' is made up of the – in principle contestable – claim 'you took that money' and the ejaculation 'Boo!') Yet ultimately, or so Ayer contended, where there is complete agreement on the facts, but disagreement on their value, there is no right or wrong in the matter. To say, for instance, that someone has 'a distorted or undeveloped moral sense ... signifies merely that he employs a different set of values from our own'.[31]

In short then, in both knowledge and morals, although for rather different reasons, Ayer denied that philosophers or indeed any other experts had any special authority to tell us what there is or how to live.

Finally, it is worth noting a second feature of the book, one which, in contrast to its rejection of authority, marks it out from its time. This is the way it combines radicalism with an exemplary rigour. A lot of anger and revolutionary zeal went into the writing of Language, Truth and Logic, and its arguments had very radical practical implications: if they were accepted, religion would wither away, ideology would perish, science would flourish, social hierarchies would collapse, and, Ayer hoped, people would become more sceptical in their moral convictions, more tolerant of others' points of view. Yet he refused to give way to rhetoric and indeed never even alluded, in the way Russell, Carnap and Neurath often did, to the social and political implications of his ideas. He made his arguments as clear and convincing as he could and then left the reader to judge their worth.

From the beginning of his life to the end, he believed in an absolute ethic of reason, of truth: winning people to your point of view was important, but getting the philosophy right was more important still.

9

Iconoclast, Hedonist

Language, Truth and Logic was published in January 1936. The book, priced at nine shillings, had an attractively up-to-date appearance with wide margins, generous spacing, and large print (although it was only around 60,000 words long, it ran to 250 pages.) Oxford University Press published it in America a little less than a year later, priced $3. Elizabeth Pakenham remembered meeting Ayer shortly after its publication, when, as she put it, 'the philosophical world was humming like a beehive that has been kicked. "Freddie," I asked, "what comes next?" His black eyes glittered and he answered gleefully "There's no next. Philosophy has come to an end. Finished." '[1]

As any publisher will testify, it is hard to account for, let alone predict, a book's reception. Coverage of *Language, Truth and Logic* was better than Ayer can have expected; the *Observer*, the *Spectator*, the *Manchester Guardian*, and the *New Statesman* all reviewed it. The *TLS*, and the *Times*, however, neglected it, and American coverage was fairly thin. In addition, while most of those who did review it, like Solly Zuckerman (*New Statesman*), and the philosophers J.D. Mabbot (*Philosophy*), Susan Stebbing (*Mind*) and Ernest Nagel (*Journal of Philosophy*), were respectful, even enthusiastic, none came close to hailing it as a masterpiece. The two longest reviews, by Father d'Arcy in T.S. Eliot's *Criterion* and E.W.F. Tomlin in Leavis's *Scrutiny*, were, in fact, highly critical. D'Arcy was evidently fond of Ayer – 'I do not think that anyone, however much he may be infuriated by the argument, can be prevented from liking the author' – but pretended to see in the work a clever satire aimed at reducing the empiricist tradition to absurdity.[2] Tomlin, on the other hand, could 'not remember having met with a book written by one who claims to be a professional, if not yet a professor, that revealed such a combination of immaturity, loose thinking, and wholly unwarranted cocksureness'.[3] Nor did Language, Truth and Logic sell in huge numbers. There were four British print runs in all before the war, the first of 500, the following three of 250 each – although this was partly because Gollancz consistently underestimated demand. There are no figures for the American edition.

Yet despite the mixed reviews and limited sales, Language, Truth and Logic quickly achieved cult status among students and young intellectuals. Father d'Arcy described it as having had 'an immense success' and the biologist Peter Medawar, teaching in Oxford at this time, remembered it as 'a dazzling and revolutionary work', 'read by every undergraduate in breathless excitement'.[4] The philosopher Peter Strawson, who went up to Oxford in 1937, had what he recalled was a common experience: he read the book in 'one absorbed sitting', and then refrained from mentioning it to his tutor, who refrained from mentioning it to him.[5] Not that all Oxford's tutors were so reticent. The philosopher David Pears, who arrived at the university a year or two after Strawson, attended a philosophical discussion group led by the Master of Balliol, A.D. Lindsay, a Christian socialist. At one meeting the students made a bid to discuss Language, Truth and Logic. Lindsay picked the book up and dropped it out of a window into Broad Street and suggested another subject.

It was not just students and amateurs who took Ayer's tract seriously. Language, Truth and Logic became the most discussed book in the philosophical press in the pre-war years. By the end of 1939 Mind had published, on one estimate, no fewer than ten articles and discussion notes directly relating to its central themes, and most of the other leading journals carried articles responding to one aspect of it or another.[6] Oxford, in particular, 'buzzed' with debate about the book.[7] In the autumn of 1936 Father d'Arcy gave a series of lectures on 'Empiricism and Metaphysics', presumably occasioned by Ayer's ideas. Similarly,

Collingwood, appointed Professor of Metaphysics in 1935, devoted part of his lectures to its refutation.[*]

Inevitably, it was Ayer's treatment of morality that aroused the greatest controversy. Tomlin described the chapter on ethics as 'surely the most puerile piece of casuistry that a philosopher has ever put forward in the name of reason', and a number of articles quarrelled with it in the philosophical press.[8] Ayer himself always insisted that his emotivism was a theory about the logic of moral language, not a first-order ethical theory, and most of the strictly philosophical debate accepted these terms. Nevertheless, Ayer's chapter on ethics and religion was provocative. He might have admitted that our moral and aesthetic convictions imbue our whole vision of the world, to the point where they seem inseparable from our empirical beliefs. He might have tried to show how his emotivism could make sense of the experience of moral growth. He might have attempted to account for the fact that moral judgements, unlike mere expletives, can function as a premise in a syllogism: torture is wrong, depriving a prisoner of sleep is a form of torture, therefore depriving a prisoner of sleep is wrong. Instead Ayer chose bluntly and at points dismissively to insist that ethical concepts were 'mere pseudo concepts', and moral judgements a 'mere' matter of feeling.

Ayer's position, of course, was animated by a very 'moral' dislike of the humbug, inflated rhetoric and woolly thinking of so much religious and conservative morality. Yet it is hardly surprising that his ideas were soon being denounced as immoral. When in the late 1930s Ayer visited Westminster School as an external examiner, one housemaster pointed him out to a pupil with an interest in philosophy: 'That is the most wicked man in Oxford.'[9]

The publication of *Language, Truth and Logic* marked a new phase in Ayer's life, and not just in his professional life. A month after it appeared, Renée gave birth to a daughter. Freddie always enjoyed the company of children and was, in his own way, devoted to his own. He was moved by

---

[*] There occurred an incident which shows that Collingwood, for all of his differences with Ayer, admired the book. Gilbert Ryle was in an Oxford bookshop when he overheard Joseph and Prichard complaining to each other that *Language, Truth and Logic* had ever found a publisher. Collingwood, also in the bookshop, turned to them; 'Gentlemen, this book will be read when your names are forgotten' (*PML*, p.166).

their utter dependency but, beyond that, the empiricist in him appreciated their open-mindedness: children are, Ayer believed, much freer of conventional views than adults – they have something of Pater's aliveness-to-life about them.* Obliged, soon after the birth, to spend two nights in Oxford, he sent Renée one of the few love notes to have survived from his pen:

My sweet darling Renée
Ever since I left you I have been thinking of you and of Juliet . . . I feel infinitely happy and relieved. I realised last night how much I loved you and I am going to love Juliet, not so as to make you jealous, but very very much. Whatever the shape of her nose. I long to be with you both again.
I drank a glass of port tonight and smoked a cigar in your honour.
Expect me tomorrow before tea-time. Meanwhile take care of yourself. Good night my own Darling.[10]

In the end they called the new baby not Juliet but Valerie, and increased their reputation for eccentricity by building a wooden cage outside a window in their Foubert's Place flat, in which they placed her to get fresh air. 'The Ayers have a child and are quite happy,' Berlin wrote to Felix Frankfurter, a few months later:

There cannot be complete tranquillity anywhere Freddie is, future crises are always looming, but on the whole even they seem settled. Their prosperity, their life in London, etc. has tranquillised them a great deal, but still they are the most exotic persons, with an infinite quantity of style, whom one has ever met and refreshing and exhilarating to the last degree. Freddie's unwavering loyalty to his friends is a childlike, pathetic, very endearing quality which always moves me a great deal. The mixture of sophistication and simplicity is very odd and attractive. He grows no older and seems

---

* 'Pater's Cyrenaic programme which still attracts me in spite of the disastrous results of the attempts made in the precious nineties to "burn with a hard gemlike flame" actually corresponds to the practice of unspoiled children,' Ayer wrote to E.E. Cummings in the 1940s, 'but it is possible for adults only if it is not self-conscious, which is to say, only in so far as they remain children' (to Marion and E.E. Cummings, 19 September 1942).

permanently fixed, still anxious to be the *enfant terrible* of the philosophers.[11]

Apart from domestic changes, Ayer also began making friends in the wider world. Through his best man David Headley, he got to know Guy Burgess, who often turned up uninvited at Foubert's Place. Burgess, working for the *Times* and then the BBC and already a Soviet agent, was drunken, dirty and unreliable, but he could hold forth brilliantly on books or politics and seemed somehow to know everything and everybody. Goronwy Rees, now established in London as an assistant editor of the *Spectator*, also introduced the Ayers to new friends, including Elizabeth Bowen, whom they especially liked. Cyril Connolly, though, was the first important London figure to take Ayer up.

'I don't remember how I met Cyril,' as Ayer later said, 'but I think my entry into a wider world . . . was due to him.'[12] Connolly, a brilliant pug-faced Etonian, was then married to his first wife, Jean Bakewell, and earning a living reviewing for the *New Statesman* and the *Daily Telegraph*. He had not yet written *Enemies of Promise*, but he had already assumed the self-protective mask of the lazy hedonist that he was to display to the world in that book. He and Ayer often met in the splendid Café Royal, with its mirrored walls, red banquettes and cane chairs, then still, as it was in Oscar Wilde's day, a meeting place for artists and writers. 'Cyril was very much a man of mood,' Ayer wrote, 'but when he was in good spirits and sure of his company, he was one of the best talkers I have ever known. He had a curiously soft voice and a slow way of talking which crystallized his wit.'[13] The two men were brought together by a love of food and drink and parties, by a deep feeling for France, and, later, by their support for the Republicans in the Spanish Civil War. Revealingly, Ayer inscribed a copy of *Language, Truth and Logic*, 'To Cyril, who hates the same things as I do.'

Cyril Connolly used to say that there were two Freddie Ayers, the Oxford philosopher, and a London twin who loved to drink and dance. Whatever the truth in this joke – and it could be argued against it that Ayer's empiricism and epicureanism were two sides of the same coin – it was in these years after *Language, Truth and Logic* that he began to get a reputation for fast living. Among the men and women who knew Ayer during this period, the same memory often rustles to the surface: 'He liked dancing, didn't he?'

He was indeed a surprisingly good dancer and with the aid of his grandfather's radio-gramophone, mastered not just the standard 1930s repertoire of the waltz, foxtrot and quick step, but the Charleston, rumba, conga, tango and others as well. The best of the 1930s dance bands played at London's smarter hotels and supper clubs – Harry Roy at the Café Anglais, Jack Jackson and the Tiger-ragamuffins at the Dorchester, Carroll Gibbons and the Savoy Orpheans at the Savoy – but these were formal and expensive, and Ayer and his friends generally ended up at the smaller West End clubs: the Manhattan, the Nut House, the Bag o'Nails, or the 400 Club in Leicester Square. The music was for the most part undistinguished – the endless oom-ching, oom-ching of five-piece bands knocking out hits by Cole Porter, Gershwin, and Rodgers and Hart – but there were exceptions like the Nest, a seedy basement on Kingly Street, two minutes from Foubert's Place, where London's small black community and any black musicians visiting from the States gathered to hear and play jazz. Ayer was among those thrill-seeking whites who ventured down its steep staircase to sniff the marijuana-scented air, dance, drink and enjoy the corned beef hash offered for breakfast.

Renée played an increasingly occasional part in Ayer's new social life. Although a strong character, and in most respects a match for Freddie, she was not always at ease with his smart, knowing friends. She was also the sort of person who preferred doing things for people rather than socialising with them. Valerie provided the most natural outlet for what one friend described as 'her ostentatious modesty' and another her 'ostentatious selflessness', but Isaiah Berlin recollected that she also made a habit of picking up drunken vagabonds, including 'negroes' from the Nest, and putting them up for the night. There was at least one project, beyond Valerie, where Freddie and Renée did, however, come together: early in 1936 they began working on Renée's 'autobiography'. It's not clear what drew Freddie to this – perhaps he thought the story of neglectful mother, adventurer father and rebellious daughter was worth telling in its own right, perhaps he wanted to boost Renée's confidence – but the manuscript reads as a collaborative effort; its drama comes from Renée, its wry style from Freddie. Before starting work on the book, they managed to secure an (unidentifiable) publisher, but no more than half of it was ever written.

By the mid-1930s Austria's intellectuals, especially Jewish ones, had begun to follow their German counterparts into exile. Carnap and Neurath had both left Vienna by the end of 1935. Schlick himself would doubtless have followed, if he had not been shot and killed by a deranged student in the summer of 1936. Now Karl Popper joined the flood and arrived in London in search of an academic position. In the end he secured a lectureship in New Zealand, but not before he and Ayer cemented a friendship struck up at the Paris conference the previous autumn. Ayer, Popper remembered, looked after him 'like a hen looks after a chick, although the chick happened to be older than the hen.'[14] He introduced Popper to Ryle and Price in Oxford, Moore and Braithwaite in Cambridge and Susan Stebbing in London. Together they went to hear Russell give a paper on 'The Limits of Empiricism' at the Aristotelian Society in Russell Square in London, and Ayer encouraged Popper to contribute, in faltering English, to the ensuing discussion.

Ayer in turn wrote to Popper a few months after he had left:

It was almost humiliating to realise how much I had to learn from you. The intensity of your interest in philosophical problems makes me feel very much of a dilettante. I put the blame on my excessively humanistic education, which has made my approach to philosophy literary rather than scientific. I am trying to remedy this but I find it difficult.[15]

When Ayer wrote that he was finding his attempts to get to grips with science 'very difficult', he was not exaggerating. In the last pages of *Language, Truth and Logic*, Ayer had more or less committed himself to becoming a philosopher of science.* Moreover, it was quite explicitly

---

* Ayer seems, understandably, to have felt a certain excitement at getting to the end of the book. In the last chapter, after summarily solving or dissolving the most long-standing and important philosophical conflicts – those between rationalists and empiricists, realists and idealists, pluralists and monists – he argued that with the traditional problems of philosophy surmounted, philosophy had now to devote itself to the logical clarification of the hypotheses thrown up by modern science. It should aim, for instance, at forging a unified science of psychology, by translating the categories of psychoanalysis into those of behaviourism (Ayer was at this stage willing to give Freud's theories the benefit of the doubt), and ultimately at developing a unified science, *tout court*, by translating the

laid down in the terms of his Christ Church studentship that he was to work on symbolic logic and the philosophy of science.

Initially Ayer was enthusiastic – one of the few letters to survive from this period is from J.L Austin, responding to his request for a reading list of elementary science textbooks.[16] Then, in the months immediately after the appearance of *Language, Truth and Logic*, he undertook to write a book on causation for Oxford University Press, which he hoped would provide him with the incentive to immerse himself in physics. Yet he never got much beyond Austin's preliminary readings, and the book on causation was never written. Part of the problem was that Ayer simply lacked the aptitude. He was not technically unable – he more or less mastered Russell's *Principia*, and was genuinely excited by developments in relativity and quantum theory – but he was not especially able either.

He was, however, also distracted by other things. To begin with, it fast became clear that *Language, Truth and Logic* was by no means the final word on its subject: the work raised as many difficulties as it solved. Ayer, then, was soon attempting to answer, in a series of articles in the philosophical journals, some of the commonest objections to the verification principle, and otherwise revise and bolster his position.

Thus in the most important of these articles, 'Verification and Experience', read at a meeting of the Aristotelian Society in London in April 1937, Ayer turned to the old quarrel over the nature of primary propositions, making a contribution which he always regarded as decisive. In order to avoid the charge of metaphysics, Neurath and Carnap, supported by the young Carl Hempel, had been led to a peculiar version of the coherence theory of truth. They feared that to suggest, as Russell, Schlick and Ayer himself had done, that everything is known on the basis of sense-data, came perilously close to saying that the world was really made up of sense-data, which they took to be as nonsensical as saying that it was really made up of fire or water, or Spirit or the forces of good and evil. Instead they contended that the whole notion of a category of basic statements was metaphysical – every proposition was

categories of behaviourism into those of physics. 'What we must recognise,' Ayer declared in a final sentence that he must have lived to regret, 'is that it is necessary for a philosopher to become a scientist ... if he is to make any substantial contribution towards the growth of human knowledge'. The future lay in the lab.

open to doubt, its truth or falsehood depending not on its agreement with 'reality' but on its compatibility with other propositions.

This neatly side-stepped the whole question of the nature and corrigibility of sense-data statements and their relation to the propositions of common sense and physical science. It raised, however, objections of its own, chief among them, that incompatible systems could each be internally coherent, thus providing a host of conflicting truths. Neurath and his allies had in fact seen this objection and attempted to get round it by arguing that those propositions were true which were accepted by 'accredited observers', by which they meant the scientists of the era. They developed this position with great agility, but as Ayer now insisted, it retained one fatal weakness: it rested on a tacit appeal to the realm of fact that it otherwise sought to banish, for the only way to determining which of a range of incompatible propositions was accepted by the scientific community, or anyone else, was via the evidence of the senses. Like Schlick, Ayer believed that if any propositions were to be true at all, there must be some primary propositions which provide an 'unshakeable point of contact between knowledge and reality'. Indeed, moving on from *Language, Truth and Logic*, Ayer now went so far as to argue that there was at least one sense in which sense-data statements were incorrigible: though one could misdescribe them, whether intentionally or otherwise, one could not mis-experience them. An experience is, by definition, all that it seems to be – in having it, one knows it.[17]

Finally, political as well as philosophical distractions took up ever more of his time. Ayer had been moving leftwards for some years, and looked on in anger at the National Government's cowardly handling of both domestic and foreign affairs – a cowardice which reached new heights when Stanley Baldwin limply accepted Mussolini's invasion of Abyssinia in October 1935 and Hitler's reoccupation of the Rhineland the following March. It was the outbreak of the Spanish Civil War in July, however, and the government's hypocritical pretence of non-intervention while denying the Spanish government their right to purchase arms, that finally whipped him into activity. He and Renée both knew Spain well, and saw the issue in black and white terms: 'Franco was a military adventurer employing Moorish, Italian and German troops to massacre his own countrymen . . . The Republican Government against which he was in rebellion was the legitimate government of Spain: its supporters were fighting not only for their freedom but for a new and better social order'.[18]

By involving himself in politics, Ayer was following the trend in Oxford – by 1938 over half of Oxford's students were members of the Labour Club – and in the country at large. The Ayers were just two of thousands of young anti-Fascists who packed parcels for Spanish Republican soldiers, went to dinners and dances in their aid, and marched through London in their support. Freddie, however, possessed an unusually developed sense of justice – the product perhaps of his own childhood humiliations – and took up the cause with special gusto. 'He had the views of all of us,' Isaiah Berlin recalled, 'but to a much stronger degree. He was always ready to quarrel about politics. If he thought that someone was pro-Franco he would cross the street to strike them.'[19]

One illustration of Ayer's new interest is that he and Stephen Spender agreed in the autumn of 1936 to write a book together for Gollancz's Left Book Club in which they were to defend a liberal, undogmatic communism. It was an exciting prospect, as any Left Book Club book was guaranteed a readership of at least 40,000 – over thirty times that of *Language, Truth and Logic*. Ayer read hard throughout the autumn and Christmas of that year, although in the end, for reasons that will become clear, the collaboration did not work and Spender published a book on his own, *Forward from Liberalism*, in 1937.

Still, Ayer put his reading to use in other ways. In the summer term of 1937 he gave a series of lectures on political philosophy and in the following term he and Frank Pakenham ran a joint class on 'Some Political Theorists', devoted mainly to Hegel and Marx. Pakenham remembered that Ayer had a large undergraduate following at this time. Although no records of the lectures or classes have survived, one can guess at their general spirit. Ayer would have had little time for Hegel – the very epitome of a conservative metaphysician, ceaselessly eliding what is with what ought to be – or for the more metaphysical aspects of Marxism. He took Marx's theory of history seriously, though, believing that where it was construed empirically, it was cogent and suggestive, although probably false, and he admired the Marxists' hard-headedness and their emphasis on the importance of action. In many respects, he would have agreed with Spender's *Forward from Liberalism*, that what was needed was to reconcile communist social justice with liberal respect for individual freedom, although the politics of small-scale, participatory collectivism also seems to have attracted him. He was impressed by Proudhon's anarchism, by the guild socialism defended by Russell in *The Principles of Social Reconstruction*, and also by the revolutionary syndical-ism of the late nineteenth-century French theorist, Georges Sorel. Sorel, an arch anti-rationalist, whose hatred of representative democracy, compromise, and bourgeois culture generally, made him in many respects an ally of Nietzsche, was not a theorist that one would have expected Ayer to appreciate. Ayer, however, responded to the drama of his thought, his ethic of action, his glorification of the General Strike. Exasperated by Ayer's contemptuous dismissal of most of the 'great' political theorists they discussed in their class, Pakenham challenged him to name a thinker he admired. He remembered the quaver in Ayer's voice, as he replied, 'Sorel – a moment of glory, a spanner in the works'.[20]*

In the end, it seems, Ayer judged his foray into political theory rather a failure. He never produced the book that he must have hoped to write, even after he and Spender had ceased to collaborate, and the ideas he developed in his lectures and classes were, he came to recognise, a little thin. This may be at least partly because he lacked the deep feeling for human motivation, for the great range of forms that human values can take, that goes into the best political theory. But it was also true that Ayer himself had so narrowed the scope for moral and political thought, reducing it to the clarification of ethical concepts, that what was left could hardly satisfy his intellectual ambitions or seem adequate to the exigencies of the moment. For it followed, from Ayer's analysis of moral judgements, that all the political philosopher could do was to separate the empirical from the moral components of our political discourse, and make plain the moral choices available to us. Politics itself on the other hand – and here he agreed with the existentialists as well as with Marx and Sorel – was ultimately less a matter of reason or thought than of

---

* It is worth making the point that contrary to the charge made by Herbert Marcuse in *One Dimensional Man* (1964), and often repeated before and since, that empiricism offers an image of man as a passive receptor of experience, Ayer was attracted to political theorists – Marx, Proudhon, Sorel – who depicted man as essentially a working, active, creature. This was in fact only a corollary to the wariness of empty and inflated language that is such an important feature of *Language, Truth and Logic*.

feeling, commitment and action. As he would put it thirty-five years later: 'I am not very interested in moral philosophy, because, in the last resort, I think moral propositions or judgements are questions for decision. And ... this is almost the only point on which I agree with Sartre.'[21]

Perhaps it is not surprising that while Ayer and the French existentialists, Camus and Sartre, had very few philosophical heroes in common, they shared a deep admiration for the communist novelist André Malraux. Writing about Malraux in the 1970s, Ayer recalled that he read and re-read all of Malraux's urgent, masculine, revolutionary novels although he thought La condition humaine, which he read soon after it was published in 1933, the greatest: 'It made such a strong impression on me that for many years afterwards its principal characters and even the details of the story remain fixed in my memory'.[22] Malraux's novels of men facing up to their responsibilities – which in practice often meant toeing the communist line – spoke to Ayer as they did to Camus and Sartre. Ayer described them as 'studies in the exercise of the will': 'He is concerned with the attempt of the slaves, the common people of Spain or China, or wherever it may be, to liberate themselves from their master and he sees that this can be done only through collective action. But there have to be leaders to take the necessary decisions and impose the necessary discipline; leaders who realize themselves in action, even if they fall short of having an appetite for power'.[23]

Many of Freddie's friends involved themselves in Oxford politics: Richard Crossman and Frank Pakenham became Labour councillors and Patrick Gordon Walker was adopted as Labour parliamentary candidate for the city of Oxford. Freddie himself regularly attended the Pink Lunch Club – weekly lunches where left-leaning dons like Douglas Cole, Berlin, Harrod, Crossman, the Pakenhams and the Gordon Walkers met to discuss the issues of the day.

Renée and Freddie, however, concentrated most of their efforts on their local Labour party in London. The Soho branch of the Westminster Abbey division Labour party was a small and demoralised organisation in a Conservative-dominated area of the city. Ayer quickly succeeded in getting himself elected chairman of the branch, and set about turning the organisation around. Where the Oxford Labour party was dominated by intellectuals and much addicted to debating the merits of the Labour

Theory of Value or the totalitarian character of Plato's political theory, Soho was a genuinely poor area and here Ayer found himself amongst trade unionists, and lower middle-class *émigrés* – Monsieur Henrie, a Polish hairdresser, Mr Goldstein, a Jewish tailor, Mr Reid, a Scottish upholsterer. The branch was too insignificant to attract outside speakers, and whenever it held public meetings it fell to Ayer to provide the oratory:

My nervousness still caused me to speak too fast and I usually tried to cover too much ground instead of dwelling on one or two simple points and making sure of driving them home. There were, however, times when I was able to work myself into a passion which carried my hearers with me ... What I was worse at was stump oratory. For quite a long period, taking no pleasure in the exercise but regarding it as a duty, I used every Saturday evening to mount a step-ladder at the corner of Broadwick Street and Berwick Market, fix my eyes on two or three passing shoppers, cry out 'Citizens of Westminster' which they quite probably were not, and embark on a political discourse. Since the audience was constantly shifting I found it hard to develop a coherent argument and harder still, as my hearers drifted away from me and others failed to congregate, to continue addressing an almost empty street.[24]

It was not logical, but it was positive.

The Westminster Labour party had many communist members; indeed according to Isaiah Berlin, it was virtually a communist front.[25] If Berlin was aware of this, then Freddie and Renée must have been aware of it too. It would not, however, have greatly perturbed them. Both of them were at this time broadly sympathetic to the party. It was the Communists after all, who, in the form of the International Brigade, were offering the most effective support to the Spanish Republicans. One of Freddie's closest friends from this period, Philip Toynbee, was in fact a party member, although an extremely well born one. The grandson of Gilbert Murray, the son of Arnold Toynbee, he became in 1938 the only communist ever to be elected to the presidency of the Oxford Union. Like Connolly, Auden, Isherwood, Spender and many other privileged young radicals of the 1930s, Toynbee's revolt against authority was inspired as much by his experiences of public school, with its endless Greek, beatings, games and chapel, as by anything else. Toynbee's name had made the papers when he ran away from Rugby aged seventeen, to join fifteen-year-old Esmond Romilly, a nephew of Winston Churchill and a fugitive from Wellington. Romilly had established headquarters in the Panton Street Bookshop, a left-wing hang-out, from which he edited and published *Out of Bounds*, a magazine improbably devoted to fomenting revolution in England's public schools.

Toynbee, tall, loose-limbed, unkempt, drunk, was six years younger than Freddie. He arrived as an undergraduate at Christ Church in 1935, where he immediately joined the Communists, going to Spain as a 'Student Delegate' of the party in the Christmas of 1936. He and Freddie shared a staircase and Freddie was captivated by what he described as Toynbee's 'zest for experience, his lack of worldly caution, his physical indulgence, his ease in making friends, his addiction to journalizing, his profound changes of mood'.[26] They quickly became confidants, Toynbee playing Boswell to Ayer's Hume, and Toynbee's unpublished diaries of these years shed helpful light on Ayer's activities and views, as well as on the reception of his work. It is interesting to see, for instance, that although he was studying history, Toynbee read *Language, Truth and Logic* carefully, coming to conceive of its creed as something like a rival to Marxism. 'I wonder, am I a logical positivist – not a Marxist at all?' he asked on 16 January 1937. As Toynbee's diaries show, Freddie and Renée ('his adorable wife'), in turn, thought seriously about entering the Communist Party. Indeed in February 1937, not long after Baldwin's government renewed its commitment to the policy of neutrality in Spain and the Nationalists, backed by Mussolini, took Malaga, Freddie promised to think seriously about joining. He spent a weekend wrestling with the choice, before pulling back from the brink.

Toynbee found the basis on which Freddie had intended to join 'odd' – 'just desire for reasonable activity'. But his grounds for not joining were just as unorthodox: he claimed he could not subscribe to the dialectical materialist theory of history. 'Toynbee thought my answer was frivolous; I thought it was absolutely fundamental.'[27] Six months later, by which time the party had begun to discredit itself with its opportunism and intolerance in Spain, Freddie was 'trying hard' to persuade Toynbee to leave.

Stuart Hampshire was another young left-wing friend that Freddie and Renée made in the year after *Language, Truth and Logic* came out, and one who felt, much more strongly than Toynbee, the pull of logical positivism. Tall, blond, handsome and high-minded, he had been educated at Repton and at Balliol, before winning a fellowship to All Souls in 1936. There he began a lifelong friendship with Isaiah Berlin, who nicknamed him 'the gazelle' for his shy and gentle manner. Like Berlin, Hampshire was intellectually cosmopolitan, keeping up with developments in French and German literature. By the time he arrived at Oxford, however, he had already decided that philosophy was his main interest and socialism second. 'It was difficult,' he later wrote, 'for undergraduates then not to think about the world-wide recession, of the throwing of coffee into the sea and of the destruction of food while there was hunger among the unemployed. Children without shoes in the winter streets were not an unusual sight, and the shoe manufacturers were dismissing their workers because they could not sell their shoes.'[28] As an undergraduate he concentrated at first on classical philosophy, but then began reading the logical positivists and underwent an intellectual conversion. 'They seemed to me,' he wrote fifty years later, 'to be starting philosophy all over again in the clear light of a rational day, and outside the dusty, dark and bookish rooms of the established professors.' He does not name the philosophers who inspired this awakening, but Ayer, Oxford's chief logical positivist and an ardent proselytiser, must surely have been first among them. Certainly by the time he left Balliol for All Souls, Hampshire was already close to Freddie and Renée; over the next years their lives would become increasingly entwined.

At about the time that Ayer was thinking about joining the Communist Party, in March 1937, he and Renée went to Paris for a week. They met Cyril Connolly, who talked fascinatingly about his experiences in Spain, and Benedict Nicolson, an art-historian friend of Philip Toynbee, whom Freddie would later get to know well. Nicolson, who had never met the Ayers properly before, recorded his impressions:

At last we lunched with Ayer . . . He is a small man, with shifty eyes and an alert expression like Salvador Dali's and acutely intelligent. Every remark he made sounded a chord of originality, sincerity and brilliance combined. He was shy of me and our relations will be difficult at first ... Mrs Ayer is a young woman of great beauty and sensitiveness, very quiet and shy and clings continually to her husband. She shuns all forms of society and feels very passionately about the lower classes.[29]

There is nothing in Nicolson's journal to suggest that Freddie and Renée were anything but happy, but their marriage had, in fact, been in trouble for some time. Renée once said that she came back from hospital, having given birth to Valerie, to find lipstick on the sheets. The story is probably apocryphal, but there is no reason to doubt one of her closest friends, who remembered Renée persuading her to accompany Freddie to the cinema soon after Valerie's birth, only to find herself subjected to unsubtle advances.

Freddie's first important affair seems to have taken place in the autumn of 1936. Inez Pearn was a fair-haired young communist, a member of the Spanish Aid Committee, with 'an oval child-like face' and 'nearly perfect classical features', 'brilliant eyes', and an awkward, combative manner. She had been educated in convents in Portugal, France and England, and then spent the summer of 1936 in Spain, looking after the children of a family of rich Spanish reactionaries.[30] On returning to England, she divided her time between London and Oxford, studying Spanish literature, writing a novel and agitating for Spain. Isaiah Berlin, who introduced her to Stephen Spender, was wary of her from the beginning: 'She pretended to be of foreign birth, but she was not'.[31] But she must have had her qualities, for not only Ayer and Spender, but the painter William Coldstream and the poet and sociologist Charles Madge courted her. Ayer may, in fact, have first met her through Toynbee with whom, in October 1936, she seems to have been having an affair. What is certain, however, is that during November she and Spender became engaged, and that by the end of the same month, she and Freddie had made love.

Freddie wished it to be more than a casual affair – he was even willing to leave Renée for her – but Inez viewed it differently, and was soon deflecting what Freddie described as his 'desperate' attempts to see her.[32] Freddie and Renée went to Inez and Spender's wedding in December; it was soon after this, when Spender learned about the affair, that he informed Freddie he no longer wanted to collaborate on their book.[33]

Although Ayer was always complimentary about Spender in public, from this point on there was a coolness between them.

Other affairs followed, mainly with game upper-class Oxford undergraduates, and Ayer doubtless attempted many more. Isaiah Berlin recalled that from this time on Freddie became 'rather infatuated with sex'.[34] It is hard to know what to make of this aspect of Ayer's character, although it was important. There remained in him a deep and ineradicable strand of self-doubt: 'his sense of self-worth' 'was very frail' Dee Ayer recalls.[35] Achievements, goals, conquests, victories mattered to him. He would wake up in the middle of the night to complete the last clue of a crossword puzzle – 'There, done' – and then, happy at last, retreat to bed. 'Chess, arguments, scrabble, bridge – whatever game was being played, he *had* to win'.[36] Winning over women, moreover, mattered especially. Their love and admiration reassured him. They were more willing to indulge and forgive his vanities and insecurities than men – more impressed by his knowledge and intelligence.

But it is also true that he genuinely enjoyed the company of women and they enjoyed his. He knew how to talk to them as most English men did not. 'It is easy,' he once commented about his success with women; 'you only have to pay them a bit of notice. In this country nobody else does.'[37] There was a warmth, a playfulness, a gaiety in him that women brought out. Sartre, it was said, seduced his girlfriends by telling them about their souls, Ayer by dancing and singing, gossiping, reciting poems and playing games. Ayer, in fact, hardly set out to conquer women at all. At Eton he had admitted to sado-masochistic fantasies, and there was a deeply masochistic strain in him. He melted before women, pleaded with them, submitted to them – he was the opposite of a macho lover. Inevitably in the course of a long career, some lovers were hurt; there were unkept promises and unkind partings. Yet most remained fond and loyal friends. It seems unlikely that they would have done so, had he been a mere Don Juan.

What seems clear is that at around this time, in the second half of the 1930s, Ayer quite self-consciously adopted a code of what Toynbee called 'hedonism', scoffing at old-fashioned ideals of fidelity, friendship and married love. This was meant to be Toynbee's code too, although, much to Freddie's amusement, Toynbee had a habit of falling passionately in love and proposing at almost monthly intervals. In April 1937, after one such proposal, as the prospect of marriage loomed, Toynbee worried that Freddie's opinion of him would change once he discovered he was not 'a really successful hedonist'.[38] Later in the year Ayer 'mocked' Toynbee's 'morality and uplift' when he found himself in love with and determined to marry not one but two women. Around the same time, Ayer nonchalantly boasted 'that he'd sacrifice all his friends for the most ephemeral love affair'.[39] Of course there was an element of parody in this. As Toynbee's diaries show, more often than not Ayer was 'sensitive', 'fond', 'friendly and delightful': a few days after denigrating friendship, he was affectionately telling a dinner party organised by Toynbee, 'We, as Philip's friends must advise him. He's so hot-headed he might do anything'.[40] But Toynbee hinted at a deeper anger beneath Ayer's irreverence. One diary entry reads: 'On Tuesday I gave Freddie and Frank [Pakenham] lunch at the Union. Freddie waxed very "persecuted" after wine, burning with intense personal hatreds – rather stupid and contemptible. Frank made fun of him very nicely.'[41]

At the end of the summer of 1937 Solly Zuckerman introduced Ayer to the poet E.E. Cummings and his wife, Marion. It was an important encounter.

The couple were in England on holiday, and Zuckerman, who had met them in New York, and had to leave the country for a conference soon after their arrival in Oxford, asked Ayer to look after them. Cummings, sixteen years older than Freddie, had been born and brought up in Cambridge, Massachusetts, the son of an eminent Unitarian minister and Harvard professor. He confounded expectations by taking to a bohemian life in New York, where he worked as painter and poet and avant-garde publisher, and had a child with a friend's wife. He had established his name with an under-appreciated masterpiece *The Enormous Room* (1922), an account of his experiences under detention in France during the First World War, which centred on his discovery of the 'Delectable Mountains', four outlaws, 'so integrated within their own personalities' that prison could not touch them. They embodied the self-reliant Emersonian individuality that became Cummings's ideal.[42]

His wife, Marion Morehouse, twelve years Cummings's junior, had fled her Midwest home for Broadway before she had finished school, where she got a job as a Ziegfield showgirl. Willowy-slim and fabulously beautiful, she became one of the leading models of the age, doing much to popularise the wearing of slacks. After marrying, she took up photography, although she devoted most of her time to looking after Cummings.

Freddie and Cummings would become very close – in his autobiography Freddie described him at greater length than anyone else. It is not obvious what drew them together; Cummings, 'with his proud, slightly rugged, questing, humorous face' was something of a right-wing anarchist, an irascible and reclusive apostle of art and impulse, hostile to mass society, big business and modern government. He disapproved of Roosevelt and opposed American involvement in both world wars.[43] But there was something in his individualism, his suspicion of conventional moral standards, and his identification with outlaws and villains that appealed to Freddie, who developed a deep love of his American, *faux-naïve*, experimental verse. In 1980, talking to an interviewer about the men whom he had met and most admired, Ayer cited Einstein, Russell and Cummings.[44] (For all Ayer's urbanity and apparent equanimity, he was always attracted to strong, outspoken, sometimes self-destructive individualists – outsiders, ill at ease with the world. Rees, Toynbee and Russell are other examples, as, in their own ways, were Renée and his second wife Dee Wells.) Cummings, for his part, liked Ayer's unaffected appetite for life – his scorn for 'the pomp of must and shall'.[45] 'He forgave me ... much,' Ayer wrote, 'because he saw me, if not quite as a Delectable Mountain, at least as someone who was, in his sense, alive.'[46]

At the outset however, Freddie, who was always enthralled by physical beauty, was attracted to Marion more than to her husband, and the glamorous model seems to have reciprocated the interest. Writing to Ayer in 1975, Zuckerman recalled the first encounter in his rooms: 'You and another don who was there on that occasion were totally bowled over by Marion, and I can still see that strange smile of his flickering over Cummings's face as he registered the fact'.[47] To celebrate the end of term, Toynbee gave a cocktail party. 'It was a splendid party. Freddie and Renée came with E.E. Cummins [*sic*] and wife. Freddie got rapidly drunk and held Mrs C's hand and flirted outrageously. Later I introduced him to Maureen [a girl-friend of Toynbee] and he began to make a pass at her ... Renée was sad and alarmed – I talked a lot to her and vaguely consoled her about Freddie'. Before the party was over, though, Toynbee, too, had taken the chance to hold hands with Marion and agree 'that unconventionality was splendid'. Later in the night Toynbee bumped into the Ayers and Cummingses at another party. 'Freddie was still drunk, lyrical with joy because, as he whispered to me, Mrs C. had agreed to sleep with him'.[48]

Marion and Freddie did, indeed, make love. Stuart Hampshire remembered a week spent in Paris, a couple of weeks after Toynbee's party, with the Ayers and the Cummingses. There was much to interest them. They visited the International Exhibition, where they paid homage to the Spanish government's modernist showcase, housing Picasso's *Guernica*, and observed the menacing stand-off between the German and the Soviet pavilions, facing each other on the right bank of the Seine. Ayer – and presumably Hampshire – attended the Third Annual Congress for the Unity of Science at the Sorbonne, once again organised by Neurath, this time devoted to the creation of an international encyclopaedia of unified science. Nevertheless, relations were understandably tense. 'It was not,' Hampshire recalled, 'a good weekend.'[49] Renée must by now have understood at the very least that Freddie was enamoured of Marion – as Berlin wrote to Felix Frankfurter at this time, 'their marriage is reaching a crisis point' – and Cummings must have realised the same.[50]

Later that summer, Freddie and Renée left Valerie in a nursery school, and went together for a holiday in Annecy in the foothills of the Alps. The attempt to patch things up, however, was unsuccessful: 'I was restless and ill-humoured' Ayer recollected, 'and for the first time in ten years we were not at ease in one another's company.'[51]

10

Bright Young Things

In 1937, preoccupied with teaching and politics, and dejected by his struggles with the philosophy of science, Ayer published only one substantial paper, 'Verification and Experience'. But he kept talking philosophy, mainly, as ever, with Gilbert Ryle and Isaiah Berlin, and increasingly with Stuart Hampshire. In the spring of that year, some fourteen months after the publication of his book, he began to take part in a series of memorable philosophical discussions held in Isaiah Berlin's rooms in All Souls, which ran, with intervals, for over two years. The meetings, which met on a Thursday evening after dinner, brought together a group of exceptionally able young minds; indeed much of the history of British philosophy over the next forty years can be told in terms of the unravelling of this little knot. These meetings witnessed the emergence of J.L. Austin as a philosopher, and the birth of a lifelong rivalry between him and Ayer.

John Langshaw Austin, 'a sort of parody of a desiccated don', was a thin wiry man, with taut, alert features, half whippet, half osprey.[1] According to Ved Mehta, the blind Indian writer who attended some of his lectures in the 1950s, he had a 'flat and metallic' voice, which seemed to be 'stuck on a note of disillusion. It sounded like a telephone speaking by itself.[2] Like Ayer, he came from a middle-class family, specialised in classics at public school, turned as an undergraduate to philosophy and always regretted he did not know more science. Austin, however, retained a classicist's interest in language and philology – a concern for exact meaning, etymology and idiom. Where Ayer had a slightly obsessive interest in sport, and Quine in maps, Austin's interest was in words: he read dictionaries for pleasure. Fastidious and methodical in the extreme, he devised an elaborate set of rules for the All Souls meetings, including provision for the introduction of an electronic buzzer to govern interruptions. Wisely, they were never adopted. Having secured a first, he was elected to All Souls in 1933, a year after Ayer's failed attempt, and two years later was appointed a fellow and tutor at Magdalen. Although both Hampshire and Berlin got to know Austin fairly well during the years before the war, he was not a sociable figure, preferring to stay at home and go through Bach's violin partitas evening by evening.

Politically he was on the Left, and took a leading role in the campaign against Quintin Hogg and appeasement in the famous 'Munich by-election' fought in Oxford in October 1938. He and a colleague, the classicist E.R. Dodds, made it their business to stalk Hogg from meeting to meeting, heckling him. As Dodds recalled, Austin had a flair for this: 'Repartees flashed from him like rapier thrusts; he rarely missed an opening and never gave one'. It was Austin who coined the slogan, 'A vote for Hogg is a vote for Hitler'.[3]

Initially, Isaiah Berlin remembered, 'Austin was rather a disciple of Freddie'.[4] Ayer was, in fact, the only one of the group who, when the meetings started, had a position of his own to defend; neither Berlin nor Austin had published a single article in philosophy at this stage. But during the course of the All Souls meetings – known jokily as the Steam Intellect Society, after Peacock's *Crotchet Castle* – Austin staked out, if not a set of doctrines, then an approach which was very much his own. As Berlin has written, Austin was, broadly speaking, an empiricist, but not, like Freddie, *un homme de système*. This, in the view of his admirers, was his strength:

He had a very clear, acute, and original intellect, and because, when he spoke, there appeared to be nothing between him and the subject of his criticism or exposition – no accumulation of traditional commentary, no spectacles provided by a particular doctrine – he often produced the feeling that the question was being posed clearly for the first time: . . . the problem stood out in sharp relief, clear, unanswered and important, and the methods used to analyse it had a surgical sharpness, and were used with fascinating assurance and apparently effortless skill.[5]

The core of the All Souls group consisted of Austin, Berlin and Ayer, although they were joined by Stuart Hampshire, Donald Macnabb, a Hume scholar five years older than the others, and A.D. Woozley, another young philosopher at All Souls. The philosopher of religion Donald Mackinnon, a large bear of a man and a troubled, questing Christian, also occasionally attended. Hampshire remembered that in the group's early days, he and Ayer were especially close. 'Very often Freddie and I would eat at the George and come swashbuckling in, smoking large cigars, which, Isaiah says, I gave Freddie. This amused but also irritated Isaiah, who saw himself as the fuddy-duddy and felt excluded'.[6] Everyone involved in the meetings looked back on them with pleasure:

> We had a feeling [Isaiah Berlin once said] which was perhaps rather vain, perhaps rather conceited, that no better discussions of philosophy were occurring anywhere in the world at that moment . . . than in my room on those evenings; . . . we felt that we were talking about subjects much more interesting than those which were being discussed by our seniors, we felt that we were better at it, that we were discovering truth, that we were progressing, and the atmosphere was one of cumulative excitement.[7]

The Steam Intellects had a lot in common. They were all followers of analytic philosophy in one form or another and, as such, were unsympathetic to metaphysics and impatient with the overblown systems of their seniors. They were young, left-wing, inordinately smart and aware of it. The group shared Ayer's wariness of philosophers who set themselves up as arbiters of right and wrong, and hardly discussed moral or political philosophy. Instead the agenda was set very largely by Ayer's ardent advocacy of logical positivism; *Language, Truth and Logic* provided the target against which others hurled themselves. They argued about phenomenalism – whether talk of material objects can be reduced to talk of sense-data; about a-priori truth – whether all necessary truths are true only by definition; the verification and logical character of counter-factual statements; and the nature of personal identity and our knowledge of other minds. Long evenings were spent discussing Gregor Samsa, the hero of Kafka's 'Metamorphosis': was he an insect with the mind of a man, or a man with the body of an insect?

Isaiah Berlin afterwards played down his own part in the discussions, although Stuart Hampshire remembers that these were in fact substantial.[8] Like Austin he was sympathetic to the Cambridge and Vienna schools but disagreed with Ayer on several major issues – especially on necessary truth. Berlin argued (following Russell's 1935 paper, 'The Limits of Empiricism') that the truth that a thing cannot be red and green at the same time in the same place is neither analytic nor empirical, but an incontrovertible principle written into the universe. Ayer protested, arguing that conceding the existence of non-analytic necessity in this way created more problems than it solved and restricted the possibility for the sort of conceptual revolution that Einstein had caused in our understanding of space and time.

If Berlin's contributions were important, the running battles between Austin and Ayer tended to dominate the meetings. Although both men were natural leaders and loved nothing better than knocking an opponent down in argument, they were in other respects almost absurdly unalike. Ayer treated life like an experiment: he liked new people, new countries, new ideas, new experiences and was instinctively suspicious of anything conventional. Austin, on the other hand, was an intensely private and domestic person – a man of austere tastes and strict principles, with a mania for routine. Ayer was metropolitan, Austin was Oxonian; Ayer danced, Austin gardened; Ayer thought most morality was humbug, Austin disapproved of Ayer. These differences at a personal level were mirrored, inevitably, in their work. The hallmark of Austin's approach to philosophy was his literal-mindedness and his attention to the way language is used. He would refuse to discuss abstract principles, only concrete examples, and was already moving towards his almost Burkean faith in the coherence of ordinary language – in the concepts and categories bequeathed by time. Ayer pursued a very different path. He might claim, in the spirit of G.E. Moore, that his doctrines left the world of common sense more or less intact, but he saw it as the job of philosophy to simplify, reduce and explain away.

They quarrelled especially over sense-data. Austin was already sceptical about the intelligibility of Ayer's phenomenalism and argued that he could not see what was wrong with ordinary language as used about the external world. One can explain optical illusions, like a stick seeming bent when placed in water, without resorting to the terminology of sense-data – we do it, Austin argued, all the time. Ayer by contrast, insisted that there was an obvious distinction to be made between things in themselves and their appearances. If a stick looks bent in water then there is something that looks like a bent stick which is seen. Together, Austin and Ayer reminded Hampshire of a couple of barristers: Ayer, the prosecutor, trying to build a convincing story; Austin picking holes in his case. Austin's scepticism drove Ayer wild, and Berlin recalled him one day complaining, 'You are like a greyhound who doesn't want to run himself and bites the other greyhounds, so that they cannot run either'. Yet Berlin himself felt that the meetings were fruitful:

the intellectual freshness and force, both of Austin and Ayer, were such that although they were in a state of almost continuous collision – Ayer like an irresistible missile, Austin like an immovable obstacle – the result was not a stalemate, but the most interesting, free and lively discussions of philosophy that I have ever known.

They offered, as Berlin remembered, 'true intellectual happiness'.[9]

The meetings of the All Souls philosophers began early in 1937. Apart from their tense week in Paris and their attempt to patch things up in Annecy, there are no records of the Ayers' activities that summer. Their social life, presumably, went on as before; they went to the cinema two or three times a week, Renée looked after Valerie, Ayer wrote during the day and danced at night. He saw as much as ever of Goronwy Rees, and more than ever of Cyril Connolly. At some point Ayer's association with the Labour Party led to his working with the Westminster Housing Association, a local charity dedicated to improving housing conditions in the area. Many Soho homes still lacked baths or internal lavatories; families slept five or six to a room. In October both he and Renée stood for Labour in the local council elections, Freddie in the Great Marlborough ward and Renée in a neighbouring one. Freddie wrote a shilling pamphlet, 'Your Westminster' in which he argued for an increase in the rates, directed mainly at the rich, in order to fund better housing.[10] In a documentary filmed in 1971 Ayer remembered the campaign:

> I stood as a candidate for local government in a Soho ward, and I was opposed by a coal merchant, Mr Parks. I used to go around canvassing, mostly in Carnaby St; it was then still tailor-shops, but not at all fashionable. These were the people who did the work for the big tailors in Savile Row. They . . . were stitching until all hours of the night. And I used to go and call on them and they were very suspicious of me at first, but I eventually convinced them that I wasn't out for myself.[11]

In fact if the local residents alone had possessed the vote, Ayer's election would have been secure. The owners of local businesses in the area, however, also had a franchise so that both Freddie and Renée lost, although Freddie only by a narrow margin.*

While they were campaigning together in London, Ayer had also been busy in Oxford, giving tutorials at Christ Church, holding his class with Frank Pakenham on political theory, and continuing to attend the discussions with Austin, Berlin and Hampshire. By Christmas, though, a problem had arisen that threatened both the tone of the Thursday evening gatherings and, much more seriously, Freddie's marriage. At some point before the end of 1937, Stuart Hampshire confessed to Freddie that he and Renée had fallen in love. Ayer was at first inclined to make light of the news: 'there is no disputing tastes,' as the emotivists liked to insist. It is perhaps testimony to his distance from his feelings that he went to far as to agree to spend the Christmas of 1937 in Paris with both Renée and Hampshire, leaving Valerie in a nursery in London.

Freddie soon found, though, that even he could not ignore what had happened. The strain of being with his wife and her lover was too great.

---

* Toynbee had promised to come down in a car from Oxford and help ferry Labour voters to the polls, but got diverted by a sexual intrigue on the way. Although Freddie teased him that this cost him the election, in one respect it played into his hands. Toynbee was given to extolling the importance of love, friendship, justice and sacrifice. Freddie believed in these things too, but as the Toynbee diaries reveal, he took the opportunity to remind Toynbee that what really mattered, in morals as in metaphysics, was not high-minded talk, but the reality beyond it. (3 November, 1937)

1 Ayer's parents on their wedding day, London, 1909.

2 Freddie on his great-grandmother's knee, with his mother and his grandfather Dorus Citroën, 1912.

3 At Ascham, 1918, Freddie is near the centre, front row
– the smallest boy, with a fringe.

4 Freddie (at top of slope)
with his cousins, Jack and
Doris Holloway, Donald
and Madge Kingsford,
around 1918.

5 The College Wall XI, Eton, St Andrew's Day, 1928, Freddie fourth from right.
6 Part of the team, Freddie on left, second row.

10 The Welsh Guards, May 1940.
Guardsman Ayer second from right in front row.

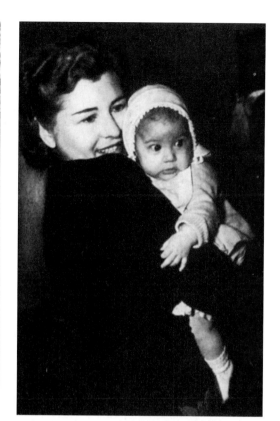

11 (*Above right*) Sheilah Graham
with Wendy, Christmas 1942.

12 (*Right*) Freddie with Valerie
and Julian in New York, 1943.

13 A.J. Ayer, by Lee Miller, late 1940s.

He decided to return to England, leaving the others behind. Taking the train from Paris, he planned to arrive in London on Christmas Eve, in time for Christmas Day, but the Channel ferry was delayed by bad weather and he found himself spending Christmas morning on the quayside at Calais, looking disconsolately out to sea. 'After some hours the fog lifted and I arrived back in London in time to have a solitary dinner at a Lyons restaurant. For once I felt a little sorry for myself but I soon plunged into a round of parties and was cheerful enough by the time that Renée returned'.[12] Early in the New Year Freddie confided in Toynbee and Toynbee confided in his diary:

> We drank martinis at Whites and he told me all. Stuart Hampshire is in love with Renée; they were in Paris *à trois* and that Freddie couldn't stand [it]. So he came home and left them . . . Really of course, Freddie is savagely jealous – without quite admitting it. He's contemplating a period of separation, Renée with Stuart, and he sowing wild oats. But could they come together after this and where does Stuart get off?[13]

The next term, Ayer and Renée continued to live together in London, but in Oxford he began an affair with a bright and lively young undergraduate at Somerville. She was a friend of Isaiah Berlin, and Berlin, who disapproved of Freddie's philandering, tried, not for the last time, to interpose himself between him and a girlfriend. ('Shaya has been rushing from one to the other urging them not to go to bed with one another,' Toynbee recorded; '– what an old fool he is.') Ayer told Toynbee about the affair and they 'agreed that seduction was enormous fun' and that they 'shared a genuinely adventurous attitude'.[14]

That Easter Ayer managed to secure the temporary separation from Renée that he wanted, by winning a scholarship from the Cleveland branch of the English Speaking Union. He was to make a month-long study tour of the US, meeting members of the ESU along the way. Ostensibly he was going to learn what he could about American philosophy, but he still did not have a secure position at Oxford and so was also on the lookout for an American job. In 1936 he had thought seriously about applying for the lectureship in New Zealand that went to Popper, but the US – scientific, forward-looking, the home of the big bands and the films that he loved most – was an infinitely more appealing option.

Ayer left for New York on 16 March 1938, throwing a party in his rooms in college before he set off. Renée and Hampshire, Solly Zuckerman, Maurice Bowra, Roy Harrod, Frank Pakenham and Philip Toynbee were all there. 'Freddie plied us and plied us with drink,' Toynbee wrote, 'skipping like a faun and [was] very drunk quite soon.'[15] The guests stayed drinking for over nine hours. Although David Cecil was present, Philip Toynbee spent a good part of the evening kissing his wife, Rachael; Freddie, too, made a pass.

Ayer set sail on the *Queen Mary* five days after the German invasion of Austria, at a point when Europe appeared on the brink of war. He and Nevill Coghill, an English don and Chaucer expert at Oxford and another ESU scholar, stood on deck, before the liner left harbour, debating 'whether it might not be our duty to withdraw from our scholarships and remain in England waiting to be called up'.[16] In the end both men remained on board. Ayer got on well with Coghill, who had visited America before. The trip was less of an adventure for him, but he indulged Freddie's enthusiasm. And enthusiastic he was. Waking up at dawn, as the liner was drawing in to New York, its skyline glittering in the sun, Ayer experienced extraordinary elation. 'Apart from the beauty of the city, which I discovered in more detail once we had gone ashore, there was a buoyancy in the air, which took possession of me'.[17]

I had the luck to arrive there [he wrote to Isaiah Berlin, at the beginning of April] on a brilliant spring day and I was intoxicated by it. I remained in an abnormally excited state for several days. I wasn't doing anything much: but merely to be there, looking at the skyscrapers and the wide streets and the bright lights excited me so much that I could not and did not need to sleep. And though the intoxication wore off, I still believe that it is a place in which I should be very happy to live . . . If they offered me a decent job in New York I should take it.[18]

The first week of the visit was spent in New York. Freddie stayed in a downtown hotel, and saw most of Marion and E.E. Cummings, who lived in their little house in Patchin Place, a cobbled cul-de-sac in Greenwich

Village. The poet shared Freddie's taste for low life (Cummings's first love had been a Parisian street-walker) and took him to a low-class burlesque review starring the legendary stripper Gypsy Rose Lee. Ayer found the review disappointing, but the two men got on famously. Cummings wrote him a short poem, since lost, in which he characterised him as a 'blithe spirit' and sent him forth to discover America like a new Columbus. 'He has dropped his wisecracking with me now,' Freddie wrote to Berlin. 'To understand him you have to know that he really is the starving artist. He very often does not have the money for a meal.'[19]

Ayer had arrived with letters of introduction, one to the young polymath art historian Meyer Schapiro, already settled in the brownstone on the corner of West 4th Street and West 11th that he and his wife Lilian, a paediatrician, inhabited for the next sixty years. Schapiro, who taught at Columbia, was at least as learned as Bowra or Berlin and, in his own less flamboyant way, just as hypnotic a talker. Ayer thought him 'very clever and nice' and the two men became lifelong friends.[20] Schapiro introduced him to Ernest Nagel and Sidney Hook, two brilliant young philosophers. Jewish, left-wing and scientifically minded, they were baked from the same batch as Ayer, although, like most of the radical 'New York Intellectuals' who came of age in the 1930s – and quite unlike Ayer or Berlin – they were from poor, working-class, immigrant backgrounds.

Hook, who, Ayer told Isaiah Berlin, 'might have been one of Mr Bick's [his father's partner's] sons-in-law', had established himself as the leading Marxist theorist of his generation; his book *Towards an Understanding of Karl Marx* had been published by Gollancz in Britain in 1933.[21] Ayer would have had some sympathy with the sort of humanist Marxism both he and Schapiro advocated. The New York Left in general, however, polarised by the Moscow Trials of 1937, did not make a favourable impression: 'I met many intelligent people of left-wing sympathies,' Ayer wrote on his return, 'but they seemed excessively concerned with the respective merits of Stalinism and Trotskyism, which can hardly be regarded as a serious issue for the American nation at the present time.'[22]

In the whistle-stop tour that followed, Ayer visited nine cities and diligently gave a lecture or a talk in most of them. But in other respects he was clearly not the best behaved of scholars. In Washington he upset his guests, wealthy patrons of the English Speaking Union, by defending Sacco and Vanzetti; in Chicago he formed 'an innocent friendship' with a night-club hostess, a Norwegian from the Bible belt, 'who seemed content to listen to me talking, whether or not she understood what I was saying'; in Champaign-Urbana he got so drunk that he cut his thumb badly on a razor blade; in Cleveland itself, he fell in with 'a fast set', mainly exiles from New York and San Francisco, and 'again made do with very little sleep, so little indeed that when toward the end of my stay I went to a relatively formal dinner at the home of one of the members of the English Speaking Union, I lost a desperate struggle to prevent myself from falling asleep quite early in the meal'.[23] Writing to Cummings from Cleveland, Ayer recounted some of his impressions and adventures:

> The English Speaking Union contains the most God awful members: you couldn't go on disliking Roosevelt if you know what allies you had … But everywhere I have been I have always managed to find someone to play with me. I find that people open out to me in this country in a way they don't in England, not only people I meet at parties, but waiters and taxi-drivers and lift-girls … I saw a disagreeably obscure floor show in Philadelphia … and my first apparently genuine burlesque show in Chicago, which I enjoyed. In Chicago, following your precept, and relying on a taxi man, I got landed in a clip joint (25 cents and tip for a packet of cigarettes; at least five dollars tip for the girl who comes and sits with you and she orders something expensive but mild to drink so that she can drink a lot of it). Any sane person would have had a drink, cut his losses and cleared out but I suddenly became obstinate. I was determined that these people who were out to pluck me had got to be made to see me and treat me as a human being even if I was ruined in the process. I even went back there with that object. I thought at the time you were probably the only person who would understand what I was doing and why I was doing it.[24]

But Ayer's trip was not all debauchery: in Princeton ('a fraud, like its gothic buildings') he visited Einstein, and in Chicago he reintroduced himself to Carnap. When Freddie had last met him, in London in 1934, he had been awed by him, but now they played table tennis together, and he became more aware of Carnap's 'personal charm'.[25] He went to

Urbana for a philosophical congress, and lectured on perception at the University of Michigan in Ann Arbor. The tour ended in Cambridge, where Freddie stayed with the Frankfurters, and met or met again the leading Harvard logicians, Quine, Sheffer, and C.I. Lewis, on whose work *Language, Truth and Logic* had drawn. He travelled back to New York for a few last heady nights, and on his final day again joined the Frankfurters, who were staying in the city. They took him out for some 'delicious' soft shell crabs at a 'luxurious hotel' before seeing him off at the docks. It was a fine conclusion to a 'strange' and magical visit – 'the spell kept-up until the end'.[26]

The English Speaking Union in London still has a copy of a report that their young scholar wrote on his return. Ayer was admirably frank, neither hiding nor flaunting his political views, or his disagreements with his mainly Republican hosts from the ESU. He was impressed by what the Roosevelt government was doing for the unemployed but regretted that divisions within the trade union movement were preventing the emergence of 'a strong labour party'.[27] Where philosophy was concerned, Ayer had found that the pragmatism of Peirce and James still had a following, but he judged that the best work was being done by symbolic logicians; he was pleased, he added, that positivism seemed to be gaining ground. 'Indeed it is in the United States that the latest development of logical positivism, the attempt by means of modern logical techniques to create a unified language of science, is receiving its chief support'.[28]

Throughout the academic year of 1937–38 Bertrand Russell was living in Kidlington on the outskirts of Oxford; during the Easter term, before Ayer's visit to the US, he had given a course of lectures at the university on 'Language and Fact' and in that and the following term he held discussions with the younger philosophers. Ayer attended these, and also saw Russell occasionally at Solly Zuckerman's house, where 'his dry manner of utterance and his astonishing memory for facts and quotations made even his small talk fascinating'.[29] The two philosophers did not at this stage, however, become friends.

Russell's lecture series and the book that came out of it, *An Inquiry into Meaning and Truth*, grappled directly with logical positivism. Ayer was proud that Russell drew on and commended many of his ideas, particularly the arguments against Neurath's and Carnap's views of protocol statements.* He was enormously impressed by Russell's powers as a teacher. 'He seemed to me then, and later, to have the great quality, which Moore and Einstein also had, of being able to talk to younger and less gifted people as though he could learn something from them.'[30] That summer the Fourth International Congress for the Unity of Science was held at Cambridge. Ayer gave a paper, 'On the Scope of Empirical Knowledge', in which he tried to answer some of the doubts about the possibility of a full-blown logical empiricism that Russell had advanced in 'The Limits of Empiricism'.

'My going away [to the US] was supposed to have cleared up a lot of the difficulties,' Ayer wrote to Cummings from Christ Church, 'but in fact nothing was altered by it: [Renée and I] tacitly agreed not even to raise the questions to which two months before we had thought we must find answers and so we have continued.'[31] By the beginning of the summer, a few months after his return from the US, Renée discovered she was pregnant again. According to Isaiah Berlin, Freddie first convinced himself that the child was his rather than Hampshire's, although the dates of his American tour told against it.[32] Berlin in fact suggested that Ayer did not learn the truth until after the child's birth, but this seems unlikely. At the very least, Ayer must have had his suspicions. In a long letter to Cummings sent in December, the first since his return from the US, full of detail about Renée and Valerie, Ayer omitted even to mention that Renée was pregnant again.[33]

Even after he admitted or discovered the truth, he and Renée decided to try to make a go of their marriage. When Renée's son was born, in January 1939, Freddie made an effort at a more domesticated life, working hard again at philosophy. They called the boy Julian David Ayer, in homage to Freddie's father, Jules, and grandfather, Dorus, giving him in name the links to Freddie's family that he lacked in blood. Isaiah Berlin suggested that there was a gesture, too, to Julien Sorel, the small, dark and romantic hero of Stendhal's Le rouge et le noir.

'Except for an odd weekend,' Ayer wrote to Cummings a few weeks before Julian was born, 'I spent the whole of the long vacation at home,

---

* In 'On Verification and Experience' (PAS, 38, 1937–38) Russell writes about Ayer's 'admirable' 'Verification and Experience', which enables him to deal briefly with certain parts of 'my subject, since I am in complete agreement with the views that it expresses'.

trying to write another book about the theory of knowledge.'[34] Ayer had, in fact, been at work on this for at least a year and a half, ever since abandoning his intention of writing a work of political theory. The new book, which he originally planned to call 'The Theory of Perception' and then 'Elements of Natural Knowledge', before arriving at its eventual title, *The Foundations of Empirical Knowledge*, was to be published by Macmillan, and represented an important step in his philosophical development. It is a considerably more sophisticated, closely argued and independently minded work than *Language, Truth and Logic*, and repudiates some of its main claims. Indeed, in most respects the gap between *Language, Truth and Logic* and *Foundations* is greater than that between *Foundations* and any of Ayer's later works. Yet it is also perhaps the least satisfactory of his major books: his arguments are not always as simple and clear as they could be – the whole effort feels slightly myopic. It was as if Ayer, stung by those who said that his first book was crude and programmatic, went too far in the opposite direction.

Perhaps the most obvious feature of *Foundations* is the space it gives to the philosophy of perception. In *Language, Truth and Logic* Ayer had more or less taken phenomenalism for granted; here though, owing no doubt to the criticisms Austin had been advancing in the All Souls meetings, he set out to elaborate a theory of sense-data – one tighter, more rigorous and characteristically purer than had ever been developed before. The hallmark of his approach, as so often, was his insistence on a very clear separation of philosophical from empirical questions.

Philosophers had traditionally, or so Ayer contended, treated sense-data theory as a *factual* theory, claiming that what we are directly aware of in perception is never a material object but only a sense-datum. They had argued that the facts of perceptual experience – that for instance things look different from different perspectives or, in the extreme case, that we seem to see things that don't exist at all – oblige us to recognise a world of 'impressions' between us and the material world, much as developments in astronomy might oblige us to recognise the existence of a new galaxy. Ayer however argued that this time-honoured reasoning was entirely fallacious. What was at stake between realists and sense-data theorists was not an empirical question but a conceptual one about the best way of analysing perception: the dispute was about language, not about facts. Thus ordinary language supplies us with linguistic resources to distinguish between the way things are and the way they seem to us (we say that the sun looks small but is in fact vast, that there appears to be a dagger in front of me, although there is none). Moreover one could, Ayer argued, more contentiously, do justice to the facts with a language that changed the meaning of 'material objects', so that all the things we perceive, even in cases of illusion, are really material objects, albeit of a very transient and mutable kind. Nevertheless, while nothing in experience forces us to employ the language of sense-data, this language has its philosophical advantages. 'For since in philosophising about perception our main object is to analyse the relationship of our sense-experiences to the propositions we put forward concerning material things, it is useful for us to have a terminology that enables us to refer to the contents of our experiences, independently of the material things that they are taken to present'.[35] In short, the sense-datum language is a technical language, invented by philosophers for the purposes of epistemological discussion.

With the case for sense-data established, Ayer was able to turn to the old problem of the relation of sense-data to the world of common sense, and the relation of the world of both sense-data and common sense to the world as described by modern science. One theory, the 'usual one', according to Ayer, had it that one could justify beliefs about the existence and character of things other than sense-data by means of a causal argument – or to put it the other way round, that sense-data are properly understood as a manifestation of something permanent and enduring beyond them. There are many variants on this theory. Thus while our sense-experiences are usually said to provide evidence for the existence of what Austin called 'the middle sized dry goods' of common sense, or the atoms and electrons of science, Berkeley described them as a manifestation of God. But as Ayer argued in a chapter on 'Causality and Perception', all these theories fall at the same (positivist) hurdle: 'it is impossible, by any valid process of inference, to make a transition from what is observed to anything that is conceived as being, in principle, unobservable' – talk of an unknowable realm of hidden objects was simply nonsensical.[36] Instead he opted for a form of phenomenalism, encapsulated in the principle that propositions which are ordinarily expressed by sentences which refer to material things can also be expressed by sentences which refer exclusively to actual and possible sense-data. On this account, 'the designations of "sense-data", "common-sense objects" and "scientific objects", do not refer to constituents of different "worlds" which lie in some mysterious way "beyond" one another, sense-data alone being observable and the other "objects" inferable as their causes', but instead belong to 'different languages which are distinguished from one another by referring to phenomena in different ways'.[37]

A story circulated at this time, that Ayer, having lost his pen, tried to console himself with the thought that it was just 'a favourable series of sense-data come to an end'. Although, doubtless apocryphal, it does capture some of the spirit of this position.

Foundations also deals with a host of other issues, with perhaps the most notable development occurring in Ayer's treatment of the problem of other minds. Where in *Language, Truth and Logic* he had boxed himself into the uncomfortable position of arguing that while statements about one's own mental states referred to inner experiences, statements about other people's mental states had to be interpreted behaviouristically, he now offered a version of the argument from analogy. On this account, the truth that one cannot experience other people's experiences is an analytic truth: any experience one has is by definition one's own. Yet there is a sense in which one might have the experiences that other people have – one can conceive of having such experiences, although then of course they would be one's own and no one else's. It is this conceptual possibility that gives us the right to generalise from our own experiences to those of others. Ayer admitted late in his life that 'none of my philosophical preoccupations have given me as much trouble as the problem of our knowledge of other minds.'[38] Nevertheless, he stuck to roughly this approach to the problem until the end.

When Ayer got to know Russell during his year at Oxford, the great philosopher was still maintaining his pacifist stance. Ayer, though, had already changed his position, along with most of his friends. While he had opposed rearmament until 1936, the menace of Mussolini and Hitler and the example of the Spanish Civil War had forced him to think again. Roy Harrod described an evening in the mid-1930s, in Christ Church Senior Common Room, when Lindemann argued the case for the need to prepare for war with Germany:

Ayer and I joined together in deploying the usual liberal arguments, and in Ayer I had an ally of no mean debating power. I remember saying gloomily to him as we walked back through the dark quad 'I do not see the answer to all that'. He gave a little shudder, like a dog shaking off water, and replied in tones equally depressed, 'No, it is difficult to see the answer'.[39]

The process of conversion had begun. By the time he and Renée were running for election in Westminster, Ayer was arguing for the need to stand up to the dictators. He looked on in dismay as, in Munich in September 1938, Prime Minister Chamberlain capitulated over Hitler's demands to the Sudetenland and campaigned against Hogg and the Munich agreement, in the Oxford by-election that October. He took a still more prominent part in a similar by-election in his London constituency, acting as treasurer of the anti-Munich campaign. 'This meant quite a lot of work as I had not only to keep the accounts but also to send out a great many letters soliciting and acknowledging donations, with no secretarial help and writing everything by hand'.[40] Neither campaign was successful, although both dented the Conservative vote.

Yet as Ayer admitted in a letter to Cummings, even as he agitated against appeasement, he was assailed by doubts and fears. Renée saw 'right from the start that the whole war scare [of September] was a fake ... I was more uncertain and also irrationally disturbed, not knowing what I wanted to happen'. He worried, he went on to explain, that many people, including his friends, were succumbing to the illusions of 1914, that this would be 'the war to end war, to protect European civilisation, to preserve our democracy ... And yet pacifism seems open to even more severe objections'. Sometimes, he admitted, he thought crudely of revenge and nothing else: 'In this mood, I see myself as a Jew avenging my people. But it is not a wholly honest mood. For what I really want is not that I should fight Nazis but that somebody else should.'[41] Ayer, indeed, seems to have been haunted, at this time, by doubts about his own bravery. In his autobiography, he recalled becoming irrationally angry with his old friend Martin Cooper when Cooper suggested that men of talent, like himself and Freddie, should not have to fight in the war. 'I suspect that the vehemence of my reaction,' Ayer admitted, 'was due to some inner conflict. I had no desire to run into danger, but I had been saying in my political speeches that we had to resist Hitler and I felt that this committed me to taking an active part in the war, if it came about.'[42]

Ayer had almost nothing to say about his activities in the year before the war, perhaps because it was overshadowed in his mind by events on the political stage. He worked hard on *The Foundations of Empirical Knowledge* but found time, in May 1939, to give a paper, 'Sense Data and Incorrigible Propositions', to the Moral Science Club in Cambridge. Writing to Isaiah Berlin, the club's chairman, Richard Braithwaite, described it as 'a striking success': 'I had relieved his fear of Wittgenstein and [John] Wisdom with a *vin de Saumer pétillant*; and he had an extremely profitable discussion with Wittgenstein that lasted to midnight. I very much hope that he'll get a college tutorship soon'.[43]

Wittgenstein's ideas had evolved since the publication of the *Tractatus* and although he refused to commit anything to print, some indication of the direction that his thought was taking was given by transcripts of his lectures that circulated in Oxford and elsewhere from the mid-1930s (the so-called 'Blue and Brown Books'). Ryle and Ayer, nevertheless, still found the *Tractatus* interesting enough to devote a class to the book. Ian Crombie, an undergraduate philosopher, attended and remembered that it was tough going and attracted a small audience.[44] In this last respect, at least, it was not representative. By the late 1930s Ayer had acquired the sort of reputation that ensures a large undergraduate following. In what became almost a routine, he would start a course of lectures in one of the university's smaller lecture rooms only to find that the pressure of numbers forced him to move to a larger one. Although he always preferred seminars and debates, Ayer was by this time an accomplished lecturer, pacing up and down the room as he spoke, words tumbling over each other in a fast-moving stream. Isaiah Berlin offered Philip Toynbee a 'wonderful turn', likening Ayer's performance to the overture to Rossini's *The Italian Girl in Algiers* – a quiet beginning and then a sudden burst into exuberance.[45]

Life at Christ Church was dominated by a quarrel over the future of the college. Early in 1939, the Dean left for a bishopric and Ryle, Ayer, Patrick Gordon-Walker and a young left-wing historian, Colin Dillwyn, led an unsuccessful campaign to laicise the college by changing its statutes to allow the appointment of a secular president.[46] The quarrel that ensued felt peculiarly significant because it reflected deeper divisions in the Senior Common Room. While the majority of older dons, who wanted to retain the link to the Church, had supported Munich, the younger ones, who wanted to break it, had not. At the end of the 1930s as at the beginning, Ayer found himself separated by a gulf from his seniors – it had been the story of his life. It was only after Hitler's occupation of 'Czechia' in March, and his repudiation of Anglo-German naval agreements in April, that Chamberlain's supporters had to admit that appeasement had failed.

With the outbreak of war in September 1939, Renée and Freddie and the two children left their little flat in London for a modern bungalow in Headington on the outskirts of Oxford, far away from the bombers that everyone believed 'would always get through'. 'The political situation makes me more and more depressed,' Freddie wrote to Neurath, in November. 'I resent above all the feeling of impotence from which one suffers at times like these, the feeling that really everything one values is at the mercy of knaves and fools.'[47]

In fact Ayer was far from inactive. Although academics over twenty-five were supposed, at least initially, to remain in their jobs, Gilbert Ryle, who was not Welsh, had managed to secure a commission in the Welsh Guards. He now stepped in once again to fix things for his old student. Late in 1939 Ayer donned a bowler hat and an Eton tie and presented himself for an interview at the Welsh Guards headquarters in St James's. Just before Christmas, he was informed that he had been accepted. Although several other dons at Christ Church also volunteered for service at this time, Ayer's conduct was brave and honourable, especially for one who feared that he was at heart a coward. For the first time, he won Dundas's full approval, while Frank Pakenham, who had once accused Ayer of propagating a philosophy that 'would destroy people's sense of duty',* was now moved to verse:

He sneers at duty with indignant voice
But trembles with a passion for the good.

* In his diaries Toynbee recorded a tea party of February 1937, at Frank Pakenham's home in Oxford, at which he, Lindemann, Harrod, Ayer and Pakenham were present. Pakenham attacked positivism. 'He claimed Freddie's doctrine would destroy people's sense of duty – a most immoral argument against the opposition of truth' (11 February 1937).

This perceptive, accurate fragment is all that is left of what Pakenham considered 'the one good poem I have ever written'.[48]

Christmas was spent with Renée and the children in Oxford. Freddie's mother and stepfather, who had moved to Brighton to escape the expected bombing, joined them. While all across Europe, arms factories churned, megaphones blared, and troops mustered, the Ayers enjoyed an eerily quiet new year.

11

War: 'My New Profession'

Although the Welsh Guards, which Ayer now joined, had been formed only in 1915, it was a member of a very old group of regiments, the Brigade of Guards. At war, the Guards were expected to play much the same role as any other division and in the Second World War they fought all over the globe. Traditionally, however, they were responsible for the safety of the monarch and during peacetime they retained this largely ceremonial function. The Guards alone kept their traditional uniform – bearskins, metal boots, swords – after the rest of the army gave them up, and it is usually they who stand on display outside Buckingham Palace, and who act out the changing of the Guard. In Ayer's day almost all commissioned officers in the Brigade came from one of the top four or five public schools, by way of the élite fee-paying military colleges at Sandhurst or Woolwich. In joining the Welsh Guards, then, Ayer was joining about the smartest, most prestigious part of Britain's defence forces – the Eton of the army.

After passing his interview before Christmas, Ayer expected, apprehensively, to join the regiment as an officer early in January 1940. His enrolment, however, was delayed, then, agonisingly, delayed again, and it was not until March that he finally said goodbye to Renée, Valerie and Julian. In the meantime, the rules governing army officers were democratised and anyone under the age of thirty-five was forbidden to receive a commission unless he had first been through a brief training in the ranks and then through an officers' training unit. So it was that when Ayer did finally enlist, he was dispatched to the Guards depot at Caterham, not far from London, for a two-month stint as a guardsman recruit.

The training of rank and file soldiers at this time was tough, often brutal; the training of the Guards especially so. Writing to Cummings at the beginning of April, Ayer likened his new home to a prison or at least 'an unimaginatively organised boarding-school', with every waking moment devoted to drill, combat training, or cleaning kit. Ayer's squad, however, was run by an 'exceptionally nice and intelligent' young soldier, Sergeant Jackson. Ayer was also lucky in being placed in a squad made up of other potential officers, so that his only contact with the ordinary guardsmen was at meal times: 'They seem nice fellows on the whole,' he wrote, 'but stupid and brutalised.'[1] Yet in some respects the ordeal was especially hard for him. He was a decade older than most of the other recruits, smaller, and less fit.

A week after arriving, Freddie wrote to Isaiah Berlin:

> I think that the best way for me to write to you is just to give you the facts and leave you to interpret them. I cannot myself judge what is and what is not significant and amusing. I am too much inside it . . . I am in what is known as a brigade squad of potential officers, with about twenty others, most of them undergraduates or boys who have just come down and gone into banks or what not . . . They are quite a pleasant lot, one or two of them rather silly but not offensive as yet and they are nearly all much more efficient than I.
>
> We sleep and live in one large barrack room, with about two feet between beds, together with one trained soldier who makes us keep the room tidy and shows us how to clean and arrange one's kit etc. . . We get up at six every morning and go to bed at ten and our sixteen hour day is very full. We do drill, and P.T. and weapon training and listen to one or two lectures (including a very incompetent defence by the chaplain of the physico-teleological argument [for the existence of God]), and what is worst of all 'shining' of boot, belts, buttons, rifles and, in my case, bath-house taps. We have compulsory two-hour shining parades five days a week and even they do not give us enough time to get everything

done ... Renée and Valerie came down to Croydon on the Saturday and Sunday to be with me, and at first they did not recognise me. My hair is cropped like a convict's, I have for me a florid colour, and my bearing is martial. And now I have begun to grow a moustache, the possession of which is said to be a means of advancement in my new profession ... I am well except that I have had trouble with my feet which got bruised by a pair of hard boots, and I have not been unhappy so far. Once or twice when sergeants and trained soldiers have been rude to me, I have been jolted back into remembering who and what I am to be suffering such things, but on the whole I have managed to become pretty successfully the submissive small boy that I am expected to be ... Write to me Shaya, it doesn't matter what. Freddie.[2]

As this letter suggests, Ayer seems to have managed fairly well at Caterham. William Bell, another recruit, remembers that he was popular with Sergeant Jackson and the other soldiers because he was obviously willing and good-natured, but also because he was a bit of 'a character' – 'they had never met anyone like him before'.[3] The writer Patrick Leigh Fermor, later to go on to heroic exploits in Greece, overlapped with Ayer at Caterham:

Freddie's battle-dress always looked too big for him. His alert, intellectual features, his surprised expression, his raised eyebrows and the amused smile which was never far off, made him somehow an unlikely figure in these martial surroundings. Frailer looking than most of the others, he turned out to be lithe, resilient and tough and he did very well at all the things recruits have to do – drill, PT, weapon-training, stripping and assembling Bren guns, bayonet-practice, 'naming of parts', and the endless spit-and-polish of 'shining parades', when pipes were allowed but no cigarettes, and no talk except about regimental history, viz, Badajoz, Salamanca, Vittoria, Toulouse and Waterloo ... Freddie's quickness and fluency and his knack of spotting the comic aspects of things were a great blessing, and I think the contrast of his rarefied academic world and this Spartan place fascinated him.[4]

Hugh Euston (later the Duke of Grafton) was also with Freddie at Caterham, but recalled only one incident: 'Of course he was a most unlikely soldier and I have a clear recollection of us queuing up for injections and Freddie in a dead faint on the floor'.[5]

At Caterham Ayer put finishing touches to *The Foundations of Empirical Knowledge* and he tried with characteristic bravado to sign its preface, 'Sergeant Jackson's Squad, Brigade of Guards, Caterham, Surrey', although Jackson declined the honour. (In the end Ayer signed it 'Brigade of Guards Depot, Caterham, Surrey' – a nice riposte to anyone who wanted to argue that the empiricism that it defended encouraged a passive ethic.) The book was published in the autumn in both the US and Britain and was very well received. Moore and Price both took the view that it was a better book than *Language, Truth and Logic*. Richard Braithwaite, writing in *Philosophy*, even went so far as to suggest that its treatment of 'the problem of sense-data ... may well be as final as anything can be in philosophy'.[6] Nevertheless, *Foundations* had less impact than it would if it had been published in peacetime – and by the time Ayer returned to philosophy five years had passed and both his own ideas and philosophical debate more generally had moved on.

After seven weeks' training in the ranks, Ayer was sent as an officer cadet to the Royal Military College at Sandhurst, which had been converted for the duration of the war from an exclusive military college into a unit offering crash courses to trainee officers. Freddie now had a bedroom to himself and was allowed out on Sundays, but he found it, in other respects, even more like school than Caterham, and once again all his fellow cadets were ten years younger. By June 1940 it was clear that Germany had won the first stages of the war. The Nazis had invaded the Low Countries and France, and although the British army had managed to ferry its troops back from Dunkirk, soldiers from the Welsh Guards' two battalions amongst them, Nazi troops were gathering threateningly on the other side of the Channel. Freddie was put to work with the other cadets building entrenchments in the country around Sandhurst and keeping guard of the college grounds at night. Ayer never went as far as his friend Isaiah Berlin in his admiration for Churchill, yet he admitted, writing to Berlin at the end of his life, that he had been moved by radio broadcasts that the Prime Minister gave at this time, calling on Britain to fight on alone.[7]

There was not much time, however, to listen to the radio. In three months the young cadets were expected to absorb a course that took two years in peacetime. Ayer was put through assault courses and took part in mock night-time manoeuvres. He was taught the rudiments of orienteering, mechanics and military strategy, and inducted into the use of Bren guns. Guardsmen were expected to mount a bicycle in soldierly fashion, as if it were a horse, and ride in formation as if they were a troop of cavalry. Freddie could barely ride a bike, but everyone was impressed by his ability to recite, almost verbatim, any lecture he heard.

Ayer found it easier than he once had to get on with men from a different background than his own. Philip Toynbee, who was also at Sandhurst and looked to him as a natural ally in disdain, was dismayed by how well his old friend had adapted to the 'ragging', rowdy banter and table-banging that was a part of army life. Sandhurst, indeed, represented an emotional milestone for Ayer, who was delighted to find that the same kind of boys who had spurned him at school, now accepted him as a friend. Talking to a group of Etonians in the 1970s, he was explicit about this: 'I had not been at all popular here and had not known how to get on with other boys and going first of all to Caterham as a guardsman recruit, and then to Sandhurst as an officer cadet, gave me, as it were, a second chance and I knew how to manage. I knew how to deal with people of your sort ... – of your ancestor's sort'.[8] The young Andrew Cavendish (later the Duke of Devonshire), with Ayer at Sandhurst, had 'never met anyone like him before', but recalled him fondly. 'He was a peculiar mixture. On the one hand I remember he was always well turned-out and clearly had made a great effort to get where he was. On the other hand, he could not resist teasing and mocking military authority. I can see him now in the ante-room with a glass of port, being very amusing, laughing at it all'.[9]

Ayer got on adequately at Sandhurst, getting a better rating as a prospective officer than he believed he deserved, but he worried terribly, especially about Valerie and Julian. As invasion looked increasingly likely, many wealthier parents sent their children to the US and Renée decided to do the same. 'As we were still in a state of alert at Sandhurst,' Ayer wrote later, 'I was not able to get leave to say goodbye to them, and I learned of their imminent departure through a telephone call from Renée, which left me in tears, not knowing when I should see any of them again.'[10] In New York the Ayers were taken in by a wealthy, upright, New York family, the Godleys, who lived at Rye in Westchester County, on the outskirts of the city. The Godleys made the evacuees feel welcome, but Renée had hardly arrived before she left again to make her way back to England, leaving the children behind.

In *Part of My Life*, Ayer put her move down to her discomfort at living at the Godleys' expense,[11] but she was naturally restless, and anyway seemed to find a strange pleasure in giving her children away. She had several other children during the war, although not with Freddie, which she gave to friends to adopt. It was an extreme manifestation of her 'ostentatious selflessness'. Renée, moreover, had another motive for returning to England: she wanted to be with Stuart Hampshire. Isaiah Berlin was in New York at this time and remembered a long and intimate conversation with Renée, in which she complained that Freddie had no depth. 'Freddie, she is sure, is happy more or less wherever he may be,' Berlin reported in a letter to Marion Frankfurter: 'he may need nursing but not spiritual comfort, having, she suspects, no such needs. She regards him quite obviously as a toy character, lost in a serious world, who had once taken her in, by whom she is deceived no longer'.[12] Returning to London, she found time, between her pregnancies, to get a job as a motorbike dispatch rider. Like Freddie's mother before her, war offered Renée opportunities denied her in peace.

In the first half of 1940, Ayer's mother and stepfather had moved from Brighton to Somerset, out of the way of the Luftwaffe's bombs. Reine had suffered a form of sclerosis for several years, which caused her to shake. This added to her general air of vulnerability. After Freddie joined the Guards, her sclerosis worsened. Freddie had little chance to see her. At the end of the year he heard that she was dangerously ill, but by the time he reached her bedside she had died. She was only fifty-three. In his memoirs Freddie wrote kindly about her – 'it was sad that, having found happiness in her second marriage, she was given so few years to enjoy it' – but just as he treated his father's death, so he treated hers as parenthetical to his own life story.[13] He gave the episode the same space as a subsequent paragraph on his attempts to learn how to drive.

By the time Freddie finished his training at Sandhurst at the end of September, Britain, its colonies and dominions were fighting more or less alone. The threat of Nazi invasion had receded, but the Blitz had begun.

Having successfully passed his exams, Ayer was appointed, a month before his thirtieth birthday, second lieutenant and posted to a training battalion at Sandown Park, near Esher. Like Caterham and Sandhurst, Sandown was not far from London; at night the fires that licked the capital gave off a soft glow. Freddie was now back in circles in which he felt more at home. There was a surprising number of artists and writers amongst his fellow officers, including the novelist Richard Llewellyn Lloyd and the painters Rex Whistler and Simon Elwes, as well as Gilbert Ryle. The officers had soldier-servants ('batmen') to do their valeting and look after their equipment and handsome blue and khaki uniforms. Everyone remarked how good Freddie looked in his – 'like a chasseur alpin,' according to Isaiah Berlin.

Ayer was given a platoon to train and command, but although he occasionally lectured on the historical and political background to the war, most of the real training was done by non-commissioned officers. 'I am,' Ayer wrote to his editor at Macmillan, 'in the state, so common in the army, of having comparatively little work to do here and yet not being able to find time to do anything else.'[14] The officers often escaped their barracks for an evening on the town. Talking fifty years later, Ayer recalled that in the time-honoured military fashion, his fellows often ended the evening with 'tarts', although 'this was never my style'.[15] Patrick Leigh Fermor remembered him 'dancing with a beautiful girl in the crowded but softly lit penumbra of the Four Hundred, a marvellous night club we were both fond of. I remember him as resplendent in blue patrols, scarlet piping and glittering new pips. We often met here and in the Nut-House, The Slip-In, Frico's, the Boogie-Woogie and similar haunts. He loved dancing and night clubs and girls, and they loved him'.[16]

Early in the new year of 1941, after five busy empty months at Sandown, Ayer was accepted on a course in Cambridge devoted to training officers in the interrogation of German prisoners. During his time at Cambridge he secured temporary membership of Trinity College, and Wittgenstein called on his rooms. Ayer, however, was out and felt it would be too familiar to return the call – perhaps he was more scared of Wittgenstein than he admitted.

The month Ayer spent in the university city proved a pleasant enough interlude, especially as Goronwy Rees, who had startled everyone including himself by enlisting in the Territorial Army five months before the outbreak of war, turned out to be one of the course's tutors. With the training over, Ayer expected to be dispatched abroad to one of the Welsh Guards' regular battalions, where he would finally see action. This, of course, had been the point of joining up in the first place, yet he seems to have become increasingly worried that 'the more rigorous standards' of the regular battalions 'would show up my deficiencies'.[17] It was probably fortunate, then, that although his Cambridge examiners reported that Ayer's 'knowledge of spoken German does not fully qualify him to undertake interrogation duties', an old friend from Christ Church who worked for the Intelligence Corps offered him a job in London as an interrogator. This, with some misgivings, he accepted.[18] Goronwy Rees wrote about war: 'Here all is chance, accident and absurdity'; he was drawing on his own experiences but Ayer's career bears him out.[19] When the war had started Ayer was determined, as he told Cummings, 'to go right into it', yet he spent the next four years in a variety of sometimes improbable jobs, trying, never altogether successfully, to find an effective outlet for his talents.[20]

One of his colleagues in his new job at the London district headquarters of the Intelligence Corps in Curzon Street was Francis Hare, the Earl of Listowel, a soft-spoken, left-wing Etonian, a few years older than Ayer, who had written a doctorate in philosophy and a book on aesthetics. Listowel found Freddie 'a god-send; he was such good company', and remembered the work they did: 'Most of the prisoners that came to us were German sailors who had been intercepted in the Atlantic. All they were obliged to offer was their name and rank or number, but we found that they wanted to talk and told us about their lives. Freddie and I felt very sorry for them. They were depressed and lonely and insecure'.[21] At this stage Freddie and Renée were living apart, she in Chelsea, he in a service flat in Pall Mall, but they still saw one another often and when Ayer introduced them, she and Listowel began a long love affair. For many years he was a rival to both Hampshire and Ayer.

Listowel recalled another task that he and Ayer were given in addition to interviewing prisoners. The intelligence service was worried about the amount of secret information that seemed to be leaking into the open; the two philosophers were sent to pubs and bars around London to fraternise with soldiers and officers, or simply sit and listen to the conversations of their neighbours, in order to assess who was talking to whom. In this way, they often ended up in the Café Royal.

Needless to say, this was far from Ayer's only social life. Talking fifty years on, Listowel offered the outlines of an image into which the post-war Ayer would settle: he had a pool of girlfriends and was out most nights, but even when drunk he somehow remained cool-headed, and never let his social life affect his work. Ayer's principal girlfriend from this time was Kathleen McColgan a heavy-drinking journalist. McColgan had read philosophy at Oxford, agitated for the Spanish Republicans in London, and then, with the outbreak of war, had drifted into journalism, writing about politics for the *Evening Standard*. She introduced Ayer to her friends, the photographer Lee Miller, one of the most beautiful women of her day, and critic and art collector Roland Penrose. Ayer was naturally seduced by this wonderfully cultivated and glamorous couple and he and McColgan, who lived in Penrose's house in Hampstead, spent several weekends with them in their Picasso-laden farmhouse in Sussex. Literary life in wartime London centred firmly on 'the *Horizon* crowd', the group of writers who contributed to the famous literary monthly which Cyril Connolly edited with Stephen Spender. Rather surprisingly, Ayer had seen little of Connolly since the outbreak of war, but in April, when Spender married his second wife, the pianist Natasha Litvin, Ayer attended the party that Connolly hosted in the South Kensington studio maisonette he shared with Peter Quennell and Arthur Koestler. A photograph taken by Cecil Beaton shows Freddie mingling with Connolly, Sonia Brownell (later Orwell), Louis MacNeice, Guy Burgess and the architect Erno Goldfinger among others. Ayer alone sports a uniform. Natasha Spender remembers that he brought his good friend Guy Burgess with him.[22]

Not long after this, in September, Connolly and Freddie fell out. Walking home from a restaurant, the Ivy, one night with Frank Pakenham and Philip Toynbee, Ayer began to speak maliciously about Connolly, quoting Virginia Woolf: 'I do not like that smarty-boots Connolly.' The blackout was on, the street dark, when out of the fog Freddie heard a voice: 'Not so loud, Freddie.' It was Connolly.[23] Although outwardly they remained on friendly terms, Freddie's patron never quite forgave him. Many years later Connolly was to tell Anthony

Powell that Ayer was best thought of as 'one of those knowing little French intellectuals'.[24]

This was an exciting time to be in London – war loosened class boundaries and social and sexual proprieties – and Ayer enjoyed cavorting with his friends. He made no secret of the fact, however, that he found his work for the Intelligence Corps boring and futile, and as soon as he heard of a secret service job in New York – a position which, he was told, could well lead to undercover work in South America – he expressed interest. In his memoirs Ayer wrote that at this point he and Renée were on the verge of living together again – presumably with the plan, now the threat of imminent invasion had gone, of calling the children back from the US.[25] When the New York job was offered to him, however, he took it: the work appealed and if he stayed, Renée could follow him, and together they could set up home with Valerie and Julian.

Ayer's Welsh Guards file shows that on 29 September 1941 he was transferred from the Guards to 'Inter-Services Research Bureau', one of the covers used by the Special Operations Executive (SOE). The very existence of SOE was a secret, although by the end of the war, a fairly open one. It is only recently that its archives have begun to be released. The organisation was formed in July 1940 with the purpose of promoting sabotage, propaganda and other forms of resistance behind enemy lines as a desperate attempt to plug the gaping hole in British strategy caused by the collapse of France. Not everyone approved of SOE. The intelligence service viewed it as a rival, the armed forces tended to see it as a drain on their resources, and the Allied governments in exile argued that resistance was their own affair. It had Churchill's backing, however, and a number of buildings were found for it around Baker Street. By the time Ayer joined, it had grown into a large organisation with separate sections for each occupied country, although very little work behind enemy lines had yet been done. The American office, for which he was destined, was a special case. It had been set up (in New York, not Washington, where anonymity was less easily preserved) by British intelligence with the task of monitoring pro-German feeling in the US, and organising propaganda and other measures to counter it. From the beginning, however, its head, Bill Stephenson, a shady and unreliable Canadian millionaire, a friend of Churchill, insisted on taking responsibility for the instigation of clandestine warfare in those South American countries which it was feared might be invaded by Hitler or might elect to join the conflict on his side.

British Security Co-ordination, as Stephenson's organisation was called, was located on two floors of the Rockefeller Center, in the heart of Manhattan – a ritzy Fifth Avenue shopping spot, quite unlike the grey bomb-scarred city that Ayer had left behind. Freddie, or 'G426' to give him his new name, nevertheless found himself among friends. The head of the South American section, to which he had been posted, was Bill Deakin, a young historian whom Ayer had known at Oxford.* Deakin put Ayer to work with his undergraduate friend, Giles Playfair and they were soon joined by a third Oxonian, Gilbert Highet. He made new friends as well, including Tony Samuel, later Lord Bearstead, a young Etonian to whom he became especially close, and Tim Brooke, an elegant and charming bisexual actor with a giddy social life, who had lived in New York before the outbreak of war.

The British, united by their concern for friends and family back home, tended to socialise together. They lunched at the King of the Sea on Fifth Avenue, sleeves rolled up, napkins round their necks, enjoying the restaurant's freshly boiled lobster, and in the evening they drank martinis at the English Grill, looking over the Rockefeller Center's ice rink. Ayer got back in touch with friends he had made on his last visit to the US, including Meyer Schapiro and Ernest Nagel, although he saw most of the Cummingses. 'I am very grateful for the time that I spent with you; it was one of the nicest holidays I have ever had,' he wrote in August 1942, after a week spent at Joy Farm, the electricity-less New Hampshire farmhouse that Cummings inherited from his mother.

It was just what I needed, to be with you both, enjoying a complete physical rest and at the same time being encouraged to talk my head off. I felt I had come alive again. I honestly think that I am a much nicer and better person when I am with you, partly because of the way in which you stimulate me, but mainly because of your belief in me which I want to justify. I have never tried to analyse friendship;

* Deakin eventually left New York and was parachuted into Yugoslavia, where he worked with Tito's partisans. After the war he became head of St Antony's College, Oxford, allegedly maintaining all the while his contacts with the secret services; he became and remained one of Ayer's closest friends.

but I suppose that, at its best, it consists in enjoying and receiving the kind of confidence that you give to me. Its value doesn't even depend on our being together, much though I shall miss you if I go away.[26]

During this holiday, Cummings painted a vivid oil of Ayer; dressed in an open shirt and reading a book, he looks thin and agile and intent.

The job of the section of BSL that Ayer had joined was to establish a network of agents ready to go into action if any part of the southern half of the continent should fall into enemy hands. 'They seemed,' remembered one colleague, 'to be engaged mainly in planning a scorched earth programme and arranging for suitable people to be brought out from South America to receive courses in demolition and sabotage.'[27] Two weeks after Ayer arrived on 7 December, 1941, the Japanese bombed Pearl Harbor and the US entered the war. Roosevelt quickly claimed South America as a US sphere of influence, and while the British retained the agents that they already had in the field, they no longer felt able to add to their number. Ayer's hopes of being sent into one of the Spanish-speaking countries were dashed, and he spent most of the next eighteen months writing 'conscientiously humourless' reports on the activities of the various Fascist and anti-Fascist groups in Argentina, Chile, Peru and Uruguay.[28] The only significant break in this routine came when he was sent, halfway through his stay, to 'Camp X', a large, British-run, paramilitary school, carefully hidden on the shore of Lake Ontario in Canada, devoted to training would-be agents in clandestine warfare. Courses included lessons in how to shadow a man and escape surveillance, how to use a knife and make simple hand grenades, and how to evade capture by blinding an assailant with a box of matches. For the rest of his life, Freddie was able to boast that he could kill with a few well aimed slices of the hand.[29]

In New York Ayer had his own apartment, on 34th and Park Avenue, but spent weekends upstate, in Rye, with the children's adopted family, the Godleys, enjoying their wealthy East Coast style of life. Neither Julian nor five-year-old Valerie recognised him, but it was some consolation that they both seemed happy in their new home. In accordance with the tentative plan they had made in London, Ayer now wrote to Renée asking her to join him, only to receive a telegram announcing that she wanted a divorce. Ayer was surprised and upset – and not just for the children. There was a strand in his character – half loyal, half passive – which meant that for all his promiscuity, he was generally reluctant to end relations. He wanted to stay married to Renée.

This news from London was not the only upsetting development in his personal life. Since arriving in New York, he had begun an alliance with the Hollywood journalist, Sheilah Graham, Scott Fitzgerald's last love, which had taken an unexpected turn.

Sheilah Graham, who once described herself as 'a fascinating fake', was six years older than Freddie, born in London into a working-class family of Russian Jews. Her father died when she was a baby, and she and her mother had shared a basement room with a woman who took in washing. Her earliest memories were of the stinging smell of soap, mixed with that of the boiled potatoes on which they survived. At six she was sent to an East End orphanage, returning at fourteen to care for her mother, who was suffering from cancer and died a few years later. Sheilah worked as a maid and a salesgirl, demonstrating toothbrushes, but at seventeen married a businessman of forty-two who taught her table manners and helped her rid herself of her cockney accent. Changing her name from Lily Sheil to Sheilah Graham, she got a job working as a chorus girl in London as one of 'Charles Cochran's Young Ladies'. Freddie and his mother might have seen her on one of their visits to the West End.

From the theatre, Graham turned to journalism, selling articles about London shows to the penny press. In 1933 she left her husband and moved first to New York and then Los Angeles, where she secured the position of Hollywood columnist for the North American Newspaper Alliance. She was beautiful in a cherubic, wide-faced way, clever and witty. It was in 1937, at a party which she later claimed not quite truthfully was to celebrate her engagement to the Marquess of Donegall, that she met Scott Fitzgerald. It was, she said, 'love at first sight'. (Graham appears as Kathleen Moore, Monroe Stahr's last love in *The Last Tycoon*.) She had fabricated an aristocratic past for herself – a Chelsea childhood and a finishing school in Paris – but when the story broke down under pressure from Fitzgerald's questions, he offered to guide her education and designed an elaborate reading course for her; in the bestseller that she wrote about their relationship, *Beloved Infidel* (1958), she described herself as Eliza to his Henry Higgins. The great author died in her apartment in December 1940, a year before Freddie arrived in New York.[30]

One can see what Ayer would have liked about Graham. She was smart, resilient and sexy and she had no illusions about herself. The pair had first met at a party in London a few months before Freddie moved to the US. They had not had an affair then, but within a month of his arriving in Manhattan she was pregnant by him – perhaps it was an accident, but at thirty-seven, it is possible she wanted a child. 'When she found that she was pregnant,' Ayer explained fifty years later, 'she disappeared for a few weeks without saying anything to me. When she returned to New York, she told me that she had married Trevor Westbrook in order to legitimate her child. I was still in the process of divorcing my first wife and anyway, as Sheilah knew, was not prepared to marry again so soon.'[31] Westbrook, a self-made industrialist, had been put in charge of Britain's wartime aeroplane production by Lord Beaverbrook. Like Ayer, he had met Graham in London in the summer of 1941, but they *had* had an affair. When he turned up in New York, at just the time she discovered she was pregnant, she told him she was four months gone with his child, and persuaded him to marry her. Soon afterwards she announced she had lost the child, and soon after that she was pregnant again. It was, as Graham and Ayer's daughter would later describe it, 'an audacious layer of lies'.[32]

Ayer never recorded what he thought about these deceptions, although he must have felt that, far away from home, in the midst of a war, with a wife in London pregnant with the child of another man, a son who was not in fact his in Rye, and an illegitimate child expected in New York, that his life was running dangerously out of control. He and Sheilah nevertheless remained friendly, and when she unexpectedly went into labour while they were dining together a few days before the baby was due, Ayer escorted her to the hospital. He sent his new daughter – Wendy Westbrook – a silver porringer as a Christmas present that year, but never came to see her in hospital or contributed to her maintenance in any way. When Wendy occasionally visited Ayer in London, he was pleased to see her, and she came to think of him as a 'special friend', but he seems to have been more than happy to follow Graham's wishes and keep his real relationship to her a secret. Indeed, he and Graham were both discreet to a fault, neither mentioning the other in their various volumes of autobiography.

Early on in his time in New York, Ayer took on the job of reviewing films for the *Nation*. He wrote only four 'round-ups' in all. He liked *Kings Row*, singling out Ronald Reagan's performance as the legless playboy, but reserved most of his enthusiasm for a new version of Charlie Chaplin's *The Gold Rush* – 'the art of miming . . . brought to perfection' – and Paul Strand's *Native Land*, a radical documentary about 'the workers' struggle against native oppressors' which he urged his readers to see.[33] Because Ayer was not officially allowed to work for anyone but the British government, his name could not appear in the *Nation*. The pseudonym he used in its place, P.H. Rye, is interesting: it was intended in part as an allusion to his children's American home, but also to Heraclitus's saying 'Panta rei' – 'Everything flows'. The cinema offered, in especially intense form, life rather as Ayer conceived it: something both fleeting and engrossing, a Paterian succession of sensations to be savoured and then forgotten.

Graham was not the only woman around. Ayer had a long affair with a British Security Co-ordination secretary, who was or became a friend of the Cummingses and he also went out with 'the young and pretty' Jean Gordon-Duff.[34] Her half-brother, Tony Bower, a gregarious, homosexual red-headed epicurean – Maurice Bowra once described him as 'a gossip columnist without a column' – became one of Ayer's closest New York friends. Bower, who had been a near contemporary of his at Oxford after which he earned a living as a professional bridge player, had what Ayer described as a 'zest' or an 'appetite' for life, a quality which he prized above all others.* Through Tim Brooke, his friend at BSC, he met Lauren Bacall, then around eighteen and just breaking out from working as a night-club hostess into modelling: at a party together, they made a recording on which she sang 'Chattanooga Choo-Choo' and he recited Marvell's 'To his Coy Mistress'. Ayer was no Humphrey Bogart, and was

---

* Bower was a friend of Jeanie and Cyril Connolly, Isherwood and Auden. Half-American, he had been educated at Marlborough and Oxford, where Ayer had known him slightly. He worked briefly on *Horizon* before moving to New York. He appears as 'Ronny' in Isherwood's *Down There on a Visit*, a character whose 'impudent, attractively comic face keeps breaking into grins, and his round blue eyes sparkle with a lit-up gaiety which is in its way courageous, because he isn't as carefree as he tries to appear' (quoted in Jeremy Lewis, *Cyril Connolly, A Life*, London, 1997, p.298).

hardly yet an intellectual star, but there was something in his alert, sensuous face and intellectual vitality that won these beauties over. In his fast, excited voice, Marvell's seductive, hedonistic lines somehow made sense.

Like Tim Brooke and Bacall, Ayer was often at Mabel's, a little night club in the East Fifties where Mabel Mercer sang French love songs from the 1920s and '30s. It was here that he met Elizabeth von Hofmannsthal and her husband Raimund. The daughter of the 6th Marquis of Anglesey and train-bearer to the Queen at George VI's coronation, Liz had an impeccably aristocratic pedigree, but had shocked her family by marrying 'a wandering penniless divorcee' – and one, moreover, from an enemy country.[35] Tall and thin, with fine magnolia skin, blue eyes and pitch-black hair, Ayer described her as the most beautiful woman he had ever known, and he remained half infatuated with her for the rest of his life. Raimund, a handsome, chivalrous character, and one of life's natural hosts, was the son of the Viennese poet Hugo von Hofmannsthal. A staunch anti-Nazi, he left Austria early in the 1930s, and ended by becoming an American citizen; when Freddie first met him he was working as executive in the Time-Life empire. Like Guy de Rothschild, also working for BSC and another friend from this time, Raimund looked up to Ayer as something of a mentor in both philosophy and politics. Raimund, in turn, took Ayer 'to such places as the Stork Club and El Morocco', which Ayer would 'never have thought of visiting on my own, and somehow contrived to transmute the contemporary world of café society into the Vienna of his father's librettos. He had an extraordinary power to make one participate in his romantic view of life, however little relation it may have borne to fact'.[36] The von Hofmannsthals were a cultured, strikingly glamorous couple who came to play an important part in Ayer's life. After the war, he often holidayed with them both in their *Schloss* in Austria.

Ayer had been working hard on improving his Spanish since his arrival in New York and by the summer of 1942 he could write to the Cummingses that he was capable 'of carrying on a reputable conversation if the other party speaks slowly'.[37] Early in 1943, plans were made to send him and Guy de Rothschild as secret agents to Argentina, but in the end the mission was cancelled. Once again Ayer, who had been passed over for promotion within BSC, was frustrated with his work and, as he told it, asked to be transferred.[38] Isaiah Berlin, however, had a slightly different version. According to him, Freddie had become highly critical of the way the BSC was being run. 'He thought the set-up was a racket; second-rate people doing nothing', and said so to everyone he met, despite Deakin warning him against it. 'Stephenson got to hear about it and accused Freddie of disloyalty and Freddie was removed'.[39] Ayer seems to have found it easy enough to remain discreet about Wendy, but here at least, his belief that one should tell it as it really was, won out.

12

'Good Enough, if Largely Unauthorised'

In the new year of 1943, after the British had defeated Rommel at El Alamein, Allied troops had taken most of French North Africa and the war had at last begun to turn in the Allies' favour, Ayer's request to be transferred back to Europe was granted. Late in March or early in April, he and the children left New York. It was a terrifying time to be crossing the Atlantic – sinkings were at an all-time high – and Ayer was naturally anxious for his charges, but despite the sighting of an enemy submarine, the convoy arrived safely in Liverpool on 21 April. The following day they travelled to London, where, after three years, Valerie, seven and Julian, four, were reunited with their mother.

> The children have adapted themselves to their new life in England with Renée [Ayer wrote to New York] as happily and easily as they adapted themselves to their life with me on the boat: and she naturally is delighted to have them back. My meeting with her was extraordinarily free from drama. We got on extremely well together, without any awkwardness or strain ... Stuart and the Earl are still very much in evidence, particularly the Earl, whom I like a lot. He is a mild mannered, sensitive, cultivated, high principled man, simple in his tastes, to meet perhaps a little colourless. Even if his wife would divorce him, I doubt, however, if Renée would marry him; or Stuart either, as things are now.[1]

The children's adaptation was not in fact quite as easy as Freddie here hopefully suggested. They had been used to all the luxuries the US could offer – eggs, oranges, pineapples, cookies and candy-canes – and could not help finding ration-gripped Britain wanting. That December, Freddie and Renée, with the help of Listowel, made a great effort to lay on a good Christmas for them both, but could only find a puny tree and few sweets or presents. Julian glanced at the tree and the pathetic offerings beneath it and gave his verdict: 'It isn't any much, is it?' His words became a family phrase.

Reporting to Baker Street, Ayer found, not for the last time, that SOE had no job for him. Rees's 'chance, accident and absurdity', however, came into play again, and he was soon offered a position with an SOE unit in Accra, in what was then the Gold Coast (now Ghana). Against his better judgement, Ayer accepted the position: 'I was so overwhelmed by their recognition that I could be useful to them anywhere that I simply said yes'.[2] Early that summer he set off with 'two second-hand tropical suits, a solar topee, a pair of dark sun glasses, yards of mosquito netting and a trunk full of philosophical books', on a Dutch ship to the African colony.[3] On the way he undertook to re-read Kant's *Critique of Pure Reason*, and, in the early stages of sunstroke, underwent a remarkable epiphany, during which he understood for the first time the full force of Kant's arguments. Unfortunately, once he had recovered from his fever, he was never able to regain the insight. Kant remained, as he always had been for Ayer, something of a closed book.

Judging from Ayer's accounts, his short time in Accra was like a farcical version of his career in New York. He was in the capital just long enough to savour a Saturday dance at the King George V Memorial Hall:

They have a wonderful dance called the High Life, which is jungle music more or less adapted to the ball room, very erotic. Cutting out a ferocious looking quartermaster, I procured a partner of whom I can remember only that she was very black, like artist's umber, a pleonasm of darkness, had thick inhuman hair and a lithe graceful body and was wearing a pair of blue shorts: and I capered around with her like a dervish. I don't think I have ever enjoyed a dance so much.[4]

Otherwise, he did not like what he saw of colonial life. Living conditions were 'a combination of luxury and squalor', the British officers lazy and snobbish. Nevertheless, Ayer was willing, as he explained to the Cummingses, 'to adapt myself to anything if the work justified it', and his real complaint was that it manifestly did not. The original reason for SOE's presence in the Gold Coast had been the supposed need for surveillance of the neighbouring French colonies, the governors of which had stayed loyal to Vichy. But by the summer of 1943 Vichy no longer exercised any sway over the continent, and Ayer found the SOE unit woefully underemployed and dominated by a mood of 'cynical inertia'.[5]

Within three days of arriving he let it be known that he did not think he could be a useful addition to the team and asked for a transfer; according to an SOE report he was 'almost hysterical and rather incoherent' in making the point. The colonel of the unit, who wanted to believe in the importance of what he was doing, was so angered at Ayer's behaviour – 'his whole attitude is one of feeling that the work here is beneath his dignity' – that he immediately lodged a complaint to London and placed him on 'disciplinary recall'.[6] After only nine days in the unit, Ayer was interned in a camp of 'rough, heavy-gambling gold-miners' to await the next ship home. He could well have faced a formal punishment if it had not been for the fact that the colonel was killed while flying back to Britain at the same time as Ayer was making the passage by boat. As it was, he was merely 'mildly reproached' by the authorities at Baker Street and appointed to work on France.[7] If nothing else, the episode showed that, despite Ayer's increased social grace, he had not lost his ability to antagonise his superiors.

The decision to place Ayer in a French section of SOE was much better than the one that sent him to the Gold Coast. He was bilingual, knew France well and loved it. It occupied the place in his affections that was properly due to Switzerland: he felt partly French. More than this, he was moved by the determination and the courage of the Resistance and identified with this sort of warfare; he had been a philosophical and political partisan himself throughout the 1930s.* As in New York, so

* The Resistance, incidentally, provides a good example of what Ayer believed to be the inadequacy of utilitarianism – its inability to do justice to all our moral sentiments. According to utilitarian standards, it would probably have been right to cooperate with the Vichy regime, at least at first. There was little reason to fight for what seemed, in the summer of 1940, a lost cause: the

back in London, Ayer found himself surrounded by familiar faces, including that of Robin Brook, his old schoolfellow, now the supervisor of SOE's French sections. He recalled that Ayer made a request to be sent into France as a secret agent. Perhaps remembering Freddie at Eton, however, Brook seems to have worried about Ayer's capacity to get on with people in situations of extreme stress. He also doubted that he had the physical and technical resources an agent needed.[8] An SOE report from this period describes him as 'intellectually brilliant but, we think, possibly more suited to office work than for leading men in the field'.[9] Instead, Ayer was appointed a political adviser to RF section. Where SOE's F section was responsible for sending British agents into France, RF section had the job of liaising with BCRA (Bureau Centre de Renseigment et d'Action) – De Gaulle's own special operations organisation. It trained and equipped BCRA's agents, arranged their sorties to France and ciphered or deciphered their communications from the field. The Free French were famously jealous of their prerogatives, and would have liked to take charge of all clandestine action on French soil, but they made a virtue of necessity and got on well enough with their SOE counterparts. RF's offices in Dorset Square were just a few minutes from De Gaulle's secret service headquarters behind Selfridges on Oxford Street, and Ayer spent his days walking from one to the other for meetings.

The French had been slow to take to resistance but by the time Ayer joined RF, the movement had mushroomed. The first of the Maquis, the brigades of young men who went into hiding in the hills of southern France, rather than be conscripted to work as slave labourers in Germany, appeared late in 1942. The situation, however, was extremely complex. There were over a dozen major movements from Combat, Liberation and Franc-Tireurs et Partisans on the left, to L'Organisation de Résistance de l'Armée and the Confrérie de Notre Dame on the right. The Communists had different aims and methods from the Gaullists, socialist groups from Catholic ones; there was a secret newspaper for almost every cheese. Six months before Ayer joined RF, Jean Moulin, working under De Gaulle, had succeeded in constructing a common front

---

numbers who resisted at this stage were tiny, their effects were bound to be negligible. Yet, as Ayer pointed out many years later, 'it is they whom we admire' ('The Scope of Reason', *International Institute of Philosophy Proceedings*, 1985, p.275).

of all the political bodies which were organising resistance and the Conseil National de la Résistance had been formed, meeting for the first time in Paris in May. Then, late in June, Moulin was captured and tortured to death, and the entire organisation, created with such pains over many months, fell apart. BCRA and SOE had to start again, but this time the French agreed on a less centralised approach and resistance was henceforth organised through regional military delegates.

It was Ayer's job to try to monitor this state of affairs, assessing the strength, aims, tactics and political allegiances of the various Resistance groups. This information was important to SOE, who were not happy to rely entirely on De Gaulle's version of developments, but was doubtless also passed to the Foreign Office, which was already beginning to worry about what would fill the vacuum left if and when the Nazis were expelled from France. Ayer debriefed agents, and read reports, underground news-sheets and radio messages from the field. Almost as much of his information seems to have come indirectly from the interception of Nazi and Vichy messages, as it did directly from those working for the Resistance.

A long memorandum by Ayer on the history, current condition and future prospects of the French Communist Party and associated groups has survived, in which, among other tasks, he distinguished the 'five communist organisations now known to be operating in France', assessed their strength and analysed their working methods.[10] The report was written in September 1943, the same month that Ayer was at last promoted to captain, and shows that he was a clear-headed judge. While recognising that the Soviet Union, in spite of its egalitarian features, was 'essentially a bureaucratic dictatorship',[11] he acknowledged the achievement of the French Communists who 'for the last 2 years, ... have contributed more than any other single group to the maintenance of active resistance in France'.[12] It is an outstandingly perceptive and incisive report, drawing on a wide range of sources and involving some clever detective work. That Ayer was so good at this type of analysis reminds us that he was an intensely political animal and – not necessarily the same thing – one with a feel for political reality. It helps counter the impression of a certain simple-mindedness that his necessarily more abstract writings on political philosophy might give.

At about this time Ayer was, in fact, working on the first piece of political philosophy he ever published and his first work of philosophy for three years. Called 'The Concept of Freedom', his article appeared in Connolly's *Horizon* in 1944 and represents the distillation of a book on the same subject which (like another on the concept of time) 'refuses to take shape'.[13]

By this stage in the war an Allied victory seemed more or less certain. Perhaps with this in mind, Ayer began by warning against confusing national freedom, 'the elimination of foreign rulers', with individual freedom, before arguing a number of points about the second. Predictably, he first rejected any theory like Rousseau's or Hegel's which made freedom dependent on obedience to a higher moral or political authority. However, he refused the most simple liberal alternative, that of crude 'negative freedom', according to which freedom of the individual is to be measured solely in terms of 'his power to do what he himself actually wills'.[14] As he argued, there are two other criteria that apply to the assessment of an individual's liberty. In the first place, we tend to consider the extent of an agent's field of choice. It is not enough that someone has everything he wants. It also matters that he should have rich, developed wants: 'It is by this criterion that most social and economic, as opposed to penal, legislation is judged to be productive of freedom; for by raising people's standards of living and improving their education, it serves to widen their field of choice'. Secondly, we take into account the provenance of a person's desires: 'The ideal of freedom which [this] presupposes is that a man's choice must depend as little as possible upon external factors, including the will of others, and as much as possible upon himself'.[15] So we deny that someone is free if all his desires and beliefs are the product of a totalitarian education, hypnosis or brainwashing.

'The Concept of Freedom' thus sketched a rich and sophisticated version of liberal freedom. The problem was, as Ayer felt obliged to admit at the end of his article, this conception was open to one troubling objection. According to the third criterion he had identified, that of provenance, it was right to say that a person who has been programmed to make certain choices is not truly free. Yet, or so Ayer contended, there is no reason to think that our own haphazard upbringing and education do not determine us in much the same way – at least, 'it is hard to see how any choice can fail to be somewhat conditioned' by circumstances outside one's control.[16] To be consistent then, we should accept that there is no difference between the freedom of the subjects of a scientifically planned society and our own. Ayer was here wrestling with the old challenge of determinism – the worry that if we trace reasons for our actions far enough back we will eventually reach factors in childhood or beyond for which we can hardly be held accountable. For someone, however, who prided himself on being resolute and hard-headed, Ayer's response to this challenge was strangely uncertain. While admitting that he could not live without the conventional, if illogical, conception of freedom, he went on matter-of-factly to suggest that perhaps one day, as people come to confront its illogicality, they will learn to embrace 'the advantages of a planned society'. Ayer would later regret this suggestion, but doubts about the tenability of our conception of freedom would trouble him for the rest of his life.

In March 1944, three months before the Normandy landings, Ayer was sent to Algiers, where De Gaulle's government in exile was now located. SOE was also there, running a large operation from typically luxurious headquarters, Club des Pins, a group of holiday villas in a secluded area about fifteen miles west of the capital. Driving to and from Algiers, Ayer and his colleagues enjoyed the heart-lifting sight of the Baie d'Alger full of Allied craft, assembling for the assault on France. The representatives of SOE were busy assembling dozens of three-man teams, known as Jedburghs, to be sent into France with the aim of organising internal uprisings to coincide with the invasion from the south. Ayer, though, seems to have devoted as much time to reporting on the political developments in Algiers, where De Gaulle was in the process of coming to an understanding with the Communists, as he did to analysing developments in France itself.

To improve his standing with the Free French, he was appointed a local major and given a handsome sea-view flat. As was his habit, Ayer found ways of combining his work with social life, and enjoyed wining and dining French officers and politicians. With victory now firmly in sight, he had lost most of the martial bearing that had been drummed into him at Caterham. The commander of the SOE in Algeria, Colonel Douglas Dodds-Parker, remembered meeting 'an odd-looking individual dressed in shorts, shirt and sandals' whom he took to be 'one of the

Spanish Communists, proud to wear a British Uniform'. A professional soldier and future Conservative MP, Dodds-Parker was shocked to discover that this unmilitary figure 'claimed membership of a famous Guards Regiment'.[17] As in Accra and possibly New York, Ayer had managed to make an enemy of his commander.

Not everyone, however, found Ayer's arrival so unwelcome. He made lifelong friends with the second in command, Brooks Richards, a young naval officer, and his assistant Barley Alison, 'a small, dark, intelligent, vivacious girl', later to go on to a distinguished career in publishing, who like the other women working in this branch of SOE, was misleadingly enrolled in the 'First Aid Nursing Yeomanry'.[18] According to Richards, Ayer had the 'job of going through the secret mail which came from the Resistance in France and which we had to pass on, so Freddie only had an hour or two to read it and write reports on it. It mainly contained political rather than operational material. All the reports were extremely good – in fact brilliant'.[19]

After an unhappy two-month interlude in London, 'marking, sorting and tearing up pieces of paper like a man on a conveyor belt', Ayer returned to Algeria in the middle of July, 'on a nebulous mission which I had invented for myself'.[20] He spent a month 'loafing in the sunshine – profitless, sultry days but memorable romantic evenings on the balcony of my flat with – of all things – toads for an orchestra'.[21] Algiers was now humming with preparations for the reconquest, and Ayer hoped to follow the troops over the beaches of the Riviera. Dodds-Parker, however, had other ideas. Dismayed to find Ayer back under his command, he put him out to graze in a beautiful villa in Ravello near Naples, from where part of the assault was being mounted. Disobeying the spirit if not the letter of his orders, Ayer got to France anyway, determinedly hitching a plane to Algiers and another from there to St Tropez, arriving a week or two after the first mid-August landings.

Ayer now persuaded Brooks Richards, established at a temporary general headquarters south of Lyon, to give him a roving commission as a political observer. For the first time in the war, Ayer found himself in the sort of situation he liked best, in charge of a small group, using his own initiative, with no superiors to tell him what to do. It was like being chairman of his local Labour party all over again, only in a rather more dramatic situation. His sense of adventure aroused, he disappeared in a

Bugatti with a burly peasant driver from the Corrèze, a bodyguard and a wireless operator – Major Ayer's own private army – to make a tour of south-west France. This was an extraordinary time to be travelling through the region. Hitler's troops had retreated without much of a fight but an array of armed Resistance groups, many of them communists, now vied to fill the vacuum they had left behind. Even with their official car, uniforms and *laissez-passer*, Ayer and his party were constantly stopped and searched by self-appointed 'committees of public safety' or representatives of rivalrous local warlords. Ayer enjoyed watching and occasionally intervening as events unravelled, introducing himself to the fighters whose movements he had tracked in London and Algiers, or simply gleaning what he could from ordinary Frenchmen in shops and bars. He still found time, however, to throw himself into the great *débauche de fraternité* – the wave of drinking, dancing and lovemaking – that was sweeping through France.

Ayer went first to Marseilles, which had been terribly damaged by Allied and German bombs, and then made his way to Toulouse. 'The journey was slow,' he reported, 'because of the number of roads and bridges that had been blown up but immensely pleasurable. We stopped at Nimes and Avignon and Montpellier, visited the Pont du Gard and discovered a lovely fishing village whose name I forget, where we ate dozens and dozens of oysters and mussels, washed down with a harsh white wine.'[22] Toulouse and the area around it were particularly unsettled, with rival Resistance groups and De Gaulle's newly established administration struggling for control. In the middle of September, De Gaulle went on a tour of the southern cities – Lyons, Marseilles, Toulouse, Bordeaux – in an attempt to establish some sort of order. Ayer was there when the French leader arrived in Toulouse and, having become friendly with the civilian prefect appointed by De Gaulle, Pierre Bertaux, he managed to join the official party, standing on the balcony beside the General, while he made his triumphal speech. Ayer, who was anyway disposed to identify with the Resistance groups rather than De Gaulle, disapproved of the grudging, heavy-handed way in which he attempted to impose his authority. The General went so far as to expel George Starr, a heroic Resistance leader, from France, on the grounds that he was English. Nevertheless, when De Gaulle moved on to Bordeaux, Ayer, who followed him, did his best to dissuade his contacts in the Resistance from kidnapping him and later claimed that he had 'saved his bacon'.[23]

The journey from Toulouse to Bordeaux had taken longer than expected, because, as Ayer explained to Cummings, 'we were so much feted on the way ... You see in this area, and still more as one went further West, they had seen practically no British officers since 1940, in some places we were in fact the very first – and though we had done no liberating ourselves. ... we were treated as if we had, which was always pleasant, often embarrassing, sometimes touching'.[24] After retracing his steps to Toulouse, Ayer met a 'very nice' major he had known in Algiers, and together they led a procession of two Bugattis, a large army truck, and an odd gang of civilians and soldiers, to Paris. 'We went up through Brives to Limoges, over what is perhaps the loveliest stretch of country in France, then to Chateauroux across to Montargis, because the direct road was still cut, and so to Paris by Fontainebleau,' he wrote at the time. 'We took several days over it because the truck was slow and all three vehicles broke down, but they were days well spent. We finally reached Paris towards the evening of a fine autumn day and found it looking exquisitely beautiful.'[25]

Ayer and his outfit arrived in Paris less than a month after it had been liberated, when its streets were still scattered with the remains of the barricades – railings, paving stones, plane trees – that Parisians had erected in the last days of Nazi occupation. With the storm over, the city had a strange air of calm. By now Duff Cooper and his beautiful wife Diana were established in the British Embassy building on rue du Faubourg Saint-Honoré, which was fast on the way to becoming a fashionable social and literary centre. While doing his best to seduce Martha Gellhorn at an embassy reception, Ayer was seized by a sharp pain and had to take to bed for a week. 'A silly Army doctor' diagnosed gall trouble, but it turned out to be 'nothing but excess of eating and drinking'.[26]

In October, having written a report on what he had seen in the south-west which Duff Cooper found 'excellent', Ayer headed off again for Toulouse, passing through Nevers, Lyons and Avignon.[27] From Toulouse he and a colleague went in plain clothes to Andorra to investigate rumours that German sympathisers were taking refuge in the mountain state. While he was there, one of his retinue disappeared and Ayer realised that he had helped a collaborator escape.

Many of the leading Resistance figures in the south-west were Spanish Republicans who had fought against Franco's Nationalists and taken refuge in France. Ayer's friend Pierre Bertaux asked one fighter how long he had been in the Resistance and was surprised by the answer: 'Since '36. I was at Guadalajara'. Here more than anywhere, Ayer too was in a battle he had been fighting for nearly a decade. Understandably, the Spanish soldiers hoped that the overthrow of Hitler and Mussolini would be followed by an attack on Franco's government and looked to the Allies for assistance. As Ayer recalled, 'I was naturally sympathetic to their aims, but was not sure how far my superiors would approve of my becoming involved in their plans. I therefore made use of my wireless operator to send a message to Baker Street asking for instructions'.[28] Ayer had been in France for over six weeks without ever once reporting to his superiors in London, with the result that having now at last made contact, he was immediately ordered back home – in fact a message was sent out to all SOE officers in the area, demanding that he be detained on encounter and dispatched to London. He returned to Paris at the end of October, and, after one last night of wild revels, stayed up until dawn writing a report in which, by somewhat over-dramatising the situation around Toulouse, he attempted to justify his conduct, and then, red-eyed, caught a plane to England. 'I was a little afraid that I should find myself in trouble when I got back to London,' Ayer admitted to Cummings, 'but my work was thought to have been good enough, if largely unauthorised.'[29]

Freddie was delighted to be back in contact with Valerie and Julian, who were living with Renée in Hampstead and attending 'one of those very pleasant but rather absurd' progressive schools, where children 'are encouraged to do things in groups and to express themselves by doing handicrafts. This is all right for Valerie, who has immense social talents ... but Julian is too much of an individualist to enjoy doing things in groups and his way of expressing himself is to knock things over rather than assemble them. I sympathise with him on both counts'.[30] He was a good deal less happy, however, about finding himself behind a desk again. Initially SOE toyed with making him head of a French section. But in the end he was sequestered by the Foreign Office, or more specifically its

Secret Intelligence Service, SIS, or MI6, where he worked mainly analysing reports that came in from France.

After three months in London, Ayer received notice that he was going to be transferred to the British Embassy in Paris. Duff Cooper had worked with Brooks Richards and Barley Alison in Algeria, and after taking up residence in Paris, quickly appointed them to his intelligence section. They in turn had worked with Ayer and were keen to have access to his expertise. The embassy, indeed, had written to SOE as early as October that the ambassador was 'extremely anxious to have Ayer back in France ... he is regarded as a first class political observer'.[31]

As for Ayer himself, for as long as he was going to have to wear a uniform, he would rather wear it in Paris than anywhere else. Yet as he made clear the following February in a letter to G.E. Moore, he had had enough of wearing a uniform at all:

It seems a very long time since I last saw you. In the course of the last five years I have been successively a soldier in England, a British government official in the United States, an apprentice commando in Canada, a civil servant in the Gold Coast, a staff officer in London, a political observer in North Africa, a tourist in Italy and a liaison officer in the invasion of Southern France; and I am leaving at day break tomorrow to become a diplomat in Paris. What I want, and have long wanted, is to return to Oxford and be a philosopher, but I am not finding it easy to get myself released.[32]

13

The Meaning of Life

Life in Paris remained hard during the months after its liberation. Food, fuel and clothes were in short supply. Parks and squares were haunted by the memories of family and friends killed in the war. Shrunken, hollow-eyed survivors of Hitler's prison camps hobbled through the streets. Diplomats like Ayer, however, were well provided for, and even for those who were not so lucky there were compensations. Spring had begun beautifully, with chestnut blossom, wistaria and lilacs out early, and on the night of 7 May 1945, a month after Ayer arrived, on the day after the Germans finally surrendered, Paris's great fountains and monuments were lit up for the first time since the outbreak of war. Liberation had brought a free press and in October free elections. Ayer watched with satisfaction as senior Vichy officials, including Pétain himself, now half senile, were brought to trial. It was a good time to be an English-speaking foreigner in the city. American slang, clothes and music took on an unrivalled prestige, as jazz clubs, banned by the Germans, mushroomed around Saint-Germain-des-Prés. English artists and writers were fêted. Everywhere Ayer went he found the same extraordinary thing: Parisians touched with warmth and generosity.

Ayer was very vague about what his 'Special Duties' for the War Office involved. He wore his officer's uniform, was described simply as a 'political attaché' and sat in on Duff Cooper's weekly staff meetings. But it is almost certain that he was now employed by the Special Intelligence

Service, although still doing the sort of work he had always done as analytical philosopher turned political analyst. This was delicate work: the British were worried about the possibility of a Communist coup, and the SIS kept a close eye on developments, maintaining secret contacts made during the war and developing others. Ayer, though, was more likely to be damping down fears than stirring them up; he doubted the will of the French Communist Party, and events proved him right.

After returning from New York to London, Ayer had continued to see Guy de Rothschild, the handsome and dynamic young heir to the Rothschild fortune, who was later to run the French branch of the bank. In his autobiography, Rothschild described a lunch in May of 1944, when he had bet Ayer that Paris would be liberated within a month.[1] Ayer lost the wager, but now that the city was free, Rothschild lent him his palatial home in Avenue Foch, complete with a butler, cook and well stocked wine cellar. His father, Jules, would have been delighted at this re-establishment of relations between the Ayers and his old employers. Later Ayer moved to the hôtel Castiglione, which the British Embassy had occupied. What with meals at Maxim's, commandeered as a British officers' club, parties at the embassy, hosted by Diana Cooper, and his own dinner parties chez Rothschild, Freddie was leading a glamorous life. 'As I had no work to do, and plenty of government money to spend, I had a pretty good time,' he wrote to Marion and E.E. Cummings at the end of his six months in the city. 'I have never seen Paris look so beautiful and got to know it as I never have before, discovered out of the way restaurants ... learnt to speak French really rather well, learnt something about modern French literature, saw some very good films, drank everything I could lay my hands on and saw Renoir's "Moulin de la Galette", which had been restored to the Louvre.'[2] The painting, of ordinary Parisians enjoying an outdoor dance beneath the soft sparkle of Chinese lanterns, embodied much of what Ayer loved in the French: their sensuality, elegance and joie de vivre. It was his favourite work of visual art.

There was the usual round of friends and girlfriends. Early on in his stay, Paul Willert, an art collector and a friend of the Penroses whom Ayer had got to know in London, introduced him to Nicole Bouchet de Fareins and her younger sister, Francette Drin. In their twenties and from a well-to-do Normandy family, they had played a brave part in the

Resistance, hiding English and French fighters in their Normandy farmhouse. Francette's husband had been tortured and killed by the Germans. They were left-wing, literary and well connected, with an earthy French toughness of manner. Ayer went out with Nicole, and remained lifelong friends with them both, though Francette at least felt that he was never better than when she first knew him: 'He was alert and curious about everything and thoughtful about other people – he would bring eggs to people who could not get them. He made a big sensation. Later he became much more insular'.[3] Through Francette, Freddie met Camus, then as famous as a Resistance journalist as he was as an author, and the philosopher Maurice Merleau-Ponty, although never Sartre. (Later, after Ayer had written some unfavourable articles on Sartre's work, a meeting was mooted, but Sartre responded, 'Ayer est un con.'[4]) Ayer welcomed the chance to meet his old hero André Malraux at a dinner party organised by Nicole and Francette. The leading role Malraux played in the liberation of Toulouse only increased Ayer's admiration. But unfortunately when they were introduced, something in Malraux's manner combined with a shyness in Ayer to make him almost tongue-tied.[5]

There were certain similarities between Malraux and another writer whom Ayer also met at this time, George Orwell, who was in Paris as a foreign correspondent for the *Observer*. Both men were individualists and each combined radical sympathies with the conservative values of patriotism, self-reliance and discipline in action. But where Ayer had been too shy to befriend Malraux, he got on well with Orwell, who shared his devotion to Kipling and Dickens, and they were often together. Ayer was proud of their friendship – 'He was another of those whose liking for me made me think better of myself' – and so was Orwell, who dropped Ayer's name to an old Eton master, Andrew Gow.[6]

There were also older English and American friends staying or passing through, including Tony Bower, dressed as an American soldier, Lee Miller, in the uniform of a war correspondent, and Philip Toynbee, who despite a career of drunken ill-discipline, had escaped more or less unpunished and was now dubiously employed as an officer in the Intelligence Corps. In July Cyril Connolly wrote to his girlfriend Lys Lubbock, that he had been night-clubbing in Paris with Freddie, Stuart Hampshire and Solly Zuckerman and all had 'got absolutely plastered'.[7]

Alistair Forbes, a young well-connected Boston journalist living at the embassy, remembered a picnic on the Seine with Freddie and Barley Alison. Freddie spotted an old fashioned salad-drier floating down the river, managed to catch it and used it as a wine cooler. 'He would sometimes surprise you like that. He was resourceful'.*

In the first months of his stay in Paris, Ayer spent most of his time 'with a French girl of Turkish origin, whom I got to know in Algiers', and in the last month began an affair with Isabel Delmer (born Nicholas) the estranged wife of a journalist and wartime propagandist, Sefton Delmer.[8] She had lived in Paris before the war, and now introduced Ayer to many of the leading figures of the burgeoning left-bank scene, including Georges Bataille, Michel Leiris, Tristan Tzara, René Leibowitz and Alberto Giacometti. Isabel Delmer was one of those people whose life weaves together an extraordinary range of circles – musical, literary, artistic and, in this case, philosophical. After divorcing Sefton, she married the composer and conductor Constant Lambert and then another composer, Alan Rawsthorne. Two years younger than Ayer, she trained as a painter, although she was to become best known as an artist's muse and model. She had a child with Jacob Epstein, and a long love affair with Giacometti. Francis Bacon painted her often, and there is a portrait in the Fitzwilliam Museum by André Derain. Giacometti called one of his sculptures of her 'The Egyptian', and with her narrow eyes, high cheekbones, arched eyebrows and full lips, it is not hard to see why. Ayer liked her infectious vivacity and was not put off by her drinking – in fact she introduced him to many of the all-night bars and restaurants around Les Halles.

At the end of one long evening, Ayer found himself sitting with Isabel and Giacometti at Le Sphinx, a well known café and brothel, when 'a young man who was making a disturbance by the doorway, started brandishing a revolver'. Ayer, emboldened by alcohol, attempted to disarm him and, after a scuffle, persuaded him to put away the weapon.

* Forbes had first met Ayer in Algiers, through Barley Alison. Later they were in London, during the last of the bombs – the V1 and V2 attacks. Forbes was going through 'a Christian stage' at the time. He and Ayer were in a taxi one evening, driving under Admiralty Arch into Trafalgar Square, when a raid began. Freddie started taunting him: 'This is the end, there is nothing more to it, you'll never meet your God.' It was too much for Forbes, who jumped out of the taxi 'like a debutante who had been interfered with' (Alistair Forbes, IWA, 2 September 1996).

Although Ayer was 'rather pleased' with himself, Giacometti 'saw nothing in my behaviour but a foolish act of bravado' and in the light of sober dawn, Ayer had to admit he was right.[9] He does not record what Isabel thought of his conduct although it did not seem to affect their friendship. Ayer wrote to Cummings about 'an idyllic' week they spent in the Loire before he left France – 'the sort of thing that George Moore wrote about, although I don't believe it ever really happened to him'.[10]

Ayer found himself in a city where extraordinary things were going on. 'To be twenty or twenty-five in September 1944,' wrote Simone de Beauvoir, 'seemed a great stroke of good luck: all roads opened up. Journalists, writers, budding film-makers, discussed, planned, made decisions with passion, as if their future depended only on them.'[11] It was as if the departure of the Nazis had lifted some invisible floodgates on a lake of pent-up creative energy, as Giacometti, Artaud, Genet, Dubuffet, Wols, Beckett and others poured out revolutionary new work. Existentialism, in particular, was well on its way to becoming almost a byword for philosophy. Sartre's lecture of October, 'Existentialism: Is it a Humanism?', was so crowded that the box office was flattened and men and women fainted in the crush. TOO MANY ATTEND SARTRE LECTURE. HEAT, FAINTING SPELLS, POLICE. LAWRENCE OF ARABIA AN EXISTENTIALIST, screamed a headline in *Combat*.[12] Ayer stood near the centre of this scene and met most of its leading actors, but his position was very different to what it had been in a comparable situation in Vienna thirteen years before. Now he was a critic, not a partisan.

Guy de Rothschild recalled that Ayer worked hard to master existentialism – 'It didn't come easy' – yet the essays and reviews he produced on Sartre and Camus around this time are a model of their kind; lucid, judicious and engaged, they make uncomfortable reading for those who say that the analytic philosophers of Ayer's generation were parochial.[13] Existentialism, the 'French school', was to be enormously influential in Britain over the next two decades, though less in philosophy departments than among intellectuals, novelists and critics. Ayer's own study of the movement thus gave him a certain authority, although one he generally exercised to negative effect.[14]

As already suggested, Ayer agreed with the existentialists in what was most fundamental in their ethic:

It is one of Sartre's merits that he sees that no system of values can be binding on anyone unless he chooses to make it so. I may indeed look to some authority to tell me what I ought to do, but then my decision consists in acknowledging that authority. The authority has the characteristics that it has; if they were different perhaps I should not give it my allegiance; but the possession of these characteristics does not in itself constitute it an authority either for me or for anyone else. Whatever my motives, and they may be various, it becomes an authority for me only through my acceptance of it.[15]

Moreover, he claimed to find much in the existentialists' psychology and moral code that was convincing and attractive. He acknowledged, for instance, that Sartre's analysis of man's endemic *mauvaise foi* – his addiction to playing at being what he is not – was 'often very penetrating', and he likened Camus's 'Cyrenaicism', his insistence 'on getting the most out of life', to that of his own undergraduate hero, Walter Pater – 'Not the fruit of experience, but experience itself is the end' – and admitted to finding this code 'to some degree persuasive'.[16]

Nevertheless, whatever the merits of existentialism as an attitude to life, Ayer insisted that as a philosophy, it 'displayed a startling indifference to logic'.[17] Ayer's first *Horizon* essay, a long and valiantly patient analysis of Sartre's *Being and Nothingness*, set the tone for his other writings:

[Sartre's] metaphysical pessimism, which is well in the existentialist tradition, is no doubt appropriate for our time, but I do not think it is logically well founded. In particular Sartre's reasoning on the subject of *le néant* [his belief that every state of consciousness is necessarily separated from itself by 'nothing'] seems to me exactly on a par with that of the king in 'Alice through the looking-glass'. 'I see nobody on the road,' said Alice. 'I only wish that I had such eyes,' remarked the king . . . Whatever may be the effective value of these statements, I cannot but think that they are literally nonsensical.[18]

Indeed, even in the elaboration of their moral code, where Ayer was most inclined to sympathise with them, the existentialists showed a maddening muddle-headedness. Camus offered an example. The central feature of his philosophy, at least as presented in *The Myth of Sisyphus*, was its emphasis on the absurdity of the human condition, and an important element of the absurdity, according to Camus, lay in the fact that life was ultimately 'meaningless'. Now Ayer affirmed that while life gains meaning from the ends individuals give it, 'ultimate' ends at least were not capable of justification, and if that was what Camus meant by life being 'meaningless', then he agreed with him. Where Camus went wrong, according to Ayer, was in supposing that things could somehow have been otherwise – that life might have had some transcendent purpose independent of the purpose we give it, that the universe might have been 'rational'. In effect, Camus, and the other existentialists along with him, had mistaken what is a logical necessity – the absence of transcendent meanings – for an empirical disaster.*

The existentialists' logical mistakes had, Ayer thought, a distorting effect on their moral code. For having insisted on the absurdity, emptiness and meaninglessness of life, they commended an ethic of heroic defiance. Ayer, seeing no tragedy, could not see the need for heroism. Indeed, he found the existentialists' *refus continuel*, their brave commendation of 'a total absence of hope', 'gratuitous', even 'melodramatic'. On Ayer's account, life supplied its own reasons for living – reasons, of course, that varied from culture to culture and person to person. As a hedonistic utilitarian, Ayer found justification enough in the pleasures of life, and the good one could do in making those pleasures available to others. If, on the other hand, life genuinely proved as pointless and wretched as Camus liked to claim, there was every reason to end rather than 'defy' it. In contrast to Camus, Ayer believed that suicide was, in some circumstances, an entirely honourable response to life's travails; the view that it was somehow immoral was a relic of a cruel religious ethic.

In October, Ayer was officially demobilised with the honorary rank of captain and a very hard-wearing civilian suit. Back in London, in many

---

* Ayer always refused to make a drama out of the truth in moral subjectivism. This was an important feature of his thought, one which distinguished him not just from the existentialists but from Russell as well. Like the existentialists, Russell was committed to something like emotivism on intellectual grounds but found it emotionally repugnant. Ayer never did.

ways more depressed than Paris, with weeds growing in the ruins of bombed-out buildings and cars and buses 'the most antique things in the world', Ayer thought seriously of trying to stand for parliament – of becoming 'a commissar', in Cummings's idiolect.[19] Philosophy, though, won out. Christ Church, inhospitable to the end, let it be known that although there was a place for a philosopher (Ryle having been elevated to the Chair of Metaphysics) they were not inclined to give it to Ayer. Fortunately, Maurice Bowra, now Warden of Wadham, had already offered him a position at the college and Ayer took up his new posting as a tutorial fellow and dean at the beginning of the autumn term, 1945.

Bowra was pleased to have Ayer in the nest, writing to Berlin in November, 'Freddie is very gay. He brings countless guests to hall, which is quite unusual, where none of us have any friends alive, and he enlivens us'.[20] Yet by his standards, Ayer was living very quietly indeed. 'In time,' he wrote to the Cummingses, 'I dare say I shall feel stifled, and make some violent outbreak, but for the moment it suits me very well.'[21] Renée, ever the fixer, came up to decorate his rooms. After a distinguished career in military intelligence, deciphering encoded German signals traffic, Hampshire was working for Philip Noel-Baker at the Foreign Office and Listowel had a position in the new Labour government, so 'Renée', Ayer observed, 'is virtually running the country'.[22] 'I have often thought, and she also, I think,' he confessed later in the year, 'that we might go back to each other, but there has never been a moment at which it seemed wholly feasible.'[23]

Little philosophy of note had come out of Oxford during the war, but Ayer marked that the climate had nonetheless changed; before the conflict he had been the leader of the avant-garde; now the brighter students and the young dons looked on logical positivism as old hat. He had mysteriously passed 'from being a young Turk to being, at the age of thirty-five, almost an elder statesman, without ever having known the plenitude of office.'[24] The young philosopher David Pears, however, recalled that a series of lectures Ayer gave on his favourite topic of perception during this year was extremely popular: 'He had great difficulty getting started, but he would accelerate as the lecture went on – by the end he was at full throttle'.[25] He and John Austin, fresh from a brilliant war in intelligence, where he established himself as the unrivalled authority on enemy forces in occupied France and Belgium, attempted to renew their old discussion group with a younger circle but the synergy had gone. In the summer of 1947, Austin gave the first of his lecture series, later published as *Sense and Sensibilia*, attacking Ayer's sense-data doctrines.

Ayer, however, was finding new outlets for his energies in a series of essays for London literary and arts magazines. In addition to the essays on Sartre and Camus which appeared in *Horizon*, he began writing for *Polemic*, an elegant new quarterly edited by an ex-communist, Humphrey Slater. The first edition, in the new year of 1946, featured an essay on 'Deistic Fallacies', and later numbers included an article on free will, 'Freedom and Necessity' – one of Ayer's most frequently cited and reprinted papers – and another on 'The Claims of Philosophy', first delivered as a lecture late in 1946 to an inaugural Unesco conference. Diverse as they are in subject, all these articles revolve around the big moral questions – the purposes of philosophy, the nature of freedom, the meaning of life – and in their audience and approach are quite different from anything Ayer had written before the war. Like French existentialism, they represented a response to a thirst among the war's survivors for an articulation of the most basic principles of the new world order.

The central concern running through most of these essays is to circumscribe philosophy's domain – to restrain its pretensions. Ayer found himself, not for the last time, in the ironic position of denying in public that philosophy could ever have much of a public role. 'The Claims of Philosophy' opens with a distinction between the metaphysically minded 'pontiff' and the analytical 'journeyman'. The pontiff sees it as his job to 'compete with natural science': to offer an alternative vision of reality. To the Unesco audience Ayer offered a scathing denigration of modern metaphysics – albeit as embodied in the Nazi Heidegger, rather than Sartre or Merleau-Ponty. In traditional form, as represented by Hegel, metaphysics at least tried to compete with science by out-reasoning it: 'Few men, indeed, can ever have reasoned worse than Hegel, the arch-pontiff of the nineteenth century, but at least he claimed the support of reason for his fantasies'. Heidegger, on the other hand, forced to recognise that science has a monopoly on reason, has come to decry it. His arguments have 'ceased to be, in any ordinary sense, a vehicle for knowledge'.[26]

In opposition to the pontiffs, Ayer argued that philosophy consisted of nothing more than logical analysis. The philosopher's proper role was that of Locke's 'under-labourer', sorting out conceptual problems. This conception is well illustrated by the essay on deism written for the first edition of *Polemic*, where Ayer sets aside empirical questions about the authenticity of the Bible, in favour of an examination of those genuinely philosophical arguments which claim that the universe must, as a matter of logic, have had a creator. Ayer in fact denied, in true positivist fashion, that any sense could be made of an entity existing outside space and time, on the grounds that 'in being made to transcend time, it loses all possibility of being, even in principle, accessible to our experience'.[27] But even if the existence of such a being was intelligible, deistic arguments for its existence plainly were not. The suggestion, for instance, that God must have caused the universe, on the grounds that all things must have a cause, only begs the question of what then caused God, while the 'argument from design', rather than proving the existence of God, presupposes it.

The sharp distinction on which these arguments rest between conceptual and empirical inquiry, is familiar from Ayer's earlier writings; what is new is Ayer's insistence on another point, implicit in the sixth chapter of *Language, Truth and Logic*, but now articulated for the first time. In almost all of these essays and reviews, Ayer underscores the point that philosophy cannot serve as a source of values or a guide to life. Philosophy was quite incapable of offering an authoritative answer to the question 'How should I live?'

Put negatively, Ayer was arguing for Hume's 'is–ought' gap: 'the fact that something is what it is does not by any means entail that it is what it ought to be: nor does the fact that something is considered valuable by any means entail that it exists'.[28] We can have knowledge of empirical truths and of the truisms of maths and logic, but not of values. Put positively, Ayer argued that our morality was ultimately up to us. 'The question of how men ought to live is one to which there is no authoritative answer.' 'The purpose of a man's existence is constituted by the ends to which he, consciously or unconsciously, devotes himself.' It followed, Ayer argued, now again sounding very existentialist, that 'in the last resort, each individual has the responsibility of choice; and it is a responsibility that is not to be escaped'.* This way of putting it is, in fact, not altogether warranted by Ayer's position – to argue from the existence of a fact–value distinction to the obligation to take responsibility for our actions is to violate the fact–value distinction. That Ayer should have argued in this way, however, indicates both his affinities with the existentialist ethic of individual responsibility and the difficulties he found, even when denying that philosophy had anything to say about the way people should live, in not playing the philosophical moralist. It was a tension that was to run throughout his career.

Richard Wollheim, later to become a friend and a colleague, first met Ayer in Oxford in the first half of 1946 and has left a memorable description of the encounter. Wollheim, reading history at Balliol, had called on the Oxford home of Phyllis Young, a woman of about Freddie's age, a glamorous modern painter who before the war had been married to Freddie's friend, the biologist J.Z. Young. There in Young's all-white sitting-room – white walls, white sofas, white lilacs – he found a stranger who, he quickly realised, was no ordinary person.

> He was in his late thirties, not tall, with dark wavy hair, parted near the centre of his head, which from time to time he combed back – combed back rather than brushed back – with his fingers. He was very delicate looking, slightly swarthy, with very hooded brown eyes, and the general Modigliani cast of his face was enhanced by the two upper front teeth being slightly longer than the others ... But it was the movement, the constant movement, of head, hands, fingers, hair – the playing with the watch-chain, one bit rubbed against another, the feet going backwards, forwards, shuffling, tapping, turning on his heel and *sotto voce* a stream of 'Yes, yes, yes' – it was this incessant movement, this constant stream of excitement, that so impressed me.

Wollheim conjectured that this remarkable stranger was the dancer Frederick Ashton, the principal choreographer of the Royal Ballet. (Ayer

---

* Compare this to Sartre's argument that 'existentialism's first move is to make every man aware of what he is and to make the full responsibility of his existence rest on him' (*Existentialism is a Humanism*, London, 1973, p.36).

would have been flattered, although he would rather have been mistaken for Fred Astaire.) The trio sat and talked for half an hour or so, after which Ayer made to go and Wollheim 'followed him into the night air and down the two steep steps on to the pavement, when suddenly with a daring balletic movement he leapt round me, jumped back into the house, and slammed the door behind him. I was confirmed in my misunderstanding'.[29]

Ayer was certainly attracted to Young, but he also had other interests. A repercussion of Ayer's connection with *Polemic* was the beginning of a relationship with Celia Paget, one of the two beautiful, cultivated, and much-photographed Paget twins and leading débutantes of the 1930s. Born six years after Freddie and orphaned at a young age, they had been educated at an English boarding-school and in Lausanne and spoke French and German fluently. One acquaintance, the writer Eleanor Perenyi, who met the twins in a German *pension* in Bavaria in 1938, described them as the two most attractive women she had ever known.[30] Back in London in 1936, they became friendly with Cyril Connolly, Stephen Spender and others in the *Horizon* circle. The twins, frail and keen, had an almost telepathic understanding of one another, and shared the same tastes in almost everything.

Celia, small and delicate, with an open, unaffected manner, had married a journalist before the war, but the relationship had broken down, and when she met Ayer early in 1946, she was working on *Polemic* as an assistant to Humphrey Slater. She and George Orwell, who wrote some of his best essays for *Polemic*, had become close friends, although she refused his offers of marriage. Her sister, Mamaine lived with Arthur Koestler, and the two couples – Mamaine and Koestler, Celia and Ayer – spent the Easter of 1946 together in Koestler's house in Wales, while Ayer paid court to Bertrand Russell who lived nearby. However, Koestler, a former communist turned seer, seeking to build a new 'philosophy' integrating religion and science on a high plane, and Ayer, the arch sceptic, were naturally wary of each other. Perhaps Ayer was referring to this Welsh weekend when he wrote in 1982 that 'Many years ago, Koestler told me that he aspired to become "The Darwin of the 20th century". I did not laugh at him then and do not now. Nevertheless I think he showed a lack of self-knowledge. He has proved himself a man of exceptional gifts, but his mind has displayed a religious rather than a scientific bent'.[31]

Ayer and Celia had first met in February 1946, in the offices of *Polemic*, and Ayer immediately asked her and Slater to Oxford for the weekend. Soon after, he and Celia began an affair which ran for about a year. Celia, perhaps too proud and not quite single-minded enough to capture Ayer, found him 'perfidious in the extreme' when it came to women but in other respects 'very honourable'.

> Freddie Ayer was a man in whom intellect and the senses were unusually highly developed at the expense of the faculties of feeling and intuition. In these two he was very deficient, as indeed he realised himself: only a few days after I first met him he told me he was 'a hollow man'. He genuinely loved his children and perhaps he may have felt real affection for a few close friends, but my own experience indicates that towards others, even towards some friends of long standing, though he was subject to sudden bursts of affection when he felt particularly happy and in good form, on the whole he was completely indifferent and would not go a step out of his way – would not even cross the floor at a party – to see them.[32]

Freddie and Celia's relationship, however, was quickly complicated by Freddie getting involved in a tangled romantic intrigue – 'the violent out-break' he had half anticipated in his letter to Cummings. While seeing Celia at the weekends in London, Ayer began a weekday affair with an intelligent young Oxford undergraduate, Penelope. Then, during the Easter vacation, he took a two-week holiday in Paris. There he met yet another woman, Countess Patricia de Bendern, the aristocratic, alluring, mercurial wife of John de Bendern, a dashing golfing champion, who worked under Duff Cooper at the embassy. She had been born Lady Patricia Douglas, her mother was a comedy actress, her father Francis Queensberry, an impoverished aristocrat and nephew to 'Bosie', Oscar Wilde's *jeune homme fatal*. As so often, the descriptions that survive are mainly physical: she grew up wildly beautiful, 'with marvellous deep blue eyes set in a rather mischievous *gamine* face beneath soft-brown hair'. When Cecil Beaton first saw her, at a ball in 'a meagre dress of pleated white chiffon, her hair straight as a page boy's', he took her as 'a creation of the moonlight'. There was a serious, questing side to her – she would end a disciple of Gurdjieff – but she was also an incorrigible flirt and three of her children carried names different from those of their biological fathers.[33] Isaiah Berlin had met her in Washington during the war, when she was in her early twenties, fallen miserably in love and dedicated his translation of Turgenev's 'First Love' to her.[34]

Ayer later acknowledged that part of the attraction he initially felt for Patricia might have arisen from the fact that he wanted to succeed where Berlin had failed.[35] This motive, though, was soon supplanted by what he described as a 'sudden and violent passion' of love.[36] Despite the fact that she was not only married with a child, but also pregnant with another, they were soon talking about making a life together. The evening before Ayer left for Paris, he and Celia Paget had enjoyed a romantic dinner where he had told her how much he would miss her. On his return, she was surprised to be told that Patricia de Bendern was divorcing her husband and moving to London to be with Ayer.

Ayer later insisted that he also told his Oxford girlfriend, Penelope, all about his affair with Patricia, although he 'did not wholly succeed in breaking' their relationship. Unfortunately Penelope and Patricia were friends, and met in Paris soon after Ayer's return, where they naturally both talked about him. According to Isaiah Berlin, they even compared Freddie's letters, only to discover they were identical ('he had formulae in love as well as philosophy').[37] Whatever the truth in this, Patricia discovered that the relationship between Penelope and Freddie was not quite finished, and duly wired London to say that her elopement was off. 'I did not reply to the telegram, or ask for any explanation,' Ayer recalled. 'My feelings were a mixture of regret and relief. I did not pretend to myself that I had come at all well out of it, but I already knew that I was not yet emotionally equipped for the responsibility that I had undertaken.'[38] The story has one final chapter. In an angry exchange of letters, Ayer accused Berlin of having written to Patricia, warning her off him, and, what was worse in Ayer's eyes, of not telling the truth about his actions; Berlin denied this and in turn accused Ayer of behaving like a 'Don Juan'.[39] In time the two philosophers made up, but it was not the last time that their friendship was to be tested in this way.

Ayer was back in Oxford by the end of April, feeling, he wrote to Cummings, 'rather flat, though not unhappy'.[40] Affairs improved when he was invited by University College London to put himself forward as a candidate for the Grote professorship of philosophy. UCL's philosophy department had a poor reputation but the position appealed to Ayer. University College London, the oldest of the colleges that make up the University of London, had been founded in 1828, chiefly for those excluded from Oxford and Cambridge on the grounds of their religion. It was thus a liberal college, historically associated with the radical Utilitarian cause and had remained true to its traditions, to the extent of never having established a theology faculty – just the place for a free-thinker like Ayer. Then there was London itself. By this stage Ayer knew that he agreed with Hume that the town, not the country, was 'the true scene for a man of letters'.[41] He had no difficulty, then, in accepting the Chair when it was offered to him in the summer of 1946. As he liked to point out, with pride as ever in his precocity, he was not quite thirty-six.

That summer he spent six weeks in France. He took Valerie to St Jean-de-Luz, on the southernmost point of the Atlantic coast. He had been there the summer before 'mainly to see a girl', Denyse de Bourran, 'a friend made during the war in the course of my work for SOE', and this was presumably his reason for going again now.[42] At the end of August he sent Valerie home, and then went on to the small village of La Croix, near St Tropez, where he met Celia Paget. 'We spent a fortnight there, eating and drinking and lolling in the sun'.[43]

14

Professor

From the mid-1930s to the mid-1940s Ayer's life had been dominated by politics, or politics and war, rather than philosophy. If, in his mind, philosophy and life were two separate categories life had exercised the stronger pull. Deciding against a career as a politician, and now accepting the professorship at University College London, tipped the scales the other way, and they remained there for the rest of his life. There were to be political campaigns, close friendships with politicians and frenetic socialising, but he now knew, as he never altogether had before, that he could look forward to a life as an academic philosopher.

The war had a particularly disruptive effect on UCL – most of the college had been evacuated to Wales, and the philosophy department that Ayer found when he arrived in 1946 was in a sad state. Housed in some dilapidated rooms on Gordon Square, it had no telephone, few students, and one principal lecturer, Dr S.V. Keeling, a beret-wearing Francophile and Christian-Hegelian pacifist, who disapproved of Ayer – 'the Zeitgeist' – and resented his arrival. Ayer, no longer as combative as he once was, soon learned to indulge Keeling and in most other respects these circumstances suited him very well. Here was a department without traditions or bureaucracy to hamper him – a place on which he could quickly stamp his seal.

One of Ayer's first moves was to appoint Stuart Hampshire as a lecturer. In the circumstances this sounds exceptionally charitable, although Ayer was in fact acting, at least in part, from a sense of guilt. In the process of divorcing Renée, Ayer had been obliged, reluctantly, to cite Hampshire as correspondent. In order to avoid any publicity, his lawyers had instructed him to use the address of the Headington house that he and Renée had rented in 1939. Ayer, however, or so the story went, was simply unable to identify himself as the resident of a modern suburban home, and gave his Christ Church address. As Hampshire recalled, 'In those days, adultery was no light matter', and the effect on his career was 'absolutely disastrous'. The *Oxford Times* ran a short article on the divorce, prompting the Dean of Christ Church to make representations to the Warden of All Souls, where Hampshire was still, nominally, a fellow. This ensured that it became more or less impossible for him to secure a fellowship in the university. Ayer therefore, felt some obligation to him.[1]

For two years Ayer, Hampshire and Keeling shared the teaching between them. In 1949 they were joined by Richard Wollheim, who had encountered Ayer so memorably in Oxford. A young, keenly left-wing intellectual, with an interest in psychoanalysis and aesthetics, Wollheim had been to school at Westminster and, after fighting in France, had taken a first in history and then another in philosophy. Ayer characteristically appointed him on the basis of a few social encounters and an intuitive sense that he had the makings of a good philosopher.

Thereafter he appointed his own students to lectureships. There were five in all: James Thomson and John Watling (appointed 1949), Peter Long (1951), A.H. Basson (1953), and Peter Downing (1956). These were a talented but unlikely bunch. John Watling had been a conscientious objector in the Second World War and remained politically radical after it. He had begun by studying psychology, before, under Ayer's spell, moving to the philosophy department. Thomson, an outstandingly gifted philosopher, had been attracted to the subject by reading *Language, Truth and Logic* before the war. A rear-gunner in Bomber Command during the conflict, he was 'always in the grip of an obsession: psychoanalysis, logic, chess, the dogs, horse-racing, the Stock Exchange, drink – and the two great constancies, philosophy and smoking'.[2] Long, from a Northern working-class background, arrived at the department, after hearing Ayer give a talk on the radio. Anthony Basson, though, was the most unlikely of all. Older than the others, his past was shrouded in mystery. He may have gone to Harrow, he may have got a degree from Utrecht, he may have been married, and he may have been born Cavendish, a name he later used. When he first turned up at the department he had no formal philosophical training, but already had several logical papers published in *Mind*. He became a student and a tutor at UCL at more the less the same time, leaving in the 1950s first for Khartoum and then the University of Wales. An exceptionally astute logician, he remained aloof from the rest of the gang, living off pancakes – savoury for first course, sweet for second – in a bedsit in Shepherd's Bush.

Together this group gave the UCL department a certain flavour. While the 'Oxford Philosophers' of the period, the followers and associates of Ryle and Austin, had almost to a man been educated at public school, Freddie's 'boys' (as he liked to call them) were predominantly grammar school.[3] The department was staunchly analytic in style and broadly left-wing and avant-garde in sympathies. Russell, whose reputation was in decline in Oxford and Cambridge, was revered at UCL, as, less exceptionally, was Freud. (Ayer himself had come to take a fairly sceptical view of psychoanalysis. But even he took part in a crowded debate in the early 1950s with the psychologist Cyril Burt, in which Ayer made use of Ramsey's distinction between primary and secondary systems to defend the concept of the unconscious.[4] Thomson, Hampshire and Wollheim were all much more committed Freudians.)

Yet if Ayer and his fellow teachers were bound together by a certain community of interests and commitments, Ayer never attempted to impose an orthodoxy or form a school. Everyone who knew him, even his detractors, were keen to stress this point: Ayer was a brilliant teacher, and what marked him out was the enjoyment he took in disagreement and the way he immersed his students in it. 'Freddie,' as John Watling put it, 'loved being contradicted – he was entirely different from Popper who claimed he welcomed criticism but in reality could not tolerate it. The more you voiced your opinion the better.'[5]

Empiricists have always accorded a special importance to education: minds, they hold, after all, are made not born. What is clear, though, is that quite apart from thinking teaching important – and Ayer did think it hugely important and was proud of being a good teacher – he also enjoyed it. He had an instinctive sympathy for the young, he valued their fresh and open minds, and found it easy to identify with them. Ayer's devotion to his students was in some way connected, Wollheim suggested, to the value he attached to precocity: he liked the idea that he had something to learn from them, and he was pleased when they showed the same unconventionality and irreverence that had marked him out.

Talking to Ayer's students from these days was a heartening experience. 'Keeling used to say that you should not have an opinion in philosophy until after you had studied it for twenty years, but Freddie,' Watling recollected, 'was just the opposite. In retrospect I realise that his knowledge of the history of philosophy was very limited, but he was an enormously inspiring teacher. After almost the first thing I read to him, he said "Are you going to publish that?" It was immensely encouraging. It's why we made such good progress.'[6] Coming from a working-class family, Peter Long never felt altogether comfortable socially with Ayer, Hampshire, Wollheim and their public school ways. (He remembered that on one occasion Freddie took him to his club, the Travellers', and towards the end of the meal offered him 'pudding'. Long, embarrassed, thought he was being offered a meat pie.) But he also emphasised that as a teacher Ayer was utterly blind to class – he just did not see it. 'To me he was an enormous influence and he changed my life. He was so much better than any other teacher I had had ... He seemed to me stunning, generous, marvellous; the most stimulating teacher I could have had, listening to you, encouraging you, arguing with you, making it so exciting. It was a delight'.[7] Jeremy Hornsby, a student at UCL in the late 1950s, similarly described Ayer as 'the greatest influence on my life', and remembered how if Ayer disagreed with a student, he would end the discussion with something that became almost a refrain: 'I think you're wrong, but you're in good company anyway', citing an important philosopher who sided against him in the issue under dispute.[8]

The job that Ayer set himself at UCL was to create a place where 'free-spirits' were formed. The students were taught some history but the department was hardly scholarly. Students electing to do the Hegel paper were sent to King's College, as no one at UCL could teach his ideas sympathetically. Ayer thought history important, but only as a way into the essence of the subject: the truth. 'The interesting thing,' he said, at the end of the 1940s, 'is not to find out why [philosophers] said what they did, but evaluate what it is they were saying, and how far it was significant or true.'[9] The department remained small – there were rarely more than five or six undergraduates in a year – and Ayer made a point of teaching them all personally; he took a class for first-years, and another for second- and third-years, as well as giving individual tuition to all the finalists and postgraduates. Nevertheless at UCL, unlike at Oxford, pride of place was given not to tutorials, essay-writing or lectures, but to group debate. 'It was that,' John Watling said, 'that was exceptional about the department – the amount of time devoted to discussion, and its level.'[10]

There were three main forums for all this talk: the Monday five o'clock seminar for senior students and tutors, its Wednesday counterpart for tutors alone, and monthly meetings of the UCL Philosophical Society, where a guest speaker, usually from Oxford or Cambridge, would give a paper. In contrast to the more casual way of doing things at the ancient universities, Ayer made sure that all the leading philosophers of the day were invited to talk at London – his became one of those invitations that you did not want not to get. Outsiders were welcome to wander into any meeting and did so. Most analytically minded philosophers passing through London – Max Black, Morris Lazerowitz, Alice Ambrose, Quine, Nelson Goodman, Hilary Putnam, David Armstrong – attended, but students from other disciplines also came, pulled in by Freddie's virtuoso performances, and the intellectual excitement he and his boys generated. Jonathan Miller, for instance, made his way to Ayer's seminars from University College Hospital, where he was studying to be a doctor, as did the biologist Lewis Wolpert, studying at Kings, and many more came from psychology; a number followed Watling's footsteps and actually transferred to the philosophy department in order to study with Ayer. It was a form of seduction.

As Ayer's department grew, it moved from site to site, before, in the mid-1950s, finally settling into 19 Gordon Square, a tall elegant Georgian house of just the type Ayer liked. Ayer's capacious white-walled, smoke-filled office, with an outsize couch, doubled as the department's seminar room. Whatever the occasion, someone, a student, tutor or visiting speaker, would read a paper. Richard Wollheim has described the scene:

Freddie would sit behind his desk, tipping his chair back, with his silver cigarette case in front of him, helping himself to it at regular intervals, pausing between cigarettes only to comb his hair with his fingers or to adjust the knot of his tie or to straighten the silk folds as they fell over his shirt. The paper would end. Freddie's chair would fall forward. He frowned. He took another pull on his cigarette or twiddled his watch-chain. Then he began. His reply was clear, precise, in faultless sentences, touching on every point made or not quite made. Sometimes he would stop himself in mid-flight. 'No, that's not quite right – because you could get out of it by saying . . .' and then he would invent a counter argument. It was, and it was meant to be seen as, a *tour de force*. After that the discussion was general, but if there was a silence, someone would be asked his view . . . the rules of engagement were always the same. No position was to be considered better than the arguments presented in its favour. No argument was to be considered better than the weakest link in the form in which it was presented. The most implausible counter-example was a deadly, festering threat.[11]

The philosopher Daniel O'Connor, who attended Ayer's seminars regularly, likened his young tutors – Long, Thomson, Watling – to a 'praetorian guard' and recalled the gusto with which, encouraged by Ayer, they attacked visiting philosophers. O'Connor himself gave a paper around 1950 and, although 'a friend of these people . . . was surprised by the ferocity with which they set about me'.[12] Ayer was delighted if he could say, 'Yes Strawson came down the other day', or Berlin or Wisdom or Popper or Gombrich, 'and my boys gave him a pretty rough time'.[13]* After the seminar, the discussion would adjourn to the pub. Freddie would stay for half an hour or so, the hub of attention, and then hop into a taxi and into one of his other worlds.

Inevitably, Ayer's manner and methods suited some students better than others. One of his undergraduates left a moderately unflattering

---

* Like Wollheim, the Oxford philosopher David Pears also looked back on Ayer's career as a teacher after his death. 'In London he achieved a miracle, resurrecting a moribund department and putting it in competition with Oxford and Cambridge. His colloquium soon became the best forum in the country for philosophical discussion. If you had written a paper and wanted to get it criticized so that you could improve it for publication, or, perhaps, tear it up, that was the place to read it. I used to feel that it was like a manufacturer's test of a motor-car in a simulated collision – tough but worth it' (Obituary read to the meeting of the International Institute of Philosophy, California, 1 September 1989, Ayer Archive, York St. p.3).

portrait of him in an autobiographical novel of 1958. *The Monkey Puzzle* stars an easily recognisable Mr Marble – a vain, fast-talking, chain-smoking philosophy tutor, 'always fiddling with matches'. At the beginning of the book, Catherine, a bemused and failing Catholic, finds herself in love with Mr Marble but weary of the austere kind of analytic philosophy he and his coterie practise. Towards the end, when Marble and his colleagues have failed to respond to the Suez crisis, one of the characters is more forcefully critical:

> There's your liberal philosophers for you. The ones whose facetious-ness you in the end accepted and excused saying they were good socialists anyway. No doubt they will continue to write their little articles, continue to spread their true facetious little philosophy *but* when the barricades go up, it's not that they're on the wrong side, they aren't there at all. And d'you know why? It's awfully easy. They're snobs.

Yet Catherine's own feelings remain more ambiguous, and the novel ends where it begins – in one of Mr Marble's seminars. Catherine, it seems, could not quite shake off the attraction of Mr Marble and his little techniques.[14]

Freddie loved his department, was proud of its successes, and worked hard to make it the remarkable and friendly place it became. Richard Wollheim suspected that it was 'here for the first time that he could put behind him the very real wounds inflicted on his pride at Eton, at Christ Church and in the Welsh Guards'.[15] When not eating with a friend or a girlfriend in one of his favourite Charlotte Street restaurants, L'Etoile, Bertorelli's or the White Tower, he lunched with tutors and students in a local pub – never the canteen. Once or twice a year he threw a party for the whole department at his flat.

Ayer was jealous of his prerogatives as the head of a department, and did his best to prevent outside administrators – 'clerics' – having any say in whom he appointed, which students he admitted or what he taught them. He, in turn, did not involve himself in university administration more than was necessary and, as Dean, was remembered for his expeditious, and sometimes impatient dispatch of business, although among other initiatives he instituted, or at least revived, the public lunchtime lectures that UCL still runs. Wollheim recalled that 'Freddie wanted an unacademic department. He wanted these "free spirits"; he was always rather uneasy and not altogether consistent in his views about being in a university. Part of him wanted to be a Parisian *philosophe*, doing his philosophy in cafés'.[16] 'He liked,' Peter Long remembered, 'to travel light and arrived at the department, after his morning writing at home, without papers or books under his arm.'[17]

Yet if Ayer liked to be in control of his little platoon, he did not encourage insularity. On the contrary, following Neurath and others in the Vienna Circle, he had always insisted that if philosophy was going to make any contribution to human learning, philosophers would have to co-operate closely with academics in other fields, especially scientists. Nowadays, this is very largely a commonplace: philosophy and science have drawn ever closer. But in the 1940s and 1950s, Ayer's attitude was still strikingly novel.

Ayer seems to have worked hard at improving his science in these years – a long broadcast he gave on the Third Programme in March 1948 shows that he had been mugging up on the nineteenth-century history of the subject – and he did his best to persuade his colleagues in the science departments of the relevance of philosophy to their work. Among other initiatives, he founded the Metalogical Society (inspired by the nineteenth-century Metaphysical Society), which met monthly in his flat in Whitehorse Street, or sometimes in J.Z. Young's Chelsea home, over a period of three or four years from 1949.

The nucleus of this group was formed by the UCL philosophers, Hampshire, Wollheim, Watling and Thomson, and UCL scientists, Young, Peter Medawar and Lionel Penrose, along with two amateur philosophers, Humphrey Slater and Rupert Crawshay Williams. Russell and Popper, now professor at the LSE, joined them as, for a short time, did the great Polish logician Alfred Tarski; as logician-scientists, they acted as something of a bridge between the philosophers and the others. No records remain of the discussions, but with so many biologists present they would certainly have argued about the mind–brain relation. Russell, Popper and Ayer doubted that the experiential quality of mental life could be analysed away, while the scientists were more inclined to believe that it could. On the other hand, a broadcast that Ayer gave in the summer of 1949 on 'The Physical Basis of the Mind', shows him eager to dispel the notion that there is any mystery about the relation between mind and body: it is no more surprising, he argued, that there should be causal connections between mental and physical phenomena, than that there should be such connections between purely physical phenomena.[18] Ayer was especially close to UCL's Professor of Anatomy, J.Z. (John) Young, a tall, debonair, handsome left-winger, and his second wife Ray, and the trio often ate out together. Young, a friend from Oxford, who had helped secure Ayer the professorship, took the view that he 'didn't understand much about science', but then he thought the same about Popper. Ray remembered Ayer as 'very attractive . . . he had great charm and knew how to talk to women, which so few Englishmen did'.[19]

If Ayer had some contact with scientists and other intellectuals in UCL, he had still more through his involvement in a succession of debating clubs and discussion groups that were very much a feature of post-war London life. Early in the 1950s, the biologist, evolutionist and environmentalist, Julian Huxley, a generation older than Ayer, invited him to join a discussion group devoted to 'planning a better future for mankind'. Huxley had been the first director-general of Unesco, and had set up an Institute for Human Studies with a grant from the Rockefeller Foundation, with offices off Piccadilly, and the discussion group met under its auspices. It ran for about two years and included the Polish born polymath Jacob Bronowski and the economist and environmentalist, Barbara Ward, among other luminaries. 'Meetings of this society were fairly frequent and a great many memoranda were circulated, mostly written by Julian Huxley himself, but I do not think,' Ayer confessed, 'that we contributed anything much, even in the form of blueprints, towards the progress of civilisation.'[20]

An organisation even less likely to make a tangible contribution to human progress was a discussion group-cum-dining club organised by Nigel Nicolson and George Weidenfeld, which met once every month or so in various restaurants around London. In an early meeting, Philip Toynbee and the German Resistance leader Pastor Neimöller spoke on religion. Evelyn Waugh, cajoled by Father d'Arcy into attending, put in a characteristically boorish and drunken performance: 'A lot of Jews here,' he said when he first arrived; 'which one of them is Freddie Ayer?'[21] The 'Ordinaries', as they were known, soon ran out of fuel, but they were quickly succeeded by another dining club, this time organised by

Benedict Nicolson and Toynbee, which met at Bertorelli's restaurant in Soho and lasted until Ayer's death. The Bertorelli club (no women allowed) was just the sort of cosy, familiar institution that the pre-war Ayer despised, but which he now found he liked. He joined the Travellers' Club around this time, later forsaking it for the Garrick.

It was during this period of Ayer's life that he became close to Bertrand Russell. After the war, Russell had taken up a fellowship in philosophy at Trinity College, Cambridge, and then migrated with his third wife, 'Peter' Spence, to north-west Wales. By the end of the decade, however, he and Spence had separated and Russell had moved to London, marrying his last wife, Edith Finch. Russell shared Bloomsbury's suspicion of Jews (nicely captured in Harold Nicolson's remark, 'although I loathe anti-Semitism, I do dislike Jews')[22] and one has a sense that he always remained slightly wary of Ayer – 'that Jew from Oxford', as he once described him.[23] But Ayer impressed his girlfriends by taking them to have tea with the great man; he and Russell entered into first-name terms and exchanged short, wry letters. In the summer of 1952, Russell wrote to inform Ayer of an article that had appeared in an official Soviet journal comparing him unfavourably with 'such full-grown bisons of contemporary imperialist philosophy' as John Dewey, Santayana and Ayer. 'I am trying to learn to think of you,' Russell explained, 'as a bison in the hope of becoming modern-minded.'[24] Both philosophers were united in their hostility to the linguistic philosophy of Wittgenstein and Austin, and Russell looked to Ayer to keep him informed of the latest developments and when they met they talked mainly about logic, epistemology and the philosophy of mind. 'I have respect for Ayer,' he told Ved Mehta; 'he likes information and he has a first-class style.'[25]

Yet however much Russell approved of Ayer, it would have been hard to reciprocate the admiration Ayer felt for Russell, 'a great and good man'.[26] Ayer in fact found Russell's later work very variable, and only managed a lukewarm welcome for *An Inquiry into Meaning and Truth*, when he reviewed it in *Nature* during the war. Russell was 'The Picasso of modern philosophy' – he 'has expressed himself very differently at different periods, and in each period he has exerted deservedly great influence and aroused extravagant hostility' – but this book, Ayer regretted, 'lacked the sharpness and clarity' that characterised his earlier works.[27] Nevertheless, he judged the early philosophy the single greatest contribution to the subject since Hume. Ayer also thought Russell's views on the Cold War and nuclear weapons misjudged: at this time Russell was arguing that America should force Russia into a form of world government by threatening to use the atomic bomb. But he admired his moral fervour and his aristocratic refusal to conform. When Ayer wrote that 'in the field of learning, as in politics it is only because some people are prepared to make trouble that anything of any importance gets done', he might have been thinking of Russell.[28] But perhaps too, beyond the philosophers' shared intellectual outlook, there was something else that drew Ayer to Russell. Russell had had a lonely, miserable childhood and there was a melancholy in his character that may have resonated with Ayer.

One of the first things Ayer wrote, on getting down to work after the war, was a new preface to *Language, Truth and Logic*. It is a characteristically Ayerian piece, guilelessly pointing out the errors in the book and setting out to correct them. He expressed reservations about his treatment of our knowledge of other minds, revised his account of the nature of philosophical analysis, and briefly expanded on his analysis of propositions about the past, now arguing that since it is only a contingent rather than a necessary fact that one lives at the time that one does, past events are not logically but only contingently unobservable. The statement 'Brutus killed Caesar', rather than laying down rules for the prediction of future experience, as Ayer had originally claimed, is simply a statement about what would be observed if one had lived at another time, and as such is amenable to phenomenal analysis, in just the same way as a statement about the present.[29]

He paid most attention, however, to the principle of verifiability. In a paper published before the war, Isaiah Berlin had shown that *Language, Truth and Logic*'s original formulation, which Ayer had carefully composed to allow the meaningfulness of general and hypothetical propositions that could not be conclusively verified, was in fact so liberal as to allow meaning to any assertion whatsoever. Ayer now offered a complex reformulation, but as the American logician Alonzo Church demonstrated in a review in the *Journal of Symbolic Logic* in 1949, the new formulation was as leaky as the old. Ayer had to admit, once again with admirable honesty, that he at least could not devise a formally watertight version of his famous principle, although he continued to insist that it must, in some form or another, be right.

Church's neat demolition, however, amounted to no more than a paragraph in an obscure periodical and did little to affect the success of the second edition. In October 1945, immediately after being released from the armed forces, Ayer had written to Gollancz, suggesting a reprint of the book, possibly with a new introduction: 'It is not likely to sell thousands of copies but . . . it ought to have respectable sales'.[30] This of course was very far from how things turned out. In the US, where it was published by Dover, it sold 300,000 copies in the thirty years after the war. In the same period in England, Gollancz and Penguin sold 100,000 copies between them. Translated into at least fourteen languages, it still sells 2,000 copies a year in Britain today.

Indeed, at least in Britain, it appears to have outsold all other works of analytic philosophy in the same period, attracting, and just as often repelling, beginners in the study of philosophy. The Canadian-born philosopher Ted Honderich recalled how, studying at Toronto in the mid-1950s, he 'suddenly one day happened on the book and there it was. It said that all this stuff I had had pumped down my throat should be cast into the flames. The philosophical heavens opened a bit.' Honderich was so impressed by *Language, Truth, and Logic* that he turned down graduate places at Harvard and Yale to study under Ayer at UCL.[31] Richard Pring, now Oxford's Professor of Education, had a not dissimilar experience – one that Ayer would have found particularly gratifying. He was training for the priesthood in the English College in Rome in the mid-1950s when he discovered the book, which had unaccountably made its way into the college library. He struggled with its doctrines, 'which, if true, would have made a nonsense of what I was doing', and after quitting Rome also gravitated to Ayer's department.[32]

With the new preface behind him and the essays on existentialism out of the way, it took Ayer some time to get down to more serious work. The post-war years seem to have been difficult ones for him. 'London is all right,' he wrote to Celia Goodman in 1947, 'but I feel that I am working very badly, more hand to mouth than ever and getting rather depressed about it.' That year he produced only two substantial articles: 'Thinking and Meaning', his UCL inaugural address which he never reprinted, mainly because he thought it owed too much to Gilbert Ryle, and 'Phenomenalism', a paper in which he finally repudiated phenomenalism.*

The next three years saw only one major piece each. In 'The Principle of Utility' of 1948, he offered a qualified endorsement of Bentham's principle that 'the right and proper end of government . . . is the greatest happiness of the greatest number'.† This was followed by 'On the Analysis of Moral Judgements', which furnished a more sophisticated and conciliatory version of the emotivism than the one he propounded in *Language, Truth and Logic*, and by 'Basic Propositions', in which he once again turned to the nature of observation statements, defending the view that sense-data are exactly as they appear and that the sentences that report them are incorrigible.

In the early 1950s, spurred on in part by Quine's work, Ayer's output began to pick up. These years saw the appearance of some fine, imaginative papers, on philosophical logic – 'Individuals', 'On What There Is', 'The Identity of Indiscernibles', and 'Negation' – which, among other concerns, sought to argue, contrary to the view that the world was made up of particulars and universals or individuals and properties, that in fact things were, to put it crudely, merely bundles of properties, with no underlying individualising essence or substance. To put it a little less crudely, Ayer suggested (following Quine's generalised version of

---

* Here the break was not as radical as it is sometimes made to sound. Already, in *The Foundations of Empirical Knowledge*, Ayer had acknowledged that material-object and sense-data statements were not inter-translatable, on the grounds that no sense-data proposition entails the truth of a material-object proposition (any sense-data proposition is logically compatible with there being no material objects at all) and no material-object proposition entails the truth of a sense-data proposition (some circumstance might always intervene which prevents the occurrence of the expected sense-data). In finally rejecting phenomenalism, then, Ayer was not so much revising his position as acknowledging that it could not properly be called 'phenomenalist'; speaking of physical objects is a way of interpreting our sense-experiences, rather than merely redescribing them, as Berkeley and other phenomenalists had held.

† Ayer's endorsement is qualified because, in the first place, he contended, in line with his emotivism, that the principle could never be justified as uniquely and objectively true in the way Bentham suggested it could; secondly because he thought other considerations mattered apart from aggregate happiness – most obviously its distribution, but also values that had nothing to do with happiness, such as truth. Thus he was inclined to scorn myths, taboos, hypocrisy and self-deceit, even where people find satisfaction in them. Ayer did though believe that the utility principle provided an important political standard: it was probably better, or so Ayer believed, if politicians aimed at giving people what they actually want, rather than 'what they ought to want or what they must be made to want' ('The Principle of Utility', in *Philosophical Essays*, London, 1954, p.270).

Russell's theory of descriptions) that the world could be described in a purely predicative language. This would be a language that avoided the use of what Ayer called 'indicators' – demonstratives, pronouns, proper names and definite descriptions – in favour of indefinite descriptions: a language which described the world from no particular place or time. In our ordinary way of speaking, we do indeed appear to distinguish between properties and the things that they characterise, but this appearance is fallacious. 'For if we are asked what the thing is that has the properties in question, the only informative answer that we can give is to enumerate further properties'.[33]

Altogether, however, it took him nine years from the end of the war to produce a book, *Philosophical Essays*, and that was just a collection of previously published articles. It was not until 1956 that he produced a successor to *Language, Truth and Logic* and *The Foundations of Empirical Knowledge* – *The Problem of Knowledge*. Applied to many philosophers, this rate of production would be perfectly respectable, but Ayer believed in writing books.

Part of the problem, doubtless, was that he was overloaded with work. Apart from his teaching commitments and other duties at UCL, he had accepted the job of editing what were in effect two large series of books for Penguin, one devoted to individual philosophers (Stuart Hampshire's study of Spinoza was the first to appear) and another on general topics like logic, the philosophy of science and ethics. But he was also not sure which way to go. The essays on existentialism, the meaning of life, the analysis of moral judgements, free will and Utilitarianism all suggest that Ayer might have been thinking, as he often did, of writing some general work on moral philosophy, but if so it never emerged. In 1949 he wrote to Cummings saying that he was about to start work on an introduction to philosophy for Penguin, but that never came to anything either, or at least only very gradually transmuted into *The Problem of Knowledge*.[34] Perhaps, indeed, instead of explaining Ayer's modest output by reference to his work at UCL, his work there should be explained by reference to his modest output. At least one colleague suspected the reason why Ayer put so much into his students in these years was that he was no longer confident of his ability to solve the problems of philosophy single-handedly – although he did still believe that they could be solved – and threw himself into teaching as another means by which to solve them.[35]

Yet if the years after the war were difficult, they ended well. *The Problem of Knowledge* formed part of Ayer's Pelican series and Ayer tended to consider it his best book, preferring it to *Language, Truth and Logic*. It is a masterful little work, only 80,000 words long, wise and radical at once, and written, inevitably, in Ayer's peerless, crystalline prose.

Unlike Wittgenstein, Ayer was not a philosopher who ever seriously renounced his earlier views. As David Pears once put it, Ayer's was a 'living philosophy' which adapted itself

> to new considerations and absorbed its critics' good points over many years. His writings, like Russell's, are excerpts from a continuing process of argument and the identity of his central contribution to philosophy is more like the identity of a rational conversation than a rigidly formulated thesis.[36]

Thus many of the central tenets of his pre-war writings remain, most obviously the sharp distinction between logical and empirical propositions (Ayer's hammer and sickle), and the fundamental place he assigned to his hallowed observation statements, which he continued to argue, although more tentatively than before, can be described in the language of sense-data. All propositions, Ayer still believed, had to be justifiable by reference to these, or otherwise jettisoned. But the great combative proclamations and sweeping generalisations of *Language, Truth and Logic* had gone, replaced with a quieter treatment of the problems of epistemology, and different ideas and interests were developed, as Ayer showed a new interest in the challenges of scepticism. Indeed, where *Language, Truth and Logic* was basically concerned with slaying metaphysics and cutting back on our ontological commitments, Ayer now occupied himself with the more constructive task of justifying the commitments of common sense. In the context this is not surprising. By the 1950s, in a philosophical galaxy dominated by Wittgenstein, Wisdom, Popper, Ryle and Austin in Britain, and Carnap, Quine and Nelson Goodman in the US, metaphysics no longer seemed the menace that it once had.

The feature of the book of which Ayer was proudest was its handling of scepticism – he once called it 'seminal'.[37] His innovation here was to present the various positions that have been adopted by philosophers of knowledge as responses to a radical sceptic who argues for the existence of a series of gaps between our beliefs and the evidence on which they are based. Thus the sceptic denies the validity of the transition from sense-experiences to physical objects, from the world of common sense to the entities of science, from the overt behaviour of other people to their inner thoughts and feelings, from the present to the past. Ayer neatly distinguished four standard ways in which epistemologists have attempted to bridge the gap advocated by the sceptic: naïve realism, which denied the existence of the gap between evidence and inference; reductionism, which attempted to close it by defining the things inferred in terms of the evidence for them; the scientific approach which presents the inferences as justified on inductive grounds; and Ayer's own contender, 'the method of descriptive analysis':

> Here one does not contest the premises of the sceptic's argument, but only its conclusion. No attempt is made either to close or to bridge the gap: we are simply told to take it in our stride. It is admitted that the inferences which are put in question are not deductive and also that they are not inductive, in the generally accepted sense. But this, it is held, does not condemn them. They are what they are and none the worse for that. Moreover they can be analysed. We can, for example, show in what conditions we feel confident in attributing certain experiences to others: we can evaluate different types of record: we can distinguish the cases in which our memories or perceptions are taken to be reliable from those in which they are not. In short we can give an account of the procedures that we actually follow. But no justification of these procedures is ... possible ... And if there cannot be a proof, it is not sensible to demand one. The sceptic's problems are insoluble because they are fictitious.[38]

Ayer later came to believe that his advocacy of 'the method of descriptive analysis' was somewhat underhand, amounting as it did to little more than acknowledging the truth in the sceptic's arguments, while refusing to be troubled by them. As he put it, 'my general procedure was to allow the sceptic to make his points but then to take the verdict away from him like a corrupt referee'.[39] It was as if he had let himself be lulled into complacency by the quietist turn that philosophy had taken with Wittgenstein, Wisdom, Ryle and Austin, and in later works he would attempt to argue, more positively, that our commonsense beliefs have their own rationality.[*]

There was much in the book, in addition to its ingenious schematisation of problems and solutions in the philosophy of knowledge, about which Ayer had a right to be pleased. The chapter on perception offers his most sophisticated version yet of the relation of sense-data to material object propositions. Instead of understanding talk about the physical world of independently existing and enduring objects as a shorthand way of talking about sense-data, Ayer now argued that beliefs about the physical world are best understood as a *theory* elaborated on the basis of sensory experience:

> The statements which belong to the theory transcend their evidence in the sense that they are not merely redescriptions of it. The theory is richer than anything that could be yielded by an attempt to reformulate it at the sensory level. But this does not mean that it has any other supply of wealth than the phenomena over which it ranges. It is because of this indeed, that they can constitute its justification. Accordingly, it does not greatly matter whether we say that the objects which figure in it are theoretical constructions or whether, in line with common sense, we prefer to say that they are independently real. The ground for saying that they are *not* constructions is that the references to them cannot be eliminated in favour of references to sense-data. The ground for saying they are constructions is that it is only through their relationship to our sense-experiences that a meaning is given to what we say about them. They are in any case real in the sense that

---

[*] If Ayer came to see the book as rather too accepting of common sense, it is also, it could be argued, a little insular. In the course of his argument (and very much in keeping with the pride he took in his 'boys'), he cites a number of his students and colleagues – Wollheim, Downing, Watling and Shearn. Apart from these, however, and the predictable range of dead thinkers – Descartes and Locke, Hume and Mill (although not Kant) – he cites, exclusively, his Oxbridge colleagues: Russell, Wittgenstein, Ryle, Austin and Berlin.

statements which affirm or imply their existence are very frequently true.[40]

Ayer's chapter on perception is followed by an imaginative treatment of memory, which, with an earlier discussion of the concept of knowledge, demonstrates decisively that mental imagery need play no part in the empiricist scheme of things. Ayer himself always admitted to being a very poor visualiser.

The same chapter also offers a vertiginous criticism of the common-sense belief that the past determines the future. As he argues, we might just as well say that the future determines the past, for the same relations of necessity and sufficiency obtain in both directions. We say that it is a necessary condition of my suffering malaria that I have been bitten by the anopheles mosquito, but then my suffering from malaria is a sufficient condition of my having previously been bitten. Similarly, my taking a bottle full of arsenic is sufficient to kill me, but then my dying is a necessary condition of my previously taking arsenic: 'I should not be taking the arsenic unless I was about to die, just as I should not be suffering from malaria, unless I had been bitten by the mosquito'.[41] If we do tend to find this symmetry between past and future hard to accept, and give a special potency to early events as 'causes' of later ones, it can only be, Ayer contends, because we tend to anthropomorphise causes. Not knowing what will happen in the future and knowing what has happened in the past, we find it natural to think of our actions as securing the future, and we then extend the idea to all other cases of causality.[42]

The Problem of Knowledge received almost universally enthusiastic reviews. Stuart Hampshire, who had left UCL for Oxford in 1950, complained in a review in the *New Statesman* of 'a certain tameness, a lack of impulse, as in a school work' – 'one can see from the beginning that none of the sceptical arguments are going to get out of hand; they are on a tight, light rein, familiar, domesticated animals which are taken out for a short run' – but even he welcomed it as 'a superbly executed work of analytic philosophy, exact, economical, and everywhere intelligible.'[43] Writing in the *Spectator*, Oxford's leading moral philosopher, R.M. Hare, judged the book 'so thorough, so penetrating, rigorous and up to date, and at the same time so readable and manageable that it is unlikely to have a serious competitor for many years'.[44]

By the time it appeared, Ayer was also well known as a broadcaster. BBC Radio's Third Programme, with its uncompromising commitment to serious literature, music and discussion, had been founded just after the war. Ayer gave over twenty-five talks in its first decade, on topics ranging from 'Contemporary British Philosophers', 'John Stuart Mill' and 'Jean Paul Sartre's Definition of Liberty' to 'The Physical Basis of Mind' and 'Occam's Razor and Modern Philosophy'. These last two were fairly technical and must have gone over most listeners' heads, but a 1957 broadcast on telepathy, then still a widely debated topic, was accessible enough. Ayer admitted the logical possibility of the phenomenon – although privately he was dismissive of it – only to deny that it could properly be called supernatural: all phenomena that came within the knowledge of humankind were, Ayer argued, natural by definition.[45] On one rare occasion, a whole UCL departmental seminar was convened in Broadcasting House, and Ayer and his colleagues spent an hour and a half in a live discussion of the issue of our knowledge of other minds.

In another venture, he, Solly Zuckerman and a BBC producer, Robin Whitworth, inaugurated a Lunar Society of the Air (named after the eighteenth-century group of scientists and intellectuals associated with Joseph Priestley), a series of discussions broadcast from Solly Zuckerman's house in Birmingham. The regular participants were Zuckerman, Medawar, Huxley and Ayer, although they were joined by others. Topics included the future evolution of man, telepathy (again) and psychoanalysis. There were at least eight broadcasts, beginning in the new year of 1951.

Perhaps the most memorable of Ayer's radio broadcasts from these years was a 1949 debate with Frederick Copleston, a young Jesuit philosopher with a deep knowledge of the history of philosophy and of recent developments in France and Germany. Their discussion stood out not just because both were exceptionally able debaters, but because for once the verification principle and Ayer's empiricism were being put to work in an argument against someone who really believed in metaphysics. Ayer began by offering an overview of logical positivism, describing it as not so much 'a system of philosophy', as the analysis and elucidation of concepts 'used in science or mathematics or in everyday language'.[46]

From that point on the debate largely remained focused on Ayer's ideas and beliefs, with Copleston for the most part assaying Ayer's system or doing his best to rebuff attacks from it. The main conflict between them was over the sense of metaphysics; Ayer kept returning to the point that the metaphysical propositions dear to Copleston had no content because there was no way of testing their truth. 'Suppose,' Ayer challenged Copleston,

> I say 'There's a "drogulus" over there', and you say 'What?' and I say 'Drogulus' and you say 'What's a drogulus?' Well, I say, 'I can't describe what a drogulus is, because it's not the sort of thing you can see or touch, it has no physical effects of any kind, but it's a disembodied being.' And you say, 'Well how am I to tell if it's there or it's not there?' and I say, 'There's no way of telling. Everything's just the same if it's there or it's not there. But the fact is it's there. There's a drogulus there standing just behind you, spiritually behind you.' Does that make sense?

Copleston withstood this onslaught, but only by feebly claiming that all that was needed in order to frame an idea of something was the possibility of 'some experience relevant to its formation', a formulation which seems to rule absolutely nothing out.[47]

Wittgenstein, listening to the debate in Dublin, where he had gone after resigning his Cambridge chair, took a characteristically low view of both participants. Copleston 'contributed nothing at all' to the discussion; Ayer 'has something to say but is incredibly shallow'.[48]

15

The London Freddie Ayer

Soon after the end of the war, Renée, who had been living what Ayer described as 'her peculiar, solitary, *haus frau* life' in a house in Hampstead, moved to a flat in Dolphin Square in Pimlico, a fashionable address where her suitor, Francis Listowel, also lived.[1] Ayer continued to see a great deal of her over the next decade; it was in some respects as if they were still married. He went to Dolphin Square for Sunday lunch. After the meal Renée took out a basin and lovingly washed his hair. She arranged for his flat to be decorated, repaired and cleaned. They even celebrated their wedding anniversary together.

Renée thrived on this type of relationship, administering to the men and the children in her life and skilfully managing their comings and goings, while all the time retaining her independence. Both Hampshire and Listowel proposed marriage, but she refused. Freddie, in turn, loved being looked after in this way – although he had other reasons for tying himself so closely to her. It was quite possible that at some distant date he would have a second family, but he wanted, for the time being, to get the most out of being young, relatively rich and increasingly famous. His relationship with Renée, then, gave him an excuse for not altogether committing himself to another woman.

Late in the 1940s, Freddie and Renée made the decision to move the children from their progressive Hampstead school, to more conventional boarding establishments: Valerie to a girls' school in Oxford, and Julian, first to a prep school in Wiltshire and then, as a fee-paying Oppidan, to Eton – a strange choice for two socialist parents. Renée arranged it so that Freddie saw more of Valerie than Julian and his letters of this period tend to dwell on her. They often spent weekends together in Oxford: 'I stayed in Wadham,' he remembered, 'and used to read Jane Austen to her under the trees in the Wadham garden.'[2] Freddie also took her away for a holiday every summer until she left school, generally leaving Julian behind to spend time with Renée and Hampshire. In 1945 and again in 1946 they were in St Jean-de-Luz, in '48 in the US, in '49 in the Swiss Alps and the South of France, often touring with, or visiting friends. Twice Ayer took her to the Edinburgh Festival, sweetly attending the classical concerts she liked.

Julian, nevertheless, was brought up to believe that Freddie was his father, and to all purposes he was. Julian remembers him, indeed, as a 'splendid' and 'exceptional' father – especially if you 'bordered' and did not occupy too much of his life. 'He attached no importance to biological ties at all – it was remarkable'. As Julian grew up, they talked about literature, history and philosophy, although it was sport that bound them most closely together. They went regularly to watch Spurs, and also played together, 'not just competitive games but aimless play, with balloons and balls' and the like. Freddie would occasionally arrive at Eton unannounced on a weekday afternoon to watch Julian play football on College Field, the scene of his own Wall Game triumphs.[3]

It took Ayer some time to find a home for himself. He borrowed a place in Highgate for a while, and then moved into a flat in Sloane Street belonging to Celia Paget, with a 'very pretty girl'. Thirty years later, he confessed that he couldn't remember anything about her, except that he would lie on their bed watching her comb her hair and do her make-up – she took an extraordinarily long time preparing to go out.[4] In the autumn of 1947, however, he found a highly desirable bachelor's flat in 2 Whitehorse Street, the top two floors of a narrow town house, just off Shepherd Market in Mayfair. The area was one of the smartest in London, combining grand houses and hotels with a generous spread of restaurants and a large population of high-class prostitutes more or less openly plying their trade.

Ayer's new home, situated above a tailor, consisted of four small, elegantly proportioned rooms, with a central window in each, plus a small kitchen and a bathroom. A cleaning lady, Mrs Moore, came in every day and cooked him breakfast, and the short bus ride to UCL just gave him time to complete the *Times* crossword. Renée took control of the decoration of the flat, which she painted white – Cummings's portrait took pride of place. Richard Wollheim recalled that although Ayer had a limited feeling for visual art, there was nonetheless something very aesthetic about his manner and appearance. He was always immaculately if conservatively dressed in a three-piece suit and delicately patterned tie; his face had become gentler with age; he used his eyes, and the continuous movement of his hands and face to fine effect. 'Everything had to fit together with Freddie and be elegant. His approach to philosophy was in a way very aesthetic. He told me how he wrote: he would start in the morning, never make notes, and never put a sentence down on paper, until it was perfectly formed in his head'.[5]

Ayer's social life expanded enormously in these years, owing principally to the Gargoyle Club. Situated at the top of a tall building in Dean Street, Soho, the club was founded in 1925 by David Tennant, a handsome and dissolute young aristocrat, but it was after the war that it really came into its own, playing something of the role that the Café Royal had played before it, as an inexpensive hang-out for London's artists, writers and their friends. Figures as diverse as art historian Clive Bell, writer Anthony Powell, Labour politician Tony Crosland, scientist J.Z. Young and artist Francis Bacon were all regulars. The club had private rooms for parties, and offered lunch, tea and supper to its members. Its focus was a Moorish mirrored ballroom, based on a design by Matisse. During the evenings little Mr Alexander and his four-piece band played perky renditions of mainly pre-war hits – 'Bye Bye, Blackbird', 'Melancholy Baby', 'Ain't Giving Nothing Away' – furnishing a counterpoint to some fairly serious conversation. George Weidenfeld, an *habitué* who became a friend of Ayer at around this time, remembered that 'the Gargoyle was grand enough for relatively conventional people to feel they would not lose caste if they treated it as their club and Bohemian enough for them to think that they were not at all conventional.'[6]

When opening the club in the 1920s, Tennant had said he wanted a place 'without rules, where people can express themselves freely', and his customers took him at his word. Philip Toynbee, Guy Burgess and

Donald Maclean, as well as Tennant himself, were regularly carried off to bed; considering the pedigree of the membership, fights broke out with surprising frequency. Although not himself a heavy drinker, Freddie often ended up there two or three times a week until it closed in 1952. He liked the conversation – one evening Graham Greene invited him to argue him out of his 'half-belief' in God – but it was the dance floor that attracted him most. It was only when Ayer was dancing that he was not fiddling or pacing around: it gave a formal, socially permissible outlet to his restlessness. According to V.S. Pritchett, another close friend from this period, he danced the samba especially well.[7]

Ayer once said that the Gargoyle was, more than anything, responsible for making him the well known 'social figure' he became, and it is true that in the five years after the war his network of friends expanded significantly.[8] It is not easy, at this distance, to say anything about what was inevitably a varied and ever-changing 'set' but its members were generally well born, well educated, very smart, with bohemian attitudes and manners – a group that spanned the gap between Bloomsbury and the swinging aristocrats and writers of the 1960s. In 1948 Philip Toynbee organised a cricket match on the Isle of Wight, and the team he gathered together offers a representative cross-section. Aside from Ayer himself, it included Toynbee (author and journalist), V.S. Pritchett (novelist and critic), Benedict Nicolson (art historian), Sir Martyn Beckett (architect and jazz pianist), Giles Romilly (journalist, nephew of Winston Churchill), J.B. Priestley (playwright) and Evelyn Shuckburgh (Foreign Office).

Inevitably, Ayer's London friends had connections in the country. Barley Alison had introduced him to Mary and Robin Campbell and he became a regular guest at their manor house, Stokke Farm, not far from Julian's Wiltshire school. Robin Campbell, who had lost a leg in the war while attacking Rommel's North African villa, had since turned to painting, and Stokke offered a taste of country life *à la* Bloomsbury: artistic activity, unheated rooms, walks in the country, vaguely continental cooking, rough red wine and a great deal of talk. Patrick Leigh Fermor was present for a memorable day spent catching crayfish and bathing in the Kennet. 'There was a great crayfish feast in the evening and much high spirits and Freddie suddenly burst into a *pas seul* of soft-shoe dancing, flickering about the house so nimbly one felt it would have been no effort for him to have danced up the walls, across the ceiling and down the other side without breaking step'.[9]

The Campbells' friends, Ralph and Frances Partridge, lived nearby in Ham Spray, a house that had direct links with Bloomsbury. Lytton Strachey had bought the house in 1923, and lived there with Ralph Partridge and Dora Carrington, and it remained full of paintings by Carrington, Vanessa Bell and Duncan Grant. Ayer became close to Ralph and Frances, and from early 1953 was a frequent house guest, amusing his audience by insisting that what we think of as visual 'images' are really just colourless, shapeless concepts – words in our heads.[10] Ayer's inability to visualise places or people was often remarked upon in these imaginative, artistic circles, as was his complete indifference to nature. At around the same time that he first met the Partridges, he travelled to Dublin for the 1953 Joint Session of the Mind Association and the Aristotelian Society, where the writer Robert Kee offered to take Ayer on a drive and show him some of the country. Having reached a particularly beautiful spot, Kee noticed that Ayer seemed lost in thought. 'I was wondering,' he explained, 'whether sheep think.' Kee was 'furious' and drove him back to the city.

Frances Partridge, who had studied philosophy, especially liked Ayer's company – 'Freddie Ayer, touching, slightly comic and alert as a fox terrier,' she recorded in one of her diaries – as did her close friend Janetta Jackson.[11] Twelve years younger than Ayer, Janetta had been married to Humphrey Slater, Robert Kee and a wealthy businessman, Derek Jackson, before she and Ayer became friends and briefly lovers. They holidayed in the South of France in 1954 and were often at Ham Spray together. She remembered 'how he hated to lose in a game. Even good-humoured un-grand croquet – at Stokke – made him desperate to win, so that it was awful, on a doubtful day, to be his partner . . . We had a warm detached easy relationship, talking a great deal about everything which I loved. His decisiveness, his sure and definite way of expressing himself, after that very characteristic initial hesitation, was enormously enjoyable'.[12] Not everyone, however, found him so charming; 'Freddie Ayer . . . very talkative and flamboyantly egomaniacal,' wrote Barbara Skelton, at Stokke with Cyril Connolly for a weekend in 1954: 'says he is pleased with himself because he has been doing some satisfactory work lately'.[13]

In the autumn of 1947 Valerie came down with TB, still in those days a life-threatening illness. She was hospitalised in Oxford, where Ayer went to see her almost every weekend: 'it has been a nerve-racking business but the doctors think that they can cure her,' he wrote to a friend in New York in January 1948.[14] Ayer had been invited by Sidney Hook to spend the autumn term of 1948 teaching at NYU and accepted, at least in part for Valerie's sake: she would accompany him and could spend as long as she needed recuperating with the Godleys on their farm in Morris in New York State. Ayer and Valerie took a liner from Southampton at the beginning of August, leaving Renée in charge at Whitehorse Street, and spent the late summer of 1948 with the Godleys. After the privations of Britain, America seemed ambrosial. No sooner had he arrived, however, than he was struck with a severe attack of piles, and hospitalised.

At the end of the summer Valerie returned home, her health recovered, and Freddie moved to Manhattan to take up his duties at NYU. Sidney Hook arranged for him to teach a course at Bard, the liberal arts college close to Rhinecliff, a two-hour train ride north of the city. This was the first time Ayer had taught in the US, and he was shocked by the ignorance and parochialism of most of his students – especially those at Bard. His old friend, Tony Bower, now an editor at *Art in America*, was also looking for somewhere to live, and the two men moved into a mean little apartment on Sullivan Street in the West Village.

While in New York, Ayer found himself at the centre of a controversy about his ethical views. Giles Romilly, a friend of Philip Toynbee, whom Ayer knew only slightly, wrote a poorly researched article for the *New Statesman*, in which he described a visit to Oxford, where he claimed to have come across a group of Fascist undergraduates taking their inspiration from *Language, Truth and Logic*. The book, he claimed, had 'acquired almost the status of a philosophic Bible' in the city.[15] The philosopher, C.E.M. Joad, who had made a name for himself as a broadcaster, had recently been convicted of travelling on a train without a ticket, and now sought to use Romilly's article to rehabilitate himself with the BBC. He wrote an article for the *Statesman*, which he later expanded into a book, in which he argued that *Language, Truth and Logic* did, indeed, by divesting life of any purpose, create the negative climate in which Fascism flourishes.[16]

Ayer's position on the question of the relation between emotivism and substantive ethical propositions was complex. He wanted to insist on the logical fallacy of attempting to deduce statements of value from statements of fact, while at the same time suggesting that emotivism at least disposed one to take a progressive view of the world, undermining, as it did, the belief that tradition, Church or state could ever possess the authority to dictate how to live. Whether or not he was entitled to occupy these two positions at once is a matter of debate, but either one alone was enough to refute the claim that positivism somehow sanctioned fascism. As Ayer contended in a letter to the *New Statesman*, responding to Romilly's article, it was a matter of historical record that 'Fascists have hitherto tended to favour some form of metaphysics and . . . have been hostile to positivistic ideas, in so far as they were aware of them'.[17]

These arguments notwithstanding, Oswald Mosley himself attempted to pay a call on Ayer in London, when he was in New York. Worse for Ayer, *Time* got hold of the story, interviewed him just as he was taking up his duties at NYU, and published an unflattering photograph of him, along with a short but insinuating interview, describing him as 'a wan and wispy philosopher . . . the son of a small businessman', who taught that it 'means nothing to say "That man is good to support his mother"'.[18] Ayer was upset: only five years earlier Russell had been divested of his professorship at City College because of his views on religion and marriage.

The four months spent in New York had their moments. He met Auden properly for the first time and liked him. *Partisan Review*, the house journal of New York's liberal Left, gave him a party, and he saw a good deal of the Schapiros and the Cummingses. But the few letters that have survived suggest that he did not enjoy his visit. Indeed, this is the one occasion that we have evidence of Ayer coming close to, if not quite a breakdown, then at least nervous depression. Writing to the Cummingses, whom he had been to visit in Joy Farm in August, he expressed in unusually warm terms what they meant to him: 'I count you the best friends that I have. There is no one else with whom I feel so much at home. And if ever I needed friends I need them now.' Running through his grievances, he cited Bard, where the dullness of both students and teachers had made teaching 'an appalling nervous effort', and left him 'depressed and exhausted'; the article in *Time*, the 'wanton malevolence' of which had given him an 'unpleasant shock'; and the West Village apartment which looked 'like a seaside bungalow', with no kitchen and a phone he had to share with his neighbours.[19] Perhaps the after-effects of his illness contributed to his dejection. Possibly he was worried about his failure to make any real philosophical progress: he became anxious, around this time, that his philosophical powers were declining. Writing to Cummings after his return to London, he himself put it down to 'something in the atmosphere': 'It is a silly vague phrase, but it does express something that I came to feel very strongly. The atmosphere seemed to me hostile to people like ourselves. I have always thought that the intellectual ought to dominate his environment . . . but during the months in New York I came for the first time to see how difficult this might be'.[20]

Recalling this period in his memoirs, Ayer inevitably made light of his depression, admitting only that he had written 'despondently' to a London girlfriend, Jane Douglas, who came out to stay.[21] When she returned to England, he started a more serious affair with Angelica Weldon, 'a femme fatale with a marvellous body', from a wealthy upper-class, East Coast family.[22] Weldon had moved to London at some point after the war, and became a friend of Cyril Connolly and the circle around *Horizon*. Ayer had first met her 'years before' when she was still living with her husband, but she had since left him for a love affair with Henrietta Moraes, Francis Bacon's favourite model, a leading Soho figure, and, like Angelica, a great drinker and night-club goer. At the end of the semester, Freddie, Angelica and Tony Bower went on a driving holiday through the South, passing through Virginia, North and South Carolina, Georgia and Alabama. These states 'were not so prosperous as they have since become', Ayer remembered, 'and I was depressed by the ramshackle houses in which many of the Negroes seemed to live and frightened by the aura of sultry violence which pervaded so many of the small and dusty towns through which we passed'.[23] New Orleans, however, where they ended their trip, was a delight. 'I was happy to drink Pernod in its bars but slightly embarrassed by the scantily clad girls who stood bumping and grinding on the counter a few feet away'.[24]

After spending Christmas in Houston with his old friends Jean and Michael Judd, Freddie returned to London early in 1949, to teaching, the

Metalogical Society and other commitments, and Angelica followed him, moving into Whitehorse Street. The experiment was not a success and she moved out in the autumn, when she took up with a younger man, John Maclarent, causing Ayer a stab of jealousy'.[25] Angelica and Freddie remained friends, but she became progressively more depressed and killed herself in January 1954, prompting the suicide of her young lover in turn. Ayer ends one of his chapters in *More of My Life* by retelling the story in a characteristically matter of fact fashion: 'She rang me on the night of her death, without giving me any hint of her intention, which may not yet have been formed. I do not think that I could have done anything to save her'.[26]

Ayer celebrated New Year's Eve of 1949–50 at a party given by an actress friend Bunty Howard. Just as the clock struck midnight, he found himself looking into the face of a young, dark-haired woman, whom he kissed. Jocelyn Rickards, slim, small and dark, had the appearance of a sexy pixie, with a *retroussé* nose, a serene, sensual round face and large round eyes. She had been born in Melbourne in 1924, into a prosperous middle-class family and as a child moved to Sydney, where she eventually went to art school. She had been in London only a year when she and Ayer had their new year's kiss, but she and her sometime boyfriend, a handsome and successful fashion photographer called Alec Murray, had quickly built up a fashionable circle of young actors, artists and designers. Jocelyn and Freddie's relationship took off slowly and it was several months before they became lovers. She remembered that a few days after Ayer finally 'bedded' her, they found themselves walking in Green Park together: 'I was so obviously happy that Freddie asked why I wasn't able to say I loved him. I laughed and said I loved him, but didn't think I wanted to get married'. He was delighted: 'no man was ever more pleased to hear that I was not hell-bent on marriage'.[27]

For their first year together Freddie and Jocelyn tended to see one another alone: she liked 'the warm anonymous cocoon he wove around' her, and would make herself at home in his flat, waiting for him to return from one of his parties.[28] Later, beginning with a large party at the old ICA in Soho, he began to introduce her to London literary life, from which she came to draw many of her closest friends, including Graham Greene, with whom she had an affair, Robert Kee, George Orwell's widow, Sonia, and Cyril Connolly's wife, the enchanting Barbara

Skelton. Ayer in turn liked her younger, faster crowd of friends, becoming particularly close to Alec Murray. Murray and Jocelyn shared a large flat in Eton Square with the ballet critic Peter Williams, where she and Freddie frequently had parties. They went more often still to the Gargoyle, usually dining first at L'Etoile. Freddie, Jocelyn found, was the only man in her life she was ever able to dance with: 'Our bodies moved together relaxed and unselfconscious in a single light-hearted rhythm'.[29] In June 1951 the Cummingses made their first post-war visit to Europe, and Freddie and Jocelyn spent a week with them in Paris.

Like most of the women to whom Freddie became seriously attached, Jocelyn Rickards was a foreigner, with few of the doubts, fears and scruples of English women of her class. She was alert and open-minded, outspoken and ambitious, almost in fact domineering, with a zest for gossip and art, food and drink, and a great capacity for friendship. Ayer encouraged her to paint and disapproved when she more or less gave it up for a successful career as a costume designer. She found him wonderful and 'loved him with a single-minded devotion'. He 'would coruscate and dazzle' in public 'like a hummingbird' – at least if the public were admiring enough – and she remembered in particular his wit with words: in bed at night, he would construct acrostics for her.[30] But she detected what she later described as 'dreadful underlying anxieties which emerged in his sleep, when he would cry out "No, No, No". On one occasion he sang in a dirge-like voice, "I'm always on the outside, on the outside always looking in"'.[31]

Early in their relationship, they established a principle of absolute honesty. Freddie had taken a former student, a woman, to dinner one night and when Jocelyn asked about it, he blithely reported that they had parted after the meal. Jocelyn challenged him, feeling certain that they had made love – 'I could see it running like a film in my head' – and then proceeded to tell him exactly what she thought had occurred. Ayer confessed she was right. From that moment on they were, according to Jocelyn, entirely honest with each other. Not that there was much that either might have wanted to hide, at least at the beginning. For the first two years they were in one another's company most of the time, and Ayer became more or less faithful.

In the last week of June 1950, Ayer travelled to West Berlin to attend the first meeting of the Congress for Cultural Freedom. The congress, an international meeting of writers, scholars and scientists, had been organised by Melvin Lasky and Koestler, by this time a violent anti-communist, and funded indirectly by the recently created CIA. Intended as a Western, liberal counter-blast to a series of Soviet-backed conferences that met in East Berlin, New York and Paris in the late 1940s, it coincided with communist North Korea's invasion of South Korea. For a moment, the world seemed on the brink of a third world war. Sidney Hook, another old communist turned zealous cold-warrior, and a veteran conference-goer, reckoned it 'the most exciting conference' he had ever attended: 'The news of Korea broke just before the initial session at the Titania Palace. The meeting opened with a period of silence, memorising those who had fallen in the struggle for freedom. There was considerable uncertainty whether the Russians would move against West Germany. Instead, though, of being subdued, the delegates to the congress responded with élan to the threat of Korean events. The meeting became very militant in its denunciations of the Soviet Union'.[32] Ayer, who read a paper defending political tolerance, including even the tolerance of communists, was less approving of what he judged to be the hysterical, uncritically pro-American atmosphere, and he and Hugh Trevor-Roper made themselves unpopular by thumping the table whenever a delegate expressed support for American intervention in the conflict. Returning to England, Ayer did his best to persuade Russell to resign from his honorary presidency of the congress. Koestler was furious at Ayer's efforts to sabotage the project and they barely spoke for three years.

If anything Ayer was, during these years, an anti-anti-communist. Celia Paget recalled a conversation between Ayer, Humphrey Slater and Russell about whether Stalin or the Pope was the greater force for evil; Russell and Slater considered Stalin by far the worse, but Ayer thought the Pope had a serious claim. Ayer, nevertheless, wrote occasionally for *Encounter*, a magazine devoted to the anti-Soviet cause and widely and rightly rumoured to have been funded by the CIA. His contributions included 'Nihilism' (published much to Ayer's disapproval as 'Philosophy at Absolute Zero'), a lively and imaginative essay of 1954 in which he argued, once again, that the fact that the universe itself is purposeless is no ground for repudiating existence, or morality or anything else that nihilists repudiate.[33]

The Berlin congress was just one of many similar meetings Ayer now attended every year. He was exceptionally assiduous in this respect – no philosopher of his generation can have lectured as widely or attended more conferences. There was much, of course, that Ayer liked about these journeys: he enjoyed the sights, the meals and the new faces; and he relished performing. But beyond this, he brought to his travels the same attitudes he brought to UCL: a liberal-empiricist appreciation of the importance of a free exchange of views, especially between nations – a sense that, however pleasant it can be to stay at home and write, philosophy is a collective and, to a great extent, an oral enterprise. In the late 1940s he made his way, more or less uninvited, to three of the annual meetings of the Association des Sociétés Philosophiques de Langue Française, in Bordeaux, Strasbourg and Grenoble respectively, where he must often have been the only Anglophone philosopher present.

Ayer seems to have given up attending these conferences when he came to the conclusion that he could not learn from the French and they would not learn from him, but he lectured irregularly at the Sorbonne – for the first time on 'Truth' in January 1951 – and more often in Belgium, where there was a greater interest in analytic philosophy, and where he acquired a following. Lecture tours took him to northern Italy in the summer of 1952, and Denmark and Sweden in the autumn. In 1953 he attended the eleventh World Congress of Philosophy in Brussels: it was his first world congress, but from that point on he was at most of its five-yearly meetings until his death. The same year saw his election to the Institution Internationale de Philosophie, a French-based organisation devoted, like the world congresses, to bringing philosophers from different countries together. From 1953, when he was first elected to the congress, to 1978, when he began to attend less regularly, he had missed only three of its annual meetings, despite the fact that its debates were rarely of high quality.

Two longer journeys in the early 1950s stand out. In May 1951 Ayer was invited to Peru to celebrate the 400th anniversary of the University of San Marcos at Lima. He and Jocelyn were at the height of their romance, but she later burnt his letters and as no others have survived, nothing is known about the visit other than what can be gleaned from his memoirs: that after the congress at Lima he visited some of the ancient Inca sites, and then made a short lecture tour of Chile, Uruguay and Brazil. In Santiago and Montevideo he lectured in Spanish, in Rio in French.

In the autumn of 1954, on the fifth anniversary of Mao's Revolution, Ayer was invited to join a party of writers and artists on a tour of Peking, Shanghai and Hanchow. The group included Ayer's friend, the architect Hugh Casson, the novelist Rex Warner and the painter Stanley Spencer. He liked Rex Warner, respected Casson and found Spencer 'a vile little man, boring on an unwholesomely lavish scale, intolerable, interested only in himself and women.'[34] One can, indeed, hardly imagine someone Ayer was less disposed to like than the mystical Christian misfit, who wore his flannel pyjamas under his clothes throughout the trip: the two men bickered like children.

It was five years since the Chinese Communists had taken power, the horrors of the Cultural Revolution lay in the future and the English party were on the whole impressed by what they saw. They watched a five-hour parade, in which a quarter of a million Chinese marched past. Only a fraction were military, and the great majority displayed what seemed to be a genuine enthusiasm for the new regime. 'The old Liberal in me felt that this was not the way in which people ought to react in the presence of their rulers,' Ayer wrote at the time. 'But it does suggest that the regime is not likely to be internally overthrown.'[35] Like Russell, he found Peking 'the most beautiful city in the World',[36] and was pleased to see that the traditional empiricism of Chinese thought had been allowed some space in Mao's reformulation of Marxism. On the way to China, the group visited Moscow, which Ayer likened to Victorian England. 'There is the same expanding economy, the harsh conditions of labour, the belief in a Utopia to be attained through material progress, the jingoism, a certain sanctimoniousness and moral earnestness, and almost exactly the same artistic tastes.'[37] The plane journeys to and from China were long and boring but Ayer was able to boast that by the end of the trip he had read the whole of Gibbon's Decline and Fall.

Ayer gave a radio talk on his return, 'Impressions of Communist China', but the broadcast was, even by his standards, strangely lifeless. There is no doubt that China had made a very great impression on him, especially Peking where he spent a fortnight – he was moved by the exuberance of the people, the colours of its buildings, and the serenity of its parks – but his powers of description were not adequate to the occasion. It was not as if he thought, as an empiricist, that writers had a duty simply to report the facts – philosophy had to be analytic, not literature – but when he came to describe his own experiences, however intense, the prose came out flat.

If travel became, in the post-war years, one source of intense, if not easily articulated experience, football became another. Freddie watched Spurs sporadically in the 1930s and 1940s but regularly during the 1949–50 season, and from then until he died he hardly ever missed a home match if he was in London. It was the success of Tottenham Hotspur under Arthur Rowe's management that revived his interest. On taking over the team in the late 1940s, Rowe introduced his famous 'push and run' strategy, encouraging the players to make short passes, releasing the ball quickly and running into open spaces. The speed and energy the game took on naturally appealed to Freddie; Rowe's motto, 'Make it simple make it quick', could have been his own. He was happy enough to attend Spurs' White Hart Lane grounds by himself, bantering with other regulars who knew him as 'The Prof', but he usually went with Julian, friends such as Goronwy Rees, Philip Toynbee, the novelist Henry Green, an old secret service colleague Nigel Clive or the poet and publisher Alan Ross. Occasionally he would bring a girlfriend, delighting in initiating them into the intricacies of the game.

Although Ayer's future wife, Dee, remembered him pointing out the patterns the players made on the field – 'Pretty, aren't they?' – there was nothing especially high-minded or aesthetic in Ayer's appreciation of football: the pleasure in the game, as in life, was to immerse onself in it, to identify with your chosen team – and his enjoyment was sincere and unselfconscious. Julian, not uncritical of his father, recalled that he would roar himself hoarse during a match in a genuine display of excitement, and then, sharing a cab with other supporters, 'would argue all the way home, at it hammer and tongs'.[38] Anthony Dworkin, who was taken by Ayer to some matches when he was a child, thought he liked the ritual – 'he always had a hot dog with onions' – and being part of a large male crowd: 'he enjoyed the emotions, the camaraderie'.[39] At the same time, like his enthusiasm for film and musical comedies, football made for endless conversation and gave a certain opportunity to show off.

His editor at the *New Statesman*, Karl Miller, described Ayer's appreciation as 'fact-heavy but judicious'. He liked to test co-supporters' knowledge of the game.[40]

The England of the 1950s was a place worried and confused by changing class structures, preoccupied with what was 'U' and 'non-U', but with a son at Eton, Ayer enjoyed flouting the class boundaries football set in place.[41] The media loved the unlikeliness of it all, and as the decade progressed, he became football's most famous egghead, called on to radio and television to compare the 1960 Spurs team with the Arsenal sides of the 1930s, or the 'push and run', 'continental' style with the English long passing method, or Spurs' great captain Danny Blanchflower – who became a friend of Ayer's in the 1960s and was often at his house – with Duncan Edwards of Manchester. Empiricism's critics like to argue that empiricists work with an excessively computational view of the mind – that they overrate 'knowing that' at the expense of 'knowing how', that they fail to understand that bodily skills are themselves a form of knowledge. Ayer's feeling for sport, however, like his love of dancing, is hard to reconcile with this.

By the summer of 1952, Jocelyn and Freddie had known each other for two and a half years and evolved a large network of common friends; they were very much like an easygoing married couple. It was not long, however, before the ground began to shift beneath their relationship. Jocelyn believed the problem was precisely that they were all but married: a wedding was beginning to look inevitable and she, indeed, now wanted one. In the winter of 1952, Freddie began a series of affairs. 'Girls came and went, or came and stayed,' Jocelyn recalled. 'Progressively I became part of a trio, a quartet, a quintet, and sextet (plus Renée)':

I didn't behave particularly badly, but I didn't behave well. Like an Indian tracker, I would leave signs for my rivals to read. Before I left Whitehorse Street in the morning, when the bed was already carefully made by Freddie's splendid Mrs Moore, I would go upstairs and wipe my finger across my freshly applied lipstick, turn the cover of the bed down and smear my red-tipped finger across the pillowslip. I would leave small reminders of my presence in the bathroom. And sometimes, feeling particularly malevolent, I would, when making love, scratch Freddie's back, so that the next pair of fingers could read by braille the story of my existence.[42]

Freddie, according to Jocelyn, handled his affairs and her attempts to sabotage them, 'with great dexterity. All the ladies knew about me, I knew about all of them, but none of them knew about each other'. If he had been more sensitive, he might have seen that beneath her veneer of acceptance, Jocelyn was 'wildly jealous'. Finally, owing to Ayer's lack of initiative, sex between them came to an end, and she more or less admitted defeat: 'If he so much wanted his freedom, I thought, it was better that he should have it'.[43] They were still in one another's company and remained, in the world's eyes, a couple, giving parties together and dining out. But by the time Freddie dedicated *The Problem of Knowledge* to her in December 1955, their love affair was all but over.

The most significant rival to Jocelyn during the period in which they were gradually drifting apart was Alvys Maben, like many of Ayer's girlfriends an actress, often on the radio or in supporting roles in the West End. Dee Ayer remembered her as 'beautiful and sweet – just a very nice person'. She had an unhappy upbringing in a rich Northern family – her father had named her after his car – fled to London and married a doctor during the war. When Ayer met her she was already divorced, with a flat off the Fulham Road. Eager and vulnerable, she quickly fell for Ayer and moved herself into his Whitehorse flat more or less uninvited. Alvys helped teach him to talk clearly on the radio, but in other respects the arrangement was not a success: 'I am afraid that I still subconsciously resented the invasion of my privacy, and she was too sensitive not to respond in kind'.[44] She had not been living there for more than two or three months, when she became ill. Ayer took her to Paris to recuperate and, much to his surprise, came back alone. While in the French capital, he had introduced her to a friend of his, a French diplomat whom she promptly married. Francette Drin remembered that at the time Ayer was indignant – 'I loved her' – but Francette felt he was entirely deserving of his fate. 'He was terrible, he used to boast about how many girlfriends he had, "One for breakfast, one for lunch, one for dinner." He treated Alvys very badly'.[45]

In the winter of 1955–56 Ayer suggested to Jocelyn that they spend the Easter holidays together in Rome. She had exhausted herself after nine months' work on the set of *The Prince and the Showgirl*, with Laurence Olivier and Marilyn Monroe, while at the same time nursing her friend Alec Murray through tuberculosis, and the holiday was intended to help her recuperate. At the same time, the Cummingses would be passing through the city, so it would also provide an opportunity for Ayer to see his old friends. Jocelyn at least looked on the holiday as one last chance to revive their relationship, but although they had a 'wonderful' time, her hopes proved unfounded. She remembered a night when she arranged to meet an old friend, a poet and film-maker, Nelo Risi, and Freddie went off on his own. 'Nelo and I tried to spend a night together, and humiliatingly failed because of Italian laws preventing people who hadn't all their documents with them from booking in to an hotel together. At the same time, Freddie was trying to charm a sensational blonde American girl into bed – and he failed too. It was a night of spectacular misjudgement on all our parts, and one of the most ludicrous misadventures in which I was ever involved'.[46]

They stayed in a small suite of rooms in the Inghilterra, in the centre of the city. Ayer spent each morning 'covering pages of foolscap paper with his minuscule writing, which looked as though a fly with wet feet had marched evenly from side to side across the page', and in the afternoons they explored the city.[47] The Cummingses arrived, tired and a little frustrated. Estlin was now America's most famous living poet and his readings drew crowds of thousands, but he remained an implacable opponent of mass society, irascible and reclusive. He was abnormally sensitive to noise and both he and Marion suffered from arthritis. 'Spain was icy' and Italy was 'cold, cold, cold, cold'. In Venice they had encountered motor-boats and television, in Florence motorbikes.[48] Nevertheless, Jocelyn was charmed by them both – 'of all of Freddie's friends they were the two I loved the most' – especially Cummings, who delighted her with his large repertoire of bawdy lyrics.[49]

Altogether, Jocelyn recalled, she and Freddie 'had enjoyed being with each other'. But 'returning to London was sad. I knew it was the end of the line for him and me. He did not want to marry and he still felt, in a curious way, married to that wretched Renée, who, even though they had been divorced for something like fourteen years, used to insist that they celebrate their anniversary together'.[50] It was indeed the end of their period as a couple, although Jocelyn remained the closest of any of his old girlfriends and he would turn to her again and again. Ayer sometimes regretted not marrying her – she was lively and stylish, a good organiser and a fine cook – but within eight weeks of returning from Rome he had met someone else.

16

All Change

In its files the publisher Macmillan has a letter from Ayer, dated 20 June 1956, requesting that a copy of *The Foundations of Empirical Knowledge* be sent to a Mrs Wells, at her London address. Dee Wells, Ayer's principal girlfriend of the late 1950s, grew up as 'a crafty quick witted savage'.[1] She was born Dee Chapman in 1925, to a WASP, but relatively impoverished New England family. Her father worked for the family paper, the *Providence Journal*, but a few years after Dee's birth, he moved with his wife and children to the old whaling town of New Bedford, where he became an executive in a telephone company. His wife, Dee's mother, was a depressed, unbalanced woman, capable of a 'mesmerising charm' but also 'cruel, violent and vicious': she harboured murderous fantasies and killed any animals – chickens, cats, dogs – she could lay her hands on. Dee describes her as 'the most untrustworthy, destructive person I have ever known'.[2]

Dee was formidably intelligent – Ayer would say that she was the most intelligent woman he had known – but although her brothers and sister were educated at Harvard, Swarthmore and Radcliffe, she never attended university. Having decided that 'war could not possibly be more unpleasant than home', she went north aged eighteen, and enlisted in the Canadian army. Although she remained in Canada throughout World War Two, and thus never saw action, she quickly rose to the rank of acting sergeant-major. After the conflict was over, she worked as a receptionist for the publisher Random House in New York, and then in 1947 bought a one-way ticket to Paris, where she worked at the American Embassy. In Paris she met and married Alfred Wells, an American diplomat, and moved with him to a posting in Burma. They separated amicably a few years later, however, and in 1954 Dee moved to London with their young daughter, Gully, where she secured a position with the *New York Times* writing about French and English fashion and 'London life'. Journalism was in the family blood and Dee Wells quickly made a name for herself, moving first to the *Sunday Express* and then, early in the 1960s, to the left-wing *Daily Herald*, staying when it changed its name to the *Sun*. She was hired to write book reviews, but her remit soon widened to cover film, politics and anything else she cared to write about from her left-wing feminist angle. With her courage, energy and determination, she would have made a good war reporter. Like many journalists, she wanted, one day, to write a novel.

Dee was loud, glamorous, and very funny in a tough-talking way: 'I just hate nice people – people that are good – but then I have not met many'. When Freddie was invited to the von Hofmannsthals' large estate outside Salzburg, she responded 'Their *Schloss* is everybody else's gain.' A little shorter than Freddie, she had brown hair, a straight nose, and a strong square jaw, offset by animated soft blue eyes. Her broadsides were launched, her 'mother-fuckers' dropped, in a deep bourbon drawl.

Freddie and Dee first met early in June 1956, at a ball given by Freddie's old friend Bill Deakin, in the basement of St Antony's College. At the time Dee was engaged to Labour economist Robert Neild but had been brought to Oxford by another admirer. Freddie was introduced to her and they danced the foxtrot, their performance overshadowed by Iris Murdoch, who, having landed on her bottom at the foot of the stairs, proceeded to gallop dramatically around the floor. Dee had no idea of Ayer's identity when they were introduced, and when she asked, over the music, what he did, was surprised to hear him reply 'I am a magician.' There followed an absurdly one-sided conversation about top hats and rabbits, until Ayer brought their dance to a halt: 'I didn't say magician, I said *logician*.' It was not a promising start, but she was sufficiently intrigued by this man to contrive to bump into him again on the train back to London the next day and when he suggested that they go out to dinner that night, she agreed. Freddie was still living in Whitehorse Street, and Dee had temporarily settled in the house of some friends, Sue and Basil Boothby, in Holland Park, and they were soon dividing their time between their two homes.* Dee recalled with amusement the condescension among Freddie's other girlfriends at her arrival on the scene, 'like bad news blown in from Winnetka ... When I finally captured him, they were horrified'.

Freddie had indeed a large collection of beautiful and accomplished girlfriends. There was Jean Dawney who began life as an air hostess and ended by marrying the Russian Prince George Galitzine, with a successful career modelling for Christian Dior and others in between; the gossip columns called her and Freddie 'the odd couple'. There was elegant Janetta Jackson, and the willowy, blue-eyed Joan Raynor, who later married Paddy Leigh Fermor. (The Macmillan files show that Raynor was another lucky recipient of *The Foundations of Empirical Knowledge*.) Another leading model, Bronwyn Pugh, who later married Lord Astor and converted to Catholicism, and Janey Ironside, the new Professor of Fashion at the Royal College of Art, also enjoyed his company. Ironside and Freddie often lunched together in Soho. He tried to teach her to play chess, but they had to compromise with the *Times* crossword puzzles, of which she fairly soon got the knack.[3] One bouncy girlfriend from the era, who soon realised there was no point in competing with Dee, wrote to Ayer not long after she broke with him:

Dear Freddie
By the time you get this I shall be in France and married, but at the moment I am still I and nothing has started. My father's in his tails, we leave in half an hour and I'm feeling numb, which is not unpleasant.
    I had another dream about you in the night, and this morning I

---

* Dee had befriended Sue and Basil Boothby in Burma where Boothby, a British diplomat, had been posted. By the time Dee and Freddie met, Boothby had been appointed to the British Embassy in Brussels – later he would become ambassador in Iceland – and Dee had their London house more or less to herself. Ayer was introduced to them by Dee and over the years they became close friends. Boothby was interested in philosophy and supported Spurs and the two men often went to White Hart Lane together. Sue, who belonged to the Asquith family, was 'a woman of character and charm' (*MML*, p.127).

thought I would write you this note. It is to say that you have my love and affection always.

Dee remembers that 'the four years it took us to get married saw a lot of frenzied love affairs on Freddie's part. Some men played golf. Freddie played women. He was not at all malicious – he did not want to hurt anyone. Having someone like that is much less grisly than having a drunk for a husband or someone full of malice.'

Outside of his relationship with Dee, Ayer's life went on much as before. That summer's Joint Session was held in Aberystwyth on the very un-Ayerian topics of dreams and self-knowledge. He was also presumably in Paris for the annual meeting if the IIP (Institution Internationale de Philosophie). Autumn of 1956 saw publication of *The Problem of Knowledge* and the Suez crisis – Ayer signed the inevitable letter of protest to the *Times*. He took a more individual part in another controversy – that over Colin Wilson's *Outsider*. Wilson's ruminations on outsiderhood were published in the summer of 1956 and were an enormous commercial and critical success. Cyril Connolly, Edith Sitwell, Philip Toynbee, Elizabeth Bowen and V.S. Pritchett all hailed it as a masterpiece: here at last was Britain's answer to Sartre and Camus, a work of 'real philosophy'. Ayer had no quarrel with the lower-class Angry Young Men of the 1950s – he liked and admired Kingsley Amis in particular – but he remained unimpressed by Wilson's book. In its disdain for ordinary people who work at regular jobs, its gratuitous pessimism and sloppy logic, it epitomised all that Ayer found worst in existentialism and he said so in a harsh *Encounter* review:

> Though Mr Wilson assumes, apparently on *a priori* grounds, that the great mass of people, the despised bourgeoisie, who work at jobs, are living the lives of automata, I have no doubt, that if one could undertake the research one would find that it was not at all uncommon for them to be interested in the questions of how they should live.[4]

Ayer's review is a reminder that however close he was socially to London literary society, his training as a philosopher gave him a critical vantage point on it.

In May 1957, Ayer took Dee to Russell's eighty-fifth birthday party in the Millbank flat where he and Edith stayed when they came from Wales. Meyer Schapiro, lecturing in London, went with them. The occasion stuck in Dee's mind because she saw Russell, Ayer and the young Bernard Williams talking together; they represented three generations of British philosophy, and, all slight in build with the same thin, distinguished noses and agile faces, looked like a triptych of the three ages of man.

In June 1957, a year to the day after Freddie met Dee, she was introduced to Renée for the first time. The occasion was Eton's Fourth of June celebrations and Julian, now a tall, scholarly and athletic eighteen-year-old, was at the end of his last year at the school. Renée was friendly and animated, and Dee found her charming although eccentric. She remembers asking Renée, during a picnic lunch, when she would tell Julian about his origins: 'It's not up to me. Freddie and Stuart are his parents.' And this, despite the fact that Julian's housemaster, James Parr, had written to Renée a few months before, urging her to reveal all: 'I am certain that to learn the truth from anyone (even Valerie) other than you and Freddie would be a mistake, perhaps even a danger, for him'.[5] In the event, neither Renée nor Ayer was brave enough to tell Julian the truth, and he discovered it from a girlfriend while an undergraduate at Oxford. Isaiah Berlin remembered that Julian came to him in a state of extreme distress, wanting to change his name.[6] Ayer did his best to pretend that nothing of any significance had occurred, and with time their relationship settled into its old pattern.

The IIP held its congress in Warsaw that summer. After visiting Krakow and Auschwitz, Ayer went to stay with the Hofmannsthals in their large *Schloss* in Zell-am-See, to the west of Salzburg. The house was grand and Raimund and Liz entertained in style. Ayer had been there several times before in the course of the 1950s, working in the morning, playing tennis with Liz in the afternoon. Early on in their friendship Raimund formed the view that Ayer was an expert mathematician, and despite Ayer's attempts to disabuse him of this notion, he was put to work coaching their son, Octavian, in the subject. Octavian described him as a surprisingly impatient teacher, perhaps because he had so little patience with the subject himself. He recalled, too, how Ayer would provoke the assembled aristocrats by defending the socialist cause, at one point arguing that no one should be allowed an income above a certain fairly modest amount – roughly that, strangely, of an Oxford professor. Octavian had the impression that Ayer was 'very left wing – nobody else who came to stay shared his views'.[7]

Early in the next year he was away lecturing in India and Western Pakistan. He was granted audiences with the President of the country, Radakrishnan, and the Defence Minister, Krishna Menon, as well as with Prime Minister Nehru. It was Nehru who most impressed him; the great man was charming and wise, an undoctrinaire but radical moderniser of just the sort Ayer admired. He was less pleased to discover that Bradleian idealism still predominated among the philosophers he met, their predecessors having been converted to the school by Scottish evangelists in the late nineteenth century. Instead of talking, as he had planned to do, about the fashionable topic of 'Philosophy and Ordinary Language', Ayer found himself once again deploying Russell's and Moore's old arguments against the view that the universe was a single seamless spiritual whole.

Back in England, Ayer's broadcasting career was flourishing. In October 1956, he was invited to appear for the first time on *The Brains Trust*. The programme already had a long history. It began early in the war, when the 'trust' consisted of three men, Julian Huxley, scientist, C.E.M. Joad, philosopher, and Commander Campbell, common man. The talkative trio, who debated theoretical and practical questions sent in by listeners, were never at a loss. In 1955, the programme transferred to television and the panel, now increased to four, changed from week to week, although there were certain favourites like Huxley and Bronowski, the historian Alan Bullock, and the literary critic Marghanita Laski. It is surprising that Ayer had to wait as long as he did for an invitation, but with his first programme, he became a star performer. Between 1956 and 1961 he appeared in forty-three programmes, including the last, featuring Henry Kissinger and broadcast from New York.

Sometimes the discussions ignited – in 1960 Ayer and his old sparring partner, Father d'Arcy, quarrelled vehemently about the existence of God – but for the most part they were well mannered and discursive. The broadcast of 26 October 1957 with Aldous and Julian Huxley, and the scientist, W. Grey Walter, seems representative. The panellists agreed about the permissibility of using drugs to alleviate anxiety and about the necessity of limiting growth in the world's population. (Like the others,

Ayer thought the greatest hope lay in the development of a chemical contraceptive, but insisted, for extra measure, on the importance of combating religion.) He denied, as a matter of logic, that mystical experience could ever increase the sum of human knowledge, there being no way of verifying the existence or the attributes of the entities mystically apprehended, though he readily conceded that such experiences might be valuable in other ways to those who have them. If anything distinguished Ayer from his fellow panellists, it was his clear-headedness – the questions, after all, were philosophical. The panel was asked whether it would approve of the development of a machine capable of identifying suitable marriage partners on the basis of their interests and character traits. Ayer got right to the point when he saw that the machine was a red herring: the issue concerned *mariages de convenance* versus marriages of love. Ayer's voice, too, was distinctive. It was the lightest of them all, irregular in its pace – like a Martian who had only recently mastered talking – almost nasal and slightly grating, but it lilted in a bizarrely attractive way.

Ayer's broadcasts before *The Brains Trust* had been mainly confined to highbrow matters – or to those and football – but the 'Trust' made him famous. His first newspaper profile appeared in the *Observer* in 1957, by his old friend Philip Toynbee, who likened Ayer, like many others who wrote about him, to an animal: 'There is something cocksparrow-like about this outwardly self-confident man', Toynbee suggested in a loving and observant sketch, 'and one has to know him well before recognising that the apparent assurance conceals a real modesty and inner nervousness . . . His mind is fundamentally commonsensical, but capable of carrying the implications of common sense into far, obscure and almost dream-like regions.' This was followed by deeply admiring profiles in *The Telegraph* in 1959 and *The Sunday Times* in 1962, the latter describing him as 'the most influential philosopher in this country'.[8] Along with the profiles came the other trappings of fame: mail, abusive and admiring, invitations to talk at schools and literary societies, verses in *Punch* and cartoons in the *New Statesman*. Ayer now appeared on radio and television, talking on football rowdyism, Russell, cricket, the nature of truth, children's fiction, the non-existence of God. One could hear him *Talking Sport* with Tommy Steele, romantic literature in *Not So Much a Programme, More a Way of Life*, or the National Health Service on *Any*

Questions. He even appeared on the early evening dictionary game, *Call My Bluff*, and the pop music show, *Juke Box Jury*. At the time Ayer relished the attention – 'I am famous therefore I exist' – although later he came to regret that *The Brains Trust* had given him 'an uncritical appetite for publicity': there was an embarrassing moment on one chat show, where Eartha Kitt began to flirt with Ayer and he floundered, talking pompously about medieval literature. He was becoming well known, too, in America, although that had more to do with *Language, Truth and Logic* than *The Brains Trust*. Late in the 1950s Roy Harrod wrote to say that an American publisher had approached him, asking whether he would be interested in writing Ayer's life.[9] In 1963 Ayer was elected, along with F.R. Leavis, an honorary member of the American Academy of Arts.

One of the producers on *The Brains Trust* was a young graduate from Oxford, Catherine Dove. She later married the journalist, Charles Wheeler and the Labour MP and diplomat, John Freeman, and made a successful career as a TV producer, but in the late 1950s she and Ayer were often together. He was, she recalled, extremely vain and found the fame *The Brains Trust* brought him 'exhilarating', but he was not remotely affected. He could not bear 'emotional scenes': ' "Don't get fussed, my darling" was a stock phrase. It was very Noël Coward'. The only time Catherine ever saw him genuinely upset was in February 1958, just before he flew to India, when seven members of Manchester United's team were killed in the Munich plane crash. Then he cried.[10]

Early in the summer of 1958, Ayer had been obliged to make a flying visit to the US, to attend Valerie's wedding. Having worked for a short time as an assistant producer at the BBC, Valerie had moved to New York, and there met her future husband, a young philosophy student. Ayer felt she was getting married for the wrong reasons, not least of all to escape 'her mother's over-powering influence', and the marriage did indeed quickly break up.[11] (Renée, now living once again in Hampstead, did not herself go to the wedding, 'Mummy G' – Mrs Godley – standing in.) Ayer had been a devoted father, but one senses that from this point a certain distance entered into their relationship. A kind and loving person, Valerie was neither especially glamorous nor particularly academic, and it is hard not to feel that he slightly lost interest in her: she certainly felt jealous, whether justifiably or not, of Dee and Gully.

By the time of Valerie's wedding Ayer and Dee were very much an established couple – after his return from the US, they holidayed together with Gully, Francette Drin and a mutual friend, Jo Saxe, in a house Saxe owned outside Paris – and in many ways they were well matched. More sociable than Renée, more political than Jocelyn, she was, like them, an outsider. Looking back on their relationship in the last year of his life, Ayer reflected that they were both 'iconoclasts and shared the same sense of humour'. He loved the way things happened around her: she was always throwing parties, giving dinners, making new friends. She admired his clarity of mind and stubborn sense of justice.

That September Ryle drove Ayer to Venice for one of the five-yearly meetings of the World Congress of Philosophy. Ayer found the journey rather a strain. Driving across a particularly flat part of France and running out of things to say, Freddie asked Ryle whether he was a virgin. Ryle replied tersely that he was. 'And if you were to sleep with someone, would it be more likely to be a boy or a girl.' 'Boy I suppose'. They drove on in silence.* The truth was that he and Ryle had little in common except philosophy, and even here they found less to agree on than they once had. Ayer thought Ryle's masterpiece, *The Concept of Mind*, with its attack on the existence of private thoughts and feelings, a provocative but in many ways simplistic book and his writings of the 1950s and 1960s often take issue with it. Ayer's paper for Venice, 'Meaning and Intentionality' – a thumbnail sketch of meaning in terms of belief – was atypically thin, or at least programmatic. His ideas on the subject, however, were fleshed out in a later book, *The Origins of Pragmatism*, and the paper at least allowed him, true to form, to commend the work of one of his UCL graduate students.

In the autumn of 1958, owing to ill health, Henry Price resigned from his position as Oxford's Wykeham Professor of Logic and Ayer decided to apply for the Chair. He thought Price a greatly underrated philosopher, and was pleased at the prospect of picking up his baton. It was negative considerations, however, that really counted. Ayer had long been arguing against the similarly directed turn taken by Wittgenstein and his followers in Cambridge and Oxford's 'ordinary language' philosophers – a turn which had done so much to bring logical positivism into discredit.

---

* Ryle, for his part, had long come to a view about Ayer's sexuality. He and the writer Paul Johnson were chatting in Oxford in the late 1940s when they spotted Ayer walking sprightly across a quad – 'might have been a great philosopher—ruined by sex' (Paul Johnson, IWA. 29 March 2000).

The Wykeham professorship would allow him to carry his argument right into the enemy camp; above all, it would give him the chance to do something to counter the attacks Austin, now Professor of Moral Philosophy, had been launching on him in his lectures. It would enable him to confront his old rival face to face.[12]

By the time of Wittgenstein's death in 1951, he had established a firm ascendancy over Cambridge; the posthumous publication of the *Philosophical Investigations* (1953) helped spread his influence further afield. It has become commonplace to say that much of Wittgenstein's later work is best understood as a very critical working over, often amounting to rejection, of his earlier thought. Where the *Tractatus* had offered a radically simple version of language, captured by the metaphor of words as pictures, his later work drew attention to the variety of uses to which language is put – to the way we use words to describe, but also to command, commend, greet, thank, curse and joke. The metaphor of a picture was replaced by that of a tool. According to the *Investigations*, philosophical puzzles arise when philosophers overlook this great range of practices or 'language games', each with its own logic, and attempt to force language into a single mould. The task of the philosopher, as Wittgenstein came to see it, is not to devise theories to deal with these problems but to 'dissolve' them by calling attention to the way language works – a job which involved all the practice, patience and dexterity that goes into the untangling and mending of fishing nets. This method was well illustrated by Wittgenstein's treatment of 'mental psychology', where he sought to show how the empiricist belief in an inner self, made up of sense-data and mental images, arises from neglect of the way we actually use phrases like 'it hurts', 'it seems to me' or 'I remember'. Indeed Wittgenstein famously denied the very possibility of a private language, a language that refers to inner experiences. Language, he contended, must be public.

Ayer was never remotely convinced by this 'private language argument'. He first criticised it in an article in the *Proceedings of the Aristotelian Society* in 1954, and returned to the attack time and again over the next thirty years. Wittgenstein's case against the logical possibility of a private language rested on what was in effect a *reductio ad absurdum*: the inventor of a private language used to refer to mental sensations would not be able to distinguish between actually using a word properly and just thinking it was being used properly; there would be no objective linguistic rule against which he could check his own usage; but if there is no distinction between really getting it right and just thinking we have got it right, then the concept of rightness has no content at all. The problem with this position, Ayer contended, was that even in the case of a public language, the same situation arises: I can check my understanding of a term against other people's usage or against dictionary definitions, but then, in turn, I might misunderstand the meaning offered to me. Ultimately, Ayer argued, all language rests on what he called an act of 'primary recognition', which itself contains no guarantee that the recognition is valid.

Beyond his objections to the private language argument, Ayer had an interestingly ambivalent attitude to Wittgenstein's later philosophy. He found it hard to glean exactly what Wittgenstein wanted to say, and in so far as he could, he disagreed with the general drift of his thought. Yet reading the *Investigations* he felt the power of the writing and the suggestiveness of the examples and was thus never able to dismiss it in the way Russell and, to some extent, Popper did. There was less ambivalence, however, in Ayer's view of Wittgenstein's followers, like Elizabeth Anscombe and Norman Malcolm. In the 1960s he published an uncharacteristically tough attack on Malcolm's Wittgensteinian treatment of dreams – his argument that dreams were not private experiences but dispositions to tell untrue experiences when waking. Ayer told Chris Coope, a student of the early 1960s, that one could write one of Malcolm's essays while doing something else.[13]

Oxford philosophy of the 1940s and 1950s was more indebted to Wittgenstein than it liked to admit. Ryle had become a close friend of Wittgenstein in the 1930s and *The Concept of Mind*, published in 1949, owed a great deal to Wittgenstein's example. Friedrich Waismann, one of Wittgenstein's closest Viennese associates, arrived in Oxford just before the war and his imaginative examinations of the varieties of grammar won him a following and provided another conduit for Wittgenstein's ideas. And of course Wittgenstein's 'Blue and Brown Books' circulated in samizdat even before the appearance of *Investigations*. Nevertheless, Ryle and Austin were important thinkers in their own right, who developed Wittgensteinian ideas in original ways, and when at the end of the war they found themselves the leading figures in a university flooded with mature and eager students, they set about, fairly self-consciously, building up what became known as the 'Oxford' or 'ordinary language' or 'linguistic' school.

Ryle did much to help found this school. His book *The Concept of Mind* was its flagship, the journal *Mind*, which he edited, became its official organ, and the Oxford B.Phil. in philosophy, which he established after the war, served as its principal training ground, educating a generation of young students in what Ryle liked to call 'The Revolution in Philosophy'. Indeed, at an institutional level, Ryle reigned supreme, exercising an unparalleled power over philosophy appointments in Oxford and beyond.

Yet for all of Ryle's industry and reach, it was Austin who did most to shape the character of 'linguistic philosophy'. Austin wrote very little – by the time of Price's retirement, his published works ran to no more than three lectures, four symposium papers and a few reviews, published over a period of thirty years – but his qualities as an interlocutor and lecturer ensured that his influence over Oxford in many ways resembled Wittgenstein's over Cambridge. Like Wittgenstein and Moore before him, he was a philosopher who mesmerised his audience, generating something very like discipleship; his writings cannot possibly convey the importance that his ideas seemed to take on in his presence. Where he differed from Wittgenstein, and disapproved of him, was that he discouraged anything like a cult of personality: he wanted to put philosophy on a collective footing, convinced that it was only if philosophers worked in teams (very much like the intelligence teams he had built up during the war), each tackling different aspects of a problem, that the subject could make progress. The vehicle by which Austin sought to realise this conception – and the main source of his influence over Oxford philosophy – was a weekly meeting that he ran, 'Austin's Saturday Morning'. In a move of which Ayer would not have approved, he restricted attendance to philosophers junior to himself, thus effectively ruling out the presence of Price and Ryle and others who might have challenged his authority.

The guiding idea behind Austin's work was his belief that the language of any community provides its users with a near flawless set of tools with which to guide themselves through the world, and that if academic philosophy had not made the sort of progress characteristic of, say, medicine, it was because it had failed to pay sufficient heed to the way words actually work. Austin did as much as Wittgenstein to alert philosophers to the performative dimension of language – to the way saying is often doing. As Austin conceived it, then, philosophy needed to devote itself to the systematic study of the diverse logics of different linguistic practices and, within practices, the precise meaning of different terms. In one well known essay, 'A Plea for Excuses', he engaged in a minute examination of the use of words like 'inadvertently', 'deliberately', 'mistakenly', 'intentionally', in order to show how ordinary language furnishes the resources to discriminate between different shades of responsibility ignored by those philosophers who talk in terms of a simple opposition between determinism and free will.

The same approach is evident in Austin's treatment of the problems surrounding perception. Austin was a powerful, irreverent, often scornful speaker and his lectures attacking Ayer's, and to a lesser extent Price's, views on perception won him a large student following. His main complaint was that Ayer's doctrines rested on a distinction between the direct perception of sense-impressions and the indirect knowledge of material objects which has no counterpart in our language or experience; ordinary language, he argued, offers us means of discriminating appearances from reality without having recourse to the jargon of sense-data. Even some of Austin's closest admirers, like Isaiah Berlin, admitted that in the 1950s he became almost too combative and slightly rigid in his adherence to ordinary language.[14] Nevertheless, he was an utterly individual thinker and under his and Ryle's leadership English philosophy took on a rare energy and sense of purpose. Those who worked with and under them, like Peter Strawson, Herbert Hart, R.M. Hare, Geoffrey Warnock and J.O. Urmson, came to look back on the 1950s wistfully as a time when anything seemed possible. Bliss was it in that dawn to be alive, but to be young was very heaven.[15]

Ayer was the first to acknowledge the importance of respecting our everyday conceptual schemes. The job of philosophical analysis was not, he had always argued, to populate the world with new entities, but to make sense of the knowledge offered us by science and common sense. He had in fact engaged in just the sort of linguistic analysis practised in Oxford, when in his article 'Freedom and Necessity' of 1946 he invoked the distinction between being caused to do something and being forced or constrained to do it, in an attempt to argue that it did not follow, at least on the basis of ordinary language, that because an action has a cause, it is not done freely. But he was no longer happy with that paper and could never, more generally, be reconciled to Austin's approach. As he argued in a number of papers he wrote towards the end of the 1950s, the weakness in Austin's position was that there was no reason to suppose that our conceptual schemes are entirely coherent. Free will provides a good example: 'For', as he wrote in 'Philosophy and Language', a paper of 1960, 'those who are troubled by this problem are perfectly well aware that we are in fact trained to distinguish between cases in which an agent can "help himself" and those in which he cannot. Their trouble is that they do not see how this distinction can be justified.'[16]

A similar objection could be made to Austin's treatment of perception. Perhaps he was right that the language of sense-data theory was completely alien to 'the plain man'. The point remained that, as the sceptic saw, our perceptual judgements tend to affirm more than is warranted by the deliveries of our senses, thus raising important philosophical questions about whether and how they are justified.

Ayer, who had begun his career as the scourge of giddy metaphysical speculation, now found himself in the unexpected position of arguing that Austin had gone too far in the opposite direction. He had taken to its extreme a tendency which had been present in analytic philosophy from the beginning, and to the fore in the work of Moore, the later Wittgenstein and Ryle – to leave the world just as it found it.

If it is clear from Ayer's and Austin's published writings that each found the other hugely overrated, it is also evident, from those who knew them, that there was, by the 1950s, little personal sympathy between them. Ayer objected not only to Austin's views but also to his approach to students, whom, Ayer felt, he sought to convert. Perhaps Austin, who had once been under Ayer's spell, disliked him all the more intensely for it. As Geoffrey Warnock, one of Austin's closest followers, put it:

The fact is that Austin and Ayer were grossly, almost ludicrously incompatible, antipathetic characters. Austin was a respectable, rather severely upright, formal and straight-laced, dedicatedly domestic husband and *père de famille*. He not only did not pursue or even contemplate the *vie de bohème*; he would not allow it even to be discussed, thereby diverging markedly from the more usual Oxford liking for gossip. This led, of course, to his being regarded by Freddie with (on personal not professional terms) a rather uneasy mixture of incomprehension, derision and utter boredom; while he viewed Freddie (again in purely personal terms) with a kind of moral horror, as recklessly frivolous and self-indulgent in personal relations, and rather short on such virtues as truthfulness, care, loyalty and concern for others. (Of course that mirrors almost exactly the view he tended to take of Freddie's philosophy.) I don't believe Freddie ever had any understanding of the depth of pure disapproval that he aroused in Austin – just as he could never have taken seriously the provincial, private, monogamous home-body life that Austin lived.[17]

Ayer's hostility to Austin, then, gave him a mission. He once said that philosophy in Cambridge would have taken a happier course if Ramsey had lived to challenge Wittgenstein; Ayer saw himself as playing Ramsey's unfulfilled role in Oxford.[18] The election to the Wykeham professorship, however, first had to be secured. Ayer applied in December 1958, and Russell and Isaiah Berlin both wrote testimonials. Berlin's is not accessible, but Russell's was commendatory, if typically laconic:

I am writing to confirm that I consider A.J. Ayer exceedingly suitable for the post of Wykeham Professor of Logic in the University of Oxford. I have followed his work since he was quite a young man and have always found that it showed a high order of ability. I am confident that he will be found capable of inspiring a sustained interest in his subject on the part of his pupils.[19]

Ayer's election, however, was far from a foregone conclusion. Of the seven electors, Austin, as might have been expected, opposed Ayer in favour of the young Peter Strawson; so, more surprisingly, did Ryle, who voted for the historian and logician W.C. Kneale. In the end only two of the five philosophers among the electors – Anthony Quinton from New College and John Wisdom from Cambridge – supported Ayer, although he also secured the votes of the two non-philosophers, the Vice-Chancellor and the Warden of New College. The result was that Ayer was invited to occupy the Chair but not before Ryle and Austin resigned from the electoral board. They claimed that they did so in protest at the way the election was run rather than at its result, but as Ayer suggested, 'to say the least their gesture was open to misconstrual'.[20] Getting the chair, Ayer found himself in an ironic situation. He joined the three most important interlocutors of his youth, Berlin, Austin and Ryle, as professor: the radical young things of 1930s Oxford philosophy had come of age. Two, though, had opposed his entry into the club. Ryle's vote, in particular, must have hurt. Perhaps it says something about his feelings that although there is a letter from Austin among his papers congratulating him on his election, Ayer drily noted in his autobiography that Austin never wrote.[21]

As it turned out, the differences between the linguistic philosophers and their opponents almost immediately took a public turn. In November 1959, *The Times* published a letter from Bertrand Russell in which he attacked Ryle for having refused to review a new book by Ernest Gellner, *Words and Things*, attempting a systematic demolition of Oxford philosophy. Gellner had become acquainted with Austin while studying at Oxford and conceived a deep dislike for him: 'I had the impression of someone very strongly obsessed with never being wrong, and using all kinds of dialectical devices to avoid being wrong'.[22] In *Words and Things* Gellner offered a clever if over-simple indictment of Oxford philosophy, as at once superficial, conservative and most of all evasive. In its triviality – its obsession with words and its jocular, often facetious tone – it was very much, he argued, the product of a leisured class.

Ayer wrote to Russell supporting his position, but never publicly involved himself in the heated quarrel that ensued. He did however take up cudgels in his inaugural address of November 1960, 'Philosophy and Language', when, after paying fulsome tribute to Price, he sought to draw a distinction between a proper attention to language as the medium in which all concepts are expressed, and a less helpful inquiry into the 'niceties' of ordinary usage; as Ayer later admitted, 'one of my purposes was to drive a wedge between [Austin's] approach to philosophy and that of either Ryle or Wittgenstein'.[23] By then though Ayer was striking at shadows. Early in the winter of 1959–60 Austin had become ill and by February, five months after Ayer had taken up his chair, he was dead.

Their disagreement did in fact have one final round: in 1962 Geoffrey Warnock published *Sense and Sensibilia*, an edited version of Austin's lectures on perception, and Ayer responded five years later with 'Has Austin Refuted Sense Data Theory?' But it was a pedestrian paper, in which he identified seventeen distinct arguments against sense-data theory in Austin's lectures and then proceeded to knock them down one by one. The battle that had been going on between the two men for thirty years ended on a feeble note.

In the autumn of 1959, just as Ayer was taking up his professorship, he and Dee embarked on living together. Ayer approached the move with the wariness characteristic of his feelings towards most women – but the fact that he could contemplate it at all seems to have been testimony to a change in his relations with Renée. In 1957 Francis Listowel had accepted the position of Governor-General of Ghana, a move which led to a final break with her. Renée was unable to conceal her sadness from Freddie, and this, as he wrote, 'had the effect of bringing about my own liberation'.[24] It was clear at last, even to Freddie, that Renée's lovers mattered to her at least as much as he did. A few years later Renée and Hampshire married. Continuing his and Ayer's lifelong game of musical chairs, Hampshire had by that time taken up the professorship at UCL. In the 1950s the two men were still on moderately friendly terms, but gradually relations worsened, so that 'by the end of their lives they could hardly be in the same room as one another'.[25] Ayer once described Hampshire, not altogether in jest, as 'a very wicked man'; Hampshire in turn found him increasingly hard to bear:

> Freddie became a different person in the years after the war. From being a man of the Left, he became Establishment. From being anti-club he joined them and was always having lunch at the French Embassy. He came to see himself as an important cultural figure. He is almost the only person whom I have ever known who really changed. Gaiety and heterodoxy gave way to self-consciousness. From my point of view it was downhill.[26]

In the winter of 1958–59 Dee had found a small, sturdy but dilapidated four-floor Georgian house in Conway Street, off Tottenham Court Road, in the heart of Fitzrovia. Ayer agreed to buy it and Dee took charge of its conversion and decoration. In August he wrote to Marion Cummings saying that the house was ready: 'I agree that I should probably not make a good husband. We don't in fact plan to get married, at least not straightaway, but for various reasons, including the attitude of Gully's father, it may be difficult for us not to. And anyhow, the point is not so much being married as living with one person. My being away at Oxford during term may or may not make it easier. We are both full of forebodings, but it seems feeble to back out now, having got so far'.[27] Two months later Dee wrote with the news that they had finally moved in. Freddie 'so far has at least *said* that he feels cheerful, even if sometimes one catches him looking wistfully out the window toward the bright lights of Mayfair'.[28]

17

Oxford, New York, Toulon

Ayer's tenure of the Wykeham chair coincided almost exactly with the years that he lived with Dee Wells. It was a period in his life defined by the two poles of London and Oxford. Negatively put – and sometimes negatively experienced – the one provided relief from the other. Ayer was forty-nine and with greying hair when he took up the professorship, and must have done so with a certain foreboding. Original philosophical work does not come any easier with age – indeed, he found it increasingly hard, as he was the first to admit, to keep up with technical developments in logic and the philosophy of maths and science. He had, too, mixed feelings about Oxford. It had treated him badly as a young man and, anyway, the cloistered city hardly appealed to his metropolitan tastes. Richard Wollheim remembered chauffeuring him to New College in the autumn of 1960: 'He was in high spirits all the way there. As we approached the Headington roundabout, he spotted the carved wooden sign which says "City of Oxford". Freddie turned towards me. "My heart sinks," he said. "It always has at the sight of Oxford."'[1]

New College of the 1960s was admittedly a less prejudiced place than Christ Church of the 1930s. Large and rich, it is also among the most beautiful of Oxford colleges and Ayer secured one of the best sets of rooms, overlooking the college garden. In addition to a living-room and bedroom it included a study which doubled as dining-room for the lunch parties that he liked to give. As usual he left the decoration of his rooms to a woman, in this case Dee. She did not share Renée's modernist taste, but her yellow walls and ivy wallpaper nevertheless struck Freddie's graduate students as the height of sophistication. Ayer tried to spend two, at the most three, nights a week at Oxford, and this entailed squeezing in a great deal of work when he was there. As well as his undergraduate lectures, which attracted an enormous audience, he had in his first years up to fifteen graduate students to supervise – at least a day and a half's tutorial teaching a week. David Wiggins, newly arrived as a young philosophy tutor at New College, recalled that to begin with Freddie 'was, by his standards, rather nervous'.[2]

Ayer must have realised that he could not hope to have the impact on Oxford philosophy that he had had on UCL. He worked hard to establish joint degrees in philosophy and mathematics, and philosophy and physics, arguing that philosophy has almost always developed, from Thales to Mach, in union with science. It was only with the rise of Romanticism that the two had become separated, much to the detriment of philosophy. Otherwise, in terms of his contribution to the sub-faculty, he is remembered, as at UCL, as an efficient and above all brisk administrator. Peter Strawson, who succeeded Ryle to the Chair of Metaphysics in 1968, found him 'a good judge' when it came to appointments and in other ways reliable. Others complained that he could be impatient, even contemptuous, in disagreement.

At New College he simply kept away from administrative affairs: 'We did not like to ask him to sit on committees – he was too grand and easily bored,' Alan Ryan, then a young politics tutor at the college, recalled.[3] Nevertheless Ayer did his best to enliven New College's Lenten social life and was generally liked by his colleagues; he could talk French literature with Merlin Thomas, American politics with Herbert Nicholas, the Spanish Civil War with Raymond Carr. For many years he turned out for the fellows' team in their annual cricket match against a team of the college choir school. On his first appearance he scored seventy-four not out, more than the rest of the team put together. 'His batting was very much in character: quick, bold, militant.'[4]

Perhaps his closest friend was New College's senior philosophy tutor, Anthony Quinton. He got into the habit in the mid-1960s of having a weekly dinner with Quinton and his American wife, Marcelle, a sculptor, at their flat in the centre of the city, playing chess with Marcelle or talking philosophy with Tony. Surveying Ayer's work after his death, Quinton came to the fairly devastating conclusion that Ayer had made no original contributions of note; among scientifically minded philosophers, Quine and Popper were the more important. In the 1960s, however, Quinton, a large feline polymath, was something of a disciple as well as a friend. He remembered Ayer as a 'soldierly little fellow' with 'a very strong sense of duty', but he was struck, above all, by his 'remarkable freedom from malice'. This was a quality 'that gave him an almost childlike innocence by comparison with contemporaries of similar gifts and interests'.[5] Marcelle described him in similar terms: she admitted he was vain, and could be insensitive, as well as extraordinarily unobservant – 'the most unvisual person I have ever met'. But he was also 'completely without guile ... The thing about Freddie was that you saw his vices immediately, and spent the rest of your life discovering his virtues.'[6]

Never a willing administrator, Ayer devoted himself to philosophy, working harder over the next decade and a half than he ever had before. In addition to his lectures, which he changed from year to year so as to keep them fresh, he initiated 'informal instruction' in the form of a weekly seminar, open to undergraduates and graduates alike: they proved 'oases of spiritual refreshment for graduate students who found the Oxford philosophical scene rather insipid'.[7] Students read short papers, but Ayer, in his element, directed discussion. Most of his time, however, was taken up with his supervision of graduate students. Almost everyone agreed that he was an outstandingly gifted and devoted teacher, quick-witted and willing to pursue an argument wherever it led. Peter Lipton, who wrote a thesis offering a coherence theory of explanation under Ayer's supervision early in the 1960s, found their discussions 'enormously stimulating ... I would usually leave them with the feeling that I wanted to go on working for the next ten hours, only to collapse half an hour later, as the high wore off.'[8]

In addition to his lecturing and teaching, Ayer also set up in his first term a Tuesday evening group to rival Austin's 'Saturday mornings'. With philosophers like Peter Strawson and Michael Dummett attending, there was no question of Ayer dominating the group of regulars that evolved, but the conviviality of the meetings, like the presence of alcohol, owed a lot to him. Over the years they became an Oxford institution, attracting the best of each new generation. They are still running today.

It is not easy to pinpoint the direction of Ayer's thought during the early years of the 1960s, although there are signs in a number of essays, notably 'Philosophy and Science' (1962), that he was becoming increasingly interested in questions of ontology and relativism – questions about the relation between experience and theory, and the extent to which 'what counts for us as the world depends upon our conceptual system' – an interest stimulated by his reading of the American pragmatists in the late 1950s which would be taken further later.[9] Two essays, however, half logical, half moral, do stand out from this period: a discursive and imaginative lecture on 'Fatalism', delivered to the Oxford University Humanists in 1960, and a narrower more combative counterpart, 'Man as a Subject for Science', the Auguste Comte Memorial Lecture for 1964, delivered at the London School of Economics. 'Man as a Subject for Science', almost Ayer's only foray into the philosophy of social science, has often been reprinted, but both essays deserve to remembered not only for their philosophy, but, like all Ayer's writing, for their verve and grace.

As their titles would suggest, the two essays complement each other: both broach the related questions of the extent to which human behaviour is subject to causal law, and the bearing of the answer on the problem of free will. Ayer acknowledges that 'the idea that man somehow stands outside the order of nature is one that many people find attractive on emotional grounds', but insists, true to character, that this is no reason for thinking it true.[10] In the main, in fact, 'Man as a Subject for Science' represents an attempt to challenge this ideal – to defend the theoretical possibility, championed by Hume, the Utilitarians and the positivists, of developing a human science on the model of biology, chemistry or physics. Here Ayer was arguing against the position, made fashionable by Ryle and Wittgenstein, that we typically explain human actions not by identifying their causes but by redescribing them in terms of motives, intentions or purposes, or more generally in terms of norms and context. Indeed, Ryle had contended, in buttressing his position, that very often it is not even possible to identify any separate occurrences – what he called 'ghostly thrusts' – which can be said, on the model of the natural sciences, to be the cause of an action. Against this, Ayer argued that while it is obviously true that we explain actions by identifying motives and intentions, motives and intentions function as causes. There is nothing about human conduct, Ayer concluded, that entails a priori that it was in any way less law-like than any other sort of natural process. For this reason Ayer did 'not think that we can exclude the possibility of discovering a causal scheme into which human behaviour can be made to fit, not only in outline, but even in detail'.[11] It might for instance become possible to account for every facet of human behaviour in neurological terms.

The relation of this to the stubborn problem of free will was, as Ayer admitted, far from clear. He was inclined to argue that the development of a theory that enabled us to predict behaviour accurately would threaten our sense of ourselves as free agents, while consoling himself, in a rather unscientific spirit, with the thought that such a development remained in practice very unlikely. 'The chances that we could actually use a physiological, or even a psychological, theory to plot the course of our destinies in detail appear very small'.[12] That Ayer should have identified with the project of developing a science of man, while welcoming its likely failure, reveals something of his doubts and ambivalence in this area.

By the time Ayer took up his professorship, he and Dee were contemplating marriage. Ayer, though, had qualms. One day in 1960, he invited himself for lunch with Jocelyn, then living with the playwright John Osborne. In his autobiography, Osborne describes coming home to their flat in Lower Belgrave Street after Ayer had left:

I found Jocelyn, her face streaked with tears, more upset than I had ever seen her. It confirmed my view that Ayer was possibly the most selfish, superficial and obtuse man I had ever met, spitting out his commonplace opinions to an audience mystified by the tricks of manipulated sleight-of-mind. He had announced that he was contemplating marriage to an American, but was undecided whether the match fulfilled his standards of wisdom and self-esteem. He offered his ex-mistress a two-card choice: he was prepared to marry the American unless Jocelyn should feel impelled to offer herself as an alternative. Anyone less kindly would have kicked this pear-shaped Don Giovanni down the stairs and his cruel presumption with him. She could find nothing to say except, 'But Freddie, it's too late'.[13]

Jocelyn published a similar, although gentler, account of the episode herself, in her memoirs.[14]

Dee and Freddie finally married in July 1960, at the end of his first year at Oxford. After a small lunch party at the Ritz, and a quiet register office ceremony, they threw a large, flower-filled party at Conway Street. For their honeymoon they flew to Dubrovnik, a popular holiday spot among Britain's intellectual Left, where they joined Dora and Hugh Gaitskell, their daughters Cressida and Julia, and Richard and Anne Wollheim. Gaitskell, in the middle of a controversial campaign to 'modernise' the Labour Party by ditching its commitment to unilateral nuclear disarmament and nationalisation, was a new friend. A keen dancer, he and Freddie had met often at the Gargoyle, but it was Dee, whom Gaitskell adored, who really brought them together. Ayer admired him, liked what he inevitably described as his 'zest for life', and shared his version of socialism, with what Ayer described as 'its primary emphasis on social justice and its avoidance of Marxist shibboleths'.[15] Their only quarrel occurred when Ayer made a favourable remark about Russell: Russell's support for disarmament made it impossible for Gaitskell to acknowledge his importance as a philosopher.

The Gaitskells were guests of the Yugoslav government, and the Ayers, as their friends, were also treated royally. They accompanied the Labour leader and the President of Croatia on a cruise along the Montenegrin coast in the President's yacht, meeting Yugoslav officials on the way. The Wollheims had with them a young beauty, Vanessa Jebb, later to marry the historian, Hugh Thomas. Showing off to her, Ayer dived into a rough sea and, a weak swimmer, nearly drowned before finally securing a foothold on some rocks. The ordeal had shaken him profoundly and gave him a temperature. He looked on from his bed as Dee and Gaitskell argued over whether he was well enough to travel. Gaitskell wanted Ayer to rest in Dubrovnik, even at the risk of their missing their flight from Venice back to London. Ayer saw it as testimony to Gaitskell's power of character that he should have got his way: Dee was 'an exceptionally strong-headed woman – but her will was no match for his'.[16] Back in

London, the Ayers remained in regular contact with Gaitskell, taking a place in his 'Hampstead set' of intellectual, metropolitan right-leaning MPs, and a year or two after their Yugoslav holiday Gaitskell told Ayer that he intended to make him a peer. Ayer was devastated by the Labour leader's sudden death early in 1963 and always counted it 'a factor in Britain's political decline'.[17] Unlike a certain simple-minded strand in both Utilitarianism and positivism, Ayer appreciated that there was more to politics than the application of manifestos and programmes. Effective political leadership involved a sense of reality – a feeling for what matters, but also for what is possible. Gaitskell, he believed, possessed this quality to a rare degree.[18]

Under Dee's influence, Ayer became more politically active at this time than he had been since the war. He became friendly with most of the Labour leadership – Roy Jenkins, Denis Healey, Shirley Williams, Michael Foot, Tony Benn, Richard Crossman and Tony Crosland (by then married to Dee's good friend, the American journalist, Susan Barnes) – and during the 1959 election he wrote and broadcast in their support. In October 1960, not long after returning from Yugoslavia, Ayer helped organise a statement signed by sixty academics from London and Oxford, supporting the position Gaitskell had taken at that year's Labour Party conference opposing unilateral disarmament, although he admitted that the whole issue of nuclear policy was an exceptionally difficult one: 'I do not think it a bad thing that there should be a division of opinion among the supporters of the Labour Party on the subject of the hydrogen bomb. I think it might have the effect of making a Labour Government more sensitive than the Conservatives have so far been to the dangers inherent in the accumulation of atomic weapons, and less disposed to rely on them blindly for our defence.'[19]

Perhaps no political party has ever contained as many former dons and intellectuals as the Labour Party of this period. Ayer found it easy to feel at home. It would be wrong to assume, however, that he had much to offer his new friends by way of political philosophy, a subject about which he held negative views. A lecture given at Bristol University in 1965, 'Philosophy and Politics', offers a clear expression of his thinking at this time. Ayer had always believed that the scope for political philosophy was necessarily limited: because ultimately values were a matter of conviction rather than truth, the most that philosophy could do was to provide a clear and rigorous articulation of political choices. In the Bristol lecture, however, he went a step further, arguing that there were additional reasons why, at the present time, intellectuals had little to offer by way of political ideas. His point was simply that the last two hundred years had seen the intellectual triumph of liberalism – at least in the West. There were, of course, rivals within the liberal tradition – Ayer defended a very egalitarian version of liberalism against what he argued was the Conservatives' grudging, opportunistic acceptance of the welfare state – but there were no longer serious rivals to it. Absolutist and divine right theories had long since been discredited; Marx offered an interesting theory of history but had nothing to say about how society should be run; Fascism, fortunately, seemed to be a thing of the past. The New Left had admittedly presented itself as an alternative to both Marxism and liberal social democracy, but reviewing its manifesto of 1960, *Out of Apathy*, Ayer had argued that its positive proposals were 'disappointingly vague'.[20]

In many ways, what Ayer was saying about 'the end of ideology' was a 1960s commonplace. But it shaped his conception of what politics had come to involve in interesting ways. If, in the 1930s, his politics had an existentialist tinge – it was about choosing a set of political values among others and adhering to it – he now thought about political activity in a rather different way, as the struggle to ensure that politics was conducted according to the widely recognised norms:

> For most of us participation in politics takes the form of protest; protest against war, against the aggressive actions of the major powers, against the maltreatment of political prisoners, against censorship, against capital or corporal punishment, against the persecution of homosexuals, against racial discrimination; there is still quite a lot to be against. It would be more romantic to be marching forward shoulder to shoulder under some bright new banner towards a brave new world. But I don't know: perhaps it is the effect of age. I do not really feel the need for anything to replace this mainly utilitarian, mainly tolerant, undramatic type of radicalism. For me the problem is not to devise a new set of political principles, but rather to find a more effective means of putting into operation the principles that most of us already profess to have.[21]

That there was need to remain vigilant in support of liberal principles is well illustrated by something Ayer discovered about Eton at this time. In the autumn of 1960 Ayer was surprised to learn that a friend, June Osborn, widow of the German pianist, Franz Osborn, had a son who wanted to apply for a scholarship to Eton but was debarred from doing so because of a statute requiring that the fathers of Collegers should be British by birth. Ayer knew that this statute had not been in place when he was at the school – otherwise he could not have been admitted – and, catching a whiff of anti-Semitism, he wrote to Eton's headmaster, asking when and why this statute had been passed.[22] The headmaster passed the matter on to Sir Claude Elliott, a jovial, small-minded philistine who had been headmaster before the war.[23] He wrote back explaining that the requirement had been introduced in 1945. Elliott could not quite remember why the statute had been passed – perhaps Eton someone suggested, had been copying Winchester – but had voted for it and now defended it on the grounds that it prevented College getting 'too many boys who, though themselves British subjects, were alien in outlook and difficult to assimilate into the intimate life of college'. Elliott was particularly concerned that the 'early development' – indeed 'over-maturity' – of 'sons of Southern Europeans and the Middle Easterners' might 'exert a most undesirable influence' on British boys. It would be better for everyone if foreign families were given one or two generations 'to acclimatise'.[24]

Ayer responded with a politely threatening letter, suggesting that at the very least the 1945 statute had 'a flavour of anti-Semitism' and announcing that unless the Provost undertook to ask Eton's governing body to consider its repeal he would have no choice but to make the existence of the statute 'more widely known'.[25] On 6 February 1961, Ayer took up Elliott's invitation to meet at the Travellers' Club to discuss the matter over lunch. According to a memorandum Elliott made after the meeting, he again explained that College did not want 'too many boys of foreign outlook' and insisted on the importance 'of not allowing any kind of foreign element to get too strong'. Ayer, on the other hand, 'clearly thought that we ought to get the cleverest boys possible into College, regardless of their background and, though he did not say so, I think he would approve if we had no nationality qualification at all'.[26] According to Ayer, the Provost actually admitted that the statute had been aimed primarily at excluding Jews from the school, and this mainly on the grounds that they were 'too clever' or at least 'clever in the wrong way', although he also worried that they would not play the Wall Game.[27]

The outcome of the lunch was a bargain, according to which Elliott promised to put Ayer's objections to a fellows' meeting, and Ayer agreed not to bring the statute to the attention of the press for a year, while reserving the right to lobby fellows individually. To Ayer's disgust, however, the fellows proved, to a man, 'utterly useless'. 'I have enormous contempt for people who have no public courage,' he later told an interviewer, talking about the affair.[28] It looked as if Ayer had made a very bad bargain, when help came from an unexpected quarter – a Conservative government. Late in the winter, Ayer found himself alone in a train compartment with Sir Edward Boyle, a liberal-minded Treasury minister, Old Etonian and one of Ayer's few friends in the government. Boyle promised to raise the issue with the Prime Minister, Macmillan. Macmillan, an Old Colleger himself, then wrote to Elliott, 'in a private capacity', objecting to the anti-Semitic tone of the statute. The Provost was not a man to quarrel with a prime minister and within a month Eton's nationality requirement had been repealed.

Ayer came out of this intrigue very well. Noel Annan, a fellow of Eton at the time, was embarrassed at not having reacted as fast or as firmly, and Ayer was thrilled, as Dee recollects, at its outcome: 'It was a once in a lifetime triumph; it meant *everything* to him.'[29] Over thirty years earlier he had tried and failed to have corporal punishment banned at Eton; now he had done something to make it a more civilised place.

Ayer thought well of Macmillan as both a man and a politician, but had been hugely disappointed by his victory in the 1959 election. It was some small compensation that this was followed by a brilliant revival of Spurs' fortunes over the next two years. In 1961 they became the first team this century to win 'the double' – both the League Championship and the FA Cup. Ayer and Julian were there together at Wembley on 6 May to watch the clinching match against Leicester, played out to a chorus of 'Glory Glory, Hallelujah'. That same week he wrote about the triumph for the *New Statesman* under the aptly entitled headline 'Cock-a-Double-Doo'. It is a proud, enthusiastic piece, which gives full rein to his taste for sporting counter-factual speculation: only two of the players, he argued – Jones and Blanchflower – could clearly command a place in a current world eleven; Spurs, he thought, had performed better than any English team since the war, though the Manchester United side, which was broken by the Munich air crash, ran them very close. He was not sure that they would have beaten the great Arsenal sides of the 1930s, 'though it is perhaps in their favour that the game is probably played nowadays at a faster pace'.[30]

In the autumn of 1961, Ayer spent a semester as a visiting professor at City College in New York. First he went to Santa Barbara, the meeting place of that year's IIP held on the theme, 'Tolerance, its Foundations and Limits', and then he and Dee moved into a painting-filled brownstone on the Upper East Side belonging to the art-historian John Richardson. In New York, as ever, Freddie had a giddy social time, seeing, particularly, a great deal of Tony Bower. Early on in their stay, they acquired some sea-horses. Dee was struck by Ayer's sadness when, back in London, the creatures died: 'He loved pets – he identified with them in a way he couldn't always with people.' City College did not have a strong academic reputation so Ayer was the more impressed by the liveliness and dedication of his mainly Jewish students, detecting in them, perhaps, echoes of his own boyhood ardour. The atmosphere in his classes was 'as exhilarating as the best of my Oxford seminars'.[31]

The US had strong emotional associations for Ayer. He and Dee spent a long weekend on Joy Farm with the Cummingses, who had, in a concession to modernity, finally installed electricity in the farmhouse, and saw them often during the fall in New York. It was to be the last time he would see the poet, who died of a brain haemorrhage within the year. In his intense individualism and political scepticism, Cummings belonged to the generation that came before Ayer, the generation of the 1920s. Yet as different as they were, they had sustained a close friendship over twenty-five years. At some point, probably late in his life, Cummings wrote Ayer a birthday poem:

Considering the gravity of your language
and the levity of your nature
(or, at times, the levity of your language
and the gravity of your nature)
it is clear that keeping your balance

comes easier than it does to teetering us.
You walk on tightropes as if they lay on the ground,
and always, bird eyed, notice more than we notice you notice; and the
observation follows always with the clarity
of a wire slicing cheese.[32]

It nicely pin-points the combination of seriousness and gaiety that
Cummings admired in him.

The US had emotional associations of another sort as well. It was a
country in which Ayer had a child. Soon after the birth of Wendy,
Sheilah Graham had moved to Los Angeles, where she built up an
extremely successful career as a Hollywood gossip columnist, author and
broadcaster – her column alone was syndicated to 178 newspapers – and
had another child, a son. The father of this second infant may or may not
have been her husband, Trevor Westbrook, but the marriage had broken
up conclusively by the early 1950s and the children remained with their
mother in California. Wendy was never given any idea of her relation to
Freddie, but there was contact between them. Sheilah and the children
came to England every year or two, from 1954 onwards, and always
visited Freddie at Whitehorse Street, where he made a point of singling
Wendy out for attention, becoming her 'special friend and admirer'. On
her first visit to London, Ayer took her to a bookshop and after quizzing
her about what she had read, bought her *Tess of the D'Urbervilles*.[33] On
another trip he showed her around the Tate Gallery's Turners. 'We had
our particular moments,' she later wrote. 'They were not numerous but
they were special.' Although the two had comparatively little contact,
she was by nature academic and Freddie became a model. The friendship
influenced her out of all proportion to the time she spent with him: 'It
helped me to define who I was and wanted to be.' Ayer in turn kept a
close enough eye on her development to know that she had gone to
college at Bryn Mawr; due to go there himself to deliver a lecture, he
must have mentioned her name to the authorities, for Wendy was given
the job of showing him around. 'After his lecture we took the train
together to New York and had a drink in the city before going our
separate ways. Somewhere, I remember, we passed a television set tuned
to a football game, and Freddie made fun of the players' pink pants. I

remember thinking how easy he was to be with and what fun he could create out of silly little things'.[34]

In November Dee returned to England, leaving Ayer with more than a month to spend in New York. He soon made a new friend in Marguerite Lamkin, a belle from Louisiana, married several times, who made a career for herself coaching actors in her singsong Southern accent. She attended one or two of Ayer's City College lectures, introduced him to Christopher Isherwood and his young boyfriend Don Bachardy, and remembered accompanying him to Harlem one night to hear George Plimpton play the piano. Lamkin also took him to have lunch with Di Antonio, Henry Geldzahler and Andy Warhol. Ayer became close to both Geldzahler, who was on the way to becoming director of the Museum of Modern Art, and Antonio, a documentary film-maker, loud and outrageous. Lamkin was struck by Ayer's very wide circle of friends: she saw him, for instance, in the company of Jean Campbell, Beaverbrook's granddaughter and a journalist friend of Dee, who was later to marry Norman Mailer, and at the parties of Mrs H.J. Heinz, who was married to a Heinz food heir. She also recalled that he loved to lunch: 'I have never had so many long lunches with anyone in my life.'[35]

Among their outings, Ayer and Lamkin visited one of Warhol's happenings together. Ayer was nonplussed. Soon afterwards, he was asked to a very different and much more alluring gathering. As a means to strengthening the image of Camelot, President Kennedy had inaugurated a series of evening seminars which members of the cabinet and their wives were expected to attend. Arthur Schlesinger persuaded the Kennedy administration to invite Ayer to talk on philosophy.

The meeting took place after dinner at the Schlesingers' house and numbered about thirty. Ayer was disappointed that the President himself was not present but the proceedings were conducted by Robert Kennedy. Ayer spoke about the nature and (inevitably) the limited scope of philosophy and about his own philosophical views. It was, Schlesinger recorded in his diary, 'a virtuoso, dramatic performance and produced lively results'. Halfway through Ayer's talk, the President's sister Eunice Shriver, seated in the front row of the audience, leant over to her neighbour and whispered loudly, 'Is it possible that this man does not believe in God?' After it was over, Walt Rostow, an old ally of Kennedy, then in the State Department, attacked Ayer for rejecting the Platonic notion of the ideal state. Ayer deftly parried his blows. Then Robert Kennedy's wife Ethel asked him why he had nothing to say about Thomas Aquinas and they began to argue about the French Catholic neo-Thomist philosopher Jacques Maritain. Ethel plodded doggedly onwards, getting more confused as she went, until Robert spoke, quietly but firmly, from the back of the room: 'Drop it, Ethel.' She obeyed at once.

The British Ambassador, David Ormsby-Gore, worried that one of her majesty's subjects had caused offence, succeeded in getting Isaiah Berlin invited to talk to a subsequent gathering. Schlesinger, again writing in his diary, judged that 'The Kennedy's were more enlivened than annoyed by Ayer', but Berlin remembered Ethel complaining about his predeccessor's very 'disagreeable' behaviour. Berlin, always the more politic of the two, managed to smooth the feathers Ayer had ruffled.[36]

At Easter 1962 Ayer was invited on an official visit to Leningrad and Moscow, the first non-Marxist Western philosopher to be honoured in this way. Just returned from talking to the Kennedys, it was suddenly as if he was the world's philosophical ambassador. Over nine days he delivered five lectures on four topics, 'Contemporary British Philosophy', 'Pragmatism', 'Truth', and 'The Concept of a Person'. Together they were intended to give a full overview of developments in analytic philosophy and his position on them. He used the opportunity to make contacts and pave the way for future interaction between philosophers of the East and West, but in his lectures, and more directly in the discussions after them, he argued against dialectical materialism, contending that the claim that all movement in nature is born of conflict was simply too general to be properly verifiable.

Returning home, Ayer wrote and broadcast about his impressions. His comments to the effect that Marxism was giving way to a more intelligent empiricism – 'The spirit of revisionism has not yet conquered Soviet philosophy; but one can almost hear the beating of its wings' – ensured that invitations to return to Russia and write for Russian journals were cancelled.[38] Misjudging the extent to which dialectical materialism was still a sacred ideology, he was admonished as a purveyor of idealism in the *Kommunist*, the Communist Party's leading theoretical journal, although this concerned Ayer less than the news that his hosts had been made to suffer for inviting him.

During the few remaining weeks of the Easter holiday, Ayer, Dee and Gully went house-hunting in Provence, staying with their good friends, Bill and Pussy Deakin in their home in Le Castellet. On the second day of their search, they found something that suited them well: a very old small three-storey farmhouse in the hamlet of La Migoua, high above the town of Le Beausset, fifteen kilometres north-west of Toulon. It was a tall, narrow, crooked, low-ceilinged farmhouse, with no garden to speak of, but magnificent views. Ayer loved the area with its sunshine, markets and cafés, its restaurants and *fêtes*, and spent a part of every summer there for the rest of his life. Sitting under a lime tree on the small terrace that functioned as entrance hall, garden and dining-room, he spent the mornings working at his daily quota of words. (Dee was amazed at how he could shut himself off from the hubbub around him: 'he worked in a world of his own.') In the afternoons he warded off boredom with detective novels, chess, pétanque and other games or was chauffeured with the children to the beach.

There was, too, over the years, an enormous and often distinguished succession of guests. The Deakins lived nearby; Roy and Jennifer Jenkins, Richard Wollheim, Bryan Magee, Bernard and Shirley Williams, as well as various of Ayer's students came to stay. The Ayers gained some local standing when, in the mid-1960s, they confronted the mayor of Le Beausset on his way downhill with a cortège of cars. Dee refused to back up, saying that the road was full of holes. 'Madame,' said the mayor, 'I am mayor of this commune, I am responsible for the roads and I can assure you that they contain no holes.' While making this speech he stepped back into a hole and fell over. Ayer shouted '*Espèce de collaborateur!*' out of the window and he and Dee stood their ground. For Ayer, indeed, as for the locals, the area was rich in memories of the war. His old friend, Francette Drin, who had been in the Resistance in the north of France, bought the house adjoining theirs. Pierre Bertaux, who had played a leading part in the Resistance around Toulouse, and whom Ayer had first met a few weeks after the liberation, drove up for the day most summers. A number of his neighbours had fought with the Maquis.

Soon after buying the house at La Migoua, Freddie and Dee befriended Lorna and Roger St Aubyn, a wealthy couple with a large house nearby, who spent most of their time in Provence. Roger was a handsome, well-read, cynical character, who had trained as a doctor, but lived in great style off the money of his American wife. Ayer liked him enormously. Their son, Edward St Aubyn, thus grew up around the Ayers, and in a trilogy of coolly observed autobiographical novels published in the early 1990s (*Never Mind, Bad News, Some Hope*), he left portraits of them both. Anne Moore is an American journalist for the *New York Times*. Funny, perceptive and maternal, she is always ready to identify with the underdog: 'Anne had to guard against her wish to save people, as well as her habit of pointing out their moral deficiencies, especially as she knew that nothing put the English man more on the edge than a woman having definite opinions, except a woman who went on to defend them.'[39] As the novels' protagonist, Patrick Melrose, is first bullied and abused by his father, then, as a young man, turns to drugs, Anne is the one figure who shows any sympathy or understanding. St Aubyn's novels, however, offer a less sympathetic depiction of the eminent, and eminently vain, philosopher Sir Victor Eisen. 'The almost Edwardian clothes, the pretentious house and the claret-stained anecdotes' are described as 'part of the camouflage that a Jewish intellectual would have to take on, along with a knighthood, in order to blend into the landscape of conventional English life'.[40] Both portraits are constructed with artistic licence. However, St Aubyn confirms that Dee was one of the few adults to see through his father and understand the wretchedness of his, St Aubyn's childhood. And St Aubyn was not the only one to feel that Ayer set a high price on 'social acceptance.'[41] Dee too described him as an 'ace faker' – the ordeals of his childhood had 'taught him that he had to fit in if he was going to survive'.

18

Benthamite Saint

Early in the 1960s Emily Boothby, the teenage daughter of Dee's friends, Basil and Sue, who was later to marry the novelist Piers Paul Read, came to live with the Ayers in their house in Conway Street. They were, she remembered, enormously busy – out or entertaining almost every night. But she saw a very domestic side to Ayer. 'We watched a programme every night called *Tonight*. There was a big fat dachshund called Monster, which Freddie adored, and he doted on Gully. It was a happy period in their life'.[1] Dee also recalled these years with fondness. 'Freddie was at his very best in the early Sixties, very upright and open-minded. He was happy in himself and fair. He was certainly the nicest man in the world'.[2]

In the summer of 1962, Dee became pregnant and in April gave birth to a dark-haired boy, Nicholas. Dora Gaitskell and Nicole, the Duchess of Bedford, became the boy's secular godmothers and Russell agreed to be appointed godfather. Ayer savoured the fact that Russell's secular godfather was John Stuart Mill, and Mill's, Bentham. When Ayer finished his second volume of autobiography in the early 1980s, he ended it flatly with the birth: 'We registered him as Nicholas Hugh Ayer, Hugh in memory of Hugh Gaitskell and Nicholas because the name appealed to us.' His secretary, Guida Crowley, however, who typed the manuscript, urged him to speak from his heart, so he added, truthfully, 'My love for this child has been a dominating factor in the remainder of my life.'

A year after Nicholas was born, the Ayers bought an elegant five-storey early nineteenth-century house in Regent's Park Terrace, between Camden Town and Primrose Hill. Dee gradually transformed it with Liberty linen curtains and a collection of portraits of nineteenth-century prize bulls. Dora gave them the Gaitskells' dining-room table. Dee was to tell a journalist a decade later, 'Our community life is mainly sitting in each other's kitchens', but these were not ordinary kitchens.[3] Jonathan Miller, Victor and Dorothy Pritchett, Angus Wilson, Alan Bennett, the novelist Alice Thomas Ellis and her publisher husband Colin Haycraft, George Melly, Claire and Nicholas Tomlin, all lived in the same enclave. The area became known for the famous people who lived there.

The focus of these houses tended to be not, as it had been fifty years before, the first floor drawing-room, but the basement kitchen, generally converted into a 'knock-through' kitchen/dining-room. Here, over a glass of wine and Brie, the writers, actors and performers talked of their friends in the Wilson cabinet, of books and holidays and of the dilemma faced by socialists rich enough to send their children to a fee-paying school. It was a style of life satirised in Marc Boxer's cartoons for the *Listener* about a trendy young careerist couple from Camden Town, Joanna and Simon Stringalong, who worked for the BBC, affected all the correct political views, and worried anxiously over their dinner parties. Following Ayer's success in *The Brains Trust*, Dee too became a television star, appearing four evenings a week with two other journalists, Alan Brien and Benny Green, on *Three after Six*, and on *That Was The Week That Was* and *Not so Much a Programme, More a Way of Life*. Her outspokenness became well known. In May 1965, a Goya was stolen from the Duke of Wellington and Dee explained to an audience of millions what she thought the police's procedure would be: 'What they want to get is the poor hopeless little nut into the station and beat him up and let him fall down a couple of flights of stairs, and then say: "Well, we've dealt with that ruffian", in that splendid police way'.[4] One Marc cartoon depicted a man showing some guests around his Camden Town house: 'And this,' he says guiding them into a child's room, 'is where we lock the children when my wife lets fire on TV.' Among his new neighbours Ayer became especially close to Colin Haycraft, and the Pritchetts: 'Victor,' Dorothy Pritchett recalled, 'loved him.'[5] Ayer also liked Jonathan Miller, at least until the 1970s, when he became convinced that he and Dee were having an affair.

Ayer once admitted that he had not been a very good father to his first children – 'more like an uncle'.[6] Nicholas's birth gave him a chance to do better and over the years an unusually strong bond developed between them. 'I think,' he once said in an interview, 'that parenthood is a very strong form of love, in some ways the strongest of all, perhaps because it is so much less greedy than other forms of love, because it is more altruistic.' As the context makes plain, it was his relationship with Nick that he had in mind.[7] As Freddie saw it, playing with Nick was his part of the domestic contract; more or less everything else fell to Dee. Ayer always, according to Nick, seemed to be writing but would usually stop instantly if Nick wanted to play. 'Ball games, board games, chess, anything – he was brilliant like that. There was never any doubt in my mind that he loved me, simply because when he was around, he always had time for me'.[8] Dorothy Pritchett remembered that Freddie, when not at football matches, would spend Saturday afternoons kicking a ball around the park with Nicholas, trying to instil devotion to the game – although it never became a part of the meaning of life for Nick, as it was for Freddie.

Being a doting parent is, of course, not quite the same as being a good one. Ayer might have loved Nick, but he could not control him. Dee resented the fact that it always fell to her administer discipline, Ayer's strongest words of admonishment being, 'Please Nick, don't be a bore.' The parent–child relationship, however, is a special case and it seems clear that in general Ayer had an exceptional way with children. He adored Gully and she him: 'I remember thinking as a very small child – and all through my life – that the best thing about him was how utterly *reasonable* he was'.[9] Gully's testimony is borne out by others. Ayer liked children with their keen inquiring minds and they liked the way he talked to them as if they were adults. Sue Boothby remembered Ayer playing a variation of I-Spy, when one of her children asked him whether the object he was thinking of was near the object he was in fact thinking of – whether x, in other words, was close to x. He replied that the question was nonsensical, explaining later that an object can be identical with but not near to itself.[10]

As the 1960s unrolled, Ayer found himself taking a prominent role in a range of campaigns and public commissions, very much in accordance with the 'undramatic' principles of protest he had advocated in 'Philosophy and Politics'. George Weidenfeld liked to describe Ayer as a 'Benthamite Saint' and Ayer was, indeed, thoroughly Benthamite, in the way he devoted himself to what he saw as the public good in these years.

In 1965 Ayer succeeded Julian Huxley as president of the British Humanist Association. Nowadays the Association is not much of a force, but in the 1960s it had a large membership and Ayer worked hard on its behalf, addressing meetings, campaigning for funds, writing policy statements and editing books. James Hemming, who worked alongside him, remembered him as 'conscientious and puckish'.[11] The Association had been founded in 1963 as the union of a number of 'ethical' and 'rationalist' organisations, and as such was emphatically atheistic; as president, Ayer nevertheless argued that it would be a mistake for it to embark on an anti-clerical crusade: the churches were, on the whole, less powerful than they had been, and anyway had become – in a way Ayer must have found rather galling – increasingly progressive. Instead, he argued that humanists should concern themselves with social reform: there was, he explained, 'a logical reason for this':

> In one sense, humanism is a harsh doctrine. To insist that life has only the meaning that one succeeds in giving it, that we have only this short amount of time to experience any happiness or accomplish anything of value, is all very well for people who are living in easy circumstances and have been given the opportunity to develop intellectual and cultural interests. For those who are ignorant, helpless, and in material want, it is small consolation to be told that their miseries will end with death; and throughout history the majority of human beings have been in this condition. It would, therefore, be insensitive if not hypocritical for humanists to preach their doctrine unless they believed that the values which they set upon human experience and achievement were capable of being realised not merely by a privileged minority but by mankind in general. Even if they cannot be assured that this will ever be so, they at least have the moral obligation to do what they can to make it possible.[12]

This passage, from 'Humanism and Reform', an essay published in

Encounter, gives neat expression to the link that Ayer saw between atheism on the one hand, and the sort of radical utilitarian politics he favoured on the other. Humanism, however, was far from the only cause Ayer championed during this time. In the early 1960s he became chairman of the Campaign against Racial Discrimination in Sport, which, among other goals, campaigned for a sporting boycott of South Africa, and vice-president of the Society for Reform of Abortion Law – a position also held by Dee. On a smaller scale, he was one of the leaders of the campaign that began in the mid-1960s and succeeded in getting women admitted to New College. He rendered public service of a rather more official kind when, in July 1962, he was invited to join the Plowden Commission set up by the Department of Education and Science on the future of primary education in Britain: it was over four years before the commission delivered a hugely influential report. From the beginning, Ayer had reservations about the sort of progressive 'child-centred' approach to primary school learning that it advocated and said later that he regretted not having written a dissenting report, although, as he admitted, he did not really have the expertise to do so.[13] He did, however, dissent on religion, arguing that religious education should cease to be obligatory and was indeed 'not a suitable subject to be taken in primary schools'. He also succeeded, as he later put it, 'in obtaining a recommendation, by now very widely accepted, that corporal punishment be abolished in primary schools'.[14]

In 1965, at a time when adoption was still almost entirely in the hands of the churches, Ayer became a founder and first president of the Agnostics' Adoption Society, an organisation intended 'to help would-be adopters from minority as well as majority groups, people from all religions or none', and in particular to find homes for 'babies which other agencies have classified as difficult'.[15] According to Mary James, later director of the society, Ayer helped secure a large anonymous donation, which made the society possible: she described him as 'a good hand on the tiller, a nice person to have behind you, urbane and humorous'. Among other duties, he chaired the annual general meetings, 'knocking them off very quickly. He was not happy if they fell on the same day as a football match'.[16]

Unlike many of the other causes Ayer involved himself in, adoption was one in which he could be said to have at least an indirect interest.

He had always believed that, when it came to relations between parents and children, upbringing was far more important than biology: he found it, he would say, natural to think of Julian as his son, and did not feel too much compunction about not owning up to Wendy. Indeed, when he eventually resigned from the society in 1985 it was in part because he objected to its policy of avoiding, where possible, inter-racial adoption. Perhaps there is, here, a connection with Ayer's philosophy. Whereas metaphysicians tend to believe in the existence of essences underlying appearance, Ayer, as an empiricist, did not – like Berkeley and Hume before him, he thought of objects as mere 'bundles' of properties. The two contrasting positions had a famous airing in the 1970s, when essentialists Saul Kripke and Hilary Putnam argued that certain sorts of objects, including persons, are defined by single necessary features; in the case of persons, their parental origins or their names. Ayer vehemently disagreed, having already argued, notably in *The Problem of Knowledge*, that there was no one defining feature of a person's identity. Almost any aspect of an individual – his parents, time of birth, character, race or appearance – could be very different without making him a different person from the one he is, although of course there will be a point at which identity ceases to hold.[17*]

In the same year in which Ayer joined both the humanists and the Agnostics' Adoption Society – 1965 – he became one of six members of an *ad hoc* Oxford committee on Vietnam, devoted to organising university 'teach-ins'. He was thoroughly opposed to American intervention in South-East Asia, and vocal in his criticism of the Wilson government's refusal to take a firmer stand against it.

The *Times* index for the autumn of 1968 shows no record of any contribution to the conflict over Vietnam, but Ayer's name crops up in a host of other contexts. In October he wrote to the paper arguing against sporting contact with South Africa. In the first half of November its news pages carried two reports, one recording that Ayer had been one of the signatories of a letter to the Russian Prime Minster, Mr Kosygin, asking

---

* Ayer's tendency to downgrade the significance of origins can be seen, too, in his attitude to works of art. After the war, he and Benedict Nicolson took part in an informal debate at Philip Toynbee's house on the Isle of Wight, in which Ayer defended the view that authenticity in art was of no special value; there was no reason to value an authentic El Greco more than a perfect reproduction of one. Nicolson disagreed (Martyn and Lady Priscilla Beckett, IWA, 7 November 1994).

for tolerance in a civil disobedience trial, the other describing a speech he made to a society campaigning for the abolition of corporal punishment. (Ayer argued that spanking and caning were not only cruel in themselves but often had a sexual motive, something he had learned at first hand at Eton.) He signed another letter at the end of November, condemning a series of anti-Semitic student prosecutions in Poland, and one more in the middle of December pleading for action to help the famine victims of Biafra. Ayer was, indeed, one of the great letter-writers of the era. One of Marc's cartoons had the Stringalongs looking forward to a campaign against the construction of an urban motorway through the literary groves of NW1: 'It's my great opportunity,' says Simon, 'to be listed under the magical cross-heading "from Professor Ayer and others".'

Of all the organisations with which Ayer was involved in the 1960s, he felt that the most effective was the Homosexual Law Reform Society (HLRS). He had been one of the original signatories of a letter to the *Times* in the summer of 1958 calling for the legalisation of homosexual relations between consenting adults as recommended by the Wolfenden Report of the previous year. This and other letters had led to the creation of the HLRS as an organisation devoted to educating public opinion about homosexuality, as well as lobbying parliament and the media. After 1965, when the parliamentary battle for reform was joined in earnest, the society did all it could to assist the sponsors of private members' bills and its headquarters, off Piccadilly Circus, became an unofficial whips' office.

Dee had long used her columns and television appearances to criticise the existing laws and the horrible roll-call of blackmail, persecution and suicide they generated. It was she who suggested to Anthony Grey, the society's newly appointed secretary, that Ayer might be willing to become president, as, in September 1963, he did. As Ayer was almost too quick to point out, the appointment had the great advantage that 'as a notorious heterosexual I could never be accused of feathering my own nest'.[18] Ayer's greatest asset, according to Grey, was his name: he gave the organisation credibility. But although he did not do a great deal of active campaigning, according to Grey he proved himself an effective president:

His chief contribution was to use his contacts to help us put the organisation on a sound financial footing. He attended important committee meetings and was incisive in his contributions. I remember one or two occasions when I saw his abilities at full stretch: we had some tiresome people around, always promising and never delivering, and I saw Ayer demolish them. What impressed me was not what he did but his efficiency in doing it ... He saw through the hypocrisies and obfuscations of politicians and recognised what had to be done. He had one of the most penetrating intellects I have ever come across.[19]

It is characteristic of Ayer's preference for short incisive interventions, in politics as in philosophy, that after the reform in the law in 1967 (much helped by Ayer's great friend, the Home Secretary, Roy Jenkins), he argued that the HLRS should be wound up, instead of becoming, as it did, a permanent pressure group.

Behind Ayer's support for homosexual law reform was a Russellian, which is to say basically a Utilitarian, view of sex. This saw sex as a natural drive, to be fulfilled – not, as Puritanism had it, to be suppressed. 'I have always thought morality has very little to do with sex, or at least that sex is one aspect of morality but not a terribly important one,' Ayer said in an interview he gave in December 1966. 'Compared with the questions of whether or not to drop an atom bomb, what one thinks about the war in Vietnam, what one thinks about racialist questions, the question of who goes to bed with whom, is surely only of the faintest interest. I mean by all means let them enjoy themselves so long as they don't harm anybody.'[20]

This position had implications for marriage. Like Russell, Ayer believed in romantic love, and doubtless would have acknowledged that in some cases it can sustain itself through a lifetime. He thought, however, that at least a great minority of people were not naturally monogamous, and for that and other reasons he argued that marriage should be understood first and foremost not as an inviolable pledge of sexual fidelity but as an agreement to share the upbringing of children. 'Marriage,' he said, talking to the *Times* 'Women's Page' in 1968,

should be absolutely reciprocal. There should be complete equality between husband and wife and no nonsense about such things as who is head of the household. I also think that far too much emphasis is placed on fidelity. A brief affair by husband or wife should present no difficulty in any stable marriage. To take a hypothetical case: if I went off and made love to somebody else, I would not object if Dee did the same. Nor would I expect this to cause any breakdown in our marriage or life together.[21]

The case was in fact hardly hypothetical. Ayer had affairs from the beginning of his marriage to Dee: no sooner was the honeymoon over than he took up with several old girlfriends. In London, Dee had to get used to him disappearing in the afternoon to play 'chess' with various lady-friends, or simply to 'sit and read' in one of his clubs, and Oxford provided further scope for his intrigues. It became a joke among undergraduates at New College that you could tell when the famous professor was entertaining – he placed his shoes on the windowsill. (One student, who had a room opposite Ayer, used a pair of binoculars to monitor him, until one day he looked through them to find Ayer staring back through a pair of his own.)[22]

Whatever the Russellian view of marriage might prescribe, few of us are immune to jealousy. Dee, though, recalls that she was upset as much by Ayer's 'remoteness' as by his girlfriends. It was not just that, for all of his feminist principles, he did nothing around the house (other than make his bed – a trick he had learned at prep school) but that although warm in his way and wonderfully public spirited, he seemed to lack deep feelings.

Talking to a journalist in 1971, Ayer admitted that he was not given to introspection:

I wonder whether I do even have an image of myself? I suppose if you ask me questions about my character, I would have opinions about most of them, I would say: 'Yes I am X' or 'I'm not Y' [but] I don't think that I have an image of myself in the sense that I am much concerned with my own character. I don't think I'm all that much interested in myself. I'm much more interested in trying to solve philosophical problems, or in what's happening around me, or how my little boy is getting on.[23]

But Dee thought that Ayer was not even very interested in other people. She recalled that:

He was observant about people and a good judge of intelligence, but he was not interested in their psychology. He did not try to understand them as an analyst does and most of us do to some extent. If someone died he would not miss them – he enjoyed their company while they were there but that was all. If a cleaner or a secretary or someone left, he never mentioned them again. It was out of sight, out of mind . . . He knew he was different. He did not know how, but he knew he did not know what the rest of us were talking about when we spoke of feelings. It was strange because when I met him, I knew here was a good, kind man. And he really cared passionately about justice and fairness. But certain things were missing. The first time I got an inkling of this was when, in very early days, I said, rather wistfully, after a great old friend of mine had died, 'I'm feeling sad. You know how all of my friends keep dying', and he responded 'No, how?'[24]

Dee came to feel that it was not just that Freddie could be dispassionate, but that there was something positively awry in his make-up. In her mind, his detachment was tied up with unusual traits that she noticed: the way he had to have a chain to play with when he worked (she kept spare chains around the house) and then when working, could shut himself off from the rest of the world; his devotion to games; his love of routine; the minute handwriting, or his complete inability to visualise. 'He used to say,' Dee remembers, 'that thinking in images was primitive. He said it so often that I asked Russell whether he thought it was true. Russell said it was "Nonsense, absolute nonsense".' During a dinner party at Stephen and Natasha Spender's St John's Wood home, the conversation turned to musical and visual imagery. Natasha asked Ayer what he saw when he thought of Paris – was it the Eiffel Tower or perhaps Notre Dame? He thought for a moment: 'A sign saying "Paris".'[25]*

Beyond his domestic life, Ayer's career ran on in what was now its familiar course. He was in Mexico City in September 1963 for the five-

---

* 'At one extreme,' Ayer once wrote in 1968 in connection with C.S. Peirce, 'there are those whose powers of memory and imagination are exercised by giving verbal descriptions rather than by forming mental images: at the other, those who require even abstract reasoning to be cast in a diagrammatic mould. Peirce . . . belonged decidedly to the latter class.' Ayer to the former (*The Origins of Pragmatism*, London, 1968, p.133).

yearly meeting of the World Congress of Philosophy – he found that he could still get by in Spanish – and then, under the auspices of the British Council, lectured on 'Other Minds' in Caracas, Venezuela. In 1964 he flew to Florence for a IIP congress, and the same event took him to Copenhagen in 1966 and Liège in 1967. He often returned to Central Europe in these years and in 1966 gave a series of lectures at the University of Budapest. In some respects he found the city much as it had been when he had visited it from Vienna in 1933. 'The same gypsy bands serenaded the customers in the animated cafés and restaurants; there appeared to be no shortage of food or drink; the entertainers in the night-clubs were not afraid of engaging in political satire'.[26] He was depressed, however, by the prevalence of doctrinaire Marxism in the philosophy department. A Marxist of a very undoctrinaire kind was the great literary theorist György Lukács. Ayer secured an invitation to visit him in his apartment where they spoke for two hours, although without really understanding one another.

Ayer liked to mark Russell's birthday. For his ninetieth, in May 1962, he organised a large dinner party at the Café Royal, at which, along with the Duke of Bedford, the head of Russell's family, Julian Huxley and E.M. Forster, Ayer gave a speech, comparing Russell favourably to both Locke and Voltaire. He was still paying his respects four years later, although this time with a letter:

Dear Russell

I write to send you my very best wishes for your birthday. It is a long time since we have met ... but I hope that you are well, and that you will have many other anniversaries, some of which I hope that we shall have the chance of celebrating together.

I am on sabbatical here [in London] this year and am devoting my leisure to writing a book in which you will very largely figure. It is to be called 'Pragmatism and Analysis' and consists in studying the work of Peirce, James, Moore and yourself. It is going more slowly than I had expected, but I have nearly finished with the two pragmatists. I find that their theories are much less crude than they are commonly represented as being. In particular, I think that there is still a great deal to be said for James' Neutral Monism which you developed in your *Analysis of Mind*. At least it is a serious attempt to deal with an important problem, which is not true of much of what has recently been passing for philosophy. However I think that we are moving into better times. At least the 'ordinary language' movement seems to be played out.[27]

On Russell's ninety-fifth birthday his wife gave a party in Wales which Dee and Ayer attended. It was the last time he saw his hero alive, although Russell lived for another three years. Like most of Russell's old friends, Ayer did not altogether approve of his militant denunciation of American military and foreign policy, his contention that the US and the USSR were 'morally equivalent' or his calls for unilateral disarmament, and he disliked Ralph Schoenman, the left-wing American who ran Russell's political campaigns. But he followed Shoenman's prompting in nominating Russell for the Nobel Peace Prize in 1962, and even after Russell's death kept his reservations more or less to himself.

In November 1965 Ayer passed a personal milestone when he wrote and broadcast what was, in effect, his first exercise in autobiography, 'The Making of a Logical Positivist'. Nevertheless, as his letter to Russell indicates, he was also producing new material. Originally he had planned to write a book based on the Whidden lectures he had given as long ago as 1957 at UCL, comparing the founders of American pragmatism and the British analytic tradition. When, however, he began reworking the section on the pragmatists he concluded that their ideas were so rich that they merited a book of their own. He briefly considered fleshing out the work with a section on John Dewey, usually counted as a leading pragmatist, but soon thought better of it: 'My reason for ignoring him was not only that he wrote very badly ... but that ... it did not strike me that he had anything interesting to say'.[28]

The result was *The Origins of Pragmatism*, first delivered as a series of lectures while Ayer was Visiting Professor at Massey College, University of Toronto in 1967. The volume, dedicated to the von Hofmannsthals, came out in 1968 in both Britain and the US to mixed reviews and never sold well. As Ayer himself put it, 'The American devotees of Peirce found it insufficiently scholarly and other readers, who might have been interested in some of my own ideas which it incorporated were put off by its title'.[29] It is true that its combination of textual exegesis and critical commentary is tough, relentless and somewhat myopic: as Richard Rorty, writing in the *Philosophical Review* complained, 'There is no particular pragmatist thesis which Ayer is especially anxious to defend or confute. There is no single topic carried through the book and no dominating idea which organises it'.[30] Nevertheless *Origins* involved Ayer in an impressive intellectual leap – the pragmatists were still very little known in Britain* – and in several respects represented an important landmark in his development. It not only constituted his first semi-historical publication, but more importantly it gave a full statement of ideas more often associated with a later book, *The Central Questions of Philosophy* – the first full statement of what he once described as his last 'constructionist' phase.[31]

Ayer typically passed fairly quickly over the metaphysical and religious dimensions of the pragmatists' work. He was keen to refute the heresy that either Peirce or James was willing to let the truth of empirical or logical propositions be decided on grounds of usefulness or expediency alone – in these areas, they adhered to objective standards. Nevertheless he showed himself moderately tolerant of James's thesis that moral, metaphysical and religious beliefs should be counted true where they satisfy human needs; or if he did not endorse the thesis, he did not dismiss it either. Although religious, James at least acknowledged that almost nothing could be said about God's powers and the way he was supposed to exercise them. He was a very sceptically minded metaphysician.[32]

Having in this way dealt with the pragmatists' most famous doctrines, Ayer turned to what Rorty admitted was 'a thoughtful, lucid, perspicuous reconstruction and criticism' of Peirce on belief, truth and scientific method, and James on radical empiricism. Ayer thought Peirce a greater philosopher than James; indeed, he thought him, with Frege, the greatest philosopher of the nineteenth century. Oddly, though, it was James who stimulated Ayer to the last and most interesting section of the book, in which he attempted to build on James's radical empiricism in order to show how the self and the world might be constructed out of the flow of

---

* On first reading them properly in the 1950s, Ayer quickly found that Peirce and James were much more sophisticated than Moore and Russell, for instance, had supposed.

'pure experience'. Ayer himself was particularly pleased with his critical treatment of what he described as 'James's attempt to make good Hume's failure to analyse personal identity in terms of a series of experiences'.[33]

As good empiricists, James and Ayer followed Hume in regarding the self as 'a bundle of perceptions'. Like Hume, they saw no reason to assume the existence of what is variously called a pure ego, or soul or mental substance. As James had argued, the introduction of such an entity explained nothing that could not be equally or better explained without it: 'The Spiritualists do not deduce any of the properties of the mental life from otherwise known properties of the soul. They simply find various characters ready-made in the mental life, and these they clap into the soul, saying "Lo! behold the source from whence they flow"'.[34] Hume, however, having rejected the existence of the soul, had to admit that he could not find a way of connecting perceptions into the separate bundles that make up a person. In this way he cast the concept of personhood itself into doubt. James and Ayer, on the other hand, sought to develop a convincing analysis of the 'relations between perceptions in virtue of which they [are] collected into a unitary self'.[35]

One obvious criterion of personhood that Ayer at least considered was provided by the body. On this analysis, all or part of what would be required for two experiences to be experiences of the same person is that they are attached to the same body. The weakness of this approach, Ayer suggested, was that it debarred one from describing 'even the most extreme cases of multiple personality as cases in which the same body is occupied, simultaneously or successively, by different persons' or from admitting cases of disembodied experience or the embodiment of a single person in different bodies.[36] As an alternative Ayer drew on James in developing an account which made personhood entirely a matter of a certain relations between experiences. What makes a person a person, he argued, is the fact of 'sensible continuity' of thought and feeling. Thus two experiences belong to the same self if they occur at the same time or immediately after one another, or are linked indirectly by a chain of directly related experiences, or alternatively, if one of them represents, directly or indirectly, a memory of the other.

This analysis had one serious flaw that Ayer never seems to have acknowledged: it gave excessive weight to mental over bodily continuity. As Bernard Williams would argue a few years later, even in an instance of absolute mental discontinuity there are grounds for saying that some form of personhood survives. The knowledge that one's body is to be subject to torture, for instance, remains disturbing despite the knowledge that one is going to have one's own brain removed and someone else's put in its place.[37] This flaw aside, however, Ayer was later to admit that he could not quite make his Jamesian analysis work – it depended on a concept of memory which itself depended on the concept of a person, and was thus circular. The rather lame conclusion at which Ayer was forced to arrive was that both physical and mental criteria enter into the ascription of personhood, although these might, at least in theory, collide: in such cases 'there would not be any true or false judgement of identity'.[38] Nevertheless Ayer's Jamesian analysis set the pattern for a similar handling of the concepts of time, space and the material world, all of which, like the self, he attempted to present as theories with respect to raw experience.

The tendency of *The Origins of Pragmatism* was, as a number of reviewers noted, to minimise the pragmatist and emphasise the positivistic strain in Peirce's and especially James's thought. As Morton White complained in the *New York Review of Books*, Ayer portrayed James as 'something like a logical positivist'.[39] There was one respect, however, in which Ayer had become willing to concede a great deal to pragmatism. In the last section of the book, 'On What There Is', and again in a lecture, 'What Must There Be?', that he gave before the Israeli Academy of Sciences and Humanities in Jerusalem in the spring of 1968, not long after finishing the book, Ayer offered a thoroughly pragmatist treatment of ontology.

Questions concerning the fundamental nature of what exists – questions about the 'ultimate furniture of the universe' – have always, of course, been central to philosophy. The tendency of the logical positivists had been to attempt to sidestep them by arguing that issues of existence only properly arise within established fields of inquiry, like mathematics, science or history, with their own criteria of truth and falsehood. Carnap for instance had drawn a famous distinction between internal questions which arise within the framework of a given conceptual system – such questions as 'Is there a greatest prime number?' or 'Are there abominable snowmen?' – and external questions which bear on the framework itself – for instance, 'Do numbers really exist?' or 'Are there physical objects?' He admitted the first as legitimate and proper but dismissed the second as metaphysical.[40] Ayer himself had inclined to this approach in *Language, Truth and Logic* and remained attracted to it. By the time of *Origins* and his Israeli lecture, however, he felt obliged to acknowledge that it offered too easy a way out.

There was, he now admitted, a real conflict between rival ontologies, between, say, James's experientialism (the view that the world is made up of experiences, with physical objects merely 'entities of reason'), naïve realism (the view that it is made up of the physical objects of common sense belief, and perhaps minds and their contents), and physical realism (the view that it consists of nothing but invisible waves and particles). For one thing, the entities of common sense and science compete for the same space. It is hard to say how we can consistently think of some area as being exclusively occupied both by a continuous solid coloured object and by a collection of discontinuous, volatile, colourless particles.

Ayer was in fact dismissive of James's position. The doctrine that the world is built out of experience was grotesquely self-centred. Experiences give us access to the world, but they play a very small part in it: they only came into being with conscious life and will disappear when it dies out.[41] The only real alternative was between naïve and scientific realism. And here Ayer now advanced the pragmatist argument that because there is no fact of the matter at stake, ontology is ultimately a matter of choice:

> When it comes to such philosophical questions as 'Do things exist unperceived?' and 'In what form do they exist: as we perceive them or as physicists depict them?', the point is that they cannot be settled by experiment. They ask for an assessment of the framework in terms of which experiments are to be interpreted . . . we do not have to admit these questions: we are probably better advised not to admit them. But if we do admit them, then in answering them we are not straightforwardly reporting what there is, but deciding what there is to be.[42]

Not that the decision was entirely arbitrary. The problem was that, or so Ayer argued, there were good arguments on both sides, with the result that no decision was going to be altogether comfortable. Physical realism had the advantage that it was scientific: 'Once we have learned even a little physiology, it is hard to think of colour as anything but a causal property of physical objects, and the removal of colour brings down the whole edifice'. On the other hand, as Ayer admitted, he found it hard to think in scientific terms of the things to which he was emotionally attached: 'When I think of my small son in absence, I cannot bring myself to picture him as a group of electrons: if I get so far as the way he would look like in an X-ray photograph, I am doing very well'.[43]

What Ayer's Jerusalem audience made of this is not recorded. Ayer never wrote about this, apparently his first and only visit to Israel, or about Israel in general – a subject about which, as both a Jew and an Enlightenment universalist, he had ambivalent feelings. He did though admit that he generally supported Israel in its conflicts with the Arabs, 'for atavistic reasons,'[44] while insisting that assimilation was a real possibility. 'A great deal depends on the attitude of the Jews themselves: whether, for example, they are prepared to marry Gentiles. In fact there are many cases in which assimilation has been successful, to the point where the Jewish strain in a family has ceased to be remarked'.[45] Indeed, in a review of Sartre's highly conjectural treatment of 'the Jewish question', Anti-Semite and Jew, written for the Spectator a few months after his return from Israel, Ayer laconically suggested that the establishment of Israel had, paradoxically, made the route of assimilation an easier one to take. The creation of a Jewish homeland had led to 'Jews becoming a member of a nation state, on a level with other nation states', so allowing assimilated Jews to regard Israel in much the way that some Americans regard 'the countries from which their ancestors emigrated'.[46] This, and other brief remarks in a similar vein, was all that Ayer contributed to the century's great controversy over Zion.

Ayer was back at New College in time for the student unrest of May 1968. In Oxford this involved scarcely more than a few feeble sit-ins and the odd march. These self-styled 'uprisings' nevertheless represented a disenchanting experience for him. He had, of course, always prided himself on understanding the young and agreed with the rebels that there was much to protest against, above all Vietnam. He objected, however, that their complaints made no sense: 'First they say they want one thing, then another – their demands are incoherent'. Ayer had no time for

Marcuse, the intellectual godfather of the movement and a prominent critic of positivism, and the students' talk of 'alienation' and 'the tyranny of modern reason' struck him as so much romantic twaddle.[47] 'He felt,' Richard Wollheim observed, 'that he had been robbed of his natural basis with young people.'[48]

That September, at the end of a summer spent as usual with Dee, Nick and an almost grown up Gully, at La Migoua, Ayer dashed off five articles for the *Evening Standard* on 'Rebels and Morals'. The series attempted to come to terms with the changes in Britain since the war – with the rise of 'the permissive society' and its discontents. The result was true to character. Ayer was full of ideas and insights. He pointed out that there is no simple sense in which Britain has become a more permissive society: an increase in sexual, reproductive and other freedoms has been matched by an increase in governmental regulation of the economy. He suggested that the quarrels between and within the generations could be understood as a conflict between two rival systems of Christian morality – one a puritanical work ethic which attaches value to worldly success and the other an ethic of compassion. He contended that the Western democracies, despite their many achievements, had proved unimaginative about education and about working conditions and, in particular, undervalued many types of labour. 'In the troubles that have occurred at various universities,' Ayer noted, 'hardly any of the demonstrators have been scientists. By and large, the young scientist is doing work that he finds interesting and thinks important: and he knows that if he is any good at all, society will set a comparatively high price upon his services. On the other hand the arts student who has nothing to look forward to except an underpaid job in the teaching profession . . . or the routine of an office, naturally feels disgruntled.'[49] Ayer, however, failed to develop his ideas at any length or explain quite how they fitted together. The idea of writing a book based on the articles – urged on him by various publishers and Dee – came to nothing.

Soon after Ayer's articles in the *Standard*, there occurred an important development in his private life. At a function at the American Embassy, he was introduced to Vanessa Lawson. Born in September 1936, Vanessa was thirty-two, ten years younger than Dee, twenty-six years younger than Freddie. The daughter of a rich and prominent Anglo-Jewish family, the Salmons, owners of the Lyons catering empire, she had trained as a

ballet dancer but at nineteen had married Nigel Lawson, one of many
suitors. They had three children in quick succession, Dominic, Nigella
and Thomasina, followed six years later by their last, Horatia. Nigel
Lawson had attended Ayer's lectures at Oxford, and, in gifts and
ambition, if not in politics, in many ways resembled him. He quickly rose
to become City editor of the *Sunday Telegraph*, before, at thirty-four being
appointed editor of the *Spectator*. (Jonathan Aitken identified him as one
of the 'Young Meteors' in his 1967 book of that title.) In 1974 he became
a Conservative MP. The couple lived in grand style in a large house in
Kensington. The journalist Peregrine Worsthorne remembered how the
first time he saw Vanessa she entered a room with her three children in
procession behind her. All were 'perfectly dressed in old-fashioned
clothes, the whole family looking as if they had stepped straight out of a
Visconti film set'.[50]

Vanessa, unlike Jocelyn and Dee, did not have a career. Her
attractions lay elsewhere. Dominic described her as 'a very accomplished
wife and *saloniste*. She threw a good party. She was popular among my
father's constituency party. She knew how to dress, how to decorate and
so on, although she disliked playing the role of an MP's wife'.[51]
Photographs show an unusual beauty. Small, slim and dark, she had a
long sensuous face, huge brown eyes and the bearing of a dancer:
everyone likened her to Nefertiti. She was not herself especially political,
preferring artists and writers to MPs, and she had made something of an
art out of mocking her husband Nigel, whose manner she found orotund.

Vanessa in fact had become unhappy in her marriage. In the 1970s
there was to be a famous dinner in a Brighton restaurant, during a Tory
party conference, when Vanessa persuaded Worsthorne, then associate
editor of the *Sunday Telegraph*, to exchange shirts with her. The act was
meant to illustrate a little fantasy of Vanessa about how much better men
and women would look if they swapped wardrobes, although later
Worsthorne came to see it in a larger context, as part of her 'attempt to
transcend the political life to which her husband's career seemed to
condemn her'. A few days after the event, Worsthorne received a card:
'Next time you want to lose your shirt, put it on a horse.'[52]

Soon after Freddie and Vanessa met, her father, Felix, died. This,
Dominic believed, may have increased Ayer's attractiveness: 'Freddie
would have been about the same age as Felix. And Felix was an

intellectual, although more highbrow than Freddie.'[53] Ten years later Vanessa herself likened Freddie to her father in being 'basically sweet natured but completely self-centred', although in an apologetic letter she quickly retracted this: 'I feel you are no more self-centred than the rest of us, it is simply that you don't try and camouflage it, and as that is coupled with your gentleness and good manners, it makes for the well known charm'.[54] Whatever the source of their affinity, they were soon immersed in an intense love affair. Almost from the beginning, the relationship was centred in Oxford; Vanessa and Freddie would generally get the train up together on a Tuesday morning, have a picnic lunch and often dinner together, before she slipped back to London, although occasionally, during the week, Freddie would appear at the Lawson house for lunch. 'When Freddie and Vanessa first met', said Marcelle Quinton, 'I remember him saying, "I have just met someone I am absolutely in love with". They loved each other the way people do when they think it's their last chance.'[55]

19

Central Questions

If, as he approached sixty, Ayer took stock of his achievements, he might have started with the fact that his views now had a firm and central place in the history of twentieth-century philosophy. The position he defended had become canonical, which was strange considering that it was hard to find anyone who agreed with it. Logical positivism, as represented by *Language, Truth and Logic*, was probably the school that undergraduate philosophers knew best, but it was a school that, from the beginning, most were taught to refute. This state of affairs was mirrored further up the profession. Philosophers as different as Quine, Strawson, Iris Murdoch, Saul Kripke and Charles Taylor defined themselves against its tenets. This did not seem to shake Ayer's confidence – in the 1970s he produced some of his best books – but it did change his position in the field: the young Turk had become an old chestnut. In 1969 the philosopher of mind, Daniel Dennett circulated the first edition of a satirical lexicon, based on the names of well-known philosophers. Freddie was included: '**Ayer** (from Spanish, *Ayer*, meaning yesterday) To over-simplify elegantly in the direction of a past generation.'[1] When Ayer went to give a lecture at Sussex, Roy Edgley, a local Marxist philosopher, was heard to say that he had enjoyed seeing 'such an important episode in philosophical history revived before him'.[2]

As befitted an elder statesman, early in 1969 Ayer was invited to put himself forward as Warden of Wadham. At first he was keen to apply, but he withdrew his candidacy at the last minute. 'I managed to persuade myself,' he wrote to Isaiah Berlin, 'that I wanted [the position] but as the months have gone by I have come to realise that being the head of a college would be likely to give me more pain than pleasure.'[3] Others however insist that he dropped out of the race because he had been told that he was likely to lose to another contender, his old stalker, Stuart Hampshire. If this was the indeed the reason why Ayer withdrew his name, then according to the librarian at the college, he was right to do so. Ayer had made an unfavourable impression on younger tutors, who, when invited to meet him, found him 'arrogant and pompous'.[4] In the end the position went to Hampshire. When, in the course of the decade, Ayer was approached by other colleges, he turned them down.

If the 1960s ended badly, the 1970s began well. Two weeks after retiring from the Wadham race, Ayer was given a knighthood in the New Year's honours list. He accepted readily enough, saying the things that socialists say on these occasions: 'I don't feel strongly about the honours list in general, but given that it exists one goes along with it', or, 'It's good for the profession, and for Oxford'. Later in the decade he was made a chevalier of the French Légion d'Honneur and a knight of the Order of Cyril and Methodius, 1st Class (Bulgaria). These bagatelles flattered his vanity. Around this time he joined the Beefsteak Club, a conservative gentleman's club off Leicester Square; it was noticed that while Harold Macmillan announced himself through the intercom as 'Harold Macmillan', Ayer preferred 'It's Professor Sir Alfred Ayer'.

Despite the jokes and the accolades, however, Ayer was far from a spent force. He worked harder on philosophy than he had ever done before: early in 1970 he spent a semester at Harvard, where he delivered the William James lectures; on the same trip he also gave the Dewey lectures at Columbia. He turned both into books; the first *Russell and Moore, the Analytical Heritage* furnished a counterpart to *The Origins of Pragmatism* and displayed Ayer's now familiar brand of textual exegesis and critical commentary; the second, *Probability and Evidence*, constituted a more abstract treatment of the problems surrounding induction. In 1972, when *Probability and Evidence* appeared, Ayer also published a short 'Fontana Modern Master' on *Russell* and a year later he produced *The Central Questions of Philosophy*. These four books overlap and together form an elaboration of the 'constructionist' phase in Ayer's thought that had begun with *The Origins of Pragmatism*. They represent his last philosophical push.

The monograph, *Probability and Evidence* (dedicated to Goronwy and Margie Rees) is the least constructive and for that reason the least interesting of this cluster, and the reviews were predictably muted. One of Ayer's more technical efforts, it sets out to demolish the various attempts that have been made to justify induction – the inference from what has passed to what will be. Ayer agrees with Hume's 'marvellous chain of arguments' – 'one of the most brilliant examples of philosophical reasoning that there has ever been' – to the effect that although we are bound to rely upon our past experience as a guide to the future, no procedure of the kind can offer us any assurance of success.[5] Ayer followed Hume in rejecting as nonsensical the view that the laws of nature are somehow metaphysically necessary, and have, in some unspecified way, to obtain in all imaginable worlds. Instead he argued that what are called 'natural laws' are just a special class of empirical generalisations – those that we are willing to project on to imaginary instances. With the universe, as he liked to say, 'it is just one damn thing after another'. But if this is so, then there is no guarantee that the regularities observed in the past will continue to obtain in the future; appealing to the fact that they once obtained is clearly to argue in a circle. The purported solutions to the 'problem of induction', like the frequency theory of probability associated with Reichenbach, and the logical theory, associated in different variants with Keynes, Carnap and Harrod, all foundered in a similar way: they smuggle assumptions about the uniformity of nature into their premises.

Ayer's little book on *Russell* was finished in September 1971, a few months after *Probability and Evidence*, and came out to almost universally good reviews. Mary Warnock, writing in *New Society*, praised it as 'one of the best expositions of the work of one philosopher by another that has ever been written'.[6] Anthony Quinton found it both 'crystalline and meaty'.[7] Bernard's Crick's review in the *New Statesman* – 'a brilliant and very useful book' – and the one in the *New York Times* – 'one could hardly ask for a better guide' – were also superlative.[8] Admiring, critical, engaged, it is indeed, along with Ayer's 'Past Master' on Hume, his most successful introductory book.

The reception of *Russell and Moore* was less enthusiastic. 'Ayer does not range very widely,' Bernard Williams complained in the *Observer*, 'beyond the exposition and criticism of particular arguments and positions of the two philosophers and there are points when the book tends to sink a bit discouragingly between two stools, where the treatment is too analytical to give much historical insight, but the philosophical rewards are too slight to make the discussion of the Russellian or Moorean topic worthwhile in its own right.'[9] Ayer himself came to agree with this verdict, so perhaps it is worth saying that, though out of print, *Russell and Moore* still reads as a fresh and incisive engagement with the two founding fathers of twentieth-century analytic philosophy. The value of this book, as of all Ayer's quasi-historical work, lies in its seriousness and sense of proportion. Ayer sticks to the most central, which are also the most difficult questions, and does his subjects the honour, as he did his students, of treating them as if they still had something important to offer.

In the winter of 1972–73 Ayer was invited to give the Gifford lectures at the University of St Andrews. Although the lectures were founded in the nineteenth century for the purposes of 'Promoting, Advancing, Teaching and Diffusing the Study of Natural Theology', Ayer devoted only one lecture, the last, to the philosophy of religion, in which he rehearsed his arguments against the existence of God. Instead he set out to write something that he promised George Weidenfeld, his new publisher, would offer an up-to-date rival to Russell's best-selling 'shilling shocker', *The Problems of Philosophy* – a book that would furnish a general introductory outline as well as a mature statement of Ayer's views. George Weidenfeld accordingly extended a handsome advance.

As a successor to *The Problems of Philosophy*, *Central Questions* was a failure, and although it was published in paperback by Penguin, never outsold Russell's book. The problem was familiar: Ayer demanded too much of the reader. In fact the book is denser, and so in some respects harder than either *Language, Truth and Logic* or *The Problem of Knowledge*. Judged on its merits, though, *Central Questions* has a strong claim to be Ayer's best work – cool, lucid, and regal. It opens with a chapter on 'The Claims of Metaphysics' very different in tone from 'The Elimination of Metaphysics', the first chapter of *Language, Truth and Logic*. Ayer still insisted that it was vain to attempt, as metaphysicians from Plato to Bradley had done, to rival or supplement empirical science. Nevertheless, he now suggested that metaphysical arguments, like Zeno's for the unreality of movement or McTaggart's for the unreality of time, while ultimately unconvincing, do raise important philosophical questions. The metaphysical tradition does, it turns out, have some value, albeit of this mainly negative kind.

With the discussion of metaphysics behind him, Ayer turned to the main theme of the book. This is the theory of knowledge, still conceived as it was in *The Problem of Knowledge* as the attempted rebuttal of a particular type of sceptical argument: the insistence upon an unbridge-able gap between our claims to knowledge – about physical objects, other minds, the past and the future – and the evidence on which such claims are based. Thus Ayer argued that when one identifies the object in front of one as a table, one attributes a range of properties, such as that of being tangible, of being accessible to other observers, of having a position in physical space and time, which are certainly not vouchsafed by anything in the content of one's present visual experience. The sceptic alights on this argument – essentially a watertight substitute for the leaky 'argument from illusion' – to question the legitimacy of the inference from sense-experience to the existence of a physical table.

But if Ayer frames the problem much as he had done in *The Problem of Knowledge*, he now offers a different response – one first outlined in *The Origins of Pragmatism* and *Russell and Moore*. This was in effect an adaptation of Hume's account of the working of the imagination in the first book of the *Treatise*. But where Hume had simply explained how features of experience lead us to belief in an external enduring world of physical objects (a belief which, on Ayer's interpretation of Hume, Hume maintained had no justification), Ayer argues that the general features of our experience do in fact warrant our beliefs about the physical world; that belief in the physical world is a hypothesis borne out by our experience, albeit not a hypothesis of the ordinary sort. He speaks of 'constructing' or 'positing' the physical world, and it is important to appreciate that he is not merely suggesting, as he did in his phenomenal-ist days, that physical language represents another way of talking about percepts. He is postulating a genuinely new realm of entities and facts above and beyond the sensory level.* That is why he is able to describe

---

* Ayer's intention, it should be stressed, was not to offer an empirical account of the process by

his theory as 'a sophisticated form of realism'.[10] Under the dominion of the theory which is erected on the basis of our primitive experience, the existence of physical objects becomes a matter of objective fact.

We start with the occurrence of what Hume called sense-impressions or percepts, entities which are, for Ayer, neither private or public, physical or mental. Ayer then sets out to show how, from the way in which percepts are ordered, we are entitled to develop concepts of time and space and the existence of what Ayer calls 'visuo-tactual continu- ants', central among which is a certain body. This is the observer's own body, though not yet characterised as such. This is about as far as a lone observer could be expected to go, which is to say that a Robinson Crusoe would not get very far in developing an objective conception of the world. If, however, we imagine a Crusoe being introduced into a larger community of Men Fridays, then he will find that for the most part the testimony of his interlocutors corroborates his own account of the world. He will also find, however, that his interlocutors tell what Ayer calls 'subsidiary stories' which do not fit in with his account of the world and that he tells stories which do not fit in with theirs – stories based on dreams, hallucinations and other private experiences. 'From this he infers that the events which these subsidiary stories describe are events that exist only for him and correspondingly that the events which occur in the subsidiary stories that the others tell are events that exist only for them. The making of the private–public distinction thus goes together with the acquisition of self-consciousness and the attribution of consciousness to others'.[11]

At this point in the story, as Ayer tells it, the observer already recognises that visuo-tactual continuants can exist unperceived. This insight is now extended to the point where it is unnecessary to their existence that they ever should be perceived, or even that there should be any observers to perceive them. From here it is a short step to understanding that these independently existing objects are in fact causally responsible for our percepts – that they are objective, our percepts subjective. This is an important and characteristic feature of Ayer's theory; it makes sense-impressions epistemologically fundamental

which children come to acquire a picture of the objective world – the categories of the commonsense view of the world are embodied in the language they learn – but to analyse the logic of commonsense beliefs.

in the sense that they are the foundation of our knowledge, but ontologically marginal in the sense that they turn out to occupy a very minor place in the picture of the world that is built up on their basis. As Ayer puts it, our commonsense understanding of the world thus 'downgrades its starting-point in much the same way a self-made man may repudiate his humble origins'.[12]

This relationship between subjective experience and the commonsense world is, finally, paralleled in the way in which common sense leads to the development of scientific theories which in turn account for common sense. Most of our life we spend in the midfield of common sense. One might, though, step forward and lose oneself in sense-data – this is to live life as Pater described it – or, in cooler moments, step back into the white-coated scientific point of view.

Writing a decade later in a monograph on Ayer's work, the philosopher John Foster judged that Ayer's logical construction of the physical world was probably the best thing he ever achieved. It revealed Ayer 'at the height of his powers, and displaying an artistry and virtuosity which it would be hard to surpass'.[13] The sections devoted to it in *Central Questions* constitute a wonderfully elegant and exciting piece of writing.

In later chapters of *Central Questions* Ayer turns to the old problems of our knowledge of other minds and of the past. Just as with his account of our knowledge of the external world, Ayer is now operating with a very sophisticated body of theory, carving a subtle course between the extravagances of a soft-minded realism on the one hand, and a crude reductionism on the other. It is worth stressing, however, that Ayer's position is still thoroughly empiricist. The external world is constructed on the basis of sense-data, if not reducible to it, and his scheme of things allows no place for necessary causation, no spiritual self, no God, no objective values, no 'transcendent' meaning to life.

There was, in fact only one question on which Ayer displayed emphatically anti-empiricist, tender-minded tendencies – although this was a very important one. Over the years he had slowly rethought his position on free will. In his best-known discussion of the subject, 'Freedom and Necessity' of 1946, he had attempted to find a way round the problem of determinism by appealing to the ordinary language distinction between voluntary and involuntary actions. Ayer argued that to say that an action has a cause is not the same thing as saying that it is forced: not all causes are constraints. By the time of *Central Questions*, however, he felt obliged to admit the inadequacy of this analysis on the grounds that either human actions are entirely governed by causal laws, in which case they follow one another with law-like inevitability; or they are not, in which case they occur by chance. In both cases they are beyond our control. Yet instead of arguing, as he might have been expected to do, that we should learn to live without a belief in free will, Ayer had to admit that he looked on this prospect with repugnance. He found himself (as he would put it in 1980) 'in a dilemma'. Given his belief that the concept of desert is empty, if not meaningless, 'it appears to follow that I should set myself to cultivate an objective attitude towards myself and others, and to welcome an ordering of society in which it was generally prevalent. What should concern me morally would be just the beneficence of the conditioning. At the same time I have to confess that the prospect of any such Brave New World repels me'.[14] Even this great apostle of truth found that a belief in freedom and responsibility was one illusion that he could not live without.

Ayer's private life had also been eventful. In 1970 Dee and Nick had travelled with him to Harvard for the first semester, during which he was giving the William James lectures, and it proved, in many ways, a happy time. They were accompanied by Guida Crowley, who had now been Ayer's part-time London secretary for four years and had gradually become a close friend and confidante; *Central Questions* was dedicated to her. Nick, who had not been happy in his London school, settled into his American one with gratifying ease. The Harvard philosopher, Burton Dreben, remembered that Dee and Freddie made 'quite a stir' on campus.[15] They saw much of Diana and Lionel Trilling, the psychologist Jerome Bruner, the philosopher and literary theorist I.A. Richards, and Stephen Spender, who was teaching in Connecticut and stayed with the Ayers at weekends.

Dee remembered spending a long weekend in a hotel in New York, where they saw Tony Bower, now an art dealer, for the last time – he was murdered by a boy-friend a year later. They also received a visit from the actress, Joan Fontaine; she and Freddie had evidently been old friends. Dee got the distinct impression, as Fontaine looked down at her scrambling with Nick on the floor, that she thought that, as wives went, Dee was a very unglamorous choice.

Michael Lockwood, a young Oxford philosopher, also saw Ayer in New York. He had first attended Ayer's 'informal instructions' at New College in 1963 and recalled that while philosophically he seemed a rather isolated figure, these seminars were extremely well attended. Ayer was an 'extraordinarily effective performer, quick-witted and witty'. Ayer supervised Lockwood's thesis, entertained him in London, both at home and at his club, and in every way encouraged him in his career. On one of these occasions – lunch at the Garrick – Ayer set about ranking himself as a philosopher. 'I am a *much* better philosopher than Austin, although not quite as good as Quine'. 'Most people think like this', Lockwood reflected, 'but few will admit to it. It was the guileless nature of his vanity that made it more charming than objectionable'.

By 1970, when they met in New York, Lockwood was teaching at City College, his doctorate unfinished. Ayer invited him to a party he gave in his hotel rooms, where he too was introduced to Joan Fontaine. On another evening Ayer took him out to a bar and set about imploring him to finish his thesis – 'Do it for me, Michael, do it for me.' Freddie was in effect attempting a *seduction*, although not to his usual end. 'It was an utterly charming display'.[16]

Yet if the Ayers' American interlude proved successful and happy, it was, paradoxically, while they were there that Dee first became aware of Ayer's relationship with Vanessa, who regularly sent love-notes to their Lowell Street home. Her realisation that Freddie was embroiled with another woman inevitably dealt a blow to the Ayers' marriage, but matters worsened on their return to London, with the entry of two other lovers into the household. It had always been understood that Freddie and Dee would have an open marriage, but from the beginning it had been Ayer who had made almost exclusive use of the freedom thus provided. Then in 1971 Dee began an affair with Hylan Booker, a man the gossip columnists described as 'a glamorous black fashion designer'. Booker, an American, was, at thirty-three, thirteen years younger than Dee – around the same age as Julian. From a middle-class Detroit family, he came to England in the 1960s with the American Air Force, and managed to secure a place studying fashion at the Royal College of Art. After graduating, he began by working for the French house, Worth, and was quickly promoted. Gully describes him as 'dreamily handsome, charming and delightful'. He was also 'a very loving father', doing a good job of bringing up a daughter, from a failed marriage, on his own. On learning about the affair – and Dee was soon sporting Hylan's clothes – Ayer assumed that it could not last long. Dee and Hylan, however, remained together for over a decade – for what Dee describes as her years of 'sex 'n' drugs 'n' rock 'n' roll'. Ayer, of course, hardly had the right to object, although he did mind that Dee carried on the relationship in what he thought was an unnecessarily public manner. He was always more discreet.

Not long after meeting Hylan, Dee started work on a novel. It eventually came out in October 1973, a few months after Ayer's *The Central Questions of Philosophy*, although two books could hardly be more different. Like most first novels, *Jane* is partly autobiographical; unlike most, it became an international bestseller, translated into seven languages and selling more than a million copies worldwide. Its heroine, Jane Cornell, is a radical young American movie critic for a 'rabble rousing' English daily, who possesses Dee's fast talk – she hates 'smart bombs and dumb people'. Jane is modern in her career and in her politics but above all in her love life, and the novel's plot revolves around her dilemma in choosing a father for her soon-to-be-born baby from among the three very different men who share her bed: Franklin, a black American civil rights lawyer temporarily teaching at Cambridge, Anthony Wiltshire, a hopeless English aristocrat with a large 'compost heap' in the country, and Tom, a young cockney cat-burglar, whom she first meets when he falls through the skylight of her Covent Garden loft. *Jane* is a fast moving and very funny example of commercial feminist fiction and is still sometimes taught as such in the US. Yet almost as striking as its heroine's spirited independence is its author's intense hostility, amounting at this stage in her life to something like hatred, for the English upper classes, and by extension the English generally. As the novel develops, Anthony Wiltshire and his ruthlessly snobbish family are defined in opposition to Franklin and Tom. It is not hard to identify traces of the men in Dee's life with those in Jane's. If the black American Franklin carries echoes of Booker, there are elements of Ayer in Anthony – not least of all in his insularity. 'After long stretches with Anthony you got the feeling you'd been playing tennis against a brick wall . . . When you play a wall the only energy in the game is your own. You have to begin it. You have to keep score. You have to decide when the game is over and who, if anybody, won. And it's only you that gets sweaty and tired'.[17]

Now that both Freddie and Dee each had a lover, their lives had taken on a certain symmetry, but it did not remain that way for long. In the summer of 1973 it was decided that Freddie and Nick should go to La Migoua alone, and Dee found an attractive French student studying law in London to accompany them. Beatrice Tourot was in her late twenties, from a good French family, feminine, loving and intelligent. A 'pure bourgeois girl', she first resisted Freddie's gentlemanly advances and that summer, their friendship remained platonic. At some point in the next year, however, they became lovers. Nick remembers it this way: 'It got to the stage when Dee could not bear to go to France with Freddie, so she found Beatrice, who was living in London, to take him there and look after him. She made a huge effort to be liked, and succeeded. From that moment she was permanently in our lives. She could do all the things that Freddie loved – organise dinners, parties and outings. She was fun and charming and great with children. I am not sure how Freddie loved her, but he did'.[18] There is no doubt that Beatrice was important to Ayer, but he also touched something in her. Writing to Ayer years later, she would describe him as 'l'être le plus significatif de ma vie'.[19]

Beatrice and Freddie's love affair continued for a number of years, running parallel with his relationship with Vanessa, and of course with Dee. They saw each other in London, where she continued to study and work, but most in Le Beausset. Just as London was associated with Dee and Oxford with Vanessa, so Freddie's relationship with Beatrice was centred on summers in the South of France. In theory it all seemed very tidy, although in reality it was less so – the women did not much like each other, but Ayer either cared for or felt committed to each. Something he said in a letter in the 1980s applies to this period as well: 'You might think that as I get older I would learn how to manage my affairs better but the reverse seems to be true.'[20]

Those journalists, then, who came to profile Freddie and Dee and found them 'particularly happy' were under a misapprehension.[21] Nick remembers that in their arguments Dee was the great shouter. Freddie would just tremble quietly: 'That woman, she is intolerable.'[22] In the

20. Vanessa Lawson and
Horatia, mid 1960s

21 With Vanessa,
c.1980.

22 Freddie and Dee
on their remarriage,
1989.

14 A.J. Ayer, by Jane Bown, 1954.

15 With Jocelyn
Rickards, in the
Hotel Inghilterra,
Rome, 1956.

16 With
Elizabeth von
Hofmannsthal, 1957.

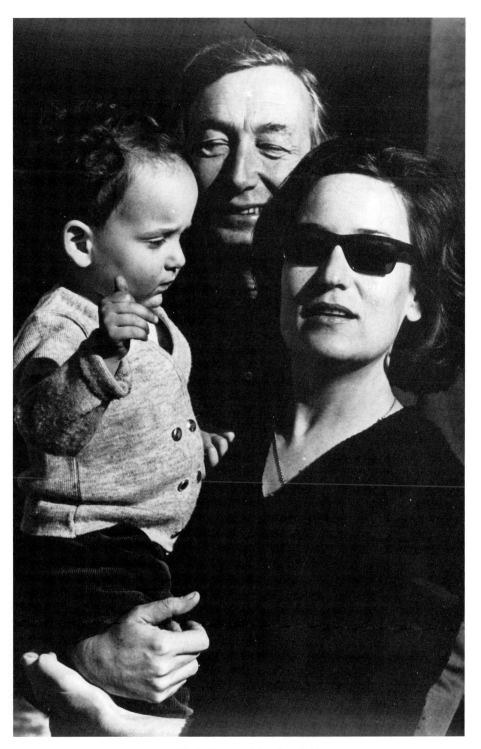

17 With Dee and Nick, 1964.

18 With
Gully and Dee,
mid 1960s.

19 'The
Thinkers'.
Freddie with
Nick and friends,
1961.

23 Wendy Fairey, John Bayley and Iris Murdoch with Freddie at Marylebone Registry Office.

24 Freddie with Julian, early 1980s.

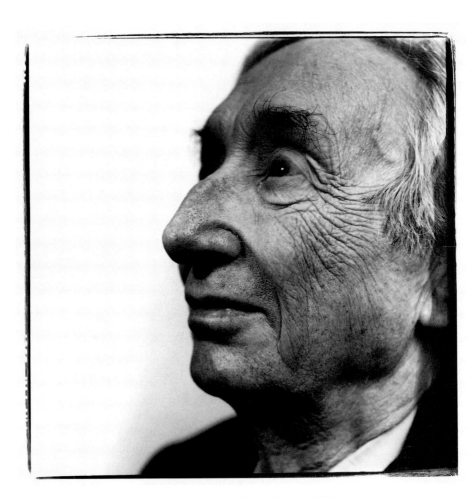

25 A.J. Ayer by Steve Pyke, 1989.

circumstances it might have been natural for Ayer to press for divorce, and a number of friends, including Margie Rees, Goronwy's wife, urged him to do so. It was not in Ayer's nature, however, to make domestic decisions for himself – 'He would,' as Gully put it, 'rather do anything than do something' – and so he stayed.[23]*

As Freddie's and Dee's various relationships developed, they came to lead increasingly separate lives, and after 1974 their large house was rearranged to reflect this: Freddie took a bedroom and study and bathroom on the ground floor, while Dee took over the one above. They saw their young lovers during the week, and lived and to some extent socialised together at the weekends. It was *Private Lives*, 1970s style. By October 1973, Nick, now aged ten, had been moved from a local state primary school to a private prep school. (Ayer had earlier defended this type of move in an article in the *Sunday Times* on the grounds that there was no point in sending a child to a poor school if the example was not going to be followed, which it was not. To do so would be sacrificing a child to no end. Nevertheless, his position was criticised in the press, and he received a full and angry mail-bag.)[24] Nick was also going for regular sessions at the Tavistock, a centre for child psychotherapy in Hampstead. 'Dee's more keen on it than I am,' Ayer told a journalist. 'They're very Freudian. I'm not at all sure that everything has that much to do with sex. He was suffering from depression last year . . . Dee thinks it will help.'[25]

In the meantime, Ayer had allowed his relationship with his daughter Valerie to deteriorate. In 1971 she married a second time, to Brian Hayden, 'a charming and talented psychologist' who taught at Brown, and they settled in Providence, Rhode Island, where she ran children's art classes at the Rhode Island School of Design.[26] Valerie and Hayden were happy together but she resented Gully and Nick and came to feel that Ayer had forgotten her. 'She cites,' her new husband wrote, 'forgotten birthdays and the like. Much of this sentiment is from Renée

---

* Perhaps these years taught him something. In Ayer's later work there is a slight shift in his view of the will. Writing in 1964, he had stated it as almost a tautology that 'given a choice of actions people attempt to perform the one which they believe will have the consquences that they most prefer'. Writing at the end of his life, he recognised that this, far from being tautologous, was not even always true: 'For my own part, I quite often find myself failing to do what I most want, owing to weakness of will or a moral scruple to which I subscribe with ill grace, or simply to inertia' (Ayer, 'Reply to Martin Hollis', *Ph.A JA*, p.240).

... However, the problem remains: Valerie herself feels that you do not really care.'[27] It was the complaint that everyone made about Ayer: 'out of sight, out of mind'.

Of course Ayer had another daughter in America. Dee had done as much as Freddie to keep up contact with Wendy Fairey, his child by Sheilah Graham. Now teaching English literature at City College, she came over to England every two or three years and occasionally saw Freddie when he was in the US. In summer 1975 she rented a cottage in Sussex with her husband and two children. Freddie and Dee drove down to see them, but the visit was not a success. Nicholas was bored and Freddie, although showing some interest in his grandchildren (it was his first and only encounter with them), spent most of the afternoon watching football on television. Dee believed that Wendy should be told about her relation to Freddie and that same summer invited her for lunch. When she arrived, Dee made an excuse and went out, leaving the pair alone. But if Dee hoped Freddie would reveal his secret, she was disappointed. Father and daughter settled on the sofa.

> A cat nestled between us, and we both began stroking it. Neither of us, I think, felt entirely at ease. I was sharply aware of Freddie's physical proximity, and remembering his reputation as a seducer of women, I wondered if he found me attractive. He was sixty five and I thirty three. My thought was that he was too old for me, but I certainly felt his appeal. Nothing happened except that we both kept stroking that cat.[28]

Perhaps it is not surprising that after *Central Questions*, Ayer should have stopped for breath. Over the next few years he produced very little philosophy, turning instead to autobiography. In 1974 he published only one substantial article, a criticism of Karl Popper on truth and verification; in 1975 he did slightly better, with two papers; 1976, though, was the first year since the war during which he appears to have published no philosophy at all. Almost the only significant paper from this period is 'Identity and Reference', a long reply to Saul Kripke's famous 'Naming and Necessity' of 1972, in which Kripke had attempted to resuscitate essentialism – the doctrine that necessity adheres to things in themselves, rather than arising from the way we define them. Ayer conceived a violent and very public prejudice against Kripke, a brilliant but unsociably intense young American, partly because he disliked his manners – they had encountered each other in Oxford and the US – but mainly on the grounds of his theories. Bernard Williams found himself standing next to Ayer in the line for a buffet at an IIP conference in the mid-1970s, when the conversation turned, as it tended to with Ayer at this time, to Kripke. 'Earlier in this century,' Ayer expostulated over his plate, 'a few of us moved philosophy on a notch or two. I am not going to live to see it put back.'[29] As Ayer's long and powerful essay makes clear, he could not understand how Kripke, whose arguments he found 'perverse', 'disingenuous' and 'absurd' (strong words for him), was being heralded as a great American logician, a successor to Peirce, Quine and Goodman.

If Ayer's philosophical output fell off in these years, he nevertheless found that he was as busy as ever, the invitations to chair charities and pressure groups and to broadcast his views on television, giving way to an endless stream of rather less glamorous requests to talk to schools, student groups and literary societies. He also continued to take a leading part in the annual round of philosophical conferences. Indeed, as president of the IIP from 1969 to 1972, he played a leading part in helping the Bulgarians organise the World Congress of Philosophy which took place at Varna in 1973, a colossal event, gathering together hundreds of philosophers from all over the world. As usual at this time, philosophers tended to divide along East–West, Marxist–non-Marxist lines, although, as Ayer noted in a closing address, debate between them was hardly ever joined: 'Like characters in the Chinese theatre, the protagonists jump up and down and make hideous faces at one another but they do not exchange many actual blows'.[30] Ayer, for his part, insisted on the need to put aside the crude oppositions between empiricists and dialecticians, idealists and materialists, that had dominated philosophy for too long, in favour of a closer focus on concrete problems. These remarks, like the proceedings as a whole, were innocuous enough. Nevertheless, as Ayer came to realise, the secret police were monitoring all that went on: when voicing his dissatisfaction on failing to get room service in his hotel, the room's bugging system soon brought up an apologetic porter.

By the 1970s Ayer had become somewhat disenchanted with undergraduate teaching, which, due to the ever increasing ignorance of students and the growing importance of exams, had, he complained, become a species of 'cramming'. Nevertheless, he remained a force among Oxford philosophers and a brilliant teacher. Jonathan Glover, a student from the mid-1960s, recalled that he 'went to Freddie's philosophy classes, and he paid us the intimidating compliment of treating our ideas as equal to his own, subjecting them both to the same devastating analysis. And later, when we were both Fellows at New College, he continued to assume that the undergraduates were as likely to be right as we were.'[31] The American writer and intellectual, Leon Wieseltier, became a graduate student of Ayer in the mid-1970s and also remembered their tutorials with pleasure:

I liked him enormously. He was like an eighteenth-century rationalist voluptuary – he could have been one of Diderot's friends. I remember asking him about Camus: 'I don't know his work well, but he and I were friends: we were making love to twin sisters in Paris after the war.'[32]

It was not the sort of reply Kant or Hegel would have given.

Beyond philosophy, sport remained, as Ayer got older, as important as ever. 'I was watching Tottenham Hotspur only last Saturday,' he said in an interview on his seventieth birthday. 'I still find that I can make this identification, I can be taken out of myself and be wholly concerned with how my side is doing.'[33] He went regularly to Spurs matches, with Julian, who was now writing and lecturing on education at Middlesex Polytechnic or with Basil Boothby or other friends. In 1970 Gully, slim, blonde and glamorous, had gone up to conquer Oxford, where she quickly paired up with Martin Amis. Amis and Ayer had little in common but they played ferocious games of chess. Writing in the *Independent on Sunday*, the novelist left a memorable account of the philosopher's strange way with objects:

Twenty years ago I drove the late A.J. Ayer to White Hart Lane to support Tottenham Hotspur. On the way Ayer smoked three cigarettes. For his first butt he disdained, or did not see, the obvious – and butt-infested – ashtray, favouring the naked tape-deck with the fiery remains of his Player. (The tape-recorder itself had been stolen, true, but the empty console had the word PHILIPS clearly stamped on it.) His second butt he squeezed into the base of the hand brake, his third he ground out on the speedometer. The high point came with his third spent match, which, with incredible skill, he balanced on the bare ignition key, where it wobbled for at least three seconds before dropping inexorably to the floor.[34]

Just as Ayer remained loyal to Spurs, despite the fact that, as he had to admit, 'since the great days of Danny Blanchflower they have seldom played well', so he remained loyal to Middlesex. The journalist and historian, Geoffrey Wheatcroft, who became a friend in the 1970s, shared his interest in cricket: 'We used to go to Lord's', he recalled, 'to watch, and do the *Times* crossword between overs, when I wasn't enjoying exquisite examples of Freddie's didacticism: "Do you know how many members of the present Middlesex team who are not black were not educated at Oxford or Cambridge?" He was genuinely learned in cricket as in many other subjects, though it might be said that he let you know this'.[35]

Ayer's social life was also set in a well established groove. Dee recollects that they saw most of Goronwy and Margie Rees, then living in a small house in Shepherd's Bush. They met regularly either there or at Regent's Park Terrace, for dinner and stormy games of bridge. They also usually spent New Year's Eve together.

Yet if, as Dee suggests, Ayer's life ran on a familiar, almost institutionalised course, with seminars, cricket, football, bridge and various supper clubs and meetings coming round on a reassuringly regular basis, his relationships with women remained as unsettled as ever. He and Vanessa still met weekly at Oxford – undergraduates had noted 'a beautiful witch-like woman who often came in with him to dinner' – although Nigel Lawson, an Opposition whip and himself involved in an affair with a parliamentary assistant who later became his wife, urged discretion. When Ayer died, he left behind a series of letters, notes and poems from Vanessa, many on small scraps of paper, often in pencil. Whimsical and self-deprecating, they are loving, but also, often depressed; she suffered, as she admitted, from 'dark moods'. In 1974, in a moment of despair, she had taken an overdose, because 'I couldn't be a political wife with Nigel and I knew I wasn't up to bringing up Nicholas and giving you a good social life'.[36] Later, before the 1979 election, she told Lawson that she wanted to leave him with his girlfriend, their house and the children, and get 'a basement flat of my own'.[37] Ayer for his part was devoted to her. 'Be on my side,' he said to her in Provence, in the summer of 1980. But he continued to court other women, telling Jocelyn Rickards, after Raimund von Hofmannsthal's death in 1974, that he would like to marry Liz if only she would have him.

Appropriately, Ayer spent the last years of his professorship writing his autobiography, *Part of my Life*. He signed a contract for the book ('Autobiography') with Collins in January 1975 and it appeared two and a half years later, in June 1977 – a year before his final retirement. Ayer worked hard on the memoir, which ends with his arrival at UCL in 1947, but enjoyed the task. He had a vivid memory for the facts if not the emotions of his early adulthood, and found that although initially he could recall little of his childhood, memories slowly trickled back. Collins launched the book with a party at Oxford. Freddie's cousin and childhood playmate, Doris Bamford, came. It was almost the only time she and Freddie had met since the war. His first remark was, 'Wouldn't Grandpapa have been proud?'[38]

Ayer found it hard to arrive at a title for this book, rejecting Christopher Hitchens's suggestion, 'The Leisure of the Theoried Class'. No one seems to have noted an aspect that he must have liked in the one he finally chose: not the hint that there were some aspects of his life he would not divulge, but the implication that philosophy was, and only ever could have been a part of his life. 'There is philosophy and then there is all of *this*,' Ayer had said to Isaiah Berlin half a century before. All his books hitherto had dealt with philosophy; *Part of My Life* was to deal with '*this*'.

Part of My Life is certainly dense with incident and observation, and contains some acute and funny characterisations. His depiction, for instance, of the young J.L. Austin, whom he compared, 'with his steely spectacles, his slight taut figure, and . . . light belted mackintosh' to one of Michael Collins's followers, is memorable. Ayer, too, was admirably even-handed. 'To the best of my ability I wrote nothing but the truth, but I did not tell the whole truth,' he once remarked, and this seems fair.[39] There is a great deal that remains unsaid – Ayer for instance, never mentions Sheilah Graham or their daughter Wendy, or identifies

Hampshire as the 'younger man' with whom Renée had fallen in love –
and many lovers and unrequited passions go unrecorded. But Ayer never
intentionally misleads his readers or describes events in a way that could
be said to be self-serving. He points to the shortcomings of his work more
often than its strengths, plays down his unjust treatment at Eton and
Christ Church, and hardly does justice to either his extraordinary
intellectual precocity or the impact that he had on British philosophy*

But despite its merits, *Part of My Life* makes for a frustrating read. The
problem is that Ayer's wry, measured tone denies us any insight into his
inner life. His appetite for experience, his capacity to live for the
moment, his philosophical zeal, his courage, anger and kindness are
barely hinted at. Russell, in the first volume of his autobiography, had
written movingly about the ways in which his sense of loneliness and his
need for certainty propelled his work and life. Ayer's motivations,
however, remain a mystery. Perhaps, as befitted a man who denied the
existence of a substantive self, he simply lacked any very deep sense of his
identity. Or perhaps, for all of his achievements and renown, he was still
scared of exposing himself. Russell, after all, was an aristocrat, with the
confidence that generally entails. Ayer was most emphatically not. He
could write about his past, but that did not mean that he had altogether
escaped the anxieties and humiliations of his youth.

Ayer was proud of *Part of My Life* but it received very mixed reviews.
Mary Warnock found that for all of his intelligence, 'there seems to be a
lack of curiosity, and particularly a lack of inquisitiveness about other
people'; deep down, she wrote, Ayer seemed 'bored'.[41] John Sturrock,
writing in the *New York Times Book Review*, judged it 'vain' and 'arctic':
'His life . . . is here in creditable, at times engrossing detail; but there is
strangely little self to go with it. Ayer's record of experience is all fact and
no feeling'.[42] Frederic Raphael was still more damning: 'A systematic
prejudice against speculation has created, it seems, a Narcissus incapable
of seeing himself, and hence others'.[43] There were many other kinder
reviews, but Peter Strawson, writing in *Books and Bookmen*, was one of
the few to hit a note of unqualified enthusiasm, arguing that the book
offered a modest, frank and generous account of a remarkable life.[44]

* John Wisdom, who had known Ayer since the 1930s, wrote to him after reading the book:
'You don't come across as someone trying desperately to renovate philosophy and to make rationality
central'. John Wisdom to Ayer, n.d. (c.1977).

Twenty years go quickly and in October 1977, a few months after the publication of *Part of My Life*, Ayer began his final year as professor. Ayer in fact attempted, with the unanimous backing of the philosophy sub-faculty, to get his professorship extended by a year. To his furious indignation, however, this move was blocked by the University Hebdomadal Council, thus seriously diminishing his pension. 'I've never involved myself in university politics,' he told one reporter; 'even so it's difficult to know how and when one makes enemies.'[45]

Anthony Grayling, Ayer's last graduate student at Oxford, remembered him fondly. 'He was a teacher of the very first rank, prepared to explore everything. He'd say, "I don't like the way you want to approach this but never mind, let's see how it would work out."' Freddie too, it seems, liked Grayling, and after dinner and a few drinks would often open up.

> I remember him saying, 'You know, I always think that one day someone is going to point a finger at me: "You are a fraud. You got into Eton and to Christ Church, you were an officer in the Welsh Guards, you became Wykeham Professor at Oxford and you secured a knighthood. But underneath you are just a dirty little Jew-boy."' That was why he cared so much about the little signs of esteem – why he retold the story about Wittgenstein or Einstein thinking he was very clever, and why he had such mixed feelings about *Language, Truth and Logic*. He used to say, 'They only give it to undergraduates to pick holes in'. He worried that other philosophers did not think that he was as good as he was famous. That, too, was why Austin's very personalised attacks hurt so much. He'd say, 'I didn't ask to be ridiculed, you know.'[46]

Despite, or perhaps because of, the status of *Language, Truth and Logic* as an undergraduate punchbag, Ayer allowed himself to devote his last graduate seminar to the book. John Parry, an undergraduate at New College, attended these as well as Ayer's last lectures, on logical atomism, recalling that they were 'neither embarrassingly empty nor exceptionally full'. A New College student society, in which Parry and another student, Richard Sheahan were involved, also invited Ayer to give a valedictory talk. It drew over a hundred students and went on late into the night.

Ayer 'reminisced about everything': about Eton, about Prichard and Joseph and about his being taken up and then dropped by Wittgenstein and about his disapproval of Kripke. He talked about the professionalisation of philosophy ('on the whole a good thing') and the changes he had seen among students ('we were more mature but more snobbish'), and about the development in twentieth-century philosophy ('The answers are not much clearer, but the questions are'). According to Sheahan, 'He held the room for hours; it was an extraordinary performance'.[47]

20

Retirement

As chairman of the judges of the Booker Prize, Ayer spent the summer of 1978 reading novels. Iris Murdoch won with *The Sea, The Sea*, but it is hard to believe that the tender-minded Platonism she defended as a philosopher worked in her favour with Ayer. In September he travelled from Le Beausset to Düsseldorf for a World Congress of Philosophy and then went on to Florence for another conference, on 'Levels of Reality', at which he read a paper attacking the new vogue for essentialism, to which the Harvard philosopher Hilary Putnam replied. Halfway through the Florence meeting, Ayer was struck down by bronchitis and embarked for the first time on a serious effort to give up smoking – an effort which he said 'augurs badly for my work'. He was not ageing well. At sixty-eight his hair was still thick, his eyes still sparkled and he retained his machine-gun delivery. But with hooded, baggy eyes, sagging jowls and a loose mouth he could look almost debauched. His paunch, he lamented, 'grows more and more obtrusive'.[1] A lifetime of smoking began to take its toll and, with the onset of emphysema, he was almost permanently short of breath. The signs of mortality were hard to ignore.

Ayer was not, however, the sort to whom retirement came naturally and he continued to work almost as hard as ever. He undertook a great deal of lecturing, mainly in the lucrative North American market, but devoted most of his energy to books. Over the last decade of his life he nearly reached his Stakhanovite target of a book a year. His writings of this period – as much historical and autobiographical as philosophical – have their merits, but it is hard not to feel that Ayer's determination to write 500 words a day, come what may, made him less discriminating than he should have been. His pension proved to be worth very little, so he needed the money that his books brought in, but he had anyway got into the habit of writing and liked the attention that it brought; he wrote, therefore, whether he had something to write about or not.[2]

With retirement forced upon him, Ayer was obliged to give up his rooms at New College in favour of a smaller set in Wolfson, a modern graduate college on the outskirts of Oxford. He preferred to be at the centre of things and complained about the food and the informal dining arrangements, although Vanessa liked the anonymity this new hideaway provided. That October Ayer began a happy six-year visiting professorship at the department of philosophy at the University of Surrey – a strong, practically minded department run by Brenda Almond, an old UCL student. A few years later Almond also persuaded Ayer to become founding president of the Society for Applied Philosophy. At first sight, Ayer, who had always argued for a separation of philosophy from ethics, seemed an unlikely choice to head an organisation devoted to debating euthanasia, abortion, trade union rights and the like. Yet although he still denied that morality could ever be made into anything like a precise science – 'I doubt very much, for instance, that I hold a coherent moral theory' – he had, as he admitted, come to appreciate that there was an important role for philosophy in clarifying moral choices. 'We did all at one time retreat to a rather insular position,' he told the *New Yorker*'s 'Talk of the Town', 'a position I find not altogether tenable today'.[3]

Engaging in a piece of applied philosophy himself, he wrote a long piece for the *Times* in November 1981, defending Leonard Arthur, a doctor accused of murder after prescribing a course of strong analgesic drugs to a three-day-old Down's syndrome baby rejected by its mother. Arthur's defence had argued that the drugs had not been prescribed in order to hasten the baby's death, but to relieve it from suffering. Ayer, however, went further. While acknowledging that the issue was fraught with difficulties, he suggested that if a severely handicapped child faces a life that is very likely to be unhappy and 'is to be condemned to an institution where there is a strong possibility that it will suffer deprivation and be a burden to others', then it should not be suffered to live. In the

same article Ayer admitted that he had himself joined the suicide group
Exit, an organisation devoted 'to providing the information which makes
death easier to embrace'.[4]

In March 1979, Ayer set out on a three-week lecture tour, beginning at
Trent University, Ontario, where he gave the four Gilbert Ryle lectures:
'Hume's Philosophy, A Reappraisal'. 'The lectures really were a success,'
Ayer wrote to Vanessa, 'which is good for my morale – a full house every
night actually – a bigger audience at the last lecture than at the first'.[5] His
host, Alan Orenstein, had arranged a gruelling round of dinners, parties
and classes but Ayer did 'not blame him: it is rather a feather in his cap (I
say immodestly) to have got me here'. Anyway he still found that he got
'caught up' in the performance – 'well I don't need to tell you after all
these years what I am like'. From Trent Ayer went to Toronto and
Montreal ('Some Problems about Perception'). Then, after a family
weekend in Providence with Valerie and her husband Brian, he travelled
on to lecture in Houston. His letters to Vanessa that have survived from
this time are tender – 'I do love you and wish you in my arms'[6] – but he
valued the freedom these trips gave. In Houston he quickly struck up a
relationship with a young psychologist and they spent three or four days
together going to movies and museums. It was exactly the sort of tidy
romance Ayer liked: he bought her flowers; she wrote to say she loved
him.

Before leaving for Canada, Ayer had secured a contract with Oxford
University Press to turn his lectures on Hume into a short 'Past Master'.
The book came out in both the US and Britain early in 1980 and
reminds us that, much as Ayer admired Russell, Hume was his real
master. Ayer argued for ways of improving on Hume's formulations and
departed from him on many details; political philosophy aside, however
(Hume was liberal conservative), Ayer agreed with him on all the major
questions – or at least, he agreed with almost all the views he attributed
to Hume. The book offered the uniquely concise, incisive commentary
which had become Ayer's hallmark and received warm reviews. As Barry
Stroud later noted, however, it provided no general account of the
character of Hume's philosophy, focusing instead on individual doctrines.[7] Ayer did half acknowledge that Hume was at least as interested in
offering an 'experimental' account of the workings of the mind, as he was
in conceptual analysis – or at least he suggested that Hume was 'guilty' of

running the two together.[8] But he never appears to have doubted that he was best treated as an analytic philosopher in the Viennese mould.

While Freddie was lecturing in Canada and Houston, Vanessa bought a flat in west London. With the 1979 election almost secured, Nigel Lawson felt it was safe to begin divorce proceedings. At around the same time Freddie and Dee also at last agreed to part, and Regent's Park Terrace was put on the market. Dee and Hylan planned to move to New York. Nick, attending a progressive day school in Hampstead and by now a punk (Ayer wept on the day he came home with a purple Mohawk haircut), was to finish his O levels and then choose whether to remain with his father in Britain or follow Dee to the US.[*] The only question was what to do with Freddie. It was widely assumed, not least by him, that Vanessa would look after him. Jocelyn Rickards, however, who so often seemed to find herself embroiled in Freddie's domestic problems, was surprised to get a phone call from Vanessa: 'I am enjoying living on my own, I don't think I want Freddie.' Jocelyn rang Dee to give her the news. 'Dee said: "Well she has got to take him. You've got to tell her she has got to take him".'[9] The story is corroborated by a letter from Vanessa among Ayer's papers:

> Darling One, I would like to stay in my Parson's Green hovel. I promise to look after you in your London flat. Please can we leave it like that. You know I love you but if I give up my own self, I give up too much. . .[10]

What was meant to be a game of musical chairs looked like becoming pass the parcel.

In the end, however, Vanessa relented and Ayer moved in with her and Horatia in the new year of 1980. (Horatia remembers the insensitivity with which he arrived, a new stepfather, and took it for granted that he was there to be looked after.) That summer Dee left for

---

[*] In the summer of 1978 Dee had taken Nick on a tour of the western States. It was so hot that the zippers scattered over his shirts and trousers burnt his skin. Nick was bullied into writing to Freddie, but as his postcards show, however much father and son loved each other, they were products of very different educations: 'Dear Dad, How are you? O.K. good. Fuck its amazing here. We just left Kit and Gayle and are at the Grand Canyon. It's also really hot . . . Don't forget to feed the Hampster. Shit I forgot your in France now' (no date).

New York: 'I am giving up the unequal struggle to become a true English lady,' she told the *Evening Standard*, in a departing shot.[11] She and Hylan took an apartment in the Chelsea Hotel, while they looked for a place of their own. Dee and Freddie now began to wrangle over a divorce settlement and Dee recalls that for two or three years relations became very 'bad' between them. Freddie's letters of the period abound with angry complaints about 'blackmail' and 'extortion'.

In March 1980, after a long and painful illness, Renée died of cancer. She and Freddie had remained friends to the end. A month later she was followed by Liz von Hofmannsthal. Dee, then still in London, was struck by the equanimity with which Ayer accepted both events.

In the summer of 1980, Ted Honderich, now a lecturer in philosophy at UCL, observing that Ayer seemed rather 'gloomy', led a campaign to get him a further, seventieth birthday honour – a Companionship of Honour or, what Ayer really wanted, a peerage. Honderich, having arrived from Canada to study under Ayer at UCL in 1960, had been disappointed to find that Ayer had emigrated to Oxford. The two had little contact over the next two decades until Honderich joined the Bertorelli's dining club that Ben Nicolson had founded and which Ayer still attended. Honderich, a large, animated, sociable figure, combined a passion for philosophy with left-wing views and a taste for drink and blazing conversations. These were features that Ayer liked in a man, and the two philosophers became increasingly close in the course of the 1980s.

'I am certainly not too proud to accept a further honour even if it were no more than a C.H. and I think I should rather enjoy making speeches in the Lords,' Ayer wrote to Ted from Vanessa's flat in May.[12] Younger philosophers like John Foster and Jonathan Glover wrote in support, as well as Lords Goodman, Blake and Longford and other venerable names. The newly elected Thatcher government, however, did not like philosophers, or at least not left-wing ones, and Honderich's campaign came to nothing. Just before his birthday in October, Ayer fell while running for a bus and broke a rib; breathing became harder still.

That summer, Freddie and Vanessa bought a house in York Street, off Baker Street, the last of Ayer's many narrow Georgian homes. The first-floor drawing-room doubled as Ayer's study, with pride of place given to the large empty round table on which he liked to work. The house, he wrote to an old girl friend, 'is a little the worse for wear, but not dangerously so, with room in it for two of Vanessa's daughters and a separate basement for my seventeen year old son. He has gone through the punk stage and now looks very presentable. He is still at sixth form college and facing examinations. I have no idea what he will do after that'.[13]

Properties tend to mark a new phase in our lives, and Ayer and Vanessa were now established in the world as an all but married couple. Horatia, still at school, lived with them, although the following summer, Nick, with school over, moved to New York, to work as a roadie and barman. Over the next few years Dee wrote often to Ayer, sharing her worries about Nick, although she too, trying to write another novel, found herself in a miasma: 'I sit all day at the typewriter, and nothing comes; it's a terrible feeling'.[14]

Back in London, Vanessa and Freddie were making new friends, eminent among them Margot Walmsley. Walmsley had worked for many years as managing editor of *Encounter*, and the salon she held at her Kensington flat tended to attract right-wingers, including Ferdinand Mount, Peregrine Worsthorne and Charles Moore. As the journalist and critic Derwent May recalls, however, Freddie and Vanessa were often there: 'I think that Margot was important to them. When couples come together they need new friends and Margot's circle helped supply them.' May liked Vanessa and respected Freddie. 'You felt his presence in a room, although he was a small compact man. He was going to be himself, which is not to say discourteous, but there was no diffidence in him.'[15]

Derwent May was not the only person to find that Ayer was still an impressive or least a noticeable presence. The Oxford political theorist John Gray met him around this period, and was struck by 'his almost pagan vitality – just vitality for vitality's sake'. Isaiah Berlin's editor, Henry Hardy, found himself sitting next to Ayer at high table in New College one night, and recalled that Ayer spent the evening trying to stir up arguments around him: 'He was extraordinarily provocative'.[16] This echoed something Berlin himself said: 'Freddie always wanted to be the centre of attention in any room'.[17]

Margot Walmsley and her friends notwithstanding, Ayer was leading a quieter life with Vanessa than he had with Dee. 'A memory,' Dominic Lawson says, 'which captures their life together is going into the drawing room and finding them reading aloud to each other, which I think a good model of a marriage.'[18] Vanessa became an avid Spurs fan, and accompanied Freddie to White Hart Lane. On Sunday nights he and Vanessa usually ate with Guida Crowley, who adored them both. Like his Oxford secretary, Rosanne Richardson, or Dee's sister, Priscilla McBride, Crowley had been close to Freddie for many years, knew everything there was to know and found that his virtues far outweighed his faults.

In July 1981, not long after Freddie and Vanessa had moved into York Street, Freddie's much-loved daughter Valerie died. It was a horribly sudden death, and the only miserably slight consolation was that Freddie was able to see her before it happened. She and Brian had come to England for their summer holiday, and were staying at York Street when she collapsed with Hodgkin's disease; a few days later she was dead. 'I will never forget the day after Valerie had died,' Brian recalled. 'Julian and I went to see Freddie and Vanessa at York Street; there were Julian and I moist-eyed and Vanessa quietly crying. Freddie focused on the clinical details and once he had got all the facts straight in his mind, he felt the conversation was over. Yet one sensed he was attempting to come to terms with what had happened. It was as if he was at one remove from the immediacy of his feelings.' 'It was,' Horatia Lawson reflected, 'the beginning of the curse of York Street.'[19]

In September 1982 Freddie, Vanessa and Horatia flew to Dartmouth College, New Hampshire, where Ayer had been appointed Montgomery Fellow. 'You have probably heard from Dee and Gully,' he wrote to Nick, 'that I am coming over in September . . . to teach for a semester in New Hampshire. They are paying me a fair amount of money and I am hoping to arrange to transfer most of it . . . to you.'[20] Although they intended to return to London at Christmas, the three of them ended by staying until March. Ayer was too busy teaching to get much of his own work done, but the comfortable house, beautiful scenery and New England good manners made their time there a great success. 'So far it is less cold than I expected,' he wrote to Nick in January, 'but they are already skating on Occam point at the end of our garden and very pretty it all looks.'[21] Valerie's husband Brian came from Rhode Island to see them and Ayer spent a number of weekends in New York with Gully, now living in the city and working as journalist, and Nick, still casting around for a future.

By this stage Vanessa's life had come to centre very firmly on Freddie.

She began to keep long diary-like notes, describing his lectures and seminars, the size of the audience, the questions asked, and she helped him in researching his books. Back in London, in March 1982, Ayer's divorce finally came through and he and Vanessa almost immediately got married. 'We wanted a quiet wedding,' Ayer told a journalist, 'so we married at the registry office down the road, with our Indian maid as a witness and her boyfriend Steve, as best man'. Steve, the leader of a Glasgow punk band, Language, was under strict instructions not to comb his hair.

Vanessa was too unconfident a person ever to be entirely happy and the marriage had its tensions. Some of Freddie's older friends complained that she kept him away from them. Nor did she get on with Nick: 'Vanessa and Horatia send their love,' Ayer wrote to him, the autumn after they got married, trying to mend a breach. 'Whatever misunderstandings there may have been in the summer, you are wrong in thinking that they do not wish you well.'[22] Yet the bond between Ayer and his new wife was unusually strong. Vanessa, Jocelyn recalled in her memoirs,

was one of the walking wounded after suffering through a long marriage to ... Nigel Lawson. Astonishingly beautiful, like a small carved ivory Egyptian figure, she set herself to create an ambience where Freddie was able to work; she cosseted and cared for him in a way no other wife had ever done. He in turn loved and protected her, helped to rebuild her shattered confidence and gave her the greatest gift it was in his possession to give, absolutely total fidelity ... It was one of the very few marriages I regarded as happy.[23]

Ayer himself admitted that this relationship was different: 'I was certainly very much in love with my first wife Renée when I married her and I was monogamous until I was twenty-six,' he told the *Evening Standard*. 'I was a romantic person and when that marriage broke up in a painful way, I suppose I grew predatory and less nice. I kept women at a distance. Vanessa got within my guard, so to speak.'[24]

By the time of Freddie and Vanessa's marriage, campaigning for the general election of June 1983 had already begun. Ayer 'detested' Mrs Thatcher and 'her pack of second rate go-go getters'.[25] 'They say "Let the devil take the hindmost",' he told Peter Strawson; 'well I don't want there to be a hindmost to take.'²⁶ He had opposed the government's attempt to take back the Falkland Islands by force, on the grounds that it would not furnish 'a long term solution to the problem' and even if it did, it would 'not justify the loss of life' or 'the emergence of the ugly face of jingoism'.²⁷ Yet Ayer, who had long described himself as 'a radical liberal' rather than a socialist, was almost as disillusioned by the Labour Party's leftward turn. He had always been in favour of closer integration with Europe, not least because he saw it as a step 'towards a federal world government', had long argued for proportional representation and a bill of rights and now wanted a written constitution as well. It is hardly surprising, then, that he should have followed many of his Gaitskellite friends into the Social Democratic Party when it was founded in 1981. Horatia Lawson remembers his disgruntlement when the new party failed to include his name in a list of supporters it published on its launch. This slight notwithstanding, both he and Vanessa voted for the SDP.

All this time Ayer had been hard at work. Meeting Stephen Spender at a New College banquet in December 1980, he told him that he was writing a history of twentieth-century philosophy: Russell's *History of Western Philosophy*, he said, had made its author a fortune and he hoped his would do the same.²⁸ *Philosophy in the Twentieth Century*, which Ayer said had caused him more trouble than any of his other books, was finished a year later and dedicated to Vanessa. After giving over the first half of the book to Moore and Russell, the American Pragmatists William James and C.I. Lewis, and Wittgenstein and the Vienna circle, Ayer turned to later developments within the analytic tradition, ending with criticisms of Kripke's and Putnam's views on necessity. Collingwood got a chapter to himself as the most sympathetic of modern metaphysicians and Merleau-Ponty was given similar treatment as 'the best representative' of phenomenology and existentialism.

A number of the reviewers politely noted that Ayer's history was really too difficult to function as a sequel to Russell's bestseller, but otherwise they were generally enthusiastic. The most forcefully critical intervention came from Hilary Putnam, an old Harvard friend, who argued in *Partisan Review* that Ayer did not have enough sympathy for the hermeneutic, interpretative turn philosophy had taken with the later Wittgenstein and others, to serve as an insightful or reliable guide: 'a reader who had only this book to go by would have to see philosophy after the early Wittgenstein as, for the most part, a series of empty and confused ideas; even the expositions become untrustworthy'.[29] Perhaps Putnam regretted the attack – when he later wrote about Ayer, he did so generously. Yet it was true that despite Ayer's opening argument that there is a sense in which the history of philosophy is a story of progress – 'As in a guessing game, the players have not yet found the answers, but they have narrowed the area in which they can reside' – the story he goes on to tell is one of decline.[30] No one since the war, Ayer seems to have believed, had quite scaled the heights achieved by Russell, Moore, the early Wittgenstein and the logical positivists. There were giants on the earth in those days.

With *Philosophy in the Twentieth Century* behind him, and nothing much else to occupy his pen, Ayer turned to a second volume of autobiography. The contract for what Ayer decided to call, for want of anything better, *More of My Life*, was signed in March 1982, although it was not until a year later, once he had got back from Dartmouth, that he got down to writing it in earnest: seven months later it was finished. Collins has in its files a letter from Ayer's editor, Mark Bonham-Carter, commenting on the manuscript:

> We are introduced to a large cast of characters, but they sometimes remain merely names – I find it difficult to tell the difference between Angelica Weldon, Alvys Maben and Jocelyn. Ryle and Price remain philosophers rather than colleagues whose personalities must have had some impact on you. I think what I am saying is that I could do with more light and shade, more contrast, that the equable flow of your prose sometimes appears to conceal you rather than reveal you, your mind and your feelings – which is after all one of the purposes of an autobiography.[31]

It is a pity that Ayer did not take more heed of Bonham-Carter's advice. The period of Ayer's life covered by *More of My Life* (essentially his years at UCL) is less eventful than that covered by *Part of My Life*, but taking this into account, the second volume is still considerably weaker than the first. (Ayer himself later admitted as much.) The book, to be sure, has its moments – there is a memorably barbed sketch of Stanley Spencer – and the whole displays Ayer's customary modesty. As Anthony Quinton put in his review, Ayer is 'much more energetic in recalling occasions when things went wrong in life than in reliving moments of triumph, these disasters being recollected with rueful amusement'.[32] Yet too often Ayer seems to be writing for the sake of writing. His accounts of travels are particularly flat. For example of Dublin: 'it did not quite come up to my high expectations. For no special reason, I formed the impression that it was living on its past glories.' Worse, however, than any longueurs, a certain chilliness sometimes enters the narrative. Twice he ends chapters with the death of very close girlfriends – Angelica Weldon from suicide, Alvys Maben in a car accident – and in neither case does it occur to him to express any sentiment. Ayer seems to have felt nothing inappropriate in transposing the 'cold beauty' of Language, Truth and Logic from philosophy to life.

In October 1983, just before writing the preface to More of My Life, Ayer again returned to Canada, although this time to McMaster University, where he delivered three Whidden lectures on the theme of 'Freedom and Morality'. The lectures later gave their title to a collection of previously published essays including 'Identity and Reference', his assault on Kripke, and 'The Vienna Circle', a lecture given at a Wittgenstein congress in Kirchberg, Austria, in 1981.

Short as they are, the three Whidden lectures – 'The Concept of Freedom', 'Are There Objective Values?' and 'Utilitarianism' – came as close as Ayer ever got to the book on moral philosophy he had always half wanted to write. Over the decades Ayer had somewhat moderated the emotivism he had advanced in Language, Truth and Logic; there he had argued that moral utterances that 'simply express moral judgements' were 'pure expressions of feeling', but by 1949 in 'On the Analysis of Moral Judgements', he was suggesting that one might be engaging in any one of a range of speech acts such as prescribing, giving leave, showing oneself favourably disposed, expressing a resolution and so on.[33] He had also admitted that originally he had neglected the descriptive component in most moral judgements – the extent to which in passing a judgement on an act, one is declaring it an act of a certain empirical type – thus exaggerating the subjective character of moral discourse.[34]

Otherwise, the broad outline of his ethical views had hardly changed over the decades. He still thought Hume's distinction between fact and value was broadly right, and he still denied that morality could be reduced to a set of simple or universalisable principles: 'I suspect that my values do not significantly differ from the liberal values of John Stuart Mill, which means that they contain a strong utilitarian element but they do not fit neatly, any more than his did, into a utilitarian mould.'[35] If he thought that there had been important contributions to moral philosophy since the 1930s he makes no reference to them. Indeed, although there are some barbed allusions to R.M. Hare, the only new meta-ethical theory that he considered at any length is the 'error theory' put forward by the Australian philosopher, John Mackie. In the first chapter of his book *Ethics: Inventing Right and Wrong* (1977), Mackie, while accepting that there are no objective values, contended that ordinary moral judgements include an implicit claim to objectivity and thus are false. Ayer's response to this argument was entirely in keeping with his positivism of the 1930s: he agreed with Mackie that there were no such things as 'objective values', but maintained that the assumption that there were, was not wrong but meaningless:

I find Mackie's [criticisms of objectivism] persuasive. What puzzles me, however, is his conclusion that the belief in there being objective values is merely false, as if the world might have contained such things, but happens not to, just as it happens not to contain centaurs or unicorns. Whereas I think that the conclusion to which his argument should have led him is that the champions of objective values failed to make their belief intelligible.[36]

Ayer was not happy unless he was writing something. No sooner were the lectures on *Freedom and Morality* out of the way than he began a short book on Wittgenstein, once again for Weidenfeld. Dedicated to Peter Strawson, *Ludwig Wittgenstein* was necessarily a slightly negative exercise, given that Ayer disagreed with so much of what his old mentor argued. One is left wondering, as Ayer himself sometimes wondered, why he thought Wittgenstein, with Russell, the only philosophical genius of the century. On the other hand, as the reviewers noted, it was at least refreshingly free from the cowed reverence of much Wittgenstein commentary. Like so many of Ayer's studies of other thinkers, *Wittgenstein* does not really have a centre – Ayer just marched from one point to the next, although he was at pains to show that Wittgenstein's repeated preference for description over theory or explanation was not reflected 'in his actual procedure at any stage of his development including that of the *Investigations*'.

> That his explanations are runic does not reduce them to descriptions: his theories do not cease to be such by being covertly laid out. Wittgenstein's whole flirtation with behaviourism is an attempt . . . to explain the operations of the mind. His suggestion that philosophy leaves everything as it was; more obviously his attempt to outlaw private languages, are both of them embodiments of philosophical theories. One of my principal objects has been to show that these theories are false.[37]

The book offers, in particular, a memorably sceptical treatment of Wittgenstein's attempt to save magical and religious beliefs from the charge of irrationality by treating them as purely symbolic or expressive or somehow internally coherent and self-validating. 'I am not myself a religious believer,' Ayer drily explained, 'but if I were I doubt if I should be content to be told that I was playing a game in accordance with a canonical set of rules. Rather I should wish for some assurance that my beliefs were true.'[38]

By now, Ayer had established a relation with the well-paying University of Texas, Houston. Having lectured there at least twice before, in 1979 and 1983, he and Vanessa returned again in January 1985, when Ayer delivered two talks, one on Wittgenstein and one on the development of his own ideas. Back in London, he began work on a book on Voltaire's life and ideas for George Weidenfeld. Ayer worried that the book 'may need more research than I have patience for', but was delighted with the £20,000 advance Weidenfeld had offered, and told everyone one about it.

That May he gave a talk in a series of Morrell Memorial Addresses on Toleration at the University of York. His contribution, 'The Sources of Intolerance', a discursive overview of the origins and varieties of modern intolerance, throws interesting light on his attitudes towards the young.

In his style and taste, Ayer was very much a man of the 1920s and 1930s. Indeed, Jennifer Trusted, a philosopher-scientist from Exeter, who made friends with him around this time, found something incongruous in the way he combined radicalism in philosophy and politics with a deep nostalgia for the dress codes and good manners of the pre-war years.[39] Yet as Ayer now argued, the decline in style and politeness since the pre-war years had its compensations: 'Aesthetically I am not an admirer of pop music, or of all the fashions in youthful dress and hair styles that successively come into vogue, but they have fostered a kinship, or at least a disregard of racial differences, which I consider much more important than the onslaught on the aesthetic sensibilities of elder persons'.[40] Ayer noted too that the new youth culture not only cut across race but to some extent across class barriers too: 'in matters of taste, my younger son has more in common with working-class boys of his own age than he has with members of an older generation. That was not true of myself fifty-odd years ago'. 'A more disquieting feature of modern youth culture,' Ayer observed, doubtless once again with Nick in mind, 'is its readiness to experiment with drugs.'[41]

Nick had been through a bad time in New York, but early in 1984 he secured a place at Bard. Ayer wrote to him regularly throughout his time in the US, and the letters show a touchingly tender father. They worry about Nick's state of mind and his health, take pleasure in his successes and never scold. Like letters from parents everywhere, they beg their recipient to reply – 'Please write to me soon. It is hateful for me to feel cut off from you'; 'I am sorry to keep nagging you but your silence does worry me'; 'I am looking forward to the letter you said you had begun to write'.[42] They tend to end in the same way – 'I miss you and I love you very much as always, Dad.' 'Le plus bel amour', as Ayer once said to Beatrice, 'est celui que l'on a pour un enfant, car il est sans égoisme'.[43]

Ayer was delighted that Nick seemed finally to have settled down, and he and Vanessa looked forward to spending a semester at Bard in the fall of 1985. Then disaster struck. Late in June, during a short holiday in Paris, Ayer noted that Vanessa was tired and weak. Back in London, it soon became clear that she was seriously ill. The doctors diagnosed an advanced case of liver cancer; she must, Horatia thinks, have known for some time that something was wrong.[44] 'My news,' Ayer wrote to Nick at the end of July, 'is not good. Vanessa is coming home today, but only for a week. Then she goes back to the clinic for the end. They have at least promised to keep her out of pain.'[45]

A few days before, while Vanessa was still in hospital, Ayer had appeared on a BBC2 studio debate about God – 'Is There Anybody There?' In a moving exchange, a member of the audience invoked his love for his wife as proof of God's existence: 'When I say "I love you" I do not mean that I, an accident, love you, an accident – something inside one says that's not right.' Ayer almost jumped from his chair in indignation, his voice shaking as he spoke: 'I must protest against the previous speaker's *grotesque* misuse of the word "accident". I have a wife too and I love her very much. When I say that I love her I do not mean that she was an accident. I don't mean she comes into the world uncaused any more than I did, or that my love does not have a psychological cause. This levity in using these words shocks me.'

At this point Hugh Montefiore, the Bishop of Birmingham, intervened:

Montefiore: You believe you and your wife are the product of an ultimately meaningless process don't you?
Ayer: If you mean that I don't think that our existence was planned by some supernatural being, yes.
Montefiore: No, meaningless.
Ayer: No, I do not accept the word 'meaningless'. I do not think my love for her is meaningless. I think my love for her has a very great deal of meaning, is very intense.[46]

It was an impressive performance, both lucid and heartfelt. Within two weeks of this exchange Vanessa was dead.

Vanessa had met her death with what one obituarist described as 'a typical, irreverent courage'.[47] She summoned an undertaker to her hospital bedside and gave him a list of detailed instructions. 'May I know the name of the deceased?' he asked. 'The deceased will be myself,' she replied. Vanessa, in fact, arranged every detail, going so far as to compose her own death notice and giving Horatia a dress to wear at her memorial service.

Despite Vanessa's own involvement, however, the arrangements were not to Ayer's liking. Although Vanessa was herself an atheist, she had organised a simple non-denominational but nevertheless vaguely religious service at Mill Hill Cemetery; just a few poems of her choice and the sixth psalm. The last, a most unchristian, vengeful verse – 'Let all mine enemies be ashamed and sore vexed: let them return *and* be ashamed suddenly' – was a characteristically mischievous choice and embarrassed the minister who was obliged to read it out. Ayer, though, did not see the joke, and on leaving the service put his arm round Jocelyn Rickards: 'I am deeply sorry you should have been involved in this ridiculous farce.'[48] The positivist in him was not yet dead.

The writer Peter Vansittart saw Ayer 'a certain amount' after Vanessa's death, and like many of his friends was touched by his very evident distress: 'He seemed terribly crushed and old – terribly crushed . . . It was terribly moving to see – I mean, the real man of feeling behind . . . this very dapper, rather vain man'.[49] Sue Boothby recalled that, asked for lunch one day, he turned up early and burst into tears.[50]

Four days after Vanessa's death, Ted Honderich took Ayer out to Bianchi's in Soho and described the evening in his diary:

He is more or less at sea, and of course very sad. They had been in connection 17 years. Said he had thought of committing suicide. Vanessa had calmly arranged all things – asked that memorial service be delayed to September when people get back from holidays etc. He was evidently grateful for the dinner, and spoke several times of the fact, at least, that he had some good friends.[51]

21

Old Age

'There was surely a bad fairy present at Freddie's birth,' Jocelyn Rickards wrote in her memoirs.[1] And it was true: Ayer had more than his fair share of bad luck. Yet of all the afflictions he suffered in old age – the breakdown in his relationship with Dee, Valerie's death, worries about Nick, ill health – Vanessa's loss was the hardest. As Honderich's diary entry suggests, he now considered suicide. Staying with Gully and her family in New York later in the year, he sat vacantly in a local park, watching her daughter Rebecca play.[2]

Vanessa and Ayer had looked forward to spending the autumn semester of 1985 at Bard with Nick. After she died, however, he postponed his visit for a year and instead applied himself to finishing the book on Voltaire. He and Vanessa had worked on it together, and, as if it were too painful to be treated as important, he dashed off the last two chapters in the weeks immediately following her death. The book came out in February 1986 in the US and in the summer in Britain. In October, Ayer could write to Ted Honderich, 'I think that I have seen most of the principal English reviews of *Voltaire*. On the whole they have damned with faint praise – I think justly. I intended to write a more ambitious book. Vanessa's illness and death prevented me. Or perhaps I was just too lazy to do enough research'.[3]

Ayer was being unfair on himself. The reviews did not herald it as a masterpiece, but a number were enthusiastic. The distinguished intellectual historian Judith Shklar welcomed the book in the *New Republic*, chiefly on the grounds that it engaged 'its subject directly in the serious philosophical argument' that his writings deserve.[4] In a review in the *New Statesman*, Justin Wintle observed that 'Ayer's Voltaire works a treat. Precisely because his approach is segmented, uneven, it allows Ayer to tackle not so much the essence as the disparate centres of an oddly protean individual.'[5]

Voltaire sets out to take the reader through its subject's early plays and poems, his writing on England, history and philosophy, and his later campaigns against religiously inspired persecution, and it does so with verve and insight. It is not surprising that Ayer should be able to write with understanding about Voltaire's sceptical Enlightenment personality – that combination of irreverence and compassion, sensuality and principle, that both men shared – nor that he should offer a lively defence of Voltaire's case against Christianity. But he is just as confident in his handling of Voltaire's historical and literary efforts.

Like the great French writer, Ayer worked with something like a universal history: he had strong and independent views on the achievements and weaknesses of the various epochs in European history from classical to modern times. He agreed with Voltaire's opinions on Pascal, but thought Rembrandt and Vermeer were at least as good as Poussin and Claude; he judged Voltaire's handling of Peter the Great 'gingerly', but shared his respect for what the Jesuits had done in seventeenth-century Paraguay 'perhaps the only place and time where the introduction of Christianity had been wholly beneficial, barring the fact that the Paraguayan Indians were not entrusted with self-govern-ment'.[6] Ayer's strength as an intellectual historian was that, while making no claims to originality, he possessed a sense of judgement and proportion, a feeling for what was valuable in the tradition to which he and Voltaire belonged.

He ended the book by warning against the mistake of assuming that because religion no longer threatened civil liberties in England, it did not do so anywhere else.

When we look farther afield and observe such things at the recrudescence of fundamentalism in the United States, the horrors of religious fanaticism in the Middle East, the appalling danger which the stubbornness of political intolerance presents to the whole world, we must surely conclude that we can still profit by the example of the lucidity, the acumen, the intellectual honesty and the moral courage of Voltaire.'[7]

Even before Vanessa died, Ayer had a very clear idea of the loneliness he would feel and began the process of getting himself re-elected to the Garrick. Soon after her death, Nigella found him a young housekeeper, Pippa Hamilton, from a smart county family and, at twenty-nine, newly divorced with two children. Pippa, who came in daily for two years, had never been to university or met 'anyone like Freddie before'. But they became friends, and she was soon not only preparing him lunch but eating it with him. Beatrice, who had been so close to Ayer in the 1970s but had since got married and started a family, also stepped in to help look after him.

Ayer's life now fell into a new pattern. When he was well, he wrote during the morning. He usually had a book to work on, the odd bit of broadcasting, lectures, and reviews. 'Surprisingly,' he told Isaiah Berlin, 'I find that as I get older I write more easily, although I am increasingly at a loss for subjects to write about.'[8] Pippa prepared lunch and, if he had made no plans for the evening, left him ham sandwiches for dinner: 'he always wanted exactly the same thing, just like the flowers in the living-room always had to be blue and yellow'.[9] Usually, however, Ayer went out to dinner with a friend, or a friend would bring a meal over to him. He ate at his clubs once or twice a week.

At one time or another Dominic and Horatia lived in the basement flat and Nigella was also often at the house, cooking for him or keeping him company. Julian, by now a successful business consultant and an active Conservative, also saw him a great deal; they became closer than they had been for many years. He and his girlfriend, Susan Butler, would cook Sunday lunch at York Street. Julian organised a chauffeur to ferry them to and from White Hart Lane and helped him try, unsuccessfully, to sell the house. All four children and stepchildren have fond memories of him, although they also spoke of his self-centredness.

Horatia liked the fact that 'he knew how to talk to women' and that he was easy to tease.[10] Nigella admitted that he could be 'selfish to a degree that is hard to explain unless you knew him well. He would come back from a dinner party and talk about what he had said, and I would say, "Who were you sitting next to?" "No idea, no idea", or "Oh just a pretty girl, just a girl". He did not think to ask.' Yet, she admitted he could be 'wonderful'. 'I suppose he had charm in the old-fashioned sense, not the charm you spray on in the morning. He was charming'.[11]

Apart from Nick, Gully was the child to whom Freddie was closest, and he spent the Christmas of 1985 in New York, with her and her husband, the television producer Peter Foges, and Rebecca in their West Village brownstone. Gully loved having him and he doted on Rebecca. Having more or less recovered from a bout of bronchitis, he returned to London before the new year, where he had an appointment for a prostate operation. 'I am just marking time, waiting to go into hospital,' he wrote to Nick at the end of December. 'Spending my days in illness and mostly in solitude depresses me.'[12]

The mid-1980s also represented a depressing time for British philosophy, as the Conservative government set about 'reallocating' spending on higher education. The departments at Surrey and Exeter, at both of which Ayer had taught, were closed and others were cut – it was a long way from those post-war days when Ayer's UCL seminars were broadcast live to the nation. Ayer wrote to *The Times* protesting against the cuts, but to little avail.[13] 'It seems,' he told one journalist, 'that I have spent my entire time trying to make life more rational and that it was all a wasted effort.'[14]

It was some consolation, then, that there was suddenly a great deal of discussion of his own work. January 1986 represented the fiftieth anniversary of *Language, Truth and Logic* and the occasion was marked by the publication of two sets of essays about the book, one issuing from a conference at St Andrews, the other from a series of talks at Durham.[15] Ayer attended the Scottish conference, and delivered the last lecture in the Durham series, 'Reflections on *Language, Truth and Logic*', in which he outlined the development of his views since 1936. When asked by Bryan Magee, in the mid-1970s, what he now thought were the defects of *Language, Truth and Logic* Ayer had blithely replied, 'Well, I suppose the most important defect was that nearly all of it was false'.[16] His Durham lecture, however, serves as a reminder that he still adhered to one of the Vienna Circle's most basic tenets – that every meaningful descriptive statement had to be cashable in the hard currency of sense-experience.

Ayer took even greater pride in the publication, at this time, of a long and detailed study of his work by a former student, the Oxford philosopher John Foster, not just because his name appeared alongside those of Socrates, Hume and Kant in Routledge's prestigious 'Arguments of the Philosophers' series, but because Foster focused on the later work, culminating in *Central Questions*, rather than *Language, Truth and Logic*. Foster finally concluded that Ayer's empiricist outlook was 'needlessly austere' and that his arguments against causal necessitation, the substantival self and objective morality were not quite convincing. His treatment, however, was admiring: 'As a curb on the conceptual extravagances of speculative metaphysics and as a guard against the uncritical endorsement of our ordinary modes of thought, this austerity has its merits, and the philosophical world should acknowledge a debt of gratitude to Ayer for his consistent pursuit of economy and rigour'.[17]

As if to crown it all, a few months after Foster's book appeared, Ayer learned that he was to be a subject of a volume in 'The Library of Living Philosophers,' a series inaugurated before the war by an American philosopher Paul Schilpp, which gathered together a collection of essays on a 'great' modern philosopher and the philosopher's replies to them – Russell, Moore, Einstein, Popper and Quine had all been honoured. *The Philosophy of A.J. Ayer* came out after its subject had died, but he had time to respond to all but two of the twenty-four essays that it included. His replies, displaying a familiar mixture of combativeness and diffidence, suggest that his mental powers remained undimmed to the end.

With *Voltaire* completed, although not yet published, Ayer set about looking for another writing project. He toyed with the notion of writing a short creed – an atheist's profession of faith – but then, early in the summer of 1986, he attended a dinner given by his wartime friend, Barley Alison. Barley sat him opposite the publisher Peter Grose of Secker and Warburg who, on the spot, offered him £30,000 for a book on any subject. Ayer immediately suggested Tom Paine. In some respects the choice was a sensible one. Paine, like Voltaire and Russell, was one of the great figures in the free-thinking radical tradition. Like them, his life combined action with ideas in a way that Ayer admired. And like Voltaire, he was more often cited than read. But, he admitted, he knew almost nothing about Paine and was not quite sure where the idea to write about him had come from.[18]

Shortly after his prostate operation of January, Ayer had been to stay with Rosanne Richardson in Oxford, and at the end of June it fell to her to escort him, Nick and his girlfriend out to Provence for the summer. Richardson became, in fact, one of a circle of women who were drawn into Freddie's life over the next few years, looking after him and enjoying his company. As Ayer admitted to a journalist when he returned to London at the end of August: 'I'd vaguely like to marry again and have someone take care of me', although candidates were warned: 'A woman who talks about my subject is wholly intolerable. A witty woman is charming.' One witty woman he saw a lot of was Cynthia Kee, a novelist and journalist, divorced from Robert Kee, who lived in a handsome flat in Ayer's beloved Fitzrovia. Cynthia came to feel that there was 'something deficient in Freddie's make-up – somehow he had been nipped in the bud as a child'. But she had been deeply touched by his and Vanessa's devotion to each other and felt responsible for him after she died. 'He was at his best when he came to dinner and there would be just my kids and some friends of theirs . . . Perhaps he identified with youth because he felt that he had missed his own childhood – he said he had hated Eton'.[19]

Another friend was a psychotherapist, Verity Ravensdale, a vivacious blonde, at the time estranged from her husband, Nicholas Mosley. They met not long after Vanessa's death at a dinner party given by Verity's Camden Town neighbours Derwent and Yolanta May. Ayer asked for her number at the end of the evening, and rang her as soon as he got home. From that point on they spoke most mornings for the rest of his life, although they never, much to Ayer's chagrin, became lovers. 'I've got nothing critical to say of him at all. I absolutely loved him; he was the brightest man. I am not usually a Florence Nightingale, but when it came to Freddie, he was such fun to be with that I would do anything for him, and if he asked me to pick him up from the airport I'd go. He danced for me, sang his favourite songs and read me Tennyson. He was life-enhancing.'[20]

Soon after Vanessa's death, Ayer made contact with a French girlfriend from the 1970s, some thirty years his junior, and an arrangement was made for her to come to stay in Le Beausset in the middle of July. It proved an emotional, physically invigorating re-encounter, culminating in a romantic night spent dancing at a Bastille Day *fête*. Talking alone after dinner one night, she asked Freddie what he would say if he found himself confronted by St Peter after he died: 'I have made a mess of my personal life, but I have taught my students to find the truth.' The woman soon returned to her family, but over the next couple of months sent Ayer a stream of love letters replete with invocations of the heavens, eternity, the spirit and other such dubiously metaphysical entities. Ayer admitted in a letter to Jocelyn that he was 'flattered' but 'also faintly disturbed . . . Perhaps it is a good thing that I am going to be away for nearly four months, for all my fear of being lonely and mildly neglected at Bard'.[21]

Ayer's connections with Bard went back to 1948, when he had taught a course at the liberal arts college at Annadale, a tiny town on the Hudson, about a hundred miles north of New York City. In 1983 he had renewed his association when he received an honorary doctorate. He was now returning for a semester as a Stevenson Fellow, committed to teaching two courses, with time off to lecture around the country. As he explained in a letter of November, 'my main reason for accepting their invitation is that [Nick] is in his third year as an undergraduate here. In the normal way I could not afford to keep him here but because I am an honorary doctor of the place they let me off the vast tuition fee . . .'[22]

Initially, as he wrote to Ted Honderich, he did not like his new life:

If I had a car, and could drive it and explore the pretty countryside, this would not be a bad place to be. As it is, I find it rather depressing. The atmosphere is friendly but the academic standard breath-takingly low. My rooms are spacious and conveniently situated, but characterless. The meals provided by the college are institutional in the worst sense of the term. The compensations are that I get to see more of Nicholas and that I am being paid and shall save (since there is next to no opportunity of spending it) a great deal of money.[23]

It was not long, however, before Ayer began to find the college 'almost tolerable'. The students were scandalously ignorant – to his disbelief not one in his class had heard of the Rubicon – but at least they were enthusiastic. Just as importantly, the college had found him a tall, blonde undergraduate from Pennsylvania to act as chauffeur, cook and companion. Stephanie Goss was a friend of Nick and, like him, a streetwise but sensitive youth with a great sense of fun. She and Freddie were soon the best of friends. 'He was,' she said, 'still very sad about Vanessa and working hard on his book on Tom Paine', but he retained a contagious appetite for life.

> He was completely without affectation. The one thing he could not stand was if you deferred to him. People in America had an idea of what an English knight should be like and were shocked that Freddie was not like that at all. You used to see him walking through college, this little old man, with a six pack of Guinness under his arm . . . It was not as with many older people, where you had to pretend to be interested. He was a brilliant conversationalist and very playful. He used to say that what he valued most was people thinking for themselves.[24]

Sometimes in the evenings, Stephanie would dress up in the style of the 1940s, in a sequinned gown and high-heels, and this unlikely pair would go dancing at a local bar, the Red Hook Inn, which had a jukebox well supplied with old hits.

Ayer was evidently enjoying himself – so much so that at the end of the semester he agreed to return to the college the following year – although not all his time was spent with Stephanie and her friends. At Bard he saw most of Mary McCarthy, another Stevenson Fellow, and her husband Jim West. During the weekends he took the train to New York where he stayed with Gully and Peter. Gully recalls that he preferred the company of young people, and generally socialised with her and Peter, although he sometimes made contact with friends of his own, including the Columbia philosopher Sidney Morgenbesser, Meyer and Lillian Schapiro, Jerome and Carole Bruner, or the *New Yorker* film critic Penelope Gilliatt, an old girlfriend from the 1960s. Although relations between Freddie and Dee had become strained during the years when they were getting divorced, their paths now began to cross again without any untoward effects. Dee had separated from Hylan and her health was poor. These experiences, Freddie reported to Horatia, had 'mellowed her'.[25] He was an easy guest, and Gully was as happy as ever to have him. She admired the way he continued to work hard into old age. When he finished the book on Paine in May, he dedicated it to her, Peter and Rebecca.

When *Thomas Paine* came out, in early 1988, it was to mixed reviews and it seems unlikely that it earned its advance. Christopher Hitchens, writing in *Newsday* found it 'exciting', and reviewers in the *Guardian* and the *Listener* described it as 'spirited' and 'robust', 'delightful', 'vigorous' and 'riveting'.[26] When Ayer discussed the book on the BBC's book programme *Cover to Cover* with journalists Polly Toynbee, Sebastian Faulks and Ruth Dudley Edwards, however, they all had the same complaint: Ayer 'lacked curiosity' and offered no insight into Paine's character and motivations. Ayer's response was disarmingly honest: 'Well, in that case I have failed.'[27]

Paine, Ayer's last book, certainly contains nothing new by way of scholarship or interpretation; as he wrote to Isaiah Berlin, 'I mugged up just enough information from some American scholar, whose name I forget, an essay of Michael Foot and, principally Moncure Conway'.[28] Ayer, however, never set out to uncover new material but, as with *Voltaire*, to highlight and defend what was important in Paine and the tradition to which he belonged. There are, accordingly, puckish chapters on *Common Sense* and *The Rights of Man*, with lively digressions on the applications of Paine's still radical ideas to the modern world. Paine's own ucompromising radicalism, indeed, seems to have had the effect of invigorating Ayer's: talking to the journalist Richard Ingrams soon after the publication of the book, he admitted that he now 'regretted' having taken a knighthood – 'I think it rather ridiculous'.[29]

Just before Christmas of 1986 Ayer returned from New York to London, where he took up his old life at York Street, eating his daily lunch with Pippa, making new lady-friends in Elsie Donald, an American writer and publisher, and Susan Baring, recently divorced from the banker Sir John Baring; and seeing a great deal of Jocelyn Rickards, Ted Honderich and Verity Ravensdale. 'He has written a letter to Susan Baring which is a kind of proposal, very tactically made. It is conceivable she will accept,' Honderich recorded in his diary in February.[30] His offer to Susan was not his last.

Honderich added, a few days later, that he realised for the first time that Ayer 'is being given up by people, no doubt mainly because of his self-centredness. To my slight surprise I am taken as his close friend. He more or less decided last night to make me his literary executor. I cannot say I was exactly asked'. From this point on, Ayer's vanity becomes something of a theme in Honderich's diary entries. Later in the year, at the end of August, he had Freddie over for a drunken lunch in his Hampstead flat with Bertrand Russell's son Conrad, and his wife Elizabeth, the publisher Catherine Lamb and others: 'Freddie was very happy and pretty embarrassing. In particular he kept bursting into exchanges of talk with pieces of self-praise. It did get a bit alarming'.[31]

At the end of June 1987, Ayer and Nick set out on their annual visit to Provence. 'I have not,' Freddie wrote, 'thought of anyone to come with us. My housekeeper would be splendid but she has a new husband whom she would not want to leave. I dare say that we can manage on our own if we buy cooked food and go to restaurants more often than we usually have. I have not yet heard from Ted Honderich when and for how long he plans to come or whether he will want to bring a girl with him. It might be useful if he did.'[32]

In the end, however, no girl was necessary. Later that month Dee suggested, via Nick, that she might come and spend some time with them, and Freddie agreed, reassuring himself with the thought that Honderich would be there 'to act as buffer'. Yet to everyone's surprise no buffer was needed: 'Dee arrived a few days after Nicholas and I did,' Ayer wrote to Jocelyn 'and has been very easy to get along with'.[33] Ted arrived two weeks later and found Ayer short of breath but otherwise on very good form, working happily on his replies for Schilpp, his taste for detective novels, gossip, philosophy and games undiminished. Honderich, too, got to know Dee for the first time.

> She has 'put cards on table' with me [he wrote in his diary at the end of his stay]. Wants to get back with Freddie – she was his second wife. (Has bad feelings against Vanessa for theft of Freddie and carelessness about Nicholas.) I am doing what I can to promote reunion. Fear to promote it openly to Freddie, however. It would be good for both of them, not bad for son. She is amazing character in the tradition of tough American women journalists.[34]

After dutifully visiting an IIP meeting in Stockholm at the end of August, Ayer returned to Bard, where he spent the autumn semester, teaching courses on *Language, Truth and Logic* and the British empiricists. In November 1987 he made a flying visit to the Southern Illinois

University at Carbondale to give the Library of Living Philosophers Honours Lecture on 'Society and Government'. 'Here everything is going pretty well,' he wrote to Ted from Bard early in the semester. 'My pupils, however, know even less philosophy than their predecessors but they are friendly and appreciative and I enjoy sharing an apartment with Nicholas and spending my weekends in New York.'[35]

On one such weekend Freddie and Gully and their friend Christopher Hitchens bumped into Wendy Fairey in a Greenwich Village restaurant, the Provençal on MacDougal Street. It was their first encounter for over a decade. In the interlude Wendy, a specialist in the nineteenth-century English novel, had become Dean of the College of Arts and Sciences at Brooklyn College. When she and Gully went to the bathroom, Ayer pointed them out to Hitchens – 'there go my two daughters' – although Wendy still knew nothing of her relationship to him. Gully now invited her to a party she was giving for Freddie's seventy-seventh birthday, although on that occasion she and Freddie hardly spoke. He 'was either being pursued by or pursuing' – Wendy didn't get the story straight – 'an imposing, extremely beautiful brunette, and when not saying hello and goodbye to other guests, seemed happily caught-up in this intrigue'. During their restaurant meeting, Wendy had suggested that Freddie might like to come to Brooklyn to have dinner en famille and Freddie had expressed interest, but he did nothing to further the plan. He had missed the last opportunity to see his grandchildren.[36]

It was at another party, given a little later in the year by the highly fashionable clothes designer, Fernando Sanchez, that he had a widely reported encounter. Ayer had always had an ability to pick up unlikely people and at yet another party had befriended Sanchez. Ayer was now standing near the entrance to the great white living-room of Sanchez's West 57th Street apartment, chatting to a group of young models and designers, when a woman rushed in saying that a friend was being assaulted in a bedroom. Ayer went to investigate and found Mike Tyson forcing himself on a young south London model called Naomi Campbell, then just beginning her career. Ayer warned Tyson to desist. Tyson: 'Do you know who the fuck I am? I'm the heavyweight champion of the world.' Ayer stood his ground: 'And I am the former Wykeham Professor of Logic. We are both pre-eminent in our field; I suggest that we talk about this like rational men.' Ayer and Tyson began to talk. Naomi Campbell slipped out.[37]

Ayer was back in England soon after the new year, having once again spent Christmas with Gully. Honderich's and Ayer's friendship was going through a testing period, Honderich putting Ayer's 'animosity' down to rivalry over three women – Elsie Donald, Sue Baring and Verity Ravensdale. In January Ayer went to Oxford to read a paper on causation to his old Tuesday group – a reply to Honderich's contribution to the Schilpp volume. Oxford's older philosophers, Michael Dummett, Peter Strawson and David Pears, still took his contributions seriously. Some of the younger ones, however, had been complaining for some years that he was irritable and out of touch.[38]

Ayer returned to the US in February 1988 to give the inaugural Lazerowitz Lecture on 'Empiricism' at Smith College in Northampton, Massachusetts. Ayer's emphysema had been worsening for some time, and, while staying with Gully, he collapsed with pneumonia and was placed in intensive care at St Vincent's Hospital. Within two weeks, however, and strictly against the doctors' advice, he was on the plane back to London, where he 'incontinently plunged' into what he described as 'an even more hectic social round than that to which I had become habituated before I went to America'.[39] All this activity took its toll and there was doubt, right up until the last minute, whether Ayer would be well enough to give the sixty-fourth Conway Memorial Lecture, on 'The Meaning of Life', which he was due to deliver at the old humanist venue of Conway Hall in the third week of May. On the day, his sense of obligation won through and he struggled through his text, badly out of breath by its end.

Ayer described the lecture as a discussion of 'the ways in which life can be meaningful even though there is no good reason to believe either in a deity or in objective values'. At its centre lies his old contention that the only meaning a life can ever have is the one it has for us. External authority, either human or divine, cannot, as a matter of logic, supply reasons to live. But if the essence of his position was familiar, his style had changed. As he grew older, Ayer's writings became increasingly informal and discursive, and in this wry and sparkling essay he glides from topic to topic – the moral implications and practical effects of a belief in hell, the unintelligibility of the Buddhist conception of Nirvana, the desirability of eternal life and the irrationality of desiring posthumous fame – hardly bothering to note the transitions on the way. The lecture also broaches themes that were new to Ayer – those, appropriately, of death and old age. He located the fear of death in the mistaken assumption that it is something that one undergoes: as Wittgenstein had suggested, death cannot be something that one suffers because one is no longer there to suffer it. And he spoke negatively about his own experience of getting old:

There are those, presumably enjoying some financial security and not in any fear of lacking warmth or nourishment, who profess to value the calm and detachment of old age. I think it was Sophocles who is said to have congratulated himself on outgrowing sexual desire. This is not an attitude that I should wish to share. From my own experiences I judge it to be true that as one gets older, one tends to live with less intensity. One is more prone to the mood of Mallarmé's 'La chair est triste, hélas, et j'ai lu tous les livres': even one's aesthetic sensibilities become less keen. It seems to me absurd, however, to regard these as compensations of age.[40]

22

Resurrection

Within two weeks of giving his lecture on 'The Meaning of Life', Ayer was in hospital again. He spent the last weekend of May 1988 eating, drinking and talking more than was good for him and by Sunday evening was running a temperature. The next day, a bank holiday Monday, he had lunch at the Savoy with his philosopher friend, Jennifer Trusted and then staggered home and collapsed. Julian, 'who', Ayer later wrote, 'is unobtrusively very efficient', arranged for an ambulance which took him to University College Hospital, where he was placed in intensive care.[1] The pneumonia from which he suffered in New York had returned.

Ayer was frail but extraordinarily resilient. Within a week, he was well on the road to recovery, when he choked on a piece of smoked salmon. He passed out and then technically he died: his heart stopped for four minutes before medical staff were able to revive him.

Having brought him back to life, Ayer's doctors expressed doubts about whether he would ever regain consciousness. The patient, however, not only recovered – within twenty-four hours he was talking – but came back with a report of a vivid experience which he had almost certainly undergone during his 'death'. He had been confronted by a bright red light, painful even when he turned away from it, which he understood was responsible for the government of the universe. 'Among its ministers were two creatures who had been put in charge of space. These ministers periodically inspected space and had recently carried out such an inspection. They had however failed to do their work properly, with the result that space, like a badly fitting jigsaw, was slightly out of joint.'[2]

Ayer could not find any of the 'ministers' responsible for space, but he realised that ministers who had been given charge of time were in his neighbourhood and remembering that, according to Einstein, space and time were one, he tried but failed to signal to them, by walking up and down and waving the watch and chain he had inherited from his grandfather. Ayer became 'more and more desperate' as his elicited no reponse. At this point his memory of the experience stopped, although when he regained consciousness, he woke talking about a river – presumably the River Styx – which he claimed to have crossed.

So here was proof of a world beyond 'the merely empirical'. Or was it? Articles quickly appeared, reporting that Ayer had returned from death to verify, variously, that there was or was not a God, that the mind did, or did not, survive the body. His experience even made it into the *National Inquirer*: 'Incredible after-life shocker! Man dies and meets . . . **The Masters of the Universe.**'[3] Ayer himself, moreover, did his bit to muddy the waters. Beatrice, who was waiting by Ayer's bed when he awoke, recalled that he seemed deeply shaken by the experience – it was as if his world-view had been thrown into doubt.[4] He told Edward St Aubyn in an interview for *Tatler* that the experience had made him a bit more 'wobbly' about the existence of an after-life and in a long but strangely obscure article for the *Sunday Telegraph* – 'That Undiscovered Country' – he seemed to imply that the experience might have been 'veridical' and that 'on the face of it' it offered 'rather strong evidence that death does not put an end to consciousness'.[5]

Later though he described himself as 'a born again atheist', and – echoing Mark Twain – insisted that the 'rumours regarding his death had been greatly exaggerated'. He now explained that all he had meant when he had said that his experience indicated that death was not necessarily the end of life, was, trivially, that the mind or brain did not stop functioning with the heart, and that he had never had any doubt that he had simply had a strange dream. The effect of the experience had not been to weaken his disbelief in the after-life, but to stimulate his interest in the conceptual possibility of the mind surviving its body or reincarnating itself in another body, and other questions in the philosophy of personal identity. The dream was a philosopher's dream, but it did not affect his philosophy.[6]

Yet although Ayer's encounter with the Masters of the Universe did nothing, in the end, to unsettle his atheism, it had other effects, almost as unexpected. He admitted to St Aubyn that there had been 'a kind of resurrection', as he started to notice scenery for the first time. Driving to France with Dee's sister Priscilla, he stopped on the mountain above La Ciotat: 'And I suddenly looked out at the sea and thought, "my God how beautiful this is" and for all these years, for twenty-six years, I had never really looked at it before'. This experience, he said, had made him feel life was 'richer' although not 'more mysterious'.[7]

His near-death experience seems to have released other emotions, too. Richard Wollheim, who went to visit him in the Primrose Hill house of Dee's sister, Priscilla, where he was convalescing after coming out of hospital, was delighted to find him very much 'like his old self – all the boasting had gone'.[8] Dee agreed, telling Jonathan Miller that 'Freddie has got so much nicer since he died'.[9] Freddie and Dee, indeed, spent part of the summer together at La Migoua and got on 'even better than last year. There has been no further talk of our remarrying,' he wrote to Honderich. 'I think we both realise that this would endanger our present good relations.'[10] Ayer also told Honderich that he had never felt intellectually more alert; mentally he had 'recovered my form of thirty years ago'.[11] It was a wonderful flowering.

Nick spent most of July and August with his father in France. Freddie wrote proudly about his skills at the chessboard – 'he had turned into a brilliant chess player, potentially better than I' – and his success with the opposite sex.[12] Nick's friend, Tom Haycroft, 'a charming ne'er-do-well, officially a writer', and his actress girlfriend, Jemma Redgrave, also came to stay.[13] Ayer was delighted by Redgrave, a skilful masseuse, and under her muse-like influence 'recovered my ability to compose light verse'. He wrote an acrostic, two lyrics ('neither of them good'), and three poems ('not at all bad') addressed to her. 'I need hardly add,' he wrote to Jocelyn, 'that my attachment to her is purely literary, though I like her very much.'[14] The acrostic, moreover, sparked off others – to Elsie Donald, Jenny Hughes and Jocelyn Rickards. And along with them came further replies to the Schilpp volume and other philosophical pieces, which, like his poems, he mainly wrote in his 'head' – 'It is as if my brain has taken to working at double its previous speed, knowing that it has not very much time left'.[15] There were also letters, including not only fond and observant pages to Jocelyn and Ted but a long exchange with Isaiah Berlin. Freddie congratulated Berlin on his collection of biographical essays, *Personal Impressions*, which he was re-reading, admitted he 'envied', although he did not 'begrudge', him his many honours and prizes, and complained about the way the Quintons had dropped him. He fondly acknowledged fifty years of friendship that, as he recalled, had suffered only one 'froideur', when, at the end of the war, they quarrelled over Patricia de Bendern. 'Julian,' he crowed, 'is devoted to me too, much more I am glad to say, than to Stuart.'[16]

Ayer was due to give the closing speech at the 18th World Congress of Philosophy in Brighton at the end of August, and had written a paper, 'A Defence of Empiricism', offering a general defence of his epistemology – what he described in a letter to Honderich as 'my cherished doctrines'. It offered little that was new but contained a scathing dismissal of modern continental philosophers, '. . . such charlatans as Heidegger and Derrida'. In the event Ayer was not well enough to attend and his paper had to be read in his absence; it was, evidently, the first congress he had missed in forty years.[*17]

By the end of the summer, Dee and Freddie, encouraged by Nick, had decided to live together again, and early in the autumn she returned to the US to sell her New York apartment. Freddie explained to Honderich that it was possible he and Dee would spend the winter in Santa Fé because of its climate: 'two months at La Migoua have done me good, but London in the winter is dangerous for me'.[18] In the meantime, Ayer, now too frail to remain by himself or easily manage York Street's stairs, moved back into Priscilla's house, only to be hospitalised again in the middle of September, although once again he quickly rallied. On leaving hospital, early in October, he moved into an elegant little garden house adjoining the St John's Wood home Jocelyn shared with her husband, Clive Donner, a film director who had become, over the years, one of Ayer's closest friends. Here Freddie was meant to await Dee's return. In the meantime, however, something had occurred that seemed to throw all plans into doubt.

---

* Ayer told the philosopher Daniel O'Connor that he had in fact engaged with Derrida at a conference in Paris at some point before this, calling him a charlatan—*un fumiste*. I have not been able to find any record of this exchange. (Daniel O'Connor, IWA – 14 March 1997).

While in hospital, Ayer had received a visit from an old girlfriend, an American in her mid-thirties, with whom he had had a brief but exciting affair in the early 1980s. The pair were carried back to their last meeting, and by the end of the day were making plans for a romantic holiday in Paris, although once out of hospital it became clear that Ayer was not fit to travel.

Over the next few months Freddie and his friend, whose commitments kept her in New York, spent only a couple of weekends together in his new garden home. Nevertheless, there developed between them an exceedingly intense and physically playful relationship, in which he discovered or rediscovered the pleasures of submission, and he was soon telling her, and others, that he wanted to spend the rest of his life with her. Ayer, so meticulous a writer, so steady in his philosophical, political and sporting allegiances, was once again allowing, indeed encouraging, his private life to run out of control. Thus was ever the pattern with him.

Slowly reality intervened, as Ayer came to acknowledge the impracticability of his schemes. When they met at the beginning of December, they both knew that it would be their last meeting for several months. She was moving to California, while Ayer was to spend Christmas with Priscilla's family and Nick in Le Beausset, where they were to be joined by Dee. During the autumn of 1988 and the New Year of 1989, however, Ayer sent his friend a series of extraordinarily uninhibited, playful love letters, apparently quite unlike anything he had written before. They offer further evidence that his brush with death had issued in a rebirth.

Ayer had other things to think about in addition to his 'princess'. He continued to reply to the Schilpp essays as they came in, and in October wrote an article for the *Spectator*, 'Postscript to a Postmortem', clarifying and elaborating on his early account of his visit to the 'other side'. Before Christmas, he went up for his last meeting of his Oxford Tuesday group. Colin McGinn, a young philosopher whom Ayer had done much to promote, recalled how 'during the discussion ... he made strenuous interventions of a wholly characteristic kind: amusing, petulant, a bit axe-grinding, exuberantly deflationary'. Afterwards he needed a taxi to take him the hundred yards from University to New College.[19]

Freddie, Nick, Priscilla and her family arrived in Le Beausset in time for Christmas. Dee, having finally sold her New York apartment, followed a few weeks later. Provence's pure, dry air soon began to have its effect; later in their stay, Dee found Ayer a yoga teacher, who further helped his breathing – although, as Ayer wrote to New York, the local doctor had forbidden 'any elaborate contortions'.[20] The first lesson got off to a bad start, when the teacher insisted that Ayer should face the east and he refused, but by the end of January he was scarcely using his nebuliser. He forced himself to write 2,000 words on the French Revolution for Dominic Lawson, now deputy editor of the *Spectator* – on the whole he was inclined to think it had been a very good thing. For the most part, however, he preferred to 'read, do *The Times* crossword puzzle and play chess'.[21]

Ayer's move to France had no effect on his feelings for his American friend, and he continued to write to her or speak on the phone almost daily. The situation, though, was more complicated than Freddie had admitted before Christmas, as he explained in a series of long, delicate letters. Since the previous summer there had been sporadic talk of Dee and Freddie remarrying, and now, he nervously but frankly explained, it was likely to happen. It was not just that Freddie had come to realise the selfishness of imposing himself on a woman over forty years his junior. Nor that he now felt under obligation to Dee. They shared, he explained, 'the same sense of humour', and the same attitude to life – they were both 'iconoclasts'. They possessed a long history and friends and family in common. The truth was that he was enjoying their life together. By the beginning of February, Ayer had not merely agreed to the idea of marriage, but acceded to it happening very soon.

Marriage, however, was not the only subject occupying the household at Le Beausset that winter. As Ayer was exchanging secret letters with his lover, Dee was exchanging them with Wendy. Sheilah Graham had died late in 1988, and Wendy, now separated from her husband, and with her son and daughter almost grown up, asked Dee to talk at Sheilah's memorial meeting. Dee had long felt that it would be good for both Wendy and Freddie if he revealed his secret ('. . . though it may seem strange', Dee later explained to Wendy, 'Freddie has a deep feeling about family – you know lineage and all that – and especially since poor Valerie died so very young') and just before Christmas, while Wendy was driving her home after a family dinner at Gully's house, Dee asked her: 'Has it never occurred to you that Freddie is your father?'[22] Dates had to be rejigged, a whole life reconceptualised, but as Wendy's friends pointed out, the evidence of the senses, or at least the photo album, worked to confirm Dee's claim – Freddie could indeed be her father.

Wendy later admitted that Ayer was exactly the father she had always wanted: famous, intellectual, debonair; she was, as she put it, 'trading up'. But by the same token he was the father she had never been allowed to have. It is hardly surprising that she greeted the discovery with a mixture of delight and resentment, 'wild hope' and despair. 'The new, I feared, would prove a chimera, and meanwhile, I would have lost the securities of the old'.[23]

Dee had suggested to Wendy that it might be best if she, Dee, tell Freddie that Wendy had worked out the truth for herself, and when she did break the news, he greeted it with ambivalence. The secret however was out, and in February Wendy received a short dry letter – Ayer would have said it was 'concise':

Dear Wendy
Your asking me to write to you is presumably the outcome of the conversation that you had with Dee after your mother's funeral. You were then feeling your way towards the truth. I am your father. Your mother and I became lovers in New York during the winter of 1941–42. When she found that she was pregnant, she disappeared for a few weeks without saying anything to me. When she returned to New York, she told me that she had married Trevor Westbrook in order to legitimate her child. I was still in the process of divorcing my first wife and anyway, as Sheilah knew, was not prepared to marry again so soon . . .
  It was an accident that I took your mother to the hospital for your birth. You arrived a few days earlier than you were expected and I just happened to be dining with her that evening. I understand her wanting to suppress it [my being the father] back at that time but don't know why she kept it a secret for so long. Perhaps she thought that you would be shocked. From the way you talked to Dee and me on the telephone I infer that you are not. For my part, I am happy and proud to own you as a daughter. I regret only that I have seen so little of my grandchildren.[24]

There followed an exchange of letters, in which Wendy, with studied casualness, suggested stopping off in London to see Freddie in the course of a trip she planned to make to Paris. Her letter hit just the right note, which is to say she appeared moderate and reasonable. Freddie now returned a much more affectionate letter – 'Your charming letter gave me great pleasure' – looking forward to a meeting in London and inviting her to stay at York Street, to which he and Dee would be returning at the end of March.[25] Whatever misgivings he had had seemed a thing of the past.

At the end of April 1989 Wendy arrived for a week's stay in York Street, a visit she later described in a short sensitive memoir, *One of the Family*: 'as I look back on my passage through that front door, it resembles nothing so much as Alice falling through the hole in Wonderland. I would meet the likes of the Red Queen and the Cheshire Cat; I would attend the Mad Hatter's tea party. Everything would seem a little peculiar, but I would accept the terms of the world in which I found myself the way one moves with matter of factness through the most surreal of dreams, only later, upon waking to marvel at its strangeness'.[26]

The visit began with a vintage Ayer act. The philosopher was working in his study with his secretary Guida Crawley. Having welcomed Wendy with some routine questions about her journey, he explained that he was trying to finish one or two things off before Guida left. He just had time, however, to subject her to his Jane Austen Quiz: What is Mr Darcy's first name? ... And where in the novel does it appear? ... And what is Mr Knightley's first name? ... And where in the novel does that appear? It says something about the qualities that Wendy had inherited from Ayer that she knew the answers to most of these questions. With the examination over, Ayer turned back to his work. He had offered no embrace, or anything else, to mark the reunion as in any way out of the ordinary.

Upstairs Dee helped Wendy unpack and they talked of Freddie and Dee's new life together – Dee joked that she saw herself as a character in *Rebecca* only she was not sure which one – and about their plans for the week. That night they were attending an opening of Iris Murdoch's play, *The Black Prince*. 'And tomorrow,' Dee announced, 'Freddie and I are getting married.' A reunion of father and long-lost daughter, remarriage of husband and wife: the strands of Freddie's past seemed to be coming together.

Freddie and Dee's second marriage was at Marylebone Register Office. The only guests, apart from Wendy, were Iris Murdoch and her critic-husband John Bayley, old friends of both bride and groom. Nick and Gully were unable to come from New York, and neither Julian nor the

Lawson children would have wanted to attend. With the ceremony over, the party moved on to lunch at one of Freddie's favourite restaurants, the White Tower on Charlotte Steet, where they feasted on pâté, the restaurant's famous duck and oranges, Grand Marnier, ouzo, white wine and brandy.

Iris Murdoch described the day as 'very moving'.[27] Lunch ran on until late in the afternoon, with talk of literature interweaving with gossip about writers and friends. John Bayley was, Wendy recalled, particularly effervescent. He relayed a quip he had heard from Isaiah Berlin '*hic biscuitus disintegrat*' ('so the cookie crumbles') and talked movingly about Tolstoy's *Anna Karenina*. The conversation turned to conversationalists, and Freddie declared that the three best he had known were Cyril Connolly, Maurice Bowra and Isaiah Berlin. John Bayley put in a word for David Cecil, but Freddie was of the opinion that David Cecil, good as he was, was no better than the people around him. Then someone mentioned the character of Mrs Lammle in *Our Mutual Friend*, but could not remember her first name; 'Sophronia,' Ayer responded, without missing a beat. 'You see what a well read father you have', he said, turning to Wendy . . . 'I am equally good in history, and you'll notice that I never even talk about my own subject'. He was in his element and Wendy marked that his breathing had improved.[28]

The rest of Wendy's stay was almost without incident, as she and Freddie – very much at his behest – pretended that there was nothing unusual about it. Ayer read, wrote, played chess and watched football on television; in the evening guests dropped round or they went out to dinner. The reunion had not gone as badly as Wendy had feared. She was touched by Ayer's courage in the face of physical discomfort and recalled some genuine exchanges of emotion: sitting chatting to friends in the drawing-room one evening, Freddie quietly said to her, 'I'm very proud of you.' In the final analysis, though, Wendy found Freddie 'disappointing': 'I wanted so much for Freddie to see who I was, and instead I found him fixed on himself'.[29]

Dee had worked hard to improve Freddie's health and by the time of Wendy's visit he was well enough to have accepted Bard's invitation to return for the fall semester. He and Dee would rent a house near the college. Early in May, he even flew alone to Barcelona to give one last lecture, his zeal for philosophy undiminished. Towards the end of the month he spent a day on his own watching Middlesex at Lord's, his favourite childhood haunt. Back at home, his breathing suddenly worsened, and that night he was readmitted to University College Hospital with a collapsed lung. Almost immediately he underwent a tracheotomy and was then placed on a respirator in intensive care. From then on he communicated chiefly by writing notes on a pad he kept at his side.

With the loss of his speech, Freddie's face took on extra expressiveness, Nick, above all, being greeted with a great beaming smile. Dee and Freddie were suddenly closer than they had been for years. Not long before he was admitted to hospital, on her sixty-fourth birthday, Freddie had given her a beautiful sonnet by Jonathan Steffen that he had cut out of the New Yorker about a troubadour who leaves his lady, only to return.[30] Jocelyn, in and out of the hospital every day, is in no doubt that she saw Freddie fall in love with Dee again. On one occasion he passed her a note: 'I love you'.

During the first three weeks vigil, Ayer's health gradually improved, but on the weekend of 17–18 June he developed a chest infection. By Wednesday there were kidney complications and over the next two days he drifted towards death. Then on Saturday, he suddenly revived and was perfectly lucid. Friends and family were overjoyed, although Freddie's main concern was that someone should find him a television on which he could watch the cricket. The improvement, however, was temporary. On Sunday he declined. On Monday he woke up, looked at Nick and said 'I am dying.' What, Nick wondered, could he say to a philosopher? The consultant failed to come that day – a stay of execution – but Freddie had always insisted that he did not want to be kept alive if there was no chance of recovery and on Tuesday the decision was made to switch off the machines. He fell into a coma and died later that evening.

Throughout his time in hospital he had remained determinedly calm and cheerful. He and Ted Honderich often exchanged clenched-fist salutes. It was a philosopher's death. Hume would have approved.

Freddie Ayer died on Tuesday, 27 June 1989 at about 10.30 p.m. Jocelyn, Dominic and Nigella had been there earlier in the evening; Dee, Nick and Horatia were present at the end. Soon after he died, it began to rain and thunder. Nick, distraught, left the room with the others, and then returned alone a little later: the nurses were already laying Freddie out. He went back again in the early hours of the morning, only to find that the body had been taken away. The respirator, though, had been restarted. Attached to it, where Freddie had been, there lay a black plastic balloon, steadily breathing away.

The death occurred too late for the next day's papers, but Thursday's and Friday's were full of it. In addition to long obituaries in all the broadsheets, the *Independent* and the *Guardian* carried front-page articles and the *Daily Telegraph* and *The Times* both ran lead features. Television, the Sunday papers, and American papers and magazines followed suit. Most of the coverage was laudatory. Anthony Grayling described him as 'perhaps the last great figure of the Cartesian tradition, that tradition of thought in which our understanding of ourselves and the world has to be built outwards from data of consciousness'. John Foster suggested that among twentieth-century British philosophers, he ranked 'second only to Russell'.[31] Robert Jackson, Mrs Thatcher's Minister for Higher Education, and the Tory philosopher, Roger Scruton, however, attacked him from the right, the one for 'enormously narrowing the range of philosophical inquiry', the other for his attempts at 'destroying the conception in which the wisdom of humanity reposes'.[32] Ayer, alas, was no longer there to answer them.

A few days after Freddie's death, a small family service was held in Golders Green Crematorium, with Ted Honderich and Freddie's old friend, the Jesuit Frederick Copleston, the only philosophers present. Ayer had said he did not want a eulogy, so instead his favourite pre-war tunes – 'Bye Bye, Blackbird', 'Oh, You Beautiful Doll', something by Fred Astaire – and one or two other favourites, were played mournfully on the organ, while family and a few friends – Jocelyn, Clive, Beatrice – filed in and then filed out. Not a single word was spoken; there was no chance for 'nonsense' there. Afterwards the whole family congregated at Jocelyn's house. The sun shone and Rebecca cartwheeled on the lawn.

Later that year, Dee and Ted Honderich organised a large memorial meeting at the Institute of Education, adjoining UCL. Over 400 gathered in a lecture theatre to hear a range of speakers talk about Ayer's life and work. Ayer's death had left hard feelings among some of his friends and family and Julian declined to attend, but most of those who mattered especially to him were there: Nick and the Lawson children, Jocelyn, Priscilla, Guida and Beatrice from London, Rosanne Richardson from Oxford, Wendy, Gully, Peter and Rebecca from the US. In one of the best phrases of the day, Ted Honderich described Ayer as a 'hussar against nonsense' – a philosopher 'whose audacity was being true to truth'. Roy Jenkins recalled his 'honesty and clarity' in argument and praised his contribution to homosexual law reform – he was 'a fine ally with whom to go into a fight'. Peter Strawson argued that Ayer's contribution to the theory of knowledge and general metaphysics was in no way inferior to Russell's; 'indeed in clarity, order and coherence' it exceeded it. And Jonathan Miller remembered him as the inspiration of Alan Bennett's 'philosophy sketch' in *Beyond the Fringe*. Dee ensured that the meeting ended on a rousing note, with a heartfelt assault on Robert Jackson, the education minister who had criticised Ayer so soon after his death.

Perhaps though it is the man himself who should be allowed the last word. A few days before Ayer returned to hospital for the last time, Ted Honderich conducted an interview with him for Radio 3. It was broadcast a month after he died. Ayer sounded breathless but as bright as ever, exhaling his words and then lunging for air. They talked about his family and schooling, the impact that the *Tractatus* had had on him and the success of *Language, Truth and Logic*. He spoke of his later books, about his admiration for Russell and his quarrel with Austin, his disappointment in both Labour and the SDP. Then Honderich asked him what he had 'pursued above all':

I suppose truth. I suppose truth. I suppose that I care more about having got something right in philosophy, if I have got anything right, than having written elegantly. Although I like that too.[33]

Principal Publications of A.J. Ayer

Language, Truth and Logic, 1936
The Foundations of Empirical Knowledge, 1940
Philosophical Essays, 1954
The Problem of Knowledge, 1956
The Concept of a Person and Other Essays, 1965
The Origins of Pragmatism, 1968
Metaphysics and Common Sense, 1969
Russell and Moore: The Analytical Heritage, 1971
Probability and Evidence, 1972
Russell, 1972
The Central Questions of Philosophy, 1973
Part of My Life, 1977
Hume, 1980
Philosophy in the Twentieth Century, 1981
More of My Life, 1984
Freedom and Morality and Other Essays, 1984
Wittgenstein, 1985
Voltaire, 1986
Thomas Paine, 1988
The Meaning of Life and Other Essays, 1989 (edited posthumously by Ted Honderich).
A full (although not complete) bibliography can be found in *The Philosophy of A.J. Ayer*, ed. Lewis Hahn, La Salle, Illinois, 1992.

Abbreviations and Notes

I have used the following abbreviations in the footnotes and end notes.

LTL: A.J. Ayer, *Language Truth and Logic*, second edition, London, 1946.

MMD: 'My Mental Development', in *The Philosophy of A.J. Ayer*, ed. L.H. Kahn, La Salle, Illinois, 1992.

MML: A.J. Ayer, *More of My Life*, Oxford (OUP paperback edition), 1985.

PAS: *Proceedings of the Aristotelian Society.*

Ph.AJA: *The Philosophy of A.J. Ayer*, ed. Lewis Hahn, La Salle, Illinois, 1992.

PML: A.J. Ayer, *Part of My Life*, London, 1977.

Interviews are cited as IWA (interview with author) followed by the date of the interview. Letters to me are cited as LTA (letter to author) followed by the date of the letter.

My interviews with Dee Ayer occurred on such a frequent basis or in such informal surroundings that it was not always possible to take notes or to place a date on a point that I owe to her. Some of our interviews however were more formal. These I have cited in the usual way.

Unless otherwise stated, letters to Ayer, transcripts and other documents, are in Ayer's files, in the possession of Dee Ayer. Letters from Ayer are in the possession of the recipient. Letters from Ayer to Isaiah Berlin are in the possession of the Berlin Archive, Wolfson College, Oxford. Letters from Ayer to E.E. and Marion Cummings are in possession of the Cummings Collection, Houghton Library, Harvard University.

A.J. AYER

PREFACE

1 Isaiah Berlin, IWA, 22 June 1996.
2 Transcript, 'Profile of Sir Alfred Ayer', Euro-Television, June 1971.
3 Jocelyn Rickards, IWA, 22 February 1994.
4 In addition to Oliver Sacks's work (*Anthropologist from Mars Seven Paradoxical Tales*, New York, 1985) see, for example, Uta Frith, *Autism, Explaining the Enigma*, Oxford, 1989, and *Autism and Asperger's Syndrome*, ed. Uta Frith, Cambridge, 1991.
5 Horatia Lawson, IWA, September 1998.
6 Philip Toynbee, 'Diaries', 2 April 1947, Vol. 20, in possession of Sally Toynbee.

1. TEACHERS, BANKERS, MERCHANTS, WIVES

1 *PML*, p.21.
2 Richard Wollheim, IWA, 17 August 1994; 'The Child in the House', *Macmillan's Magazine*, August 1878, reprinted in Walter Pater, *Miscellaneous Studies*, Macmillan, London, 1910.
3 *David Copperfield*, Everyman Library, 1991, p.154.
4 Hilda Oppenheimer, IWA, 11 October 1994.
5 *PML*, p.14.
6 Ibid., p.16.
7 Ibid., p.14.
8 Marjorie Wyllie, IWA, 24 May 1995.
9 Marjorie Wyllie, IWA, 24 May 1995.
10 *PML*, p.20.
11 Doris Bamford, IWA, 1 October 1994.
12 Doris Bamford, IWA, 1 October 1994.
13 Marjorie Wyllie, IWA, 24 May 1995.
14 *PML*, p.32.
15 Ibid., p.13.
16 Isaiah Berlin, IWA, 1 February 1994.
17 *PML*, p.14.
18 Marjorie Wyllie, IWA, 24 May 1995.
19 *Desert Island Discs*, BBC Radio 4, 28 June 1984.
20 *PML*, p.18.
21 Poppee Ayer, IWA, 15 April 1995.
22 Madge Cave, LTA, 23 October 1994.
23 Hilda Oppenheimer, IWA, 11 October 1994.
24 *PML*, p.14.
25 Ibid., p.17.
26 Marjorie Wyllie, IWA, 24 May 1995.
27 *PML*, p.17.

28 *Desert Island Discs*, BBC Radio 4, 28 June 1984.
29 PML, p.18.
30 Ibid.
31 'Women's Page', *Times*, 21 May 1968.
32 PML, p.19.
33 Doris Bamford, IWA, 1 October 1994.
34 PML, p.239.
35 Doris Bamford, IWA, 1 October 1994.
36 PML, p.19.
37 Dee Ayer, IWA, 3 November 1994.
38 Hilda Oppenheimer, IWA, 11 October 1994.
39 Doris Bamford, IWA, 1 October 1994.

2. SCHOOL-DAYS

1   *Desert Island Discs*, BBC Radio 4, 17 September 1984.
2   Gaspard Willis, *Ascham 1889–1989*, a privately published pamphlet, 1989, p.3.
3   Sir Robin Brook, IWA, 25 October 1994.
4   Cyril Connolly, *Enemies of Promise* (1938), Harmondsworth, 1961, p.175.
5   Willis, *Ascham 1889–1989*, p.5.
6   'Ayer at Eton', video recording of Open University programme E200 TV2, 1980.
7   PML, p.26.
8   Ibid., p.25.
9   *Desert Island Discs*, 17 September 1984.
10 BBC Radio 2 interview, 17 September 1984, tape in Ayer Archive, York St.
11 PML, p.27.
12 'Ayer at Eton'.
13 Transcript of 'Profile of Sir Alfred Ayer' by Louis Van Gasteren, Euro-television production, 1971.
14 Bernard Crick, *George Orwell*, London, 1980, p.48.
15 Tape recording of Michael Luke interviewing Ayer, *c.*1986, in possession of Michael Luke.
16 Sir Edward Ford, LTA, 22 May 1994
17 'Ayer at Eton'.
18 Philip Brownrigg, LTA, 5 December 1994.
19 Sir Andrew Carnwath, IWA, 12 June 1994.
20 Dee Ayer, IWA, 13 November 1994.
21 Sir Robin Brook, IWA, 25 October 1994.
22 Philip Brownrigg, LTA, 5 December 1994.
23 Sir Andrew Carnwath, IWA, 12 June 1994.
24 Anthony Blunt, *Slow on the Feather*, Michael Russell, Salisbury, 1986, p.82.
25 Sir Andrew Carnwath, IWA, 12 June 1994; PML, p.49.

26 Philip Brownrigg, LTA, 5 December 1994; Sir Bernard Burrows, IWA, 12 October 1994; A. G. Ogstan, LTA, 4 December 1994.
27 PML, p.52.
28 Sir Bernard Burrows, IWA, 12 October 1994.
29 David Wild, LTA, 25 April 1994.
30 'Ayer at Eton'.
31 Ibid.
32 Betrand Russell, *Marriage and Morals*, Unwin paperback, London, 1961, pp.30 and 31.
33 PML, pp.58–99.
34 Sir Bernard Burrows, LTA, 26 September 1994.
35 David Wild, IWA, 6 October 1994.
36 Sir Andrew Carnwath, IWA, 12 May 1994.
37 'Ayer at Eton'.
38 Edward Vernon Jones, LTA, 28 April 1994.
39 PML, p.49.
40 'Ayer at Eton'.
41 PML, p.57.
42 'Ayer at Eton'.

3. APPRENTICE

1   MMD, p.4.
2   PML, p.67.
3   'Women's Page', *Times*, 21 May 1968.
4   'Early Influences', ch. 1 of Renée Ayer's autobiography (no title or page numbers), in possession of Julian Ayer.
5   Ibid.
6   Ibid.
7   'The Making of a Roman Catholic', ch. 2 of Renée Ayer's autobiography.
8   Julian Ayer, IWA, 1 October 1998.
9   Patricia Plowright, IWA, 27 January 1995.
10 PML, p.68.
11 Ibid.
12 Ibid., p.59.
13 *College Debating Society Journal*, 39, Eton Archive, debate of 19 May 1928.
14 Ibid., 25 July 1928.
15 Ibid., 30 June 1928.
16 Ibid., 13 October 1928.
17 Bertrand Russell, *Sceptical Essays* (1928), Routledge paperback, London, 1977, p.11.
18 MMD, p.11.
19 Russell, *Sceptical Essays*, p.21.

20 Ibid., pp.54–5.
21 Nicholas Cheetham, IWA, 19 May 1994.
22 *PML*, p.70.

4. STUDENT

1   Goronwy Rees, A *Bundle of Sensations*, London, 1960, p.68.
2   William Outram, LTA, 14 July 1995.
3   MMD, p.357.
4   *LTL*, pp.113–14.
5   Ayer's writings on aesthetics are limited to a paragraph in *Language, Truth and Logic* and a short reply to a critic at the very end of his life ('Reply to Peter Kivy' in *Ph.AJA*).
6   *PML*, p.107.
7   Giles Playfair, IWA, 15 May 1995.
8   *The Oxford Magazine*, 19 June 1930; *Isis*, 18 June 1930. Ayer himself admitted talking at the union and making 'a hash of it'. 'I was painfully nervous and gabbled unintelligibly' (*PML*, p.94).
9   Henry Harvey, LTA, 19 April 1995.
10 Giles Playfair, IWA, 15 May 1995.
11 Edward Playfair, LTA, 8 November 1995.
12 *PML*, p.74.
13 Ibid., p.94.
14 Giles Playfair, IWA, 15 May 1995.
15 *PML*, p.99.
16 Clark and Powell quoted in Jeremy Lewis, *Cyril Connolly: A Life*, London, 1997, pp.107–8.
17 Maurice Bowra, *Memories, 1898–1939*, London, 1966, p.183.
18 Ayer, review of *Maurice Bowra, A Celebration*, ed. Hugh Lloyd-Jones, *London Magazine*, April–May 1975, p.101.
19 Noel Annan 'Introduction' to Isaiah Berlin, *Personal Impressions*, London, 1981, p.xxi.
20 Isaiah Berlin, IWA, 1 February 1994.
21 Ibid.
22 Ibid.
23 Ibid.
24 *PML*, p.86.
25 Richard Wollheim, 'Jesus Christie', *London Review of Books*, p.3, 5 October 1985.
26 Wollheim, IWA, 17 August 1994.
27 *PML*, p.92.
28 Patricia Plowright, IWA, 27 July 1995.

29   John Cheetham, IWA, 19 May 1995.

5. HOMECOMING

1   *PML*, p.106.
2   Jenny Rees, *Looking for Mr Nobody: The Secret Life of Goronwy Rees*, London, 1994, pp.85–6.
3   *PML*, p.107.
4   Isaiah Berlin, *IWA*, 1 February 1994.
5   *PML*, p.103.
6   William Outram, LTA, 14 July 1995.
7   Ibid.
8   'fine slippery mind': *The Diaries of Evelyn Waugh*, ed Michael Davie, Penguin Books, Harmondsworth, 1979, p.320, 8 July 1930.
9   Gilbert Ryle, 'Paper Read to the Oxford Philosophical Society, 500th Meeting, 1968', Archives of the Philosophy Library, Oxford.
10   Ted Honderich, 'An Interview with A.J. Ayer', in *Memorial Essays*, ed. A. Phillips Griffiths, Cambridge, 1991, p.210 and *PML*, p.77.
11   Ayer, 'The Making of a Logical Positivist', *Listener*, 4 May 1965, p.699.
12   Gilbert Ryle, 'Systematically Misleading Expressions', *PAS*, 32 (1932–33) reprinted in Richard Rorty (ed.), *The Linguistic Turn*, Chicago, 1961, p.89.
13   Ved Mehta, *The Fly and the Fly Bottle*, London, 1963, p.67.
14   Bertrand Russell, *The Problems of Philosophy* (1912) Oxford University Press paperback, 1967, p.32.
15   Ibid., pp.2–3.
16   *PML*, p.110.
17   Ibid., p.111.
18   'Michael Ignatieff interviews Isaiah Berlin', BBC2 television programme, 14 November 1997.
19   Ayer, 'Making of a Logical Positivist', p.700.
20   Isaiah Berlin, 'John Austin and the Early Beginnings of Oxford Philosophy', in *Personal Impressions*, London, 1980, p.102.
21   Isaiah Berlin, IWA, 27 June 1996. Ayer submitted the paper to G.E. Moore, as the editor of *Mind*, but although Moore expressed interest he asked for some major revisions, which, in the end, Ayer, getting a sense that Wittgenstein's ideas had changed, never made.
22   Ludwig Wittgenstein, *Tractatus Logico-Philosophicus*, trans D.F. Pears and B.F. McGuinness, London, 1961, 'Preface'.
23   Wittgenstein *Tractatus*, 4.0031.
24   Ibid., 6.54
25   *PML*, p.116.
26   Wittgenstein, *Tractatus*, p.3.

Notes

27 *PML*, p.115.
28 *PML*, p.113.
29 Ibid.
30 David Stephens to Isaiah Berlin, 27 July 1932, Berlin Archive, Wolfson College, Oxford.

6. MARRIAGE AMONG THE SCIENTISTS

1 *PML*, p.126.
2 Ibid., p.122.
3 Minutes of the Moral Science Club 1926–35, Cambridge University Archives, minute IX.43, 4 May 1932.
4 'On the Idea of Necessary Connection', Cambridge University Archives, Add. 8330 8A/19/1.
5 *PML*, p.135.
6 *Hayek on Hayek*, ed. Stephen Kresge and Leif Wenar, London, 1994, p.52.
7 I have found Helmut Gruber's *Red Vienna: Experiment in Working-Class Culture 1919–34* (Oxford, 1991) particularly useful in providing background to the Vienna Circle, but see also Allan Janick and Stephen Toulmin, *Wittgenstein's Vienna*, New York, 1973.
8 Ayer to Isaiah Berlin, 11 January 1933, Isaiah Berlin Archive, Wolfson College, Oxford.
9 Ayer to Gilbert Ryle, 19 February 1933, Archive, Linacre College, Oxford.
10 *PML*, p.128.
11 Sidney Hook, 'A Personal Impression of Contemporary German Philosophy', *Journal of Philosophy*, 27, No 6, 1930), pp. 143 and 147.
12 Ibid., pp. 142–3.
13 Quoted in Peter Galison, 'Aufbau/Bauhaus: Logical Positivism and Architectural Modernism', *Critical Inquiry*, 16 (Summer 1990), p.736.
14 *Neurath, Empiricism and Sociology*, ed. M. Neurath and R.S. Cohen, Dordrecht, 1973, p.46.
15 Quoted in *Neurath, Empiricism and Sociology*, p.308.
16 Quoted in *Reminiscences of the Vienna Circle and the Mathematical Colloquium*, ed. Lonne Golland, Brian McGuinness, Abe Sklar, Dordrecht, 1994, p.194.
17 W.V.O. Quine to Ayer, 6 October 1975.
18 *PML*, p.133.
19 Ayer to Isaiah Berlin, 26 February 1933.
20 Ayer to Gilbert Ryle, 19 February 1933, Linacre College Library, Oxford.
21 W.V.O. Quine, IWA, 12 October 1994.
22 Ayer to Gilbert Ryle, 19 February 1933.
23 *PML*, p.137.
24 Ibid. p.135.

7. APOSTLE

1   Ayer, 'Demonstration of the Impossibility of Metaphysics', *Mind*, 43, no. 171 (1934), p.339.
2   Isaiah Berlin, IWA, 1 February 1994.
3   John Cheetham, IWA, 19 May 1995.
4   Ayer, 'Atomic Propositions', *Analysis*, 1, no. 4 (November 1933), p.2.
5   Ibid., p.5.
6   Roy Harrod, *The Prof*, London, 1959, p.150.
7   Julian Ayer, IWA, 9 June 1995.
8   *PML*, p.84.
9   Isaiah Berlin, IWA, 7 June 1996.
10 *PML*, p.144.
11 Harrod, *The Prof*, p.62.
12 Ronald W. Clark, *Einstein, The Life and Times*, Avon paperback, New York, 1972, pp.534–5.
13 *Independent Magazine*, 2 September 1989.
14 *PML*, p.147.
15 Ibid., p.150.
16 C.A. Mace, 'Representation and Expression', *Analysis*, 1, no. 3 (March 1934), p.38.
17 Ernest Nagel, 'Impression and Appraisals of Analytic Philosophy in Europe', in *Logic without Metaphysics*, Glencoe, Illinois, 1956, p.196, reprinted from *Journal of Philosophy*, 33 (1936). Nagel's tour took place in 1934–35.
18 Alice Ambrose, LTA, 7 December 1994.
19 *Analysis*, 1, no. 1 (November 1933), p.1.
20 *PML*, pp.153–4.
21 'V.G. from S.L.', 14 December 1933, Gollancz Archive.
22 Henry Price, academic reference for A.J. Ayer, 8 February 1935, Trinity College, Oxford, Ayer Archive.

8. *LANGUAGE, TRUTH AND LOGIC* OR, THE PHILOSOPHY OF NONSENSE

1   Stuart Hampshire, IWA, 10 January 1995.
2   Ayer to Otto Neurath, 31 December 1935 in the Wiener-Kreis-Archief, Rijksarchief in Noord-Holland, Harlem.
3   *PML*, pp.169–70.
4   Solly Zuckerman, *From Apes to Warlords*, London, 1976, p.92.
5   Stuart Hampshire, IWA, 10 January 1995.
6   Zuckerman *Apes to Warlords*, p.93.
7   *PML*, p.158.

Notes

8 Isaiah Berlin, 'Felix Frankfurter at Oxford', in *Personal Impressions*, London, 1980, p.84.

9 Maurice Bowra, *Memories, 1898–1939*, London, 1966, p.317.

10 Felix Frankfurter and Harlan B. Phillips, *Felix Frankfurter Reminisces*, London, 1960, p.259: 'young steed', p.262.

11 *PML*, p.168.

12 Doris Bamford, IWA, 1 October 1994.

13 Ayer to Roy Harrod, 14 January 1935, British Library, Harrod Archive, file 71181/104.

14 Stuart Hampshire, IWA, 10 January 1995.

15 Whitehead, quoted in *PML*, pp.162–3.

16 G.E. Moore, academic reference for Ayer, 14 January 1935, G.E. Moore Archive, Cambridge University Library.

17 Henry Price, academic reference for Ayer, 5 February 1935, Ayer family archive.

18 Berlin to Felix Frankfurter, 23 August 1937.

19 *PML*, p.215.

20 Ibid., pp.174–5.

21 Ayer to Isaiah Berlin, 31 June 1935.

22 Ayer to Neurath, 19 July 1935 in the Wiener-Kreis-Archief. Ayer, 'The Criterion of Truth', *Analysis*, 3 (1935).

23 *Actes du congrès international de philosophie scientifique*, Sorbonne, Paris, 1935, published Paris, 1936, 2 vols.

24 Bertrand Russell, 'Logical Positivism', *Polemic*, 1 (1945), p.6.

25 Ayer, 'The Analytic Movement in Contemporary British Philosophy', in *Actes du congrès international*, Vol. 2: *Histoire de la logique et de la philosophie scientifique*, p.56.

26 *LTL*, Preface.

27 Ibid. p.84.

28 Ibid., pp.79–80.

29 Ibid., p.73.

30 Ibid., p.107.

31 Ibid., p.107.

9 ICONOCLAST, HEDONIST

1 Elizabeth Longford, *The Pebbled Shore*, London, 1986, p.158.

2 Martin D'Arcy, 'Philosophy Now', *Criterion*, 15 June 1936.

3 E.W.F. Tomlin, 'Logical Negativism', *Scrutiny*, 5, no 2 (September 1936).

4 Peter Medawar, *Memoirs of a Thinking Radish*, Oxford University Press paperback, 1988, p.53.

5 Peter Strawson, 'A Passionate Sceptic', *Books and Bookmen*, September 1977, p.26.

6 'Introduction' by the editors, *Fact, Science and Morality: Essays on A.J. Ayer's*

'*Language, Truth and Logic*', ed. Graham Macdonald and Crispin Wright, Oxford, 1986, p.3.

7   Elizabeth Longford, IWA, 16 September 1994.
8   E.W.F. Tomlin, 'Logical Negativism', p.215. For an example of an article quarrelling with Ayer's meta-ethics see H.B. Acton's 'The Expletive Theory of Morals', *Analysis*, 4 (December 1936).
9   David Pears, IWA, 12 July 1997.
10 [Day illegible] February 1936.
11 Isaiah Berlin to Felix Frankfurter, 3 June 1936, Frankfurter Archive, Library of Congress, Washington.
12 Tape recording of A.J. Ayer interviewed by Michael Luke, in the possession of Michael Luke.
13 *PML*, p.203.
14 Karl Popper, Introduction to Ayer's Auguste Comte Memorial Lecture, 'Man as a Subject for Science', typed manuscript, Popper Collection, Hoover Institution, Stanford University, box 56, folder 8 (no date or file number).
15 Ayer to Karl Popper, 25 September 1936, ibid.
16 J.L. Austin to Ayer, no date, but almost certainly 1936.
17 Ayer, 'Verification and Experience', *Proceedings of the Aristotelian Society*, 37 (1936–37), pp.137–56; Moritz Schlick, 'The Foundations of Knowledge', in Ayer (ed.), *Logical Positivism*, Glencoe, Illinois, 1959, p.226.
18 *PML*, p.178.
19 Isaiah Berlin, IWA, 1 February 1994.
20 Lord Longford, IWA, 16 November 1994.
21 Transcript, Profile, 'Sir Alfred Ayer', Euro-television, 1971, no page number. Iris Murdoch has always insisted on the parallels between existentialist and analytic moral philsophy. See *Existentialists and Mystics*, *passim*, London, 1997.
22 Ayer, 'André Malraux: The Early Novels', in *Malraux: Life and Work*, ed. Martine de Courcel, London, 1976, p.51.
23 Ibid.
24 *PML*, pp.179–80.
25 Isaiah Berlin, IWA, 27 June 1996.
26 Ayer, quoted in *Observer*, 21 June 1981.
27 'Ayer at Eton', Video recording of Open University programme, E200 TV2, 1980.
28 Stuart Hampshire, *Innocence and Experience*, London, 1989, pp.4–5.
29 Benedict Nicolson, 'Journals', 28 March and 1 April 1937, quoted in Vanessa Nicolson, LTA, 7 May 1995.
30 Stephen Spender, *World within World* (1951), London, 1964, pp.204–5.
31 Isaiah Berlin, IWA, 27 June 1996.
32 *PML*, p.205.
33 Philip Toynbee, 'Diaries', 14 January 1937, in possession of Sally Toynbee.
34 Isaiah Berlin, IWA 1 February 1994.
35 Dee Ayer, LTA, 11 November 1998.

36   Ibid.
37   Ayer, quoted in Peter Vansittart, *In the Fifties*, London, 1995, p.137.
38   Toynbee, 'Diaries', 7 April 1937.
39   Ibid., 3 November 1937.
40   Ibid., 8 October 1937.
41   Ibid., 11 June 1998.
42   For Cummings see Richard S. Kennedy, *Dreams in the Mirror: A Biography of E.E. Cummings*, New York, 1994.
43   *PML*, p.196.
44   'His Not to Reason Why': interview with Miriam Gross, *Observer*, 24 February 1980.
45   Quoted in Kennedy, *Dreams in the Mirror*, p.383 (poem 34, from *50 Poems*, New York, 1940).
46   *PML*, p.200.
47   Solly Zuckerman to Ayer, 20 December 1975.
48   Tonybee, 'Diaries', 11 June 1937.
49   Stuart Hampshire, IWA, 10 January 1995.
50   Berlin to Felix Frankfurter, 23 August 1937.
51   *PML*, p.205; Frankfurter Archive, Library of Congress, Washington.

10. BRIGHT YOUNG THINGS

1   Ved Mehta, *The Fly and the Fly Bottle*, London, 1961, p.51.
2   Ibid., p.51.
3   E.R. Dodds, *Missing Persons*, London, 1977, p.131.
4   Isaiah Berlin, IWA, 1 February 1994.
5   Isaiah Berlin, 'J.L. Austin and the Early Beginnings of Oxford Philosophy', in *Personal Impressions*, London, 1980, pp.104–5.
6   Stuart Hampshire, IWA, 10 May 1995.
7   Transcript, 'I Am Going to Tamper with Your Beliefs a Little', dialogue between Isaiah Berlin and Stuart Hampshire on the birth of Oxford Philosophy, for six films by Michael Chanan, 1972, pp.13–14.
8   Stuart Hampshire, IWA, 10 January 1995.
9   Berlin, 'J.L. Austin', p.115.
10   *PML*, p.181; the pamphlet proved untraceable.
11   Transcript, 'Profile of Sir Alfred Ayer', Euro-television, June 1971.
12   *PML*, p.205.
13   Philip Toynbee, 'Diaries', 16 January 1938, in possession of Sally Toynbee.
14   Ibid., 31 January 1938.
15   Ibid., 10 January 1938.
16   'Report from Mr Nevill K. Coghill, Cleveland Scholar, 1938', in the archives of the English Speaking Union, London.
17   *PML*, p.206.
18   Ayer to Isaiah Berlin, 1 April 1938.

19 Ayer to Isaiah Berlin, 1 April 1938.
20 Ibid.
21 Ibid.
22 'Report from Mr Alfred J. Ayer, Cleveland Scholar, 1938,' in the archives of the English Speaking Union, London, p.3.
23 *PML*, p.213.
24 Ayer to E.E. Cummings, 21 April 1938.
25 'Reminiscences of Rudolf Carnap', typed manuscript, Ayer Archive, York Street, p.3.
26 Ayer to E.E. Cummings, 2 December 1938.
27 'Report from Mr A.J. Ayer', p.3.
28 Ibid., p.2.
29 *PML*, p.215.
30 Ayer, *Russell*, London, 1972, p.28.
31 Ayer to E.E. Cummings, 2 December 1938.
32 Isaiah Berlin, IWA, 1 February 1994.
33 Ayer to E.E. Cummings, 2 December 1938.
34 Ibid.
35 Ayer, *Foundations of Empirical Knowledge*, London, 1940, p.26.
36 Ibid., p.231.
37 Ibid., pp.221–2.
38 *Ph.AJA*, p.598.
39 Roy Harrod, *The Prof*, London, 1959, p.150.
40 *PML*, p.185.
41 Ayer to E.E. Cummings, 2 December 1938.
42 *PML*, p.202.
43 Richard Braithwaite to Isaiah Berlin, 28 May 1939, Berlin Archive, Wolfson College, Oxford.
44 Ian Crombie, LTA, 22 March 1996.
45 Toynbee, 'Diaries', 1 March 1938.
46 *PML*, pp.217–18.
47 Ayer to Otto Neurath, 12 November 1939 in the Wiener-Kreis-Archief, Rijksarchief in Noord-Holland, Harlem.
48 Lord Longford, IWA, 16 September 1994.

11. WAR: 'MY NEW PROFESSION'

1 Ayer to E.E. Cummings, 6 April 1940.
2 Ayer to Isaiah Berlin, 21 March 1940.
3 William Bell, IWA, 15 March 1986.
4 Patrick Leigh-Fermor, LTA, 'Notes on Freddie Ayer', 20 March 1995.
5 The Duke of Grafton, LTA, 21 June 1996.

6   Richard Braithwaite, Review of A J Ayer, *Foundations of Empirical Knowledge*, *Philosophy*, 17 (1942), p.86.
7   Ayer to Isaiah Berlin, 23 August 1988.
8   'Ayer at Eton', Video recording of Open University programme, E200 TV2, 1980.
9   The Duke of Devonshire, IWA, 10 June 1996.
10 PML, p.234.
11 Ibid., p.235.
12 Berlin to Marion Frankfurter, 26 August 1940.
13 PML, pp.239–40.
14 Ayer to Lovat Dickinson, 14 October 1940, Macmillan Archive.
15 Ayer interviewed by Michael Luke, c. 1987: tape in possession of Michael Luke.
16 Leigh Fermor, 'Notes on Freddie Ayer'.
17 PML, p.243.
18 'Report on Officer Attending Interrogation Course (German)', in file 'Capt A.J. Ayer, Personal File', Welsh Guards Records, Headquarters, Welsh Guards, Wellington Barracks, Birdcage Walk, London, SW1.
19 Goronwy Rees, *A Bundle of Sensations*, London, 1960, p.131.
20 Ayer to the Cummingses, 26 May 1943.
21 Lord Listowel, IWA, n.d. (3/95?).
22 Natasha Spender, IWA, 10 March 1995.
23 PML, pp.247–9; Jeremy Lewis, *Cyril Connolly, A Life*, London, 1997, p.363.
24 Anthony Powell, *Journals, 1987–89*, London, 1996, '26 April 1988'.
25 PML, p.247.
26 Ayer to the Cummingses, 10 August 1942.
27 Bickham Sweet-Escott, *Baker Street Irregular*, London, 1965, p.131.
28 Ayer to the Cummingses, 4 August 1942.
29 David Stafford, *Camp X: SOE and the American Connection*, London, 1986.
30 For Graham see Andrew Turnbull, *Scott Fitzgerald*, New York and Oxford, 1962, p.292; Wendy Fairey, *One of the Family*, New York, 1992.
31 Letter to Wendy Fairey of mid-February 1989, quoted in Fairey, *One of the Family*, p.184.
32 Ibid., p.72.
33 *The Nation*, 154, no. 11 (14 March 1942), pp.320–1; no. 19 (9 May 1942), pp.553–4; no. 21 (23 May 1942), p.609.
34 PML, p.261.
35 Octavian von Hofmannsthal, IWA, 8 March 1995.
36 PML, p.259.
37 Ayer to the Cummingses, 10 August 1942.
38 PML, p.262.
39 Isaiah Berlin, IWA, 1 February 1994.

12. 'GOOD ENOUGH, IF LARGELY UNAUTHORISED'

1 Ayer to the Cummingses, 26 May 1943.
2 Ibid.
3 Ibid.
4 Ayer to the Cummingses, 19 September 1943.
5 Ibid.
6 'W/S. Lieutenant A.J. Ayer': report of 13 July 1943, SOE Archive, Foreign and Commonwealth Office.
7 PML, pp.265–7.
8 Robin Brook, IWA, 25 October 1994.
9 Quoted in LTA from the SOE adviser, 22 August 1996.
10 Ayer, 'French Communist Party', 7 September 1943, SOE Archive.
11 Ibid., p.21.
12 Ibid., p.3.
13 Ayer to the Cummingses, 26 May 1943.
14 Ayer, 'The Concept of Freedom', in The Meaning of Life and Other Essays, London, 1990, p.136.
15 Ibid., pp.140, 141.
16 Ibid., p.141.
17 Douglas Dodds-Parker, LTA, 30 June 1996; see also PML, p.271.
18 PML, p.271.
19 Brooks Richards, IWA, 21 November 1994.
20 Ayer to the Cummingses, 14 December 1944.
21 Ayer to E.E. Cummings, 2 January 1945.
22 Ibid.
23 Ayer quoted in Edward St Aubyn interview, 'Hot Ayer', Tatler, December–January, 1989–90.
24 Ayer to E.E. Cummings, 2 January 1945.
25 Ibid.
26 Ibid.
27 Letter from Sgt Adrian Holman, SOE Archive, 24 October 1944.
28 PML, p.279.
29 Ayer to E.E. Cummings, 2 January 1945.
30 Ayer to the Cummingses, 14 June 1944.
31 'To: AD/E, From: V/CD', SOE Archive, 27 October 1944.
32 Ayer to G.E. Moore, 28 February 1945, Moore Archive, Cambridge University Library, Add. 8330 6A/19/3.

13. THE MEANING OF LIFE

1 Guy de Rothschild Contre bonne fortune, Paris, 1983, p.186.

Notes

2 Ayer to E.E. Cummings, 14 December 1945.

3 Francette Drin, IWA, July 1994.

4 Olivier Todd, IWA, 13 December 1995.

5 Ayer, 'André Malraux, the Early Novels', in *Malraux, Life and Work*, ed. Martine de Courcel, London, 1976, p.51.

6 *PML*, p.287.

7 Cyril Connolly to Lys Lubbock, 14 July 1945, quoted by Jeremy Lewis, LTA, 28 June 1996.

8 *PML*, p.282.

9 Ibid., p.289.

10 Ayer to E.E. Cummings, 14 December 1945.

11 Antony Beevor and Artemis Cooper, *Paris after the Liberation*, London, 1994, p.197.

12 Annie Cohen-Solal, *Sartre, A Life*, New York, 1987, pp.251–2.

13 Guy de Rothschild, IWA, 9 May 1995.

14 Ayer's articles on existentialism from this period include 'Jean-Paul Sartre', *Horizon*, 12, nos 67 and 68 (1945); 'Secret Session', a review of Sartre's *Huis Clos*, in *Polemic*, 2 (1945); 'Albert Camus', *Horizon*, 13, no. 75 (1946); 'Some Aspects of Existentialism', *Rationalist Annual*, 1948; 'Jean-Paul Sartre's Doctrine of Commitment', *Listener*, 44, no. 1135 (30 November 1950); and a fine but almost entirely unknown article, 'Philosophy at Absolute Zero: An Enquiry into the Meaning of Nihilism', *Encounter*, 5, no. 4 (October 1954).

15 Ayer, 'Sartre's Doctrine of Commitment', p.634.

16 Ayer, 'Jean-Paul Sartre', p.19; Ayer, 'Albert Camus', 1946, p.161.

17 Ayer, 'Sartre's Doctrine of Commitment', p.633.

18 Ayer, 'Jean-Paul Sartre', pp.18–19.

19 Simone de Beauvoir in *Beloved Chicano Man, Letters to Nelson Algren, 1947–64*, ed. Sylvie le Bon de Beauvoir, London, 1998, 15 August 1947, p.50.

20 Bowra to Isaiah Berlin, 7 May 1995, Bowra Archive, Wadham College, Oxford.

21 Ayer to the Cummingses, 14 December 1945.

22 Ibid.

23 Ayer to the Cummingses, 15 May 1946.

24 *PML*, p.295.

25 David Pears, IWA, 12 June 1997.

26 Ayer, 'The Claims of Philosophy', *Polemic*, no. 7 (1947), reprinted in *The Meaning of Life and Other Essays*, London, 1990, pp.2–3.

27 Ayer, 'Deistic Fallacies', *Polemic*, no. 1 (1945), p.15.

28 Ayer, 'The Claims of Philosophy', p.16.

29 Richard Wollheim, 'Ayer: The Man, the Philosopher, the Teacher', in *A.J. Ayer: Memorial Essays*, ed. A. Phillips Griffiths, Cambridge, 1991, p.18.

30 Perenyi quoted in Jeffrey Meyers, *Edmund Wilson, A Biography*, New York, 1995, p.280.

31 Ayer, 'Koestlerkampf' (review of *Koestler* by Iain Hamilton), *London Review of Books*, 20 May 1982, p.8.

32 Celia Paget, LTA, 2 June 1994.
33 Quoted in Alistair Forbes, 'Lady Patricia Douglas', Obituary, *Sunday Telegraph*, 21 January, 1991.
34 For De Bendern see Michael Ignatieff, *Isaiah Berlin, A Life*, London, 1988, pp.111ff.
35 Alistair Forbes, IWA, 2 September 1996.
36 *PML*, p. 307.
37 Isaiah Berlin, IWA, 1 February 1994.
38 *PML*, p.307.
39 Ayer to Isaiah Berlin, 15 June 1946.
40 Ayer to E.E. Cummings, 15 May 1946.
41 David Hume, 'My Own Life', in *Essays*, ed. E.F. Miller, Indianapolis, 1985, p.xlvi.
42 *PML*, p.289.
43 Ayer to the Cummingses, 1 October 1946.

14. PROFESSOR

1 Stuart Hampshire, IWA, 10 January 1995.
2 Richard Wollheim, 'Ayer: The Man, the Philosopher, the Teacher', in *A.J. Ayer: Memorial Essays*, A. Phillips Griffiths, Cambridge, 1991, p.25.
3 It has been noted that all sixteen of the male philosophers most closely associated with the Oxford philosophy of the 1950s went to public school and then Oxbridge. Even by Oxford standards, its philosophers were drawn from a very narrow social base. See Jonathan Rée, 'English Philosophy in the Fifties', *Radical Philosophy*, 65 (Autumn 1993), p.16.
4 Wollheim, IWA, 17 August 1994.
5 John Watling, IWA, 9 November 1994.
6 John Watling, IWA, 9 November 1994.
7 Peter Long, IWA, 20 December 1994.
8 Jeremy Hornsby to Dee Ayer, 16 July 1989.
9 Ayer, 'Logical Positivism – A Debate', in *The Meaning of Life and Other Essays*, London, 1990, p.36.
10 Watling, IWA, 9 November 1994.
11 Wollheim, 'Ayer: The Man ...', p.27.
12 Daniel O'Connor, IWA, 14 March 1997.
13 Wollheim, 'Ayer: The Man ...', p.26.
14 Veronica Hull, *The Monkey Puzzle*, London, 1958.
15 Wollheim, 'Ayer: The Man ...,' p.27.
16 Wollheim, IWA, 17 August 1994.
17 Peter Long, IWA, 20 December 1994.
18 Ayer, 'The Physical Basis of the Mind', *Listener*, 30 December 1949, pp.1109–10.
19 J.Z. and Ray Young, IWA, 21 October 1994.
20 *MML*, p.55.

Notes

21 Ibid., p.35.
22 Geoffrey Wheatcroft, *The Controversy of Zion*, London, 1996, p.105.
23 Caroline Moorehead, *Bertrand Russell*, London, 1992, p.454.
24 Bertrand Russell to Ayer, 1 July 1952.
25 Ved Mehta, *The Fly and the Fly Bottle*, London, 1963, p.42.
26 Ayer, *Russell*, London, 1972, p.150.
27 Ayer, review of Bertrand Russell, An Inquiry, in *Nature*, 3747 (23 August 1941).
28 Ayer, 'On Making Philosophy Intelligible', in *Metaphysics and Common Sense*, London, 1969, p.18.
29 *LTL*, pp.18–19.
30 Gollancz Archive, 23 October 1945.
31 Ted Honderich, IWA, 9 March 1994.
32 Richard Pring, IWA, 23 October 1998.
33 Ayer, 'The Identity of Indiscernibles', in *Philosophical Essays*, London, 1954, p.31.
34 Ayer to E.E. Cummings, 19 September 1949.
35 Wollheim, 'Ayer: The Man . . .', p.25.
36 David Pears, Obituary read to the meeting of the International Institute of Philosophy, California, on 1 September 1989, Ayer Archive, p.3.
37 'Conversations with Philosophers – A.J. Ayer discusses with Bryan Magee', *Listener*, 31 December 1970, p.908.
38 Ayer, *The Problem of Knowledge*, London, 1956, pp.80–1.
39 *MML*, p.123.
40 Ayer, *Problem of Knowledge*, p.132.
41 Ibid., p.172.
42 Ibid., p.175.
43 Stuart Hampshire, review of *The Problem of Knowledge*, in *New Statesman*, 24 November 1956.
44 R.M. Hare, review in *Spectator*, 4 January 1957.
45 Ayer, 'The Ghosts of Versailles and Others', *Listener*, 23 May 1957.
46 Ayer, 'Logical Positivism – A Debate', in *The Meaning of Life*, p.18.
47 Ibid., pp.41 and 42.
48 Ray Monk, *Wittgenstein: The Duty of Genius*, London, 1990, p.543.

15. THE LONDON FREDDIE AYER

1 Ayer to the Cummingses, 15 May 1946.
2 *MML*, pp.38–9.
3 Julian Ayer, IWA, 1 October 1998.
4 *MML*, p.32.
5 Wollheim, IWA, 17 August 1994.
6 George Weidenfeld, *Remembering My Good Friends*, London, 1995, p.151.
7 V.S. Pritchard, talking on 'Profile: Sir Alfred Ayer', Radio 4, 31 October 1980.

8   Michael Luke, *David Tennant and the Gargoyle Years*, London, 1991, p.176.

9   Patrick Leigh-Fermor, LTA, 'Notes on Freddie Ayer', 20 March 1995.

10 Francis Partridge, *Everything to Lose: Diaries 1945–1960*, London, 1985, entry for 6 January 1954.

11 Francis Partridge, *Hanging On: Diaries, 1960–1963*, London, 1990, entry for 21 October 1962.

12 Janetta Jackson, LTA, 30 April 1998.

13 Barbara Skelton, *Tears before Bedtime and Weep No More*, London, 1993, p.182.

14 Ayer to Margery Tuck, 19 January 1948, copy of letter in Cummings Archive, Houghton Library, Harvard.

15 Giles Romilly, 'A Visit to Oxford', *New Statesman*, 26 June 1948, pp.518–19.

16 C.E.M. Joad, 'Logical Positivism, Fascism and Value', *New Statesman*, 31 July 1948, pp.91–2.

17 *New Statesman*, 10 July 1948.

18 'Truth and Consequences', *Time*, 20 September 1948, pp.74–5.

19 Ayer to the Cummingses, 19 September 1948.

20 Ibid.

21 *MML*, p.44.

22 Jocelyn Rickards, IWA, 22 February 1994.

23 *MML*, p.44.

24 Ibid. p.45.

25 Ibid., p.47.

26 Ibid., p.48.

27 Jocelyn Rickards, *The Painted Banquet*, London, 1987, p.27.

28 Ibid. p.28.

29 Ibid., p.31.

30 Jocelyn Rickards, IWA, 22 February 1994.

31 Rickards, *Painted Banquet*, p.30.

32 Sidney Hook, *Out of Step: An Unquiet Life in the 20th Century*, New York, 1987, p.433.

33 Ayer, 'Philosophy at Absolute Zero', *Encounter*, 5, no.4 (September 1954).

34 Quoted in Peter Vansittart *In the Fifties*, London, 1995, p.139.

35 *Listener*, 'Impressions of Communist China', 2 December 1954, p.942.

36 Ayer, *Russell*, London, 1972, p.250.

37 *Listener*, 2 December 1954, p.942.

38 Julian Ayer, IWA, 9 December 1995.

39 Anthony Dworkin, IWA, 15 January 1998.

40 Karl Miller, IWA, May 1997 (day unknown).

41 The terms 'U' and 'non-U' were invented by Alan Ross in 1954 and then taken up by Nancy Mitford in an article in *Encounter*. Her analysis of different language uses and to some extent mores of English classes caused a storm. See Alan S. C. Ross, Nancy Mitford, Evelyn Waugh *et al.*, *Noblesse Oblige – An Enquiry into the Identifiable Characteristics of the English Aristocracy*, London 1956.

Notes

42   Rickards, *Painted Banquet*, pp.42–3
43   Ibid., p.43.
44   *MML*, p.83.
45   Francette Drin, IWA, July 1994.
46   Rickards, *Painted Banquet*, p.52.
47   Ibid., p.53.
48   Richard S. Kennedy, *Dreams in the Mirror: A Biography of E.E. Cummings*, New York, 1994, p.472.
49   Rickards, *Painted Banquet*, p.53.
50   Jocelyn Rickards, IWA, 22 February 1994.

16. ALL CHANGE

1   Dee Ayer, LTA, 1 December 1998.
2   Ibid.
3   Janey Ironside, *Janey*, London, 1973, p.99.
4   Ayer, review of Colin Wilson, *Outsider*, in *Encounter*, 7, no. 3 (September 1956), p.75.
5   James Parr to Renée Ayer, Christmas 1956, Ayer Archives.
6   Isaiah Berlin, IWA, 1 February 1994.
7   Octavian von Hofmannsthal, IWA, 8 March 1995.
8   'Ayer Among the Marxists', *Sunday Times*, 25 March 1962; Profile – 'Philosopher', *Observer*, 15 September 1957; 'Professor A.J. Ayer', *Sunday Telegraph* February 1959.
9   Roy Harrod to Ayer, n.d.
10   Catherine Dove, IWA, 27 June 1995.
11   *MML*, p.98.
12   For Austin's career after the war, see G.J. Warnock, 'John Langshaw Austin, A Biographical Sketch', in K.T. Kahn ed., *Symposium on J.L. Austin*, London, 1969.
13   Chris Coobe, IWA, 10 October 1995.
14   Isaiah Berlin, 'J.L. Austin and the Early Beginnings of Oxford Philosophy', in *Personal Impressions*, London, 1980, p.105.
15   For an interesting, if unsympathetic, survey of linguistic philosophy see Jonathan Rée, 'English Philosophy in the 1950s', *Radical Philosophy*, 65 (Autumn 1993).
16   Ayer, 'Philosophy and Language', in *The Concept of a Person*, London, 1963, p.17.
17   Geoffrey Warnock, LTA, 15 April 1995.
18   Ayer speaking on 'Better Than The Stars' (a broadcast on Ramsey) BBC Radio 3, 27 February 1978. Taped copy in Ayer Archive.
19   Testimonial, Russell to Oxford, 9 January 1959.
20   *MML*, p.162.
21   Ibid. Austin to Ayer, 29 January 1959.
22   Ernest Gellner quoted in Ved Mehta, *The Fly and the Fly Bottle*, London, 1963, p.36.

23 *MML*, p.187.
24 Ibid., p.146.
25 Richard Wollheim, IWA, 17 August 1994.
26 Stuart Hampshire, IWA, 10 January 1995.
27 Ayer to Marion Cummings, 13 August 1959.
28 Dee Wells to the Cummingses, 26 October 1959.

17. OXFORD, NEW YORK, TOULON

1 Richard Wollheim, 'Ayer: The Man, the Philosopher, the Teacher', in *A.J. Ayer: Memorial Essays*, ed. A. Phillips Griffiths, Cambridge, 1991, p.30.
2 David Wiggins, IWA, 5 June 1995.
3 Alan Ryan, IWA, 4 June 1997.
4 Anthony Quinton, 'Alfred Jules Ayer', *PAS*, 94 (1996), p.275.
5 Anthony Quinton, IWA, 16 March 1995, and 'Logic in High Gear', *Spectator*, 8 July 1989.
6 Marcelle Quinton, IWA, 14 March 1995.
7 Anthony Quinton, 'Logic'.
8 Peter Lipton, LTA, 8 May 1995.
9 Ayer, 'Philosophy and Science', in *Metaphysics and Common Sense*, London, 1969, p.92.
10 Ayer, 'Man as a Subject for Science', ibid., p.221.
11 Ibid., p.236.
12 Ayer, 'Fatalism', in *The Concept of a Person*, London, 1964, p.268.
13 John Osborne, *Almost a Gentleman*, London, 1991 p.153.
14 Jocelyn Rickards, *The Painted Banquet*, London, 1987, p.69.
15 Ayer, 'Labour's Lost Leader', *London Review of Books*, 23 May 1979.
16 *MML*, p.191.
17 MMD, p.28.
18 Ayer, 'Labour's Lost Leader'.
19 Ayer, 'Support for Mr Gaitskell', report in *Daily Telegraph*, 11 October 1960; Ayer, 'Why I Shall Vote Labour', *Observer*, 27 September 1959. See also Ayer's contribution to Philip Toynbee, *The Fearful Choice: A Debate on Nuclear Policy*, London, 1958.
20 Ayer, 'The New Left', *Spectator*, 17 June 1960.
21 Ayer, 'Philosophy and Politics', in *Metaphysics and Common Sense*, p.260.
22 Ayer to Robert Birley, 30 November 1960, Eton Archive, file COLL/P9/119. All correspondence surrounding the affair is in this file.
23 For Elliott, see Richard Olland, *An English Education: a Perspective of Eton*, London, 1982, p.169.
24 Claude Elliott to Sir Leslie Farrer, 3 November 1960, Eton Archive.
25 Ayer to Elliott, 19 December 1960, ibid.

26 Claude Elliot, 'Conversation with Professor Ayer', 6 February 1961, ibid.
27 MML, p.198; Lord Cohen to Claude Elliott, 15 May 1961, Eton Archive.
28 Edward St Aubyn, 'Hot Ayer', *Tatler*, December–January, 1989–90.
29 Noel Annan to Ayer, 27 September 1984.
30 Ayer, 'Cock-a-Double Doo', *New Statesman*, 12 May 1961.
31 MML, p.204.
32 E.E. Cummings, 'AJA', Ayer Archive, York Street.
33 Wendy Fairey, *One of the Family*, New York, 1992, p.129.
34 Ibid., p.200.
35 Marguerite Lamkin, IWA, 14 September 1997.
36 MML, p.209: Arthur Schlesinger, Jr., Diary, 'January 14, 1962', quoted in LTA, 22 Feb. 1999; Isaiah Berlin, IWA, 1 Febuary, 1994.
37 Dee Ayer, LTA, 8 October 1998.
38 Ayer, 'How a Marxist Critic Got An Invitation to Lecture in Russia', *Observer*, 8 April 1962.
39 Edward St Aubyn, *Never Mind*, London, 1992, p.38.
40 Ibid., p.35.
41 Ibid., p.36.

18. BENTHAMITE SAINT

1 Emily Read, IWA, 28 April 1995.
2 Dee Ayer, IWA, 16 March 1995.
3 Pauline Peters, 'Lucky Them. Life with Dee Wells and Freddie Ayer', *Sunday Times Magazine*, 2 December 1973.
4 Dee Ayer, quoted in *Daily Telegraph*, 17 May 1965.
5 Dorothy Pritchett, IWA, 4 November 1994.
6 *Nova*, January 1973, p.3.
7 Ibid.
8 Nick Ayer, IWA, 7–9 September 1995.
9 Gully Wells, LTA, n.d. March 1995.
10 Sue Boothby, IWA, 24 April 1995.
11 James Hemming, IWA, 7 July 1997
12 Ayer, 'Humanism and Reform', *Encounter*, 6 June 1966, p.13.
13 MMD, p.34.
14 Ibid.
15 Independent Adoption Society, XXV Silver Jubilee pamphlet, 1990.
16 Mary James, IWA, 22 April 1998.
17 Ayer, *The Problem of Knowledge*, London, 1956, pp.176–87.
18 Ayer, *Problem of Knowledge*, pp.176–87.
19 Anthony Grey, IWA, 31 July 1997 but see also Grey's *Quest for Justice: Towards Homosexual Emancipation*, London, 1992, p.76.

20 Anthony Grey, IWA, 31 July 1997.

21 'Women's Page', *Times*, 21 May 1968.

22 Richard Sheahan, IWA, 24 May 1995.

23 'A Profile of Sir A.J. Ayer', Euro-television, 1971.

24 Dee Ayer, IWA, 16 March 1995.

25 Natasha Spender, IWA, 10 March 1995.

26 Unpublished section of MML, Ayer Archive, York Street.

27 Ayer to Bertrand Russell, 17 May 1966. Russell Archive, McMaster University.

28 MMD, p.105.

29 Ibid., p.33.

30 Richard Rorty, writing in the *Philosophical Review*, 80, no. 1 (1971), p.96.

31 The term, in fact, is Ted Honderich's, but Ayer consented to it: Ted Honderich, 'An Interview with A.J. Ayer', in *A.J. Ayer: Memorial Essays*, ed. A. Phillips Griffiths, Cambridge, 1991, pp.213 and 223.

32 Ayer, *The Origins of Pragmatism*, London, 1968, p.220.

33 MMD, p.33.

34 William James, quoted in *Origins*, p.265.

35 Ibid., p.266.

36 Ibid., p.277.

37 Bernard Williams, 'The Self and the Future' (1970), reprinted in *Problems of the Self*', Cambridge, 1973.

38 Ayer, *The Central Questions of Philosophy*, London, 1973, Pelican edn, 1976, p.124.

39 Morton White, review of Ayer, *Origins*, in *New York Review of Books*, 30 January 1969, p.25.

40 For Carnap see Ayer, 'What Must There Be?', in *Metaphysics and Common Sense*, London, 1969, pp.49–50.

41 *Origins*, pp.330 and 334–5.

42 Ayer, 'What Must There Be?', p.63.

43 Ibid., p.62.

44 MML, p.129.

45 Ayer, 'Sartre on the Jews', *Spectator*, 20 September 1968.

46 Ibid.

47 Herbert Marcuse had made a famous attack on positivism and ordinary language philosophy in *One Dimensional Man* (London, 1964), itself a belated contribution to 'the quarrel over positivism' in Germany in the 1950s.

48 Richard Wollheim, IWA, 17 August 1994.

49 Ayer, 'The Revolt of the Young' (part 4), *Evening Standard*, 26 September 1968.

50 Peregrine Worsthorne, 'Vanessa Ayer', *Spectator*, 24 August 1985, p.18.

51 Dominic Lawson, IWA, 3 May 1995.

52 Worsthorne, 'Vanessa Ayer', *Spectator*, p.18.

53 Dominic Lawson, IWA, May 1995.

54 Vanessa Lawson to Ayer, 21 June 1977.

55 Marcelle Quinton, IWA, 14 April 1995.

19. CENTRAL QUESTIONS

1   Daniel Dennett, *The Philosophical Lexicon*, 7th edn, manuscript, Ayer Archive.
2   Timothy Sprigge, LTA, 6 April 1996.
3   Ayer to Isaiah Berlin, 15 December 1969.
4   Clifford Davis, IWA, 5 April 1994.
5   Ayer, *Probability and Evidence*, London, 1972, p.6.
6   Mary Warnock, review of Ayer, *Russell*, in *New Society*, 25 May 1972.
7   Anthony Quinton, review in *Observer*, 30 April 1972.
8   Bernard Crick, review in *New Statesman*, 16 June 1972 and in *New York Times*, 22 October 1972.
9   Bernard Williams, review in *Observer*, 29 September 1971.
10   Ayer, *The Central Questions of Philosophy*, London, 1973, Pelican edn, 1976, p.108.
11   Ibid., p.105.
12   Ibid., p.106.
13   John Foster, *A.J. Ayer*, London, 1985, p.x.
14   Ayer, 'Free Will and Rationality', in Zak van Straaten (ed.), *Philosophical Subjects: Essays Presented to P.F. Strawson*, Oxford, 1980, p.12.
15   Burton Dreben, IWA, 13 September 1995.
16   Michael Lockwood, IWA, 15 October 1998.
17   Dee Wells, *Jane*, 1973 Pan edn, 1975, p.25.
18   Nick Ayer, IWA, 7–9 October 1994.
19   N.d., but summer 1986; Beatrice Tourot to Ayer, 7 July 1986.
20   Ayer to Heather Kiernan, 29 March 1983.
21   Pauline Peters, 'Lucky Them. Life with Dee Wells and Freddie Ayer', *Sunday Times Magazine*, 2 December 1973.
22   Nick Ayer, IWA, 7–9 October 1994.
23   Gully Wells, IWA, 23 October 1997.
24   Ayer, No title, *Sunday Times*, 16 July 1967; For examples of criticism see 'Equality on Education – For Whom,' by E. G. West, *Daily Telegraph*, 13 November 1962 and at a later date Geoffrey Howe; letter in *Daily Telegraph*, 7 November 1969.
25   Peters, 'Lucky Them'.
26   MML, p.156.
27   Brian Hayden to Ayer, 1 March 1973.
28   Wendy Fairey, *One of the Family*, New York, 1992, p.204.
29   Bernard Williams, IWA, 16 May 1995.
30   Ayer, 'Reflections on the Varna Congress', *Proceedings of the 14th World Congress of Philosophy* (6 Vols), Paris, 1973, Vol. 1, p.843.
31   Jonathan Glover, contribution to 'Fifty Years a Philosopher', transcript of World Service broadcast, 1 May 1986.
32   Leon Wieseltier, IWA, 17 January 1995.
33   'Profile: Sir Alfred Ayer', BBC Radio 4 broadcast, 31 October 1980.

34 Martin Amis, 'Nicholson Baker', *Independent on Sunday* (1992), reprinted in Martin Amis, *Visiting Mrs Nabokov and Other Excursions*, London, 1993, p.193.
35 Geoffrey Wheatcroft, *Absent Friends*, London, 1989, p.270.
36 Vanessa Lawson to Ayer, n.d.
37 Ibid.
38 Doris Bamford, IWA, 1 October 1994.
39 Ayer, 'On Autobiography', typed manuscript, *c*.1984, Ayer Archive, p.4.
40 Isaiah Berlin, IWA, 1 February 1994.
41 Mary Warnock, review of *A Part of My Life*, in *Sunday Telegraph*, 12 June 1977.
42 John Sturrock, review in *New York Times Book Review*, 22 January 1978.
43 Frederic Raphael, review in *Sunday Times*, 12 June 1977.
44 Peter Strawson, review in *Books and Bookmen*, September 1977.
45 Quoted in 'Ayer Today', *Observer*, 25 June 1978 (No author).
45 Anthony Grayling, IWA, 11 January 1996.
47 John Parry, IWA, 28 January 1996; Richard Sheahan, IWA, 24 May 1995.

20. RETIREMENT

1 Ayer to Vanessa Lawson, 1 April 1979.
2 Richard Wollheim, 'Ayer: The Man, the Philosopher, the Teacher', in *A.J. Ayer: Memorial Essays*, ed. A. Phillips Griffiths, Cambridge, 1991, p.22.
3 *New Yorker*, 18 April 1983.
4 Ayer, 'Why the Doctor Arthur Verdict is Right', *Times*, 6 November 1981.
5 Ayer to Vanessa Lawson, 1 April 1979.
6 Ayer to Vanessa Lawson, 27 March 1979.
7 Barry Stroud, 'Ayer's Hume', *Ph.AJA*, p.610.
8 Ayer, *Hume*, Oxford, 1980, p.25.
9 Jocelyn Rickards, IWA, 22 February 1994.
10 Vanessa Lawson to Ayer, n.d.
11 *Evening Standard*, Londoner's Diary, 25 January 1980.
12 Ayer to Ted Honderich, 5 May 1980.
13 Ayer to Heather Kiernan, 9 February 1981.
14 Dee Ayer to Ayer, 15 January 1982.
15 Derwent May, IWA, 15 October 1997.
16 Henry Hardy, IWA, 4 February 1997.
17 Isaiah Berlin, IWA, 1 February 1994.
18 Dominic Lawson, IWA, 30 May 1995.
19 Horatia Lawson, IWA, 1 September 1998.
20 Ayer to Nick Ayer, 14 April 1982.
21 Ayer to Nick Ayer, 3 January 1983.
22 Ayer to Nick Ayer, 26 September 1984.
23 Jocelyn Rickards, *The Painted Banquet*, London, 1987, p.70.

24 Ayer quoted in Maureen Cleave, 'Freddie v. Ethel', *Evening Standard*, 31 August 1984.

25 Ayer, quoted by Cathy Gunn, in *Today*, 24 August 1986.

26 Peter Strawson, IWA, 10 January 1995.

27 *Authors Take Sides on the Falklands*, ed. Cecil Woolf and Jean Moorcroft Wilson, London, 1982, p.17.

28 Stephen Spender, *Journals 1939–83*, London, 1985, entry for '14 Dec. 1980'.

29 Hilary Putnam, 'After Ayer, After Empiricism', *Partisan Review*, 5 (1984), reprinted as 'After Empiricism' in *Realism with a Human Face*, Cambridge, Mass., 1990, p.43.

30 Ayer, *Philosophy in the Twentieth Century*, p.14.

31 Mark Bonham Carter to Ayer, 9 December 1983.

32 Anthony Quinton, review of *More of My Life*, Typescript, Ayer Archive.

33 *LTL*, p.108.

34 See the 'Introduction' to the second edition of *LTL*, 'The Emotive Theory of Values'.

35 Ayer, 'Freedom and Morality', in *Freedom and Morality and Other Essays*, London, 1984, pp.49–50.

36 Ibid., p.33.

37 Ayer, *Ludwig Wittgenstein*, London (Penguin paperback edn), 1986, p.137.

38 Ibid., p.92.

39 Jennifer Trusted, IWA, 12 June 1996.

40 Ayer, 'The Sources of Intolerance', in *On Toleration*, ed. Susan Mendus and David Edwards, Oxford, 1987, p.96.

41 Ibid.

42 Ayer to Nick Ayer, 26 September and 8 November 1984; 30 December 1985; 25 May 1986.

43 Ayer to Beatrice Tourot, IWA, 10 September, 1998.

44 Horatia Lawson, IWA, 1 September 1998.

45 Ayer to Nick Ayer, 31 July 1985.

46 'Choices: Is There Anybody There?', BBC2, 28 July 1985.

47 Obituary of Lady Ayer, *Times*, 20 August 1985.

48 Jocelyn Rickards, IWA, 16 September 1998.

49 Transcript of 'A.J. Ayer: Fifty Years a Philosopher', BBC World Service, Ayer Archive, 1 May 1986.

50 Sue Boothby, IWA, 24 April 1995.

51 Ted Honderich, 'Diaries', 17 August 1985.

21. OLD AGE

1 Jocelyn Rickards, The *Painted Banquet*, London, 1987, p.70.

2 Gully Wells, IWA, 20 February 1995.

3 Ayer to Ted Honderich, 9 October 1986.

4   Judith Shklar, review of Ayer, *Voltaire*, in *New Republic*, 2 March 1987, p.36.

5   Justin Wintle, review in *New Statesman*, 17 October 1986.

6   Ayer, *Voltaire*, London, 1986, pp.88 and 105.

7   Ibid., p.174.

8   Ayer to Isaiah Berlin, 3 August 1988.

9   Pippa Hamilton, IWA, 20 September 1995.

10 Horatia Lawson, IWA, 24 February 1994.

11 Nigella Lawson speaking on 'The Firefly and the Rodent', profile of Ayer, BBC Radio 4, 5 December 1996.

12 Ayer to Nick Ayer, 30 December 1985.

13 Ayer, letter to the *Times*, 12 August 1986.

14 'Sayings of the Year', *Observer*, December 1986.

15 *Fact, Science and Morality: Essays on A.J. Ayer's 'Language, Truth and Logic'*, ed. Graham Macdonald and Crispin Wright, Oxford, 1986; *Logical Positivism in Perspective: Essays on 'Language, Truth and Logic'*, ed. Barry Gower, London, 1987.

16 Ayer and Bryan Magee, 'Logical Positivism and its Legacy', in Bryan Magee, *Men of Ideas*, Oxford, 1982, p.107.

17 John Foster, *A.J. Ayer*, London, 1985, p.297.

18 Ayer to Isaiah Berlin, 3 August 1988.

19 Cynthia Kee, IWA, 5 December 1994.

20 Verity Ravensdale, IWA, 1995 n.d.

21 Ayer to Jocelyn Rickards, 8 August 1986.

22 Ayer to Heather Massie, 26 November 1986.

23 Ayer to Ted Honderich, 10 September 1986.

24 Stephanie Goss, IWA, 25 March 1996.

25 Horatia Lawson, IWA, 24 February 1994.

26 Reviews of Ayer, *Thomas Paine*: Alan Ryan, *Listener*, 24 March 1988; Tariq Ali, *Guardian*, 25 March 1988.

27 *Cover to Cover*, BBC2 television programme, 17 March 1988.

28 Ayer to Isaiah Berlin, 3 August 1988. The American scholar was in fact Professor A. Owen Aldridge, who published a study of *Thomas Paine's American Ideology* in 1984. Moncure Conway, a free-thinking humanist, had published an authoritative life of Paine in 1892.

29 'Freddie and the Benefit of Doubt', *Independent*, 14 March 1998.

30 Ted Honderich, 'Diaries', 23 February 1987.

31 Ibid., 29 February and 24 August 1987.

32 Ayer to Nick Ayer, 7 May 1987.

33 Ayer to Jocelyn Rickards, 12 June 1987.

34 Honderich, 'Diaries', 10 December 1987.

35 Ayer to Ted Honderich, 30 September 1987.

36 Wendy Fairey, *One of the Family*, pp.206–8.

37 Gully Wells, IWA, 20 February 1995.

38 Galen Strawson, IWA, 27 October 1994; Simon Blackburn, IWA, 23 December 1996.
39 Ayer, 'What I Saw When I Was Dead', *MMD*, p.44.
40 Ayer, 'The Meaning of Life', in *The Meaning of Life and Other Essays*, ed. Ted Honderich, London, 1990, p.21.

22. RESURRECTION

1 Ayer, 'What I Saw When I Was Dead', *Sunday Telegraph*, 28 August 1988, reprinted as a postscript to MMD, p.44.
2 'What I Saw . . .', MMD, p.46.
3 *National Inquirer*, 6 December 1988.
4 Beatrice Tourot, IWA, 9 November 1998.
5 Edward St Aubyn, 'Hot Ayer', *Tatler*, December–January, 1988–9; the *Sunday Telegraph* changed the Shakespearian title to 'What I Saw When I Was Dead . . .'
6 'Postscript to a Postmortem', *Spectator*, 15 October 1988.
7 St Aubyn, 'Hot Ayer'.
8 Richard Wollheim, IWA, 17 August 1994.
9 Jonathan Miller, IWA, 1 June 1995.
10 Ayer to Ted Honderich, 11 August 1988.
11 Ibid.
12 Ayer to Jocelyn Rickards, 11 August 1988.
13 Ibid.
14 Ayer to Jocelyn Rickards, 21 August 1988.
15 Ayer to Jocelyn Rickards, 11 August 1988.
16 Ayer to Isaiah Berlin, 3 August 1988.
17 Ayer to Ted Honderich, 11 August 1988. Ayer, 'A Defence of Empiricism', in *A.J. Ayer: Memorial Essays*, ed. A. Phillips Griffiths, Cambridge, 1991, p.3.
18 Ayer to Ted Honderich, 25 September 1988.
19 Colin McGinn, 'Old Scores', *London Review of Books*, 30 August 1990.
20 Ayer to friend, 29 January 1989.
21 Ibid.
22 Dee Ayer to Wendy Fairey, 26 January 1989. Wendy Fairey, *One of the Family*, New York, 1992, pp.42–4.
23 Fairey, *One of the Family*, p.217.
24 Ayer to Wendy Fairey, quoted ibid., pp.185–6.
25 Ayer to Wendy Fairey, 3 March 1989.
26 Fairey, *One of the Family*, p.13.
27 Iris Murdoch, LTA, n.d. (autumn 1995).
28 Fairey, *One of the Family*, p.224.
29 Ibid., p.230.
30 Jonathan Steffen, 'Sonnet', n.d.

31 A.C. Grayling, *Guardian*, 29 June 1989; John Foster, *Independent*, 29 June 1989.
32 Robert Jackson, letter to the *Independent*, 30 June 1989; Roger Scruton, 'The Man Who Hated Wisdom', *Sunday Telegraph*, 3 July 1989.
33 Ted Honderich, 'An Interview with A.J. Ayer', in *A.J. Ayer: Memorial Essays*, ed. A. Phillips Griffiths, Cambridge, 1991, p.225.

Index

Index

Index

Index

Index

Index

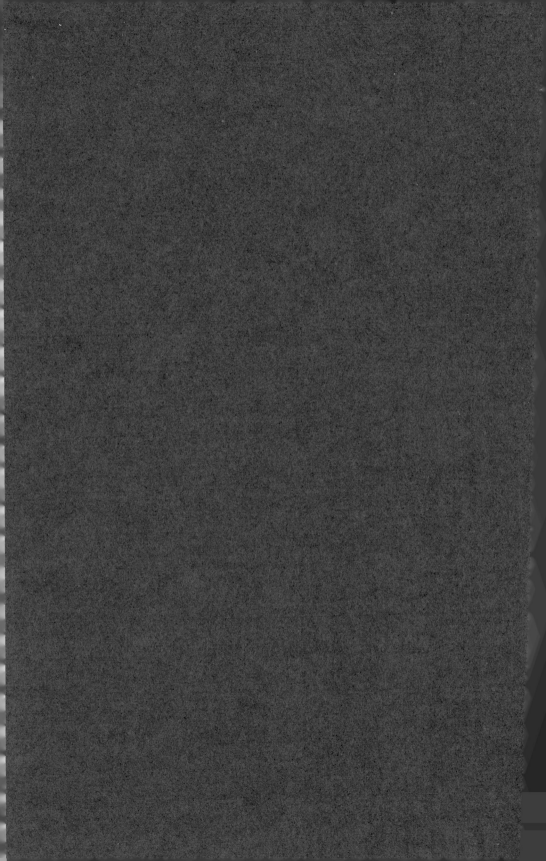